3-16

Howard Hawks; A Jungian Study

Howard Hawks; A Jungian Study

By
Clark Branson

Foreword by Judith Harte, Ph.D.

With illustrations by Marc Johnson

Garland-Clarke Editions  **Capra Press**
Santa Barbara

Published and produced in hardcover and softcover in 1987 by Garland Projects, Inc., Los Angeles; publishers of Garland-Clarke Editions/Capra Press.

Garland Projects, Inc.   Office at:
Post Office Box 5723   1610 N. Argyle Ave. #213
Pasadena, Ca. 91107   Los Angeles, Ca. 90028

DISTRIBUTED BY CAPRA PRESS, SANTA BARBARA.
Capra Press
Post Office Box 2068
Santa Barbara, Ca. 93120
Telephone: (805) 966-4590

Cover design by Don Stepp, and "John."

Library of Congress Cataloging-in-Publication Data

    Bibliography: p.
    1. Hawks, Howard, 1896-1977.—Criticism and interpretation. 2. Moving-pictures—United States—Psychological aspects. 3. Psycho-analysis. 4. Jung, C.G. (Carl Gustav), 1875-1961.   I. Title.
PN1998.A3H344 1987   791.43'0233'0924   86-32634
ISBN 0-88496-261-X
ISBN 0-88496-263-6 (pbk.)

*Dedicated to Andrew Sarris,
in gratitude for his
indispensable film criticism.*

CONTENTS

Copyright Permissions

I am grateful to the following film distributors for their prompt dispatch in granting me permission for the use of photo stills from many of the films of Howard Hawks. Thanks to: Columbia Pictures, MCA/Universal Studios, Inc., MGM/UA Entertainment Company (for the stills from United Artists and MGM Films), Paramount Pictures Corporation, RKO Pictures, Twentieth Century Fox Film Corporation, The Samuel Goldwyn Company, and Warner Bros., Inc. Copyright particulars are noted with the reprinted photos.

For permission to reprint excerpts from literary works I also thank the following publishing organizations:

The C.G. Jung Foundation for Analytical Psychology, Inc. for use of the excerpt from Edward Edinger's *Ego and Archetype*, published by Penguin Books. (Copyright (c) 1972 by the C. G. Jung Foundation, New York.)

E.P. Dutton, Inc., for use of the excerpt from Andrew Sarris's *The American Cinema: Directors and Directions 1929-1968*. (Copyright (c) 1968 by E. P Dutton, Inc.)

Indiana University Press, for the excerpts from Peter Wollen's *Signs and Meaning in the Cinema*. (Copyright (c) 1969, 1972 by Peter Wollen.)

J.G. Ferguson Publishing Company, for use of excerpts from *Man and His Symbols* by Carl G. Jung, et al. (Windfall/Doubleday. Copyright (c) 1964 by J.G. Ferguson Publishing, Chicago.)

Martin, Secker & Warburg Limited, London, for use of the excerpt from *Theories of Film* by Andrew Tudor. (Viking Press. Copyright (c) 1973 by Andrew Tudor.)

Oxford University Press, for the excerpt from *Howard Hawks, Storyteller* by Gerald Mast. (Copyright (c) 1982 by Gerald Mast. Reprinted by permission of Oxford University Press, Inc.)

Pantheon Books, a Division of Random House, Inc., for the excerpt from Laurens van der Post's *Jung and the Story of Our Time*. (Copyright (c) 1975 by Laurens van der Post.)

Reprinted with permission of Princeton University Press are excerpts from the following books:

Joseph Campbell, *The Hero With a Thousand Faces*. Bollingen Series 17. Copyright (c) 1949, (c) renewed 1976 by Princeton University Press. Excerpts pp. 73, 193-196.

The Collected Works of C.G. Jung, trans. R.F.C. Hull, Bollingen Series 20. Vol. 12: *Psychology and Alchemy*. Copyright (c) 1953, (c) 1968 by Princeton University Press. Excerpts pp. 5, 44-46.

C.G. Jung, *Psychological Reflections: A New Anthology of His Writings, 1905-1961*, ed. Jolande Jacobi and R.F.C. Hull, Bollingen Series 31. Copyright (c) 1953 by Princeton University Press; new edition copyright (c) 1970 by Princeton University Press. Excerpts pp. 115, 119.

These excerpts from Princeton University Press are also via the permission of Rowledge & Kegan Paul, Ltd., London.

Reprinted by permission of the University of California Press are excerpts from *Hawks on Hawks* by Joseph McBride. Copyright (c) 1982. Excerpts pp. 2-5, 13-18, 20, 29, 32-34, 39, 65-66, 80-83, 142.

Further copyright details regarding literary extracts and reference appear, of course, in the bibliographical back material.

Thanks also to Marc Daniel Johnson for the use of his illustrations of Howard Hawks. These illustrations are copyrighted© 1985 by Marc Johnson. All Rights Reserved.

ACKNOWLEDGEMENTS

I extend my thanks to Films Inc. and the Pasadena Public Library for providing and screening *Viva Villa!* and *Today We Live,* enabling me to economically combine a study of these little-shown films with their use in the library's film program. I am indebted to Dr. Samuel Correnti of Santa Barbara for his concise lecturing on the murky subject of Jungian psychology as well as his guidance via free consultation. Thanks too, to my mother, and to R. Thad Taylor, Dr. James Kirsch, and other associates of the Shakespeare Society of America/Globe Playhouse for conversation, moral support, and material assistance.

Further, I am beholden to D. K. Wilgus of the UCLA Folklore/Mythology program for indirectly related but valuable training which helped me in organizing a voluminously detailed project. Not least, I am grateful to Cheryl Dandridge-Perry for her help with the manuscript in terms of content as well as written-language points, and to John Dalmas, my editor.

FOREWORD

By Judith Harte

I have long been intrigued by those "tales of the psyche," otherwise known as archetypes, which exist within us in much the same way as they are expressed outwardly in myth, story and film. The capacity to discern these interactive, reciprocal parallels between psyche and art indicates a special and enviable kind of vision. Analytical psychologist Carl Gustav Jung possessed such a unique quality of vision. Jung brought to the scientific community of his time a notion which persists to the present day: the imaginative activity of the psyche has and is its own reality. If given our sacred attention, the psyche will not only permit us to know it via its product the dream, but those (archetypal) images of psyche, which exist within each individual, may also become visible when transferred onto the creative products of art and film.

While the intentions which directed Jung in his exploration of the human psyche appear to me at least to be conscious, the unprecedented discoveries which he made during the course of his explorations were unconscious and unpredictable. Such is often the case with the intentions of psyche and its subsequent manifestations within our dreams and within our art. In this sense, it is we who serve psyche, and when in service of psyche we cannot help but be impacted by the images which it produces—in much the same way as an artist produces a painting. How often have we heard an artist say, "It's as if the painting painted itself."

Filmmaker Howard Hawks, unlike Jung the psychologist, did not produce his myriad collection of cinematic renderings with the intended purpose of making conscious psychological discoveries. Hawks was an entertainer, not a psychologist; though he had the ability to express, however unintentionally, profound psychological insights. He produced his artful series of cinematic renderings much as the psyche produces a series of dreams.

What makes Jungian symbolism so pertinent for me is its uncanny ability to capture the unique way in which a dream, or even an aspect of Jungian theory, may come "alive" for the dreamer.

Let us imagine for a moment what I might say were I to write at length about the details of Clark Branson's work. Perhaps I would speak of its variety, its ingenuity, its sophistication. Then again, I might also point out the way in which Branson offers us a series of archetypal motifs and patterns which he has gleaned from Hawks's films, and through which we are able to catch a glimpse of the director's psyche as if Hawks were under the analytical scrutiny of Professor Jung himself. Were there enough time, I could even tell you how skillfully Branson has made me aware of an underlying psychological pattern within Hawks's films: namely the figures and characters repetitiously arrange and then rearrange according to a kaleidoscopic design of psychological interest.

In my estimation they reveal more about the psyche of Hawks than he himself ever intended. This complex director hides out underneath his characters, who for the most part appear on the surface as rather simple, ordinary, unsophisticated sorts speaking in the cliches of their time. With a closer look, we seem to find Hawks expressing himself as a "boy scout" whose

1

internal view of the feminine (Jung's anima), although typical of the men of his era, called forth within me a response of embarrassment as I was faced with its (i.e., Her) lack of development.

But one does not write a foreword to a literary work in order to detail its technique, or even to make technical its details. These are the things which each and every reader must independently decide.

You are about to encounter a literary work which has brought to life for its author, Clark Branson, much more than he ever proposed in his early, splendid impulse to articulate and chronicle a collaboration between the psyche according to Jung and the cinema according to Hawks.

I first met Clark on a spring day, in May of 1983. We met over what was our mutual interest in locating the similarities between archetypal or symbolic languages. Clark sought a way to reclaim the lost personal and psychological aspects of the relationshp between himself and his father, and I was attempting to help. Together we searched and researched those intellectual, psychological and symbolic sources and resources which might provide us with a clue or guide to the restoration and reconstruction of broken father-son bonds.

It is odd how time and place (or circumstance) find their own ways of tricking us into what *must* become our next (unforseeable) phase of psychological development. How could Clark and I have known that the Father he sought would be regained psychologically as a result of writing this book (then in its latter stages of revision)? Like many of the characters in Hawks's films, the figure who stood within the cloistered inner folds of Clark Branson's psyche was an adolescent boy whose need to move into and through an (archetypal) initiatory rite of passage into male adulthood would be dependent upon a Father who could act as his guide.

Again, time, place and circumstances often correct the developmental inequities to which fate has subjected us. In some curious way, Hawks—and I believe Jung, as well—became for Branson the symbolic Fathers, whose task it was to usher him through the doorway into manhood. I think that the way in which *Howard Hawks; A Jungian Study* brought to life for Clark Branson the living symbol of Father (for which he had searched, long and far) could never have been forseen by either of us during our prolonged meeting that spring day in May, 1983. In my view, this book represents for Branson the concrete embodiment and fulfillment of an intrapsychic need.

What has resulted is a job well done, by three *men*: Hawks, Jung and Branson. Such are the natural miracles and mysteries of the human psyche, when scouted by two people—who, one spring day, looked together in the wrong places for the right thing.

Judith Harte, Ph.D.
October 17, 1986
West Los Angeles, California

Judith Harte is a psychologist with an orientation in archetypal images, symbols and Jungian thought. She is in private practice in West Los Angeles.

Howard Hawks and Jean Arthur, 1939.

HOWARD HAWKS

I think most of the "art" films are bad cinema made by people who can't turn out good stuff... [Audiences] are way ahead of the critics... [This] "art" business is just people who like to talk. That's fine, let them do the talking... [The] same thing goes about directing. I don't analyze things. I found that people like the same girls I like, that people laugh at the same scenes that I do. So I just go blindly ahead and do them. I only hope the day doesn't come when they don't like it, because then I'll be very confused. But right now I don't have any doubts or hesitancy.

Howard Hawks, in an interview

To some critics:

You guys attribute strange things to me. I'm just doing the things I like
    Question: Why do you make films?
Hawks: Because it's fun.
    Question: Why have you used the same story line and characters more than once?
Hawks: When you find that a thing goes pretty well you might as well do it again.

4

INTRODUCTION

A study of the films of the late Howard Winchester Hawks proved to be a more involved undertaking than I first envisioned. Hawks's directorial style is one of the simplest—essentially one of simple story-telling by means of character interaction and development, with the camera serving like an onlooker close to the action. Yet his films are, ironically, a labyrinth when really taken to task.

This study is the result of one enthusiast's long process of fascinated, inquisitive viewing and re-viewing of thirty-nine of Hawks's surviving films. The omitted works are six little-available or lost films of his silent period, and *The Prizefighter and the Lady* (directed by W. S. Van Dyke and in part, though uncredited, by Hawks). Hawks has of course been both commercially successful and critically acclaimed as a director of international importance. There has been no lack of opportunity to view most of his films several times over, as they are continually accessible.

In this study, I have, in particular, considered his films in relation to one another as an interrelated *series*. In addition, they are examined in terms of the principal, core tenets of analytical psychology, the psychology of Carl Gustav Jung and his descendants. Jung's psychology has proven to be more than an ordinary descriptive tool. It may never have had a more penetrating application in a critical-humanities study.

The project, a task of cumulative cross-comparison among the thirty-nine films and their contents, has taken more than ten years. At about midway in the project, the process found its needed model: that of analytical psychology. Importantly, Jung was not superficially *brought* to the project, but was discovered in the very substance of the study—that is, in what was more or less naively forming in the dialogue between the films and myself, their viewer. A kind of subdrama, a level of symbolism, was very early perceived in the films. Initially, I couched it in awkward terms of esoteric philosophy (e.g., Freemasonry) and primitive culture. (Why Hawks should employ these was mysterious, though intriguing.) When I discovered Jung's psychology in the course of general reading, I quickly perceived that it pertained and related to the project in a very clear and incisive way.

Thus, commercial Hollywood and an esoteric depth psychology find intimate common ground. It can be said that, in its more or less naive way, Hawksian direction employs a Jungian-type process of symbolic expression as a feature of "method." The present work aims to show this through a comprehensive descriptive analysis: an examination of evident Jungian phenomena which in turn provides a critically incisive look into the eminent body of films concerned.

Hawks controlled his projects to an unusual degree, though working *through* his collaborators, and particularly his actors, it seems. His directorship was not one which set down letter-perfect plans to be followed, but lent itself instead to stages of improvising with co-workers. My study is hence the more illustrative of the remarkable degree to which a director—working as a director and within the Hollywood system—can influence his films, as their "author" or, as it is said in film studies, an *auteur*.

Although having majored in psychology as a university undergraduate, I was totally unfamiliar with Jung's thought until discovering it in the course of general reading in line with the developing Hawks study—specifically in Jung's *Man and his Symbols*, the well-known popular introduction to his psychology (written and edited in conjunction with close colleagues). Recognizing his pertinence, I took time off for a thorough study of Jung, covering his collected works and many works on the subject by second-generation Jungians and others. (Ref. to the Selected Bibliography.)

My experience with the Hawks films goes far in convincing me of the validity of Jung's thought and experience. The motifs and patterns of the particular film series are a cluster of data illustrating the most basic features of Jung's language. To present this is as important an aim as a study of the films for their own sake.

PART ONE: HAWKS AND JUNG

SECTION I
HAWKS AND ARCHETYPAL EXPRESSION

The films of Howard Hawks—or what I call his *series*—contain features of form and content of a special kind, namely recurrent patterns and motifs which may be designated as archetypal, in the Jungian sense. These archetypal patterns and motifs are intimately interwoven with recurrent features of a more ordinary kind.

The word "archetypal" has come to be closely associated with Jung by way of his category of the archetypal unconscious (usually called the *collective unconscious*). An ordinary dictionary will define "archetype" rather as follows. "(1) In metaphysics, the idea or essence from which an existent thing has been copied. (2) In psychology, according to the theory of Jung, an idea, image, or way of thinking that is inherited from the experience of the species and inherent in the mental life of the individual, influencing his perception of the world."

Jung's archetypal or collective unconscious is a hypothetical realm which gives rise to the entities and the patterning of myth and religion (and much else of human culture) by virtue of an unconscious "preformation" or prototyping (i.e., archetyping) of the same. Hence, the collective unconscious, in its intercourse with the external world by way of ego/consciousness, is partly responsible for the makeup of mythology, folklore, religion, and many other cultural forms. This accounts for the common patterns of religion, mythology, etc., in disparate cultures the world over. Analytical psychology holds that these common patterns do not form merely by external means and in socially determined ways but have *specifying* roots in our psychic makeup.

Jung has likened archetypes to the more familiar concept of instincts ("instincts," however, of a high order). The archetypal realm is of course unknown; but it is inferred from its clinically observed manifestations, which participate in conscious life by means of a process of active symbolism or *symbol-formation*.

These symbolic manifestations are observed in *primary* and *secondary* forms. Primary-archetypal expression is symbol-formation stemming *directly* from the collective unconscious source and emerging in certain dreams and visions, in paranormal experience, and other forms of imagination including art-formal process in some cases. A vision of a luminous, divine-like personage floating in the air would be a representation, probably, of the very deep archetype called the Self. A vivid dream of a frighteningly deformed figure of the same sex as the dreamer is likely a representation of the archetype called the shadow.

Also, the primary-archetypal can manifest *behaviorally*—acted out on the level of ego-personality and in ways more involved with social life, where the individual's behavior pattern is a symbolic expression. An unusually devoted nurse or social worker may be acting out the archetype of the nurturing mother.

Secondary-archetypal expression is symbol-formation that is more outwardly than inwardly manifest, and in *cultured* forms—in mythology, folklore,

9

religion, tradition, ritual, art, architecture, and much else. A prominent example is the trickster of world folklore (which corresponds with our own circus clown, and low-comedian), a *shadow* representation. The death/resurrection feature of world religion, mythology, and folk drama is an expression of the renewing Self (like the perennially rising-and-setting sun, when viewed as a deity). The king and queen are higher expressions of the archetypal father and mother. Again, such highly cultured archetypes have an ultimate source and substance on the primary level of the collective unconscious.

Hawks's direction and auteur dimension seem to feature archetypal expression in terms of the primary as well as the secondary level. We find the secondary-archetypal in certain evident borrowing from sources in drama, film, and elsewhere (such as folklore; ref: the 'dismemberment' motif,* discussed below and in section IV). Hawks was a considerable borrower of both archetypal and "mundane" material. Yet his particular *creative use* of borrowed secondary-archetypal material suggests a process involved with the unconscious or primary-archetypal source as well. This process is the subject—or the confident assumption—of the descriptive analysis which comprises the present study.

To begin with, it seems very unlikely that Hawks used Jungian psychology as a cinematic model. Both in terms of his films and personal testimony in interviews, Hawks displays an anti-intellectual bias, or at least an intellectual indifference (as regards the world of ideas: psychology, religion, the philosophical, "the human condition," and such). In Hawks's films, the tenets of analytical psychology are less expressed in the typical ways of their textual discussion than in fresh, "confused" ways of his own—namely, as though out of a naive, more or less unconscious (if pragmatically thoughtful) process. His films contrast with those of directors who elegantly *contrive* filmic content. Hitchcock's *Vertigo* and *Psycho* are elegantly contrived along Jungian and Freudian lines respectively, and are in this way very *conceptual.* Much of Ingmar Bergman's work is also couched in developed ideas and ideation, like that of Goddard and Samuel Fuller. In contrast, Hawks is a film-maker of pragmatic intelligence rather than one of philosophical inclination, to borrow Andrew Sarris's phrase. Relatedly, he is an "action"- or "behavioral"-type director, and his important archetypal features recur as models or devices for player-dramatics much more than as ideational content.

If we may be confident that Hawks has not used Jung's psychology as a basis for his films (and assuming that he never attended Jungian psychotherapy), then in what ways and to what extent are his patterns and motifs beholden to secondary-archetypal sources such as nodal points of literature and mythology? Put another way, how may we separate the secondary- and the primary-archetypal aspects of Hawks cinema? The series 'dismemberment' motif seems to me to be characteristic of Hawks's "translation" of secondary-archetypal material into his own, more primary-archetypal terms.

---

* Motifs and patterns peculiar to Hawks cinema are, in many instances, given single-quotation marks—not just in their initial appearances in the text, but at points throughout. This distinguishes the terms as having special meanings beyond the usual sense of the words.

In an interview, the director relates that he once met a man who was saving an amputated part of himself so that he would remain physically whole and thus be admitted to heaven. Hawks said that the idea "amused" him at the time, and he went on to use it in five films between 1932 and 1965. In view of his own 'irreligious' inclination, this attention given to the folk-religious item would seem, at first, to be out of character. But to Hawks, the item's interest and application was not religious but effectively *archetypal:* namely, concerned with the (archetypal) "sacrifice/restoration" form underlying the (secondary-archetypal) folk-religious form, and in an evidently semiunconscious way (or almost certainly not derived from Jungian study). In its instances in the films, the 'dismemberment' motif's religious association is either omitted, derrogated, or mitigated (in keeping with the series pattern of 'irreligion'). Yet in each case, the essential retained-wholeness or "restoration" aspect of the original folk-religious item is acted out in some fashion or another. Hence, the archetypal basis is retained, and even stressed. (In its *holistic* function, "sacrifice/restoration" is an expression of the renewing, archetypal Self.)

Section IV provides full discussion of the dismemberment motif in its creative, Hawksian use in ways diverging from its folkloric (secondaryarchetypal) source. (In general, Hawks seems to repress the introspective and the reflective, inclusive of religiosity—only to have the very substance of religion/myth emerge, as though semi-unconsciously, in other, more primaryarchetypal forms: as though out of psychic compensation.)

Another eminent borrowing in Hawks cinema is a venerable item from German film, the old "double" (*doppelgänger*) device in which a character shares a single identity with another character. The device, recurrent in world literature and drama, is initially used by Hawks in the early film *A Girl in Every Port,* and is basic to a number of subsequent series motifs. Yet, in common with 'dismemberment,' the "double" device is given to varying, creative use and integrative involvement with the series patterns as a whole: namely, in such ways as to make it Hawks's own.

The borrowing of secondary archetypes may, of course, be more extensive, and more important to the series patterns and motifs, than I have been able to discover. Hawks was very well-read, from his early days as a story editor, and of course well-schooled in cinema and drama. One may wonder if his patterns and motifs are more beholden than they seem to the Greeks, the Northern Europeans, the Arthurian, the Biblical, the brothers Grimm, and/or classical literature (as well as the secondary-archetypal via moviedom).

Or is his own creative process more essential, where his patterns and motifs are concerned, than such borrowings, where they exist? I am inclined to think that it is, in view of certain evidence, particularly the example of the dismemberment motif. Also, there are the parallels with mythology, discussed in section IV. These are remarkable in their ambiguity as to whether they are borrowed from Homer and Northern Mythology or whether they derive in a more primary-archetypal way of the director's own, for they are composed of well-precedented Hawksian motifs which could be their sole source.

An exceptionally creative instance of series archetyping is that of Lee Aaker/J.B. or "Red Chief," the backwoods boy who is too tough for his kidnappers in *The Ransom of Red Chief* (Hawks's episode in the omnibus film *O. Henry's Full House).* Previous to his Hawksian treatment, he is featured in a relatively innocuous O. Henry story. Patterned after several diverse figures, both male and female, in earlier Hawks films, J.B. seems to fit nearly all of the series archetypal categories: shadow, anima, anima/'animal,' and thence the all-inclusive Self. (These terms are discussed in the next section and in Appendix 1.) J. B. is in fact the most archetypally laden figure in the entire film series. He is rather clearly a Hawksian original, and not copied from a mythic source. (See further discussion in the section on the film.)

The Egyptology of *Land of the Pharaohs* is another case for discussion of the series archetypal patterns. The setting, in ancient Egypt (and filmed on location), is a renownedly mythic time and place, complete as it is, in the film, with gods, Pharaoh the living god, a high priest and fellow priests, and the holy task of building the pyramid. Yet, contrary to what we might expect, the film's archetypal import does not lie in the outward (secondary-archetypal) mythos and religiosity. Series-characteristic archetypal features are operant in the film, but in other ways than in the prevalent lore and religion of old Egypt, as we shall see. The Egyptology receives an appreciative, but common-sensical treatment (mainly in terms of the pyramid *tasks,* their engineering and labors, and peer-group concerns).

It is interesting that Hawks intensely disliked *Land of the Pharaohs.* Disowning it as he did, he was unjustly critical of it. It is one of his most interesting and essential works, from the auteur standpoint, and not unaccomplished. It is possible that (in character with his 'irreligious' streak) he hated it for the enormous theocratic, mytho-religious aspect which he could not change. (Originally, the project featured the building of, not a holy tomb in an ancient land, but a secular airfield in pre-revolutionary China; but the project had to be shifted, for reasons.)

Ironically, young J.B. of *The Ransom of Red Chief* is more archetypally laden than Pharaoh the living god of Egypt. In terms of "archetypal originality," and the emphasis of the archetypal over the religious, J.B., *Land of the Pharaohs,* and the 'dismemberment' motif illustrate, variously, where the series archetypal patterns are and, more particularly, where they are not to be found.

SECTION II
HAWKS AS A JUNGIAN SUBJECT

In more specific terms, how does analytical psychology apply to the Hawks films?

It applies in the following basic categories, which will be explained and defined in this section in six subsections: (1) The quaternity of mental functions and attitude types. (2) The archetypal shadow. (3) The archetypal anima/animus. (4) The archetypal Self, and the Self-as-*transcendent-function*. Categories (2), (3), and (4) above are part of the category Jung has termed the collective unconscious, which is discussed in this section as subsection five.

A sixth feature, a dramatic mode and pattern fundamentally present in the Hawks series, is a multifaceted version of (6) the old cultural entity of male-adolescent rites-of-passage (concerned with the transition from mother and family to male peers and thence to the tribe). This too partakes of the collective unconscious. Like much else of "basic" culture, the various rites of passage are featured in Jung's thought as having a primary archetypal basis.

The 'initiation/passage' pattern of the series combines closely with several archetypal features, in and through characters, actions, things and, in a few cases, animals—these in addition to the pattern's own ultimate "death/resurrection" feature. In the series patterns, archetypal features indeed link and merge, as they do in general.

These tenets of Jung's psychology are identifiable throughout Hawks's cinema—again, not in a static or conceptual way, but seemingly in a dynamic, creative form, and as a core feature of his directorial method.

This dynamic, creative form is well illustrated in Hawksian *anima* expression. In Jung's *Man and His Symbols,* the Marlene Dietrich character in Sternberg's *The Blue Angel* is cited as "clearly a negative anima figure." However, she is a highly developed type in the film, an exemplar (i.e., as regards "female principle," or the anima). She is highly *conceived* instead of being expressive of the anima nearer the archetypal-unconscious source. This latter proximity and condition is contrastingly suggested in the *varied* and "confused" anima expression of the Hawks series, often in other form than a female character.

The above six points, in their prominent expression throughout the series, cover a large core portion of Jung's model of the greater unconscious. Before proceeding with these points, I would provide certain other explanation and background from Jung's writings and those of his colleagues and successors.

In contrast to classical Freudian thought and its dominant Eros factor, Jungian thought posits a broader and deeper variety of features making up the unconscious psyche and its manifestations in the ego/conscious realm. Psychic energy, for its part, gets formed or channeled in more ways than as *libido,* i.e. psycho-sexually or according to the Eros factor. In Jungian psychology these ways (including the Eros form) are called archetypes. These archetypal ways/forms, again, manifest from a "preformative" source level called the archetypal or collective unconscious, a realm which is less known than inferred, and not essentially included in Freud's system.

13

Freud's psychology begins with (a) the ego/conscious realm, as in the Jungian model, but categorizes almost everything else by way of: (b) a *personal unconscious* of repressed material, partly in common with Jung's shadow category, (c) the Id, of basic instinctual energy and drives, and (d) the superego, a posited conscience entity not included in Jung's scheme (or not in the same terms).

Material of the collective unconscious is not repressed from a formerly conscious condition but is there to begin with. Although it is impossible for the collective unconscious to rise to ego/consciousness, it participates there, manifesting in the imagery of ego/consciousness and the world (again, as symbol-formation). Perhaps the ego/conscious realm was, at an earlier evolutionary stage, part of the vastly greater, *undifferentiated* collective unconscious, having recently emerged like a plant out of the soil in its separate (i.e., differentiated) category of life now. Similarly, the emerging archetypes originate in this undifferentiated "soil" or stratum.[1]

The archetypal can emerge—it can irrupt in psychosis, where the ego is shattered; or in visions or religious experience; or in other violent or dramatic ways. Less dramatically, it emerges in certain dreams, and other forms of imagination including instances of artform and, more prevalently, in the ameliorated form of *complexes.* The latter are behavioral "media of expression" closely related to the ego/conscious realm, and able to draw the individual into special, maybe obsessive patterns. They vary in their obsessiveness and in the directness of their relationship to the potent collective-unconscious level, and may comprise a normal part of psychic life and structure.

For illustration compare, in terms of a hero/Messiah complex, a religious fanatic, an ordinary conscientious clergyman, a Hitler, a sage or guru, and Jesus Christ, all of whom differ in degree and kind. (One writer speculates that Jesus had an extreme father complex: compensatory to the lack of an earthly father, as he thus became one with the archetypal father and thenceforth a Messiah.[2] In any case, archetypes can mix or overlap, and an archetypal entity/source may express itself variously in different personalities and in different cultural settings.)

The patterns of the Hawks film series seem to form a singular enough complex, involved with three or four separable archetypal factors. These factors form a *cluster,* the dynamic of which is a male-adolescent rites of passage complex, cinematically rendered in various ways. It recurs in more general association with other archetypal patterns and motifs of the series, as we will note in many specific instances later. For example, the initiation/passage of Bonnie in *Only Angels Have Wings* involves the anima (or "female principle") in Bonnie herself, and the ("sub-heroic") shadow figures in Kid Dabb and Sparks, as well as a composite expression of Self (symbolized in the Kid's two-headed coin). More generally, initiations and "hazings" of individuals in the series involve suppression of the assertive or recalcitrant anima factor: as in the "initiations" of Judith and Dorothy, respectively, into the masculine groups in *Only Angels Have Wings* and *Gentlemen Prefer Blondes.* Bonnie's case is similar. In its core instances, the initiation/passage pattern centers upon its own archetypal factor of "death/resurrection" and, subcategorically,

14

"sacrifice/restoration" (as exemplified in the basic instances of the 'fraternal return' and 'dismemberment' motifs respectively).

Next, I shall elaborate on the six points introduced earlier: which are, again, the basic analytical psychological categories of the Hawks series.

(1) THE QUATERNITY AND THE EXTRAVERTIVE SENSATION FUNCTION

For Jung, this was more a practical device than a real hypothesis.[3] Still, the quaternity of *mental functions* and *attitude types* comprises a significant part of his thought. The attitude types are *introversion* and *extraversion,* one of which tends to predominate in an individual ego/consciousness while the other, though "active" in a less conscious way, tends to be dormant. One of the four mental functions (*sensation, intuition, thinking,* or *feeling)* also tends to predominate, while the other functions are either less active or dormant. In common with the psychic opposition of the two attitudes, the functions have a polarization dynamic, as pairs of *opposites,* specifically: sensation/intuition and feeling/thinking. Like the attitudes, each member of a pair of opposites tends to "oppose" the other, in psychic life. Thus, the quaternity is usually diagrammed in terms of the functions being like the four points of the compass, with the attitudes as the upper and lower hemispheres. (See the general diagram on page 28A.)

In the Hawks films, we observe an *extravertive sensation* predominance which is a key aspect, both dramatically and thematically. It is ubiquitous in the physical, often confrontational interaction among characters—amorously, or in the manner of close-quartered peer dynamics, or in a combination of these. It is notable in the directorial tendency to replace words with action or curt implication (ref: Quita's curt, oblique acceptance of Mike's marriage proposal in *Tiger Shark),* and in a remarkable prevalence of the sense of touch, and the physical and corporeal in general. Hawksian style and theme altogether oppose (or repress/suppress) the introspective and the reflective.

Secondarily but importantly, *extravertive feeling* asserts itself—or "herself," since feeling, on the whole, functions correctively and compensatingly to the basic male-supremacistic pattern in Hawks, which, on the ego level, is bound up in group professionalism and its (extravertive sensation-functional) requisites. Some chief feeling exemplars are Tess in *Red River,* Hildy in *His Girl Friday,* and Bonnie (as well as Kid Dabb and Sparks) in *Only Angels Have Wings,* and the Frenchmen in *The Big Sky,* all of whom bring "feminine" and feeling function into the stories to major and good effect. Feeling emerges in the series by way of female characters and the "female principle" in general (namely, the archetypal anima).

In the quaternity's application here, extravertive sensation and feeling would seem to be the dual repressor of introspective *thinking.* We notice the absence or de-emphasis, and the occasional derogation of thinking or intellectuality, in Hawks. Groot in *Red River* and McTavish in *Barbary Coast* flaunt their illiteracy almost in praise of the same. In *Monkey Business,* the cerebral scientists render their definitive scene in a highly sensation-functional, tactile

15

way. Sparks, in *Only Angels Have Wings*, is the liberally educated one of the group, yet mitigatingly, this is crudely merged with his feeling-function, which he brings to the story's main turning point in serving as a go-between for lovers Bonnie and Geoff.

David Huxley, in *Bringing Up Baby* is a scientist, and as such is a burlesqued and ridiculed character. Dr. Carrington, the Nobel scientist in *The Thing (From Another World)*, is one of the most negative characters in the series: a group misfit requiring the rough "shaping up" which he receives, resulting finally in his nominal good standing with the (extravertive sensation-oriented) group. Something similar happens to David in the earlier film, in the course of his involuntary odyssey of misadventures.

In another way, the gangster, Tony Camonte, of *Scarface*, fatally disarms himself in his process of becoming more reflective. Comparably, gunman Nelse McLeod is, at length, undone by his trait of curiosity, in *El Dorado*.

As a group, the professors in *Ball of Fire* are lovable but essentially comic, parodic. They undergo an "initiation" like those of David and Dr. Carrington, as they are seduced away from their books and into physical adventure. Vashtar, the heroic architect in *Land of the Pharaohs*, is not least a manual craftsman—"the greatest man who has ever worked with stone"—and more than an armchair intellectual in any case. (He seems to be a personification of Hawks himself, who with his own engineering background, provided for the engineering aspect of the self-sealing pyramid.) Significantly, the architect is pointedly unreligious in the film. In *The Big Sky* however, Jourdonnais's religiosity, at one point, is shown as part of his feeling function—in common with Sparks and his knowledge of Shakespeare, in *Only Angels Have Wings*.

Intuition, the remaining function, is mainly absent in the series—not merely suppressed, like thinking and the introspective in general, but as though out of sight and out of mind. (In any quaternity makeup, the last, fourth function is mainly absent in this way, and often the third as well.) In the action dramas, characters may work together in a close, instinctual way (in the manner of close teamwork), but this is more behavioral than intuitional.

Even so, intuition has an eminent, almost telepathic moment in *A Girl in Every Port*, as Spike, in a fit of eerie discomfort, seems to know Bill, in the saloon, before actually meeting and identifying him as the anonymous sailor who has been "moving in on his girlfriends" all over the world. There is nothing else like it in the thirty-nine films covered. It and other examples of *premature close confrontation* between Hawks characters are part of the general series dynamic in which characters tend to act as entities of a common psyche: that is, as close-knit psychic processes which are personified in the dramatic action. The lone "intuition" instance in *A Girl in Every Port* is not a significant instance of intuition-function but, more properly, one of the 'characters as portions of one psyche' pattern. More important than Spike's vague precognition of Bill, in the film, is their being, on one level, different aspects of one and the same man, and hence intimately in contact.

All the attitudes and functions are operant in a given personality in a basic way; but they form, in one combination or another, the sort of "pecking order" observed in the Hawks films. Although the attitudinal/functional quaternity is, of late, a less accepted part of Jung's thought, we seem to have an expression of it in Hawks. In any case, *extravertive sensation,*complementary *extravertive feeling,* and repressed introspection/introversion are prominent in such a way as to require a consideration of the quaternity.

Jung considered intuition to be his own dominant function (and hence repressive of its functional opposite in sensation). Concerning this, Laurens van der Post relates:

> ...[Jung] was always having accidents and once narrowly escaped falling into a river. It was, he would tell me, borrowing from the vocabulary of his own theory of psychological types, all a result of the fact that he had been born with an inferior "sensation function," an underdeveloped sense of the reality of his physical here and now.[4]

The very opposite of this condition is a key value in the Hawks films. The action dramas are wrought in the physical here and now, often with life and death stakes resting on professional and group competence and their teamwork and timing. Similar conditions prevail in the Hawks comedies *The Twentieth Century* and *His Girl Friday.* In most of the other comedies, physical failure and mishap are featured to one extent or another, stressing the same *sensation* value, though in the negative way. Thus, in *Man's Favorite Sport?,* the somewhat introverted Willoughby's slapstick efforts at fishing and the outdoor life function thematically. Comparably, in the action drama *To Have and Have Not,* the loner Johnson's being such a poor fisherman links with his other negative traits and even, on a certain level, marks him for death.

(2) THE SHADOW

This is the first archetypal feature to be considered here, and the most prevalent of the Hawks series. This prevalence is logical, in the first place, for the shadow is in good part linked to the ego, being its immediate "underside," and very accessible to ego/consciousness. Again, it corresponds closely with Freud's category of the personal unconscious, to which the repressions, rejections, and other material not working well with ego/consciousness are relegated in the uneven course of development.

In the experience of analytical psychology however, the shadow readily assumes a *personified* form, in dreams, artform, and other imagination. This personification, a kind of subpersonality, is typically of the same sex as the bearer and of contrary or different character than that of the bearer's ego-personality. The shadow may express itself in a "bad half," as in Mr. Hyde of Robert Louis Stevenson's *Dr. Jekyll and Mr. Hyde,* or the murderous Cain of the Biblical Cain and Abel pair, to cite two of the most famous secondary-archetypal examples. Or, it may be some neutral figure, like the angel with whom Jacob wrestled in his dream; or a positive alter ego, as in the case of Jiminy Cricket of the Pinnochio story, and similar "helpful animals" of folktales. An individual's shadow may, of course, display different aspects, or manifest in different forms (in the course of his dreams, say).

The shadow (in common with other archetypal entities) is responsible for *projections* of itself to external things, situations, and people which are then perceived as bearing features actually borne (less consciously) in oneself. The shadow can be troublesome in other hidden ways, too—making one accident-prone, for example. This ego/shadow tension varies with the individual awareness or *egotization* of the shadow aspect.

As in the case of the complex, the pathology of projection is proportionate to its distortive influence. Otherwise, it is a normal part of psychic functioning, enabling one to relate to the outside. As regards artform, Hawks (for example) has shaped his films by a process of active psychic projection into the production process—by altering scripts, prodding certain kinds of responses from writers, actors, and others, and reiterating these innovations from film to film (as motifs and patterns). He has thus imparted his own shadow, anima, and other attributes to his films.

To recognize and "make a friend" of this shadowy sexual peer within is a developmental requisite, involving the recognition of one's self-concealed negative traits as well as desirable features and other qualities which, one way or another, have been repressed in the course of day-to-day ego-striving, and which the archetypal shadow assumes in the way of a sub-personality.

Although preceded by Adam and Eddie of *Fig Leaves* (1926), Spike and Bill of *A Girl in Every Port* (1928) set the precedent for the most prevalent motif of the series, which may be called the 'pals' motif. It is a motif of ego and shadow. Bill, on one level, is an expression of Spike's shadow side, dawning and pressing upon him—forcibly, violently, contrarily, yet in a friendly way, throughout the story.

Here, Hawks seems to have borrowed the older motif of the "double" *(die doppelgänger)*, a device of ego/shadow relevance, and recurrent in German film (in *The Student of Prague* [1914] and its remakes). Stevenson's *Dr. Jekyll and Mr. Hyde* is probably the most famous example of the device, which is also discerned in the characters Guy and Bruno of Hitchcock's *Strangers on a Train* (1951).

Relatedly, there is Don Quixote and the complementary Sancho Panza of the Cervantes novel, the knight and his "pilgrim shadow" in Poe's "Eldorado" and, in fact, the complementary Laurel and Hardy of silent comedy and talkies. Hawks was aware of all of these, and Poe's poem is used thematically in *El Dorado* (1966).

The *doppelgänger* device is rather blatant in its ego/shadow implication. Yet, as we shall see in our discussion of the films at length, there is more of ego/shadow interplay in Hawks—variously and creatively—than this particular secondary-archetypal borrowing, influential as it is.

(All in all, Hawks may have borrowed widely and diversely enough to be less influenced by his borrowing than by himself. For he freely modified and combined his borrowings, both archetypal and mundane, in his creative use of them.)

According to analytical psychology, the shadow comes to bear in relations with one's own sex particularly. This is another reason for its prevalence in the series, for on the whole, the Hawks films are principally and deeply about male relationships—at times to the exclusion of women or even to the extent of cryptic denials of their existence. This male-supremacy is the main reason for the psychically-compensatory pattern of the irruptive imposition or aggression of female characters, and in a more mellow way, the earlier-noted feeling-functional assertion of characters like Bonnie in *Only Angels Have Wings*.

As an archetypal entity, the shadow is inherent and dynamic in itself and not solely constituted of fragmented material purged from ego/consciousness, involved with this though it is. It is by virtue of this psychic autonomy that an archetypal entity may form a subpersonality and hence assume an integral, personified form.

The shadow is the source of certain cultural archetypes. These include the fool and the clown, the trickster (the comic, mischievous antihero of folklore), and the devil: all reversals of the norm and the ideal. The fool is the reverse of the king, and the clown the reverse of the hero. At his best, the devil is an extreme, ego-contrary trickster (an imp). At his worst (as Satan), he is the contrary shadow or underside not merely of the ego, but of the greater psyche's optimal evolution into egotization/consciousness. The composite center/circumference of this evolutionary process is the archetypal Self (discussed later in this section). The Self—as distinguished from the self in the ego sense—is represented in figures such as Christ and the Buddha: hence in reverse of the devil, who is the lord of evolutionary backsliding or cosmogonic defeat.

In the Hawks series, these highly cultured archetypes are not represented so much as a number of vague shadow figures. Among the most interesting are Norman Alden/John Screaming Eagle in *Man's Favorite Sport?* (although too little is done with him in the film), Red Buttons/Pockets in *Hatari!* and—of anima as well as shadow relevance—the steward in *Corvette K-225* and his certain descendent in Hoagy Carmichael/Cricket, in *To Have and Have Not.*

A tricksterish shadow pattern, a pronounced mischief-tending mode, is sometimes noted in Hawks films. This is eminently seen in the jungle compound group wantonly invading the town with the elephants (as "bloodhounds") in *Hatari!*—precedented by the designatedly "unhousebroken" cattle driven into Abilene, in *Red River.* But it is broached as early in the series as the two plumber pals behaving gauchely at the elegant fashion show in *Fig Leaves* (1926).

In *Sergeant York*, Alvin York and his drinking companions interrupt the church meeting with their shooting outside (in the irreligion pattern of the series). This is preceded by Zeke, the elderly churchgoer, shyly entering the meeting late with his fancy, squeaky shoes—actually a little foreboding, or a fragmented part of the uproar to come: as he, and next the hell-raisers outside, effectively converge on the religious meeting. Such 'convergence,' usually suppressive, is an important series pattern. Although Zeke is not part of York's group, he and they constitute parts of a common aggression, on one level. In *Rio Bravo*, Stumpy's interruptive levity at the formal swearing in of a deputy is similarly both tricksterish and in the series irreligion pattern, though it is in terms of the sub-pattern of denigration or mitigation of formality and ceremony. (In addition to the hell-raisers, the sermon in the earlier film is, mitigatingly [or "irreligiously"], a rather secular one about the virtues of patience and perseverance.) In *El Dorado*, the gun-battle upon and through the church is in the same mode, i.e., combining the patterns of group tricksterism and irreligion.

In the early film *A Girl in Every Port*, there is the memorable scene in the

Latin cantina where four gaucho toughs converge on Spike prior to his very narrow escape. Later in the film, Spike and Bill contrive, vindictively yet mainly as a lark, to shove an unsuspecting policeman off the dock (precedented in turn by their earlier brawling against police). These hoodlumesque portions, in particular, foreshadow the greater series shadow/tricksterish feature.

Another kind of shadow expression is seen in four instances in which a main protagonist dies: in each case, indirectly, or more symbolically, because of personal character flaws which consist of a (symbolized) irruptive shadow with anima aspect. These doomed protagonists are Tony in *Scarface,* Mike in *Tiger Shark,* Villa in *Viva Villa!,* and Pharaoh in *Land of the Pharaohs,* along with other, minor instances like Johnson in *To Have and Have Not* and Dan in *Red River.*

THE ANIMA

The next most prevalent archetypal feature in the Hawks series is the anima/animus or, in our case of the male-predominant world of the series, the anima. This is the feminine aspect inherent in every man, as the animus is the male counterpart in every woman.

In dreams and other imagination, "she" is expressed essentially in a personified and feminine form, and just as the shadow is involved in relations with one's own sex, so the anima comes to bear in man's relationship to the Other in Woman. Closely related to the Eros factor as well as the likewise archetypal factor of the mother, the anima also comprises the bearer's particular relationship with his greater psyche, including the archetypal Self (which, in an important sense, *is* the psyche as a whole, inclusive of ego/consciousness).

As the shadow relates to the ego in general, the anima relates to a man's ego/consciousness via his *persona:* the ego-extension comprising his self image in day to day relations and behavior. The anima functions compensatingly to the ego/persona, and develops or becomes more conscious after major egotization of the shadow.

In Jung's (conceived and edited) *Man and His Symbols,* a painting of a feminine demon is presented as an anima representation and "an overwhelming, terrifying vision," although a certain feature of the particular demoness alludes to "the fact that the anima contains the possibility of achieving wholeness" (p. 187). This feature is her four eyes—an invitation to development, inasmuch as the number four is able to refer to the Self (in terms of numerical symmetry, in common with a square or a squared circle, of Self-relevance). (Ref. the subsection on the Self, below.)

Whether, mythically speaking, the anima is Medusa or Muse depends on the bearer's ego/persona (as well as his ego/shadow) relationship to her, or how adequately she is "acknowledged."

Culturally, anima archetypes include the princess of fairy tales, various feminine dieties, and of course the old masculine propensity for designating ships in the feminine gender, as "she," or if conditions and treatment were bad on a voyage a "hungry bitch." A special anima-related category is the mother; thence the archetypes of mother nature or the earth mother, the divine mother (e.g., the Virgin Mary), the queen and, on the negative side, the witch or "terrible mother" in common with the evil stepmother of folktales. Popularly, movie principals like Marlene Dietrich, Mae West, and Marilyn Monroe are anima projections, of sorts, as Valentino and Errol Flynn were certain animus projections.

Amatory harmony and disharmony are a function of the relations between the man's anima and the woman's animus, a realm in each of them unlikely to be well developed, egotized. As Jung put it, bluntly, "The masculinity of the woman and the femininity of the man *are* inferior..."[5]

Jung further states:

> The persona, the ideal picture of a man as he should be, is inwardly compensated by his feminine weakness, and as the individual outwardly plays the strong man, he becomes inwardly a woman, i.e. the anima, for it is the anima that reacts to the persona. But because the inner world is dark and invisible to the extraverted consciousness and because a man is all the less capable of conceiving his weakness the more he is identified with the persona, the persona's counterpart, the anima, remains completely in the dark and is at once projected, so that our hero comes under the heel of his wife's slipper.[6]

This and other passages of Jung's basic writings closely describe an important pattern of the Hawks series, that of the recurrent threat of Woman: of female (anima) characters, things, and forces threatening to upset the hero or heroes. The male protagonists of important Hawks comedies are overwhelmed and humiliated in this way, as the male-supremacistic Hawks action drama thus "turns over" into its weak counterpart in the anima-rampant, shadow-exposed Hawks comedy. Nevertheless, the heroic and comedic modes mix, in both adventure drama and comedy, in ways both great and small, throughout the series.

Anima often *irrupts*, in Hawks films. She comes forth provocatively, often in a manner of "female tricksterism" contra the male-supremacistic viewpoint of the series. In *Rio Bravo,* she storms the sheriff's office in the form of a parcel containing a pair of feminine drawers in symbolic threat to Sheriff John Chance. In *Bringing Up Baby,* Susan, a kind of female Ulysses, drags David on an odyssey of misadventures that all but ruin him professionally (although he becomes somewhat better off with her, in gaining a stimulating mate).

Yet the anima is at other times "one of the boys," as in the example of Nikki in *The Thing (From Another World),* or, like Diana and Monique of the Hawks/Faulkner projects, she is masculinely companionable in a motherly way. In instances, she becomes companionable or one of the boys after a period or event of 'initiation/passage.' Often she has her own special dignity and, again, brings female/feeling principle to creative or salvatory effect. Male-supremacistic though the series patterns are, they are not uncognizant of the limitations of Man-on-his-own. Witness Bonnie and Geoff in *Only Angels Have Wings,* and Tess and the cowboys in *Red River.*

Even so, the ego/anima conflict is nearly always at hand, and never fully resolved, in Hawks. In the anima's functional opposition in the series pat-

21

terns, we witness a main feature of psychic life according to analytical psychology: namely, the balancing, *compensatory* function and striving of the unconscious as a whole. (It is hence no accident that the anima links rather closely with 'mandala-Centrism,' in Hawks, and hence with the all-inclusive Self which, again, entails the psyche as a whole. Ref. the subsection on the Self, below.) Directorially, this potent anima function is expressed through things and characters in addition to female characters, as the anima becomes a kind of seething, general force contra the prevailing ego of Man-the-measurer-of-all-things. Hence, certain objects and most animals are anima-aspected; and shadow figures usually carry an anima stigma. (As the general Hawks ego is overwhelmed by the Hawks anima, the Hawks ego, in being thus disarmed, is overtaken in turn by its weak counterpart in the Hawks shadow. This deep auteur condition is represented in figures of [resulting] dual shadow/anima or "male/female" aspect—who may be said to represent the Hawks ego/hero's "diagnosis.")

Hence, Mike, of *Tiger Shark* (like his predecessor in Tony of *Scarface)* is a curious "androgynous" figure, on one level. Comparably, Mother York, of *Sergeant York*, is, by cross-reference, a masculine 'pal,' in the motif, as the alien in *The Thing (From Another World)* is an out and out hermaphrodite! The remarkable J.B. of *The Ransom of Red Chief*, in clear cross-reference in the series, is descended from all these figures, and from others as well, both male and female. The many and varied instances of comedic sex role-reversal are another expression of this (hence) 'blurred sexual distinctions' pattern. The examples are very numerous and will be treated in subsequent sections.

In summary, the anima and the conflicts, contrasts, and mitigations which she imparts in the Hawks series, constitute a cinematic probe beyond the usual man-woman drama.

As powerful, and as pervasive and difficult as the anima is, in Hawks, it is natural that the only character in the entire series to be drawn in outright villainy is a woman, namely Joan Collins/Nelipher in *Land of the Pharaohs*. The film is not particularly given to realism, save in the occasionally brilliant pyramid-building aspects, and is thus the more prone to such phantasy as total villainy. (Yet female protagonists of the series are at times phantasy-simplistic in another way, namely in tending, cryptically, to lack existence in their own part: as mere anima "appendages" of the male characters. This is exemplified in the cases of Tess in *Red River* and Lotta (as well as Evvie) in *Come and Get It*, and in the early example of Tessie in *A Girl in Every Port*. This status of Woman as a mere appendage is one way that the anima is rudely suppressed in the series patterns.)

Nelipher, the Cypriot princess, enters the film out of a cinematographic "morass" of shadows, and wields a calculated pugnacity toward Pharaoh to impress and hence to woo him. This is followed by an intense, physical conflict with him (of initiation/passage relevance) whereafter she becomes his own and an associate of the pyramid cult on his terms. On another level, she is an irrupting symptom of his own decadence at this point. Thereafter she reveals herself as Villainy Incarnate, as if requiring superhuman measures for her suppression. Indeed, the antidote to Her is, finally, Man's greatest architectural achievement. In the end, she is entombed alive with Pharaoh, whom she has had murdered, and with the triumphant self-sacrificing cult elite, namely Hamar and the high priests. In the sealed tomb, the priests stand around her as, realizing what has happened, she rages in last grief on the stone floor—surrounded in turn by the tall (male) statues lining the chamber walls: again, deep within the world's greatest architectural achievement. It seems that on one level, the purpose of the Great Pyramid (i.e., Man's Work) is to bottle up Nelipher for ten thousand years! Hence, the anima is as mightily suppressed in the film as her recalcitrance is extreme; and vice versa.

Exemplary as this is, for Hawks, there are, of equal importance, the more harmonious ego/anima expressions of the series (as the psychic pendulum swings in Woman's direction): in the eventful mellowing of Henri and Catherine's sex-antagonism in the first half of *I Was a Male War Bride,* and the wonderful character of Hildy in *His Girl Friday,* amid other examples. Even so, Woman, whether at her best or otherwise, is always rendered in the series' own particular ego/masculine terms.

(4) The Self and the Transcendent Function

In Jungian thought, the Self is the formative root of all archetypal material. It is also the greater entity which wields the transcendent function. The transcendent function is the Self's active processing of archetypal material to consciousness and egotization. This proceeds through a faculty of symbolism, or *symbol-formation:* the medium through which the unconscious archetypal material may emerge in the form of *entities,* and thus be able to be grasped and dealt with by ego/consciousness to then affect the overall behavior pattern in potentially developmental ways.

The Self is a teleological entity, like an acorn from which may grow a forest of trees. A holistic archetype, the Self entails the psyche's entire, optimal course of development through all its potentially emergent archetypal entities (whatever small part of it all may be realized in the course of a life). This "path" of unfoldment (called individuation) is notably represented in the eventful path described in John Bunyan's *Pilgrim's Progress* (ref. Esther Harding, *Journey into Self).*

Again, all archetypal entities are rooted in the Self and are part of it but the anima/animus is a particular key to it. Culturally, the Self is represented in figures like Christ and Buddha, or in God himself, and in the Tree of Life of esoteric philosophy. It encompasses psychic life as a whole—the ego/-conscious, the personal unconscious and archetypal realms alike—being at once an archetypal Center and Circumference: like the manifold yet unified process of a crystal formation. As such, it is outstandingly represented by Tibetan-Buddhist *mandala* art, of squared circles of exemplary symmetry and unity in diversity. The Self can spontaneously emerge in individuals in this form too, or in many ways, geometric and otherwise (all of which may be termed *mandala-Centric).* It may be projected in an animal (which may become a tribal totem), or nearly any object (which may then take on a magical significance).

Yet the Self is, not least, inferred from the manifest, orderly transcendent function which unfolds its archetypal material is such a way as to indicate an ultimate teleological entity.

Manifest itself though it may in a composite way, in spontaneous mandala patterns or some potent equivalent, the Self is unable to be egotized. The anima/animus is very little realized (egotized) except perhaps in extraordinary individuals. Most people get little beyond an early shadow stage. (It should be stressed that anything archetypal is unrealizable at its source: namely in the Self, which is, again, the formative root of all archetypal material.)

In the Hawks series, we observe an orderly transcendent-functional process at work, particularly in the way the archetypal materials "molecularly" *cluster.* This is seen, importantly, in the 'triangle' motif in its manifold yet close-knit archetypal content, and likewise in the sundrily composite figure of J.B. of *The Ransom of Red Chief,* and in the mythic parallels in *The Big Sky* and *The Thing (From Another World).* (The latter are treated in section IV.)

The Self is also involved in the holistic function of the dismemberment and fraternal return motifs. In related aspect, a series pattern of 'mandala-Centrism' is often expressed in Hawks films. This is notable in the series dramatic/compositional pattern of 'convergence' (in which two or more characters effectively "crowd in" upon an effective Center: an object, personage, or other locus). Mandala-Centrism is observed in the related device and pattern of 'dramatized/transacted object' (in which an object dramatically links in character transaction), and in the motif of 'group-delineative/"circular" montage.' Nelipher among the priests and statues within the pyramid chamber, in *Land of the Pharaohs,* is mandala-Centric, and an important instance of the pattern. Again, mandala-Centrism is often linked with the anima, in Hawks.

These points will be further discussed, in due course, through their examples. (However, ref. also to the Summary and Description of Series Motifs and Patterns, in Appendix 1.)

(5) THE COLLECTIVE UNCONSCIOUS AND MISCELLANEOUS

The Self is the ultimate entity (and "reach") of the *collective unconscious:* a term which excludes ego/consciousness and the personal unconscious (involved with the Self though these ultimately are) and includes the shadow, anima/animus, and all possible archetypal material.

Most people adjust or live in such a way that collective-unconscious material is not drawn into their lives to a great degree—as, say, a resource for ego-striving that has gone awry. Some people seem naturally to have it nearer the surface and potentially irruptive, so that they have no choice but to deal with it (egotize it), one way or another. Hawks would seem to have been such a person.

Generally, the course of an individual's life is spent haggling with the personal unconscious, the shadow and, usually next in the development pattern, the anima/animus. Other archetypal material may be involved with these, and development (individuation) does not always proceed in an ideal pattern, as the series patterns abundantly suggest: namely in their evident *irruption en masse.*

One of the finest things about the Hawks series is the way in which the archetypal elements mix, yet are still discernible: through their cross-referencings, yet often in their own part, in their dynamic, fairly specific feeling-tones, cinematically wrought. I experienced the latter, particularly, in my first viewing of *The Big Sky*, with its abundant ego/shadow/anima clusterings richly delineating themselves (even though I had yet to be introduced to C.G. Jung).

Theoretically there are an indefinite number of at least partly separable archetypes, as the collective unconscious perpetually strives to emerge by "latching on" to things in the world, which then, creatively, may become inward/outward cultural forms. (More than being the separate archetypes themselves, the collective unconscious/transcendent function is, instead, a composite faculty for manifesting them.) Jung has interpreted an archetypal aspect in kinds of tools and utensils, and even in the ford or fording of a stream (the latter seeming to have a mythic archetype in Moses' parting of the Red Sea). The shadow, anima/animus, and (of course) the Self are, manifestly, among the most principal archetypal functions, however.

Archetypal entities carry a dangerous, undifferentiated morass to the rear of their ego/conscious emergence. Hence, the egotization process needs all the more to be pursued if begun, as it is a serious matter for emerging archetypal material to have to "give up" and regress, carrying a share of ego-consciousness with it, back into the deeper, greater unconscious realm and its potent, undifferentiated terrain with maybe a pathological result for the bearer.

In the Hawks series, this psychic morass and danger seems to be evident in general, and at particular times in the form of an expressionistic, cinematographic "morass," often linking with the thematically-prevalent danger-that-is-Woman. (Witness the shadowy morass from which Nelipher emerges, definitively, in *Land of the Pharaohs*.) All things considered, the series mandala-Centric pattern (alluding to the benign, differentiating Self) seems to be a weaker signal than this "morass" factor: with Woman/anima as the forerunner of a devouring force more than serving as the muse unto the benign Self. We will examine this "morass" pattern in important instances of the ego/shadow/anima-relevant 'triangle' motif and, at significant points, the cinematographic feature of medium-low lighting and shadow, which probably alludes to this psychic morass.

What we seem to have in the series patterns is, again, a general irruption *en masse*, like a forced surfacing of unconscious material as developmentally premature as it is extensive, as though the result of some ego-shattering trauma.

For all this, Hawks, when encountered in person, and as we might infer from the facts of his successful career and life, stands up as most balanced and good-humored of men.

(6) RITES OF PASSAGE

The preponderance of archetypal shadow material in the Hawks series links or concurs with the male-adolescent rites-of-passage pattern (i.e., as both are involved with the important series pattern and theme of male relationships).

Jungian psychology holds that initiation/passage, in addition to its attendant archetypal features (e.g., in the form of deities and tribal lore), has an archetypal aspect in and of itself: namely, its death/resurrection aspect. In common with certain tribal initiations, Masonic initiation/"ordeal" ritually enacts a death/resurrection with the candidate: to impart the death of an old condition unto a new one (much as the passage of life's end yields the mystery of death and whatever it may hold). This parallels the mythical phoenix consumed by fire and rising again from its own ashes.

Such a "death/resurrection" feature recurs in the Hawks films, importantly in the 'fraternal return' instances in *The Dawn Patrol, The Twentieth Century,* and *Air Force,* and in the holistic "sacrifice/restoration" aspect of the dismemberment motif. These motifs are, hence, central to the series initiation/passage pattern, which otherwise includes various ordeals, testings, hazings, and their transitions, usually involved with ego/shadow/anima dynamics. Tribal rites of passage violently bring the transcendent function and its symbol-formation to bear as a resource, the ego needing the emerging material to form anew (much as, at other times of ego/conscious stress or defeat, deep material can emerge in a potentially helpful complex). Tribal initiation makes use of and provides for this state of irruption, in ritual, symbolism, and attendant lore.

Less formally, there is an initiation/passage aspect in a boy's abrupt weaning from home and family into a radical new peerage when he leaves home for the first time to join the military, or to attend boarding school replete with hazing (as in the Thomas Hughes novel *Tom Brown's School Days*). Hawks's world is essentially fixated within this sort of transition-stage of the quasi-adult group of sexual peers.

In the series, this stage is perennial-like, as the rest of society is seemingly not graduated to, nor related to very positively but is, on the contrary, mainly lampooned (in the comedies). Again, this condition and pattern links closely with the series' dominating shadow aspect, involved with masculine peerage, and often combines with a crude fatalism. In *A Girl in Every Port,* probably the most influential film of the series, the condition is somewhat celebrated. It is the main point of the story, and the entire Hawks series tends to follow suit.

A violent thing by nature, initiation/passage, and its expression in the series, might link or concur with the sort of general, en masse irruption suggested in the preceding subsection. Further, the Hawksian fixation at the shadow level of male-adolescent passage, replete with archetypal irruption, would seem to involve the aforementioned imminent danger of slipping back from the needful egotization process—i.e., needing to proceed beyond the shadow and into anima development (and her part in greater and mature society, inclusive of the parental side of home and family). Thus, for all the extensive archetypal patterning of the films—including composite (mandala-Centric) expression of the Self—it is all in stunted relationship to this shadowy fixation. Consequently, the anima tends to be tricksterish or, in important instances, a "devouring" anima or "terrible mother," merged with the potent, undifferentiated morass below instead of being, more ideally, the muse unto the differentiating Self. In other instances, she is a safely "initiated" masculine peer and a participant in the shadow-fixated condition. (Ref. Jane

Russell/Dorothy's song-and-dance "initiation" with the Olympic team, in *Gentlemen Prefer Blondes*.)

This weaned but fixated condition of life, away from home, family, and normal community, and habituated with shadowy male peers, combines with a professionalistic, small-group-oriented self-sacrificial pattern (ref. *Only Angels Have Wings, Ball of Fire, Rio Bravo*, and *Hatari!* in particular). In view of this, one feels behooved to include a biographical point.

This biographical point consists of two related features: (a) Hawks's (noncombative) experience as a soldier and airman in World War I, and experience gathered from others of this peerage, and (b) his early experiences, and the experiences of associates and others, in flying and race driving. These occupational experiences, undergone in his early twenties, and which he sportingly pursued into later years, seem indeed to be the source and style of so much to be found in the films.

I have outlined above how the series patterns unfold in a way of fixated male-adolescent initiation/passage with attendent archetypal irruption. Given this, and assuming his service experience to be a biographical factor largely shaping his films, Hawks becomes a significant, and in certain ways graphic, though oblique, reflection of the particular fixation and estrangement known as the "Generation of the Front" of European social and historical significance.[7] It dwelt on the notion that veterans of the Great War were a breed and an elite apart for having come through that ordeal by cataclysm, itself a kind of initiation/passage (into the raw extremes of mass-societal, technocratic modernity). Amidst a contrastingly indolent civilian life which was unequal to postwar imperatives, this impatient elitism led nowhere but back to itself—to the veterans themselves who, unfortunately, found little or no place in normal society, and were often disinclined to join the political left.

Here, an observation of Peter Wollen's seems very pertinent:

> Hawks recognizes, inchoately, that to most people his heroes, far from embodying rational values, are only a dwindling band of eccentrics. Hawks' "kind of men" have no place in the world.[8]

This is somewhat descriptive of the "Front Generation," who gravitated to fascism (to Europe's own *collective shadow* as Jung interpreted).

The series patterns, obliquely yet somehow intimately (or archetypally), seem to reflect something of this estranged Front Generation (more so perhaps than reflecting their less earnest, sibling "Lost Generation" of similar estrangement, who likewise had their writers and figures). Hence, the Hawks film series—for all its relative lack of broader social implication or a "world view" as such—is of social-historical note.

This of course does not implicate Hawks in any fascist attitudes. He is instead a cinematic and archetypal "chronicler" of certain conditions that link in history. This is how the subject of fascism often and curiously crosses one's mind when viewing the films, despite its absence there.

In other regard, the films reflect something of the people who pioneered aviation and cars—not mentioning, however, other occupations (such as the early film industry and movie people). *Homo Hawksianus,* in Peter Wollen's term, may be applied to twentieth-century Western man more generally.

As it happens, the occupations of (a) the War and the original air corps, and (b) the air and motor professions, had many points of mergence (i.e., people in common). Capt. Eddie Rickenbacker was an exemplar of both.

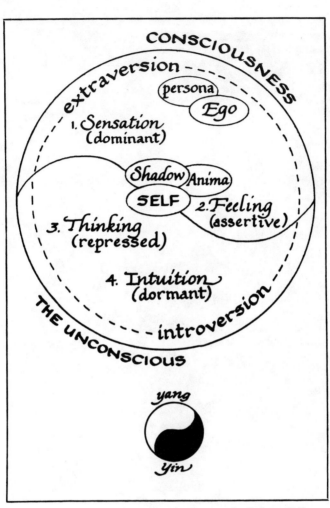

Diagram by Kathryn Callaway

The Quaternity of Mental Functions and Attitude
Types, with application to the Hawks films.

28B

SECTION III
HAWKS AS AUTEUR

In his *Theories of Film,* Andrew Tudor states: "The *auteur* principle directs our attention to groups of films having in common—the director. It asks us to isolate his conception of the world as presented in the films, and to do so in some considerable detail." The assumption of this process is "that we can learn more about a director's films by considering them in relation to one another," and that, for example, "when we have seen every 'tawdry little gangster picture,' they might really turn out to be quite good, precisely because of the insights afforded by looking at the range of a director's work." (or, put another way, because of the revealing context of a *series*). (Pp. 130-31.)

Sometimes this approach uncovers a director with special, consistent themes, and patterns of content and attendant style amounting to a manifold *outlook,* in which case we have an auteur. Although the word "auteur" is not synonymous with quality, auteurs tend to make good films.

William Wellman has some good films in his career, but his series does not reveal an auteur, as it is diverse where there would be consistencies of theme, style, and content.

Robert Aldrich seems to be an auteur of style and situation over theme and "world outlook." One is just as aware of his personal presence and hand—his filmic authorship—as with exemplary auteurs like Ford, Hawks, Hitchcock, and Capra.

Samuel Fuller, one of America's most creative filmmakers, shows great consistency and personal expression in style, theme, and other content. He is perhaps as completely an original as it is possible to be, in commercial American cinema. But because he has nearly always written his own scripts he may be considered a different type: a creator from scratch—the more in having so often worked with more wieldy, low-budget projects. The latter condition is also shared by the most celebrated work of Edgar G. Ulmer. This is different from being the personal "orchestrator" of the efforts of a team of name artists, craftspeople, and technicians with major studio connections: which is what the American auteur is, in his most significant examples—still realizing his own vision via the team effort, and throughout his series or career.

In this respect, Hawks is among the two or three most exemplary cases of the auteur approach to American film. The cornerstone of his career has been his creative control over projects. Though usually serving as his own producer, he worked with major studios and eminent co-workers, who tended to impose conditions in their turn which he managed to wield his way. He also worked with many "new faces," and considerably launched the careers of Lauren Bacall, Montgomery Clift, and others. As Andrew Sarris notes (in *The American Cinema*): "Like his heroes, Howard Hawks has lived a tightrope existence, keeping his footing in a treacherous industry for more than forty years without surrendering his personal identity (p. 54)."

Relatedly, certain of his films reveal his capacity to creatively adapt or collaborate. *Scarface* was a markedly joint effort among Howard Hughes, Hawks, Ben Hecht, and Paul Muni. In the Hawks/Faulkner projects, *Today*

We Live and *The Road to Glory*, and the Hawks/Wilder comedy *Ball of Fire*, his writers were more dominant than usual. Yet all four of these films are important in the auteur consideration.

Undoubtedly, Hawks had a way with people of more than one sort, in the industry. It seems that what he has done is *not* like Josef von Sternberg, his opposite in most ways, who managed to manipulate everything and everyone like a painter. Instead, in a person-to-person method of his own, Hawks, promptingly, would *set people and things in motion* to unfold more of their natural own. Being less inclined to unfold plots as such, his films tend to proceed "behaviorally, " via character interchange and development, wherever possible, and the stories and their dramatic progression were often worked out more or less on or near the set. The almost plotless *Hatari!* is the extreme example. (At the other extreme is *The Big Sleep*, with its involved mystery-thriller plot. Though failing to render the story in a comprehensible way, the film yet succeeds through its character dramatics.)

Most essential, however, are the Bogart and Bacall characters in their long interchange around the businesses of Johnson's wallet and then the liquor bottle, in *To Have and Have Not*. Though the sequences belong greatly to the actors, as has been testified, there is no "purer" Hawks to be found in the series.

Over his long career, Hawks and his collaborators put forth dramatic material which worked well and hence came into the series "repertoire" to be repeated in kind and in variation—in a way of "natural selection" via the director, who was also a prompter of things he was vaguely or more specifically looking for. Thus, the series patterns and motifs cumulatively came into being with the growth of the director's career.

The reader is referred to Joseph McBride's valuable *Hawks on Hawks*, consisting of interview material revealing much about the director's professional personality. (Excerpts from the book are featured in Appendix 3.)

In the following passage, Jung describes how he analyzed a series of dreams without interviewing the dreamer at all, but discovering the frames of reference internally, by way of the emerging patterns. The statement is also a good analogy of our cross-comparative method with the Hawks films and their patterns and motifs.

Now the method I adopt in the present study seems to run directly counter to [a] basic principle of dream interpretation. It looks as if the dreams were being interpreted without the least regard for context....

This procedure, if applied to isolated dreams of someone unknown to me personally, would indeed be a gross technical blunder. But here we are not dealing with isolated dreams; they form a coherent series in the course of which the meaning unfolds more or less of its own accord. *The series is the context which the dreamer himself supplies.* It is as if not one text but many lay before us, throwing light from all sides on the unknown terms, so that a reading of all the texts is sufficient to elucidate the difficult passages in each individual one.[9]

SECTION IV
The Mythic in Hawks

In this section I wish to examine something of the mythic character of archetypal imagination in specific terms of the Hawks films. The films provide well for the same.

The series patterns and the mythic compare richly, at points, due to the archetypal imagination inherent in both. In at least two instances, noteworthy parallels obtain between points of mythology and film portions. These are the Homeric and Northern European parallels respectively in *The Big Sky* and *The Thing (From Another World)*. These "mythic" film portions derive integrally from precedented series patterns and motifs and thus seem independent of secondary-archetypal borrowing from Homer and Northern Mythology. (They are discussed later in this section, in their close involvement with the folkloric 'dismemberment' motif of the series.)

(1) The Hindu Example

Initially, I would consider another series mythic/filmic correspondence, a more general or vague, yet archetypally significant parallel between (a) an item of Hindu mythology, and (b) certain basic features of *Red River* (1948): namely, the film's ego/shadow "male supremacism" and its compensatory, contrary and "enveloping" anima, which are features of the series patterns in general.

The protagonist of the myth is a demigod, an archetypal-heroic figure (whose counterpart in the film is an ego/shadow 'pals' pair in Tom and Matt). The Hindu story is of the ancient warrior-king Muchukunda, who, through the agency of the Brahmins and his father, was born of an all-male circumstance, being "born from his father's side." In the myth, the father mistakenly swallows "a fertility potion that the Brahmins had prepared for his wife; and in keeping with the promising symbolism of this miracle," it came to pass that:

> ...the motherless marvel, fruit of the male womb, grew to be such a king among kings that when the gods, at one period, were suffering defeat in their perpetual contest with the demons, they called upon him for help. He assisted them to a mighty victory, and they, in their divine pleasure, granted him the realization of his highest wish. But what should such a king, himself almost ominpotent, desire? What greatest boon of boons could be conceived of by such a master among men? King Muchukunda, so runs the story, was very tired after his battle: all he asked was that he might be granted a sleep without end.... The boon was bestowed. In a cavern chamber, deep within the womb of a mountain, King Muchukunda retired to sleep, and there slumbered through the revolving eons.[10]

Since King Muchukunda never had a mother, in the sense of an early home

31

in a womb (and it is suggested that this is how he was as heroic as he was), it may be said that he compensatorily retired to a womb as his best reward.

Encountering this story (in the above interpretive passage by Joseph Campbell), I was struck with the way it addressed the important archetypal features of *Red River,* an exemplary series adventure drama in many ways. The film's story concerns a heroic achievement, namely the founding of the King Ranch and the opening of the Chisholm Trail with the "impossible" cattle drive north to market. It likewise concerns a heroic, predominantly male circumstance, as opposed to a normally domestic situation.

Tom, Groot, Matt, the other cowboys, and the cattle constitute their own sort of "family." Inceptually, and procreatively, this is out of "the meeting of a man and a boy, and the beginning of a great herd," as Groot narrates on the sound track.*

Early in the film, Tom and Groot, with a bull tied to their covered wagon, are searching for a place for Tom to found his ranch and herd. They have left Tom's deceased fiancee behind, massacred by Indians and thus unable to bear him a son and heir. Their cows are likewise slain. Suddenly, their bull gives a lurch and a resounding grunt. As Tom and Groot turn to look around, we see that this was in the bull's detection of orphaned Matt coming along leading a cow, in delirious flight from the same wagon-train massacre. In the story, Matt will become Tom's "son" and heir, and Tom will give Matt the (recovered) bracelet he gave to his fiancee as an engagement token, as a way of validating Matt in the role and tasks of "son" and heir.

Hence, on one level, Tom "begets" a "son" by way of the reaction of his bull to Matt's cow. Further, the eventual herd out of the original kine is rather the "offspring" of Tom and Matt—and even of Groot, Cherry, Buster and the other cowboys. In this way, of Eros, their cattle ultimately beget the great herd for the heroic, pioneering drive north to market, opening the legendary Chisholm Trail.

In the film, the bracelet (which Matt will wear when he comes of age) belonged to Tom's mother. It may be said to *be* the mother, on one level (in a "compressed," objectivized form). In an anima-suppressive way, objects sometimes "replace" or "objectivize" a female character, in Hawks films. (In his book on Hawks, Gerald Mast discusses the bracelet as a metaphor of Tom and Matt, in terms of the knob at each end of its snake-like coil being like a connected pair of heads. If this is so, then the bracelet's mother/anima association is all the more suppressed. Ref. the section on *Red River.*) As a 'dramatized/ transacted object,' in the series pattern, the bracelet figures widely in the story as it passes eventfully from character to character, like a seminal talisman.

Hence Tom, Matt, Groot, and the cowboys and cattle are a kind of "family," although without women—and even without children, for, in a manner characteristic of the Hawks adventure-drama (again, removed from home and family and hence the institution of childhood), little Matt initially fights with Tom (pulling a gun on him), pointedly demonstrating a reckless spirit or hardiness beyond his age. Hence from the first, he is more a "younger brother"

---

*Certain prints of the film utilize written passages on the screen in lieu of Groot's narrating.

than a "son" ("son" though he is, there and subsequently). Yet he is even Tom's "spouse," via the engagement bracelet he is given to wear; and as, early in the film, Tom (in a homoerotic note, I think) jests that he might put a branding iron to Matt's rump, as if he were a steer.

Thus, the Muchukunda myth corresponds with *Red River* in terms of certain "motherless origins" of Matt, on one level, and the subsequent heroic achievement of the pair and the group.

Moreover, both Tom and Matt compare with the mythic king as regards ultimate compensatory anima/mother *envelopment*. In *Red River*, and in the Hawks series more generally, Woman/anima tends to lurk, like Muchukunda's fateful mountain-womb, to disarm or overwhelm the hero or heroes, who work and die in extreme situations like cattle drives, war, aviation, auto racing, pioneering, and the underworld.

At the very beginning of *Red River*, as Tom and Groot prepare to leave the wagon train in search of ranch land, Fen, Tom's fiancee, is presented as a beautiful and sympathetic but "devouring" feminine force. In parting with Tom, she, in her spoken lines, allies herself with the *night*, which will follow each of Tom's workdays, or (one might add) which "envelops" his workdays and the realm of the ranch and his masculinely important tasks (for which, however, she expresses womanly support). There he pulls back from her rich embrace, out of alarm and resistence to the temptation to take her with him (instead of sending for her later). He leaves her behind with his mother's bracelet as an engagement token. When she dies in the subsequent Indian raid on the wagon train, it is in some allusion to Tom's own psychic defense against the force she personifies: namely, to the extent of a cryptic "homicide" from his part. We will examine this in detail in the section on the film.

Late in the film, Tess enters the story. Encountering Matt, she is initially provocative and pugnacious, but soon represents an overwhelming force to him in the night/fog scene where Matt nervously stands his watch, as she seduces him into a few hours or so of comfort, there in the fog-becoming-a-gentle-rain. As we will see, when examining the "rain" scene in detail, Tess, on one level, is an irrupting, anima part of himself to which he succumbs—rather as Tom earlier had strenuously resisted succumbing to the same force personified in Fen (though Fen is not so obviously an entity from out of himself).

So it is with Tom and Matt as with Muchukunda. On one level, Fen and Tess are anima figures of the "terrible mother" kind in their early scenes. As such, they are paradoxical counterparts to heroism, namely in a compensatory way. As Jung relates:

> There lie at the root of the regressive longing, which Freud conceives as "infantile fixation" or the "incest wish," a specific value and a specific need which is made explicit in myths. It is precisely the strongest and the best among men, the heroes, who give way to their regressive longing and purposely expose themselves to the danger of being devoured by the monster of the maternal abyss.[11]

This ego/anima conflict is less acute on the part of Matt than in Tom's case, in the film. On one level, Matt is Tom's more genial shadow, and of certain

33

anima aspect. The latter is in (a) his being Tom's "spouse substitute" in a way, though particularly in (b) Tess's cryptic emergence from, or partial identity with Matt in the "rain" scene. Relatedly, Matt (it is suggested in the end) will marry Tess, who in positive anima fashion has played out a creative role in the story—like a muse now, as opposed to the initial "Medusa" in Fen (who was an expression of Tom's anima estrangement).

Characters in Hawks films tend to be personified portions of one psyche. As Matt is a mellowed Tom, Tess is a mellowed Fen. Further, Matt and Tess (as shadow/anima) are a meeting ground for Tom (ego) and Fen (the same anima, only more estranged). Though four in number, they comprise an instance of the series 'triangle' motif, which is one of ego, shadow, and anima (ref. discussion in the section on *A Girl in Every Port*).

See discussion of the hermaphroditic alien in *The Thing (From Another World)*, in subsection 4, below, and my own "U.F.O." dream in the section on *Red River*, since these relate to the Muchukunda story as well. See also Appendix 2, which contains an excerpt from Gerald Mast's discussion of *Red River* in a context of literature and myth.

(2) THE HOMERIC EXAMPLE

'Odyssey' (often alternating, in the same story, with an opposite 'close quarters' circumstance) is a series motif which varies, in extent, from an episode to, in some cases, a key part of the entire scenario. The odyssey motif has its principal beginning with the rambles of Susan and David in *Bringing Up Baby*.

Although not a film epic in the "De Mille" sense of *Red River*, *The Big Sky* is beholden to the latter film and is a considerable odyssey in its eventful story of a pioneering free-trade expedition up the Missouri River. It is possible that the film's instance of a mythic parallel derives from a particular episode in Homer, but the instance is, in key part, composed of well-precedented series patterns and motifs which could be its sole basis. Hence, the likely independence of the mythic parallel from the secondary-archetypal source in Homer's *The Odyssey*.

At one point in the upriver journey in *The Big Sky*, as the group encounters a mishap with the keelboat, Teal Eye, the Indian princess, falls overboard and is carried downstream in rough water. Both Jim and Boone, who are on shore at the time, dive in to rescue her. Boone reaches her first and brings her ashore.

Just previously, her skirt catches on a fallen tree in the river. Jim pauses to retrieve it and severely injures a finger in doing so. He complains of this to Boone before tossing the woman's skirt back to her as, ashore there, she huddles shiveringly in what remains of her clothing. In a subesquent scene, Jim has the finger amputated due to threatening infection, in a comical bout of frontier surgery with whiskey for an (internal) anesthetic.

In the film, Jim, Boone, and Teal Eye constitute an ego/shadow/anima threesome: a triangle motif instance, paralleling, to some extent, Tom, Matt, and Fen/Tess in *Red River*. (As it happens, the finger-amputation business was planned for John Wayne/Tom in *Red River*, but Wayne dissented and it was not used there).

These filmic events in *The Big Sky* correspond with a mythic item which I relate via Edward F. Edinger's book *Ego and Archetype*, where the author cites, with comment, a portion from Book V of *The Odyssey*. There, Odysseus is in trouble on the sea, and Ino, a sea goddess, comes to his aid.

> She tells him to take off his clothes and swim for it and adds, "Here, take my veil and put it around your chest; it is enchanted and you can come to no harm so long as you wear it. As soon as you touch land take it off, throw it back as far as you can into the sea." Ino's veil is the archetypal image that lies behind the symptom of transvestism. The veil represents the support and containment which the Mother archetype can provide the ego during a dangerous activation of the unconscious. It is legitimate to use this support, as Odysseus does, during a time of crisis; but the veil must be returned to the goddess as soon as the crisis is over.
>
> Another parallel is provided by the priests of the Magna Mater in ancient Rome and Asia Minor. After their consecration these priests would wear feminine dress and allow their hair to grow long to represent their service to the Great Mother. A remnant of this sacerdotal transvestism exists today in the skirts worn by the Catholic clergy who are in the service of the Mother Church. These parallels go to show that the urge of the transvestite is based on the unconscious need for a supporting contact with the female deity—the mother archetype (p. 115).

Hence, we have the following parallels between the mythic item and the film portion: Jim-and-Boone/Odysseus, the Missouri River/the sea, Teal Eye/Ino, and Teal Eye's lost skirt/Ino's veil—which clothing article Jim takes, in a manner similar to Odysseus, and, ashore with Boone and the woman, tosses it back to her, after which the pair walk away (again, in deference to the half-nude Indian girl's privacy there). In the myth, Odysseus is in trouble on the water. Similarly, Jim injures himself there, although doing so in connection with the anima-relevant object of her skirt (rather as the potent, magical veil might have harmed Odysseus had he retained it).

The "skirt" sequence in *The Big Sky* is integrally involved with the archetypal 'triangle,' 'feminine apparel,' and 'dismemberment' motifs, which have various precedence in earlier films. Hence, the sequence may be independent of the secondary-archtypal source in the Odysseus/Ino/veil portion of Homer. If so, then the mythic and the film portions parallel each other not because of borrowing, but considerably via their common archetypal source in the anima.

"Transvestism," feminine garments or "effeminate" objects and their intrusion onto a male character or into the masculine ken, are a running joke in about half the films of the Hawks series and are a particular feature of important comedies. In *Rio Bravo* (an adventure drama), there is the instance of the feminine drawers delivered to the sheriff's office previous to being passed to Carlos and Consuela at the hotel where they belong. Sheriff John Chance takes them over to the hotel, where he is the butt of some humiliation over them. Representing a challenge to the courage and prowess of the lawmen in the siege to come, the garment is a dangerous "lure." As Robin Wood has alluded, the hotel, in its general oppositeness to the sheriff's office and jail, is the setting and realm of this lure—a lure to laxity, Woman, and mishap, away from the line of duty and responsibility. In the story it proves to be a place of hero vulnerability.

Contrastingly, at the very end of *Rio Bravo*, deputies Dude and Stumpy, their job completed, pass the hotel just as Chance, who is in a hotel room with Feathers, confiscates her tights and throws them out the window. They playfully take the garment with them and proceed on their stroll about the town, in symbolic mastery now, as (in a way of initiation/passage) the lawmen have triumphed and done their job. (In this way, anima expression, including instances of the 'feminine apparel' motif, participates in the series initiation/passage pattern, at times. Usually this is in terms of anima irruption and suppression, as in *Rio Bravo*. Jane Russell/Dorothy's song and dance number with the Olympic team in *Gentlemen Prefer Blondes* provides another good example.)

In common with the red drawers early thrust upon Sheriff John Chance, there is an indignity, and on one level a taboo, in Jim's retrieving Teal Eye's skirt (for which he loses a finger) in *The Big Sky*. In the series, a male character retrieving or attending to a feminine item portends ill for him, or he is negatively stigmatized. Early in *Red Line 7000*, Mike Marsh brings Holly's luggage and clothes to her (and fixes breakfast for her), in foreboding of his later shadow/anima difficulties. In certain instances (such as Mike's), association with such items symbolizes an irruptive character flaw. In the extreme cases—where, in certain comedies, a male character is forced into feminine clothing—the "flaw" becomes complete, as he is effectively engulfed by his irrupting anima.

Though a different sort of character—a vigorous ego type instead of a vigorous, protagonistic shadow—Kirk Douglas/Jim descends, in part, from Edward G. Robinson/Mike Mascarenas of *Tiger Shark*. Mike, a heroic but flawed and doomed character loses a hand to the sharks as Jim loses a finger in behalf of a skirt. Like Tony, Villa, and Pharoah of the series—though not Jim—Mike Mascarenas is a main protagonist who (1) dies, and (2) dies in part and symbolically from "feminine forces" within his ken, represented in fancy apparel and comparable items. As indicators of character failure, on one level, these, in Mike's case, link with his obsessive hatred of sharks, which early maim and finally kill him.

A parallel example is Dan, a supporting character in *Red River*, who dies in the cattle stampede a minute after he relates his intention to buy his wife a pair of red shoes at the end of the drive. Relatedly, when they find his remains, it is noted that he was wearing checkered (i.e., fancy, gaudy) pants. These—plus the fact that he was the only married one of the group (and moreover rode a "little buckskin mare")—are, on one level, a "cause" of death. As symbolic indicators of faltered character, these irruptive anima features readily link with his stuttering (an additional stigma of ego/unconscious encumbrance).

(3) THE DISMEMBERMENT MOTIF

As it happens, 'dismemberment,' of the "Homeric" cluster of features in *The Big Sky*, is a key feature of the "Northern European" mythic parallel in *The Thing (From Another World)* as well. Before discussing the latter, I wish to examine this important motif in greater detail.

As noted in section I, Hawks obtained the motif in real life from someone who harbored it as a folk belief. The dismemberment motif was initially used in *Tiger Shark* (1932). Early in that film, old Manuel intimates to Mike Mascarenas that he (Mike) will not make it into heaven due to his missing hand, which went to a shark and is replaced now by a mere hook. In his cocky way, Mike rationalizes that gatekeeper Saint Peter, being an ex-fisherman, will make a fraternal exception for Mike since Mike is "the best fisherman in the entire Pacific Ocean." Subsequently a shark gets Manuel's legs, killing him. In spontaneous vengeance and instantly recurring consciousness of the idea, Mike and the fishing-boat crew chase and catch the shark, and "ceremonially"—all at once, as a group—'converge' upon it and beat it with clubs (before killing it) to then give the old fisherman a sea burial with it: that is, with his legs. Mike, in Hawksian irreligious fashion, gives a markedly informal service for Manuel in familiar language, as if he and "Saint Pete" were on colloquial terms. "Manuel was good fisherman," Mike says, chatting with Pete on high.

Later in the series, the motif is used humorously in *The Big Sky*. Early in the film, the physical wholeness idea is related as an Indian belief (in reference to the scalping of an enemy to cut him off from the Afterlife). When Jim, drunk for the operation, has his finger amputated and, initially realizing it, panics, the Indian idea spontaneously comes to him and he sets to searching for the finger. Others join him in his foraging, humoring him in the heated moment (although the amputated finger has in fact been thrown into the campfire).

In both these instances, the retained-physical-wholeness idea is acted out, despite earlier expressed indifference or scorn concerning it (in the series irreligion pattern). The idea is embraced in a crisis, and, in each case, the group follows through with it: respectively, in deference to Manuel, and humoring Jim in his drunken state. Thus, retained physical wholeness is played out, not religiously, but in a Hawksian, group-dynamical way, and an archetypal way.

The same 'group dynamics/contagion' pattern and "restoration" aspect are featured in the (oblique) dismemberment instance in *Air Force*. In the hospital scene, the dying Captain Quincannon hallucinates being aboard his wrecked B-17 again. His crewmen, gathered at bedside, play-act with him, as if they were all taking off in the *Mary Ann* once again, thus humoring him in his last moments, not having the heart to tell him that the airplane has been deemed beyond repair. But the crew subsequently perform the "impossible" and rebuild her, and take part in the Battle of the Coral Sea, their restorative act being essentially borne of the captain's hallucination and their own group-dynamical participation in it with him. In this way, the captain's hospital death scene and the subsequent rebuilding of the *Mary Ann* is an oblique dismemberment instance. In place of the severed limb, of course, is the wrecked and restored airplane (which Quincannon had stayed with in the crash-landing, like the proverbial captain going down with his ship, thus making the plane all the more an extension of himself).

In the way of archetypal clustering, in the series patterns, the hospital scene also hosts a 'fraternal return' motif instance: the "death/resurrection" import of which becomes one with the dismemberment instance's "sacrifice/restoration" aspect. (Ref. the sections on 'fraternal return' and *Air Force*.)

In *Barbary Coast*, the town gangsters bullyingly cut off the pigtail of a Chinese to sever him from the Afterlife. Even so, they shortly insert the same pigtail under the hat of the alcoholic Judge Harper who, in a stupor, is unaware of it as he stumbles along his way, as a "Chinaman" now. In the motif's way of sacrifice/restoration, this second prank restores the earlier dismemberment, on one level.

Again, the motif was planned for *Red River*, but was not used. It would have been an outstanding addition to that film. The interpersonal act of the primitive surgery on Tom's finger, its violent, sensation-functional imposition, its certain mayhem and, at the same time, its beneficence (medicine) would have served, on one level, as a manner of "blood pact" with the (growingly villainous) Tom, sealing his waning relationship to the group, so that he would *have* to be rejoined in the end—although there was enough in the film's dramatic development to compel this ending anyway. (Writer Borden Chase and higher-ups wanted Tom killed off, as a quasi-villain. Hawks fought for the ending and won.)

The dismemberment motif, as sacrifice/restoration, is definitively presented in the late film *Red Line 7000*. In its instance here, the motif links very explicitly with the series initiation/passage pattern, of which 'dismemberment' and 'fraternal return' are, after all, a key part.

The particular instance functions symbolically in the latter part of the film, where the story comes to a dramatic head as five characters resolve their interrelated problems through a pair of violent incidents. The resolved problems are: (1) Holly's superstitious fear of being a hoodoo to her race-driving boyfriends who have died in action, (2) Gabby's crisis in her relationship with Mike, who imagines that she is cheating on him with Dan, (3) which neurotic condition of Mike's is resolved in turn. Dan, who earlier went with Gabby, is centrally involved in one of the violent key incidents, but he has no personal problems in the story except for being in love with Holly who cannot properly reciprocate due to her phobia of jinxing him in his stock-car racing. He is something of an ego-ideal figure, one of the very few in the Hawks series.

Also resolved is (4) Ned's inflated egotism, or *hubris*, cut down to size the hard way when he loses his left hand in a crash; and (5) Julie's problem of her own sexual identity is solved, as she successfully reunites with Ned, morally supporting his recovery—inclusive of his being able to drive again.

Ned's racing accident resulting in his severed hand is the second violent incident figuring in the group's general crisis/resolution. The first incident is Mike's jealously attempting to kill Dan by running him off the track in a race, which the latter brilliantly survives unhurt, and which convinces Holly that she is not a hoodoo. That night, in Dan's motel room, further confrontation and resolution ensue. Dan and Holly are happily reunited there. Gabby comes in very distraught and concerned for Mike, having looked everywhere for him in the rain. Mike soon comes in, mopingly clown-like, with a funny-looking white rain hat, to passively take a punch from the rightly disconcerted Dan, dressed in a fine and dignified housecoat. "That's what I came for," are Mike's lines, after getting up. As he leaves, having indicated that he is through driving, Gabby rushes out to accost him in the rain, where they embrace and make up.

Next, Julie, grievously estranged from Ned, watches the stock-car races on television. (In the announcer's commentary, we hear that Mike Marsh is driving. Dan, hence, had refrained from reporting him for his offense, and Gabby was obviously supportive of his return to the track as well.) When Ned crashes and is seriously injured, Julie rushes out to catch a plane to go to him. In the next scene, Ned lies in a hospital bed with bitterness and defeatism over losing his hand in the crash. Julie is at his side. A lightning storm rages outside (paralleling the storm outside Dan's motel room just earlier, thus linking the two scenes). As Ned complains, Julie urges that he can and will drive again. How? the viewer asks. The scene cuts immediately to a future stock-car race, the camera in medium close-up on Ned's recently acquired prosthetic hand—a hook—as he skillfully uses it in steering, doing as well as ever.

In the grandstand, the three girlfriends: Holly, Gabby, and Julie, are cheerful and supportive of boyfriends Dan, Mike, and Ned on the track. This is near the end of the film, again with the characters all having solved their problems and working together again as a harmonious team, girlfriends included.

The suddenness and violence of the Mike/Dan assault and crash, and Ned's crash and dismembering, coupled with the likewise sudden and profound change in the characters and their relationships, constitute a dramatic series instance of initiation/passage. The focus on Ned's substitute hand doing the job, at the end, symbolizes the general (group) restoration. It is the same symbolism as the retained physical wholeness idea in *Tiger Shark, Barbary Coast,* and *The Big Sky,* only with a different turn in Ned's heroic *adaptation* (representing, again, the new adjustment of the group as a whole). Also, Ned's prosthetic hand is 'mandala-Centric,' and a composite expression of the Self (as it and the other dismemberings and their various restorations, in the series, involve the Self in terms of the latter's holistic function).

Relatedly, at the end of *Tiger Shark*, Mike Mascarenas seems destined for heaven for his professionalism (despite his physical incompleteness). "Mike no go to heaven," he boasts near death, "Saint Peter come and get Mike." Faintly on the sound track here, a choir sings, like welcoming angels. Thus, for all his Promethian impiety and presumption, Mike, "the best fisherman in the entire Pacific Ocean," seems to have impressed the heavenly hosts.

(4) THE NORTHERN EUROPEAN EXAMPLE

The dismemberment instance in *The Thing (From Another World)* is part of a specific Northern European mythic parallel. In section I, I related that archetypal features characteristically emerge, in the series, elsewhere than in the mythos of a setting or situation, such as it may be (indicating *Land of the Pharoahs* as one illustration). In *The Thing (From Another World)* we have a partial exception to this, as archetypal features are very much projected in the science-fictional creature, who is, after all, like a deity. Yet, in a Hawks manner, the film's substance is less in its science fiction genre features than in the *group*, their peer-centeredness and character relationships, and how they manage to beat the mortal danger upon them. Further, and importantly, the humanoid creature is, in a cryptic way, a member of the human group.

Produced by Hawks, the film's direction is credited to Christian Nyby. Hawks worked on the script as usual, and supervised, and obviously rehearsed the players. The screenplay diverges from its origins in the novelette, *Who Goes There,* by John W. Campbell, Jr. It is in fact an exemplary Hawks film in nearly all ways.

The situation is a group of Air Force men, scientists, and assistants at a North Pole laboratory/station, plus a newspaperman, on hand to cover a mysterious event which, as it turns out is a flying saucer crash-landed nearby and frozen over. Thawing it out with thermite grenades, they blunderingly destroy it, but its pilot is tossed clear, quickly freezing over again. They bring the alien back in a hewn-out chunk of ice, intending to keep it frozen until further orders from their absentee high command. But by another (human) blunder, the space creature thaws out, comes to life, and besieges them. The rest of the film is their battle of wits and forces with it, in and about the frozen-in premises, until, all other means failing, they finally conquer it with electricity.

Human-like (played by tall James Arness), the alien is of the vegetable kingdom, a manner of walking "carrot," self-reproducing from its own produced seeds. (Hence a third "motherless marvel" in our discussion, pertinent to the earlier-discussed features of *Red River* and the King Muchukunda story. See also, my own U.F.O. dream in the section on *Red River.*)

Minus animal/human weaknesses and qualities, it lives on blood, a few of the human group and sled dogs becoming its prey through the story. In an early skirmish with the dogs, one dog chews a forearm off, which the alien regrows. Moreover, the severed limb comes to life for a while on the lab table. This instance of 'dismemberment' of course compares with the earlier-discussed instances in terms of the idea of retained physical wholeness.

In the early scene where the group examines the spacecraft in the ice, they line up around its discernible edge to determine its size and shape. Discovering its roundness in this manner, a few of the group utter exclamations and comments regarding the same, one at a time in a clockwise direction around their formed circle. This ceremonial-like business suggests, on one level, a deeper relationship to the alien (who is like a part of their encircled group). More importantly, in the film, the vampirous alien is linked to the group by way of the corresponding "blood" scene in *Rio Bravo* (discussed in the section on that film). This latter scene obviously links with the 1951 science fiction film. (Further, the "ring" scene in *The Thing (From Another World)* seems to be an oblique instance of 'fraternal return,' a motif of communal reunion, in view of which the alien is all the more a cryptic group member. Ref. the section on the science fiction film.)

In Hawks films, love/affection and violence (of varying degrees) are inter-involved. In the series patterns in general, violence/opposition is less a blunt alienation of affections than a *transaction.* This is very powerful and dramatically effective at times. This series 'friend/foe' pattern probably has some basis in the director's method, which is one of relationship with the players he works with, so that, even in the play-acting itself, they may retain the same thread or more of *belonging,* whether friend or foe in the story. Hawks's basic dramatic model is the close-knit peer group, with other relationships tending to follow the same dynamics.

Basic to the friend/foe pattern perhaps, is the professional respect for, and a considerable degree of comradeship with, the captured enemy airman in *The Dawn Patrol*, with its basis, in turn, in the Great War, where airmen were known to retain a vestige of older "sporting" chivalry.

The Thing's title is part of a cluster of items in the film which parallel a specific mythic point/cluster. The word of course was familiar in fantasy fiction with reference to supernatural beings: "The Thing in the..." or "The Thing From...," and such. Previous to the film's release in 1951, there was the best-selling novelty record, "The Thing," by Phil Harris, which must have influenced the title choice (to capitalize on the word, alive in the public ear). Although the title was probably influenced by one or both of these ordinary sources, one is struck by the title's coincidence with other factors which, together with the title, constitute a mythic parallel. (Taken individually or in part, these factors mean little or nothing, of course. But occurring together as they do—and particularly in view of the crucial 'dismemberment' and 'binding' factors—they form a rather uncanny mythic parallel, I think.)

There is early evidence, dated around 600 B.C., of a Germanic religion featuring a sky-god thought to have been called Tiwaz, and whose name became Tiw and Tyr respectively among Anglo-Saxons and Scandinavians. The Romans equated this god with their own Mars and entitled him, among other names, Mars Thingus, which in turn links him to the *Thing*, which was the old Germanic assembly where men met to debate and deliberate. Later, this aspect of the god becomes added to the Viking sky-god, Thor, a god of community, law and order, politics and the like.[12]

Participants in Thing-assemblies swore in upon a sacred ring—which more generally has been a talisman for a pledge between two or more people. In a similarly general way at least, this can relate to the Hawksian peer group assembling around the frozen-over spacecraft in a circle/ring. Moreover, the ring/spacecraft shortly yields the "sky being" in the person of the alien, whom we may, as well, dub Tiwaz/Tiw/Tyr, as well as Thor. Hence, the encircled group are like the assembled Thing, and the alien the one of their acknowledgement, or Centrism (like a deity at the heart of a mandala pattern).

These parallels would be much less striking if it were not for two more particulars in the film in common with the same mythic cluster. These are the alien's severed hand, and an instance of 'binding,' a minor series motif common to *The Big Sleep, The Thing (From Another World)*, and *Rio Bravo*.

Both binding and dismembering are featured in the Scandinavian myth of Tyr, which includes a beast called the Fenris Wolf who was endangering the gods. The only hope was to bind—tie up—the wolf. But who would do it and with what? A harmless looking magic cord was produced, and the Fenris Wolf sportingly agreed to let Tyr put it around his neck if, as collateral, he would put his hand in the beast's mouth. So Tyr, the only one of the gods with

41

courage enough for it, bound the wolf and heroically lost a hand.[13] Again, early in the film the space-creature loses a hand to the sled dogs.

Binding thus becomes important in Northern symbolism. In a way of initiation, men attending certain assemblies were bound and thus humbled for the occasion.[14] In *The Thing (From Another World)* there is a part—borrowed from *The Big Sleep* (1946) and the Raymond Chandler novel in turn—where humorously, the hero-protagonist is tied up as, hence, the heroine is friendlier and freer with him (although it is a little game he plays for her affections, only pretending to be securely tied). The alien too is earlier bound in a chunk of ice, with ropes around it. In *Rio Bravo* (1959), Dude is subjugated and bound: in conjunction with certain other archetypal features, including his general initiation/passage in the film. He is also centrally involved in the "blood" scene, with its obvious ties, again, with the alien and the 1951 science fiction film. In these ways, Dude retroactively associates with the binding instance in the latter film.

The humorous binding instance with the hero and heroine in *The Thing (From Another World)* is strongly precedented in the twofold binding instance in *The Big Sleep*. Between the two films, 'binding' originates as a motif of "initiation/sacrifice" aspect. This occurs in the following manner.

The two binding instances in *The Big Sleep* are essentially one in the film, being variations of one another. The first variant is in the short, medium-shadowy scene where Marlowe ties Carol Lundgren's hands with a fancy, light-colored curtain cord at hand. The scene begins with a medium close-up on it, as Marlowe is tying his hands behind him, the cord contrasting effectively with the captive's shabby, dark leather jacket. (The business with the cord belongs to Hawks since, in the novel, the man is not bound with such a cord but handcuffed.) The cord is an instance of the derogatory, anima-relevant 'fancy apparel/item/accouterment' motif, associated there with the incompetent, nefarious, and subdued thug, who is of negative anima aspect hence. A visual touch, the fancy object echoes, a little, the gaudy (anima-relevant) decor of the pseudo-Oriental house interior.

The house was rented by Carol Lundgren's boss, Carl Gwynn Geiger, a slain pornographer/racketeer. After tying up Geiger's henchman thus, Marlowe, looking around the house, comes upon Geiger's body, lying in state on his bed, a traditional cross of fancy fabric draped over him (as in the novel). Altogether, this echoes his fancily bound cohort in the living room. Next, Marlowe phones a friend, a D.A. associate who, with a cop, comes for the culprit. The three of them then stand around the bound thug—'converged' upon him, in the frequent series compositional/dramatic pattern (which is, generally, mandala-Centric, as here: Centered upon the anima-related fancy cord, echoing in turn the fabric cross on Geiger's body). Next, the D.A.'s man and cop roughly cart the prisoner away. All in all, the little sequence is of "initiation/sacrifice" aspect. In common with other initiation/passage instances of the series, as well as the convergence pattern, it is also anima-suppressive.

In the second 'binding' scene, near the end of the film, Marlowe, subdued by the gang, wakens from unconsciousness bound with a rope, with the gang leader's wife and Vivian Sternwood present—in similar 'convergence' around him, thus reiterating the earlier scene, but in *reverse*, as the anima figures now

42

loom over the subdued ego figure of Marlowe. (This belongs to Hawks and the 'convergence' pattern since, in the novel, only the gang leader's wife is present with Marlowe). After some altercation with him, the wife throws a drink in his face and leaves the room. Vivian is then comfortingly attentive (shortly helping him to escape). This latter portion of the scene is essentially repeated with the hero and heroine in *The Thing (From Another World)*—although the earlier binding scene, with Marlowe, the bound thug, Geiger's body, and the lawmen, with its strong archetypal elements (of mandala-Centric initiation/sacrifice) is what particularly establishes the strength of the film's dual binding instance. Because of this, the dual instance is inclined toward some reuse in the series. Thus, it was (partially) reused in *The Thing (From Another World)* as an archetypal motif, hence, which effectively contributes to the Northern-Mythic parallel.

In summary then, the "Northern European" mythic cluster in *The Thing (From Another World)* is composed of the following factors: (1) The film's science-fictional title, in its coincidental verbal identity with the Thing of the old Northern tribes and deities. (2) The series-typical 'dismemberment' instance with features in common with the Tyr/Fenris Wolf myth. (3) The 'binding' scene, with (a) its strong precedence in the dual binding instance in *The Big Sleep,* coupled with (b) the likely reiteration in the instance with Dude in *Rio Bravo* and (c) the correspondence of all these with the binding feature of the Tyr/Fenris Wolf myth and Northern-tribal initiation. (4) Other features, general or circumstantial, which fit the mythic pattern. These include the alien's demigod-like character (as a more than human hermaphrodite), and its other-worldly origins, and the circle/"ring" business on the part of the group and the alien.

Secondary-archetypal mythic sources in Hawks's mind or distant memory may have had a synthesizing part in the cluster of motifs and other features. On the other hand, such influence could as well be nil. The dismemberment and binding motifs are well-precedented in earlier Hawks films, and the alien's hermaphroditic character (like that of a deity or demigod) is part of the series-prevalent 'blurred sexual distinctions' pattern (ref. particularly: the alien's precedence in the "hermaphroditic" Henri of *I Was a Male War Bride,* (1949). Further, the ceremonial-like circle/"ring" business, though not done with montage, may be considered a latent 'group-delineative/"circular" montage' instance (ref. the section on the film, and Appendix 1) and may have 'fraternal return' influence (ref. section V, and the section on the science fiction film). In short, the mythic cluster is, in all important points, thoroughly and *diversely* established in the series archetypal patterns previous to the making of the film.

The key factors of the mythic cluster are binding and dismembering. In terms of analytical psychology, a common psychic factor of archetypal initiation/sacrifice, underlying both the myth and the film, and able to be expressed in binding as well as dismembering, incline the latter features to occur (i.e., independently) in both the myth and the film. More importantly, binding and dismembering are, again, based in the series archetypal patterns and motifs, in ready "repertoire" for a Hawks project able to use them. Since archetypal features tend to occur together and interrelatedly in the series (due in part to

43

the functioning character of archetypal imagination), the appropriate patterns and motifs readily crossed paths in *The Thing (From Another World)* to form the "Northern European" cluster. Hawks need not have ever read Northern Mythology.

As Hawks selectively and cumulatively developed the series archetypal patterns and motifs from film to film, as a "repertoire" of story-telling materials, inadvertent mythic parallels were perhaps inevitable. (See also, the Gerald Mast/*Red River* excerpt, and my own discussion of the same, in Appendix 2.)

The "Northern European" mythic cluster, with its arcane initiation/sacrifice/restoration aspects, has a more "mundane" echo in the initiation/passage undergone by Dr. Carrington, the Nobel scientist and loner whose cold scientific interest in and admiration for the super-intelligent hermaphrodite override his obligation and part in the group's safety and survival. Significantly, he wears a rather "cutesy" double-breasted blazer, like a yachting coat, in an uncomplimentary 'fancy apparel' reference. Like Tom in *Red River*, he is sleepless and fatigued, and falters partly because of that. In the end, Carrington receives a broken collarbone, as "sacrificial" comeuppance.

As the group lure the alien along a passageway to electrocute it, the professor barges in with a pistol to thwart them. Disarmed, he then races forward (as the group refrain from throwing the switch) and pleadingly tries to communicate with the alien who listens for a moment, then powerfully clouts him aside and strides forward into the trap of volts (not such a bright creature after all). Later, when the newsman Scotty (very much one of the group) sends his story in by short-wave, he mentions the famous professor as having suffered injury in the course of their siege—this in such a way (to voiced approval there) as to cover his group disloyalty, now atoned for (in his being wounded and hence, on one level, punished and "shaped up"). In addition, his broken collarbone may be a significant echo of the alien's 'dismemberment' instance, in a way of "sacrifice/passage."

Thus "hazed" at the hands of the adversary, Dr. Carrington is also an example of the Hawksian turn given to an otherwise stock character or feature—in this case, the "mad doctor" of gothic science fiction—who in the Hawks setting becomes material for the group misfit who will either get killed or be forcibly straightened out. In the wartime *Air Force,* ordinary stock material takes its series-pattern slant as the rugged individualistic fighting spirit of the little B-17 group takes the form, virtually, of inspired, tricksterish, peer-centric insubordination against the larger mass of the war effort.

In *The Thing (From Another World)*, James Arness/the alien is linked with the irruptive, recalcitrant anima (as its conquest is a suppression of the same, in the frequent series pattern).

This anima connection is made in a brief but important scene. (In some prints of the film, this portion, as well as the 'binding' scene with Nikki and Captain Hendrey are edited out.) The scene in point begins with two of the group conversing in the latrine. One is shaving. (This is noteworthy. The scene is thus set in a Hawksian manner of locker-room conviviality. Shaving is very sensation-functional, and is something a player may do with his hands as part of the dramatic context. In the same mode, one character checks the other's appearance, as a soldier might, touching his uniform.) Others of the group descend on the scene in the 'convergence' pattern. Centric in this convergence instance is a *comment* (instead of the more frequent 'dramatized/transacted object,' as in the earlier-discussed instance with the fancy cord and Carol Lundgren in *The Big Sleep*). The comment bears strong anima reference. One of the men remarks that the arrival of the alien there in full siege compares with a wartime experience of his when a nurse arrived on an island of troops, causing the same sort of commotion. A joke, with a deeper implication, the femininely elicited commotion in the all-male setting of the island is, of course, the anima in retaliation against the ego-masculine predominance, one of the most common patterns of the Hawks series. Thus, the anecdotal nurse (the anima) is linked with the alien. This is compensatory for the austere creature, who is rather a stoical ideal.

In the shaving scene, characteristic though above-average series-pattern complexity is displayed. The alien is a stoical ideal and quite as "masculine" as a James Arness role would be. (It/he is reiterated in the bald, leopardskin-clad mute priests, of similar appearance and stoical bent in *Land of the Pharaohs,* who, like the alien, do not speak but utter non-verbal sounds.) Yet the stoical creature is indicated as a feature of irrupting unconsciousness in characteristic anima fashion. Moreover, the creature, although vegetable, is animalistic, and hence in the female/anima-linked 'animal' motif. As a hermaphrodite, the alien also links with the series-comedic instances in which a male character is forced into an item of feminine clothing or is otherwise lent to "female" stigma—in the pattern of the irrupting anima. Such a character is usually a shadow representation, as, in such instances, the shadow and anima cross, much as they do in Tony of *Scarface,* Mike of *Tiger Shark,* and in a different way, the brilliant instance of Mother York of *Sergeant York.*

The alien's hermaphroditic character is doubly significant in that nothing of this sort is stressed in the original novelette. Thus, the prominent series pattern of 'blurred sexual distinctions' is eminently featured in its expression of the deeper anima-entailed unconscious which, in analytical psychology, is viewed as bisexual. As M.-L. von Franz writes in *Man and His Symbols:*

> The anima is a personification of all feminine psychological tendencies in a man's psyche, such as vague feelings and moods, prophetic hunches, receptiveness to the irrational, capacity for personal love, feeling for nature, and—last but not least—his relation to the unconscious. It is no mere chance that in olden times priestesses (like the Greek Sibyl) were used to fathom the divine will and to make connection with the gods.
>
> A particularly good example of how the anima is experienced as an inner figure in a man's psyche is found in the medicine men and prophets (shamans) among the Eskimo and other arctic tribes. Some of these even wear women's clothes, or have breasts depicted on their garments, in order to manifest their inner feminine side—the side that enables them to connect with the "ghost land" (i.e. what we call the unconscious). (P. 177.)

In a number of ways, this passage compares, of course, with the earlier E.F. Edinger excerpt concerning Odysseus, transvestism, and the "feminine deity—the mother archetype." Again, the anima is closely related to the archetypal mother. This is particularly so in childhood, and on a certain level this mergence is retained, though in later stages the anima involves the female principle in other aspects, and which give rise to the greater scope of her deities.

Mythic figures, in many instances and cultures, are featured as hermaphroditic or bisexual. Concerning the primary-archetypal level of this bisexuality, Joseph Campbell writes:

> The following dream supplies a vivid example of the fusion of opposites in the unconscious: "I dreamed that I had gone into a street of brothels and to one of the girls. As I entered, she changed into a man, who was lying, half clothed, on a sofa. He said: 'It doesn't disturb you (that I am now a man)?' The man looked old, and he had white sideburns. He reminded me of a certain chief forester who was a good friend of my father." (Wilhelm Stekel, *Die Sprache des Traumes,* pp. 70-71.) "All dreams," Dr. Stekel observes, "have a bisexual tendency. Where the bisexuality cannot be perceived, it is hidden in the latent dream content" (ibid., p. 71).[15]

In *Monkey Business* (1952), the alien seems to be reiterated in the Oxly Corporation's advertising art, which shows a phoenix rising from low flames (as though in reference to the belligerent alien's surviving the fire in the 1951 film). Correspondingly, this ad art is linked with the negative anima, and is denigrated (suppressed) by the scientists in *Monkey Business.* (Ref. the section on the film.)

SECTION V
The Fraternal Return Motif

The dismemberment and fraternal return motifs are archetypally central to the broad initiation/passage pattern of the series. The preceding section dealt, in part, with 'dismemberment' and the related but more minor binding motif. In this section, I wish to examine dismemberment's companion motif of 'fraternal return,' an equally profound and important part of the series archetypal patterns. In some contrast to the series initiation/passage pattern in general, dismemberment and fraternal return are (basically) holistic rather than repressive in function, thus constituting initiation's post-ordeal "restoration/resurrection" dimension.

First, a discussion of terms, most of which have been introduced in the context thus far.

I have been using *motif* in the sense of: a recurring element used in the development of a set of related artistic works, specifically the Hawks film series. The series motifs are very specifiable or particular, while the patterns are more general and, although identifiable, are less self-contained and more diffused. Hence, in the Summary and Description of Series Motifs and Patterns in Appendix 1, the motifs are able to be enumerated in their specific instances throughout the series, whereas the patterns are too broad and "innumerable" in their recurrence, and so are only defined and listed, with illustrations, in the same appendix.

The patterns of the series "contain" the motifs, or (in my use of the term *pattern*) include both the motifs and the broader patterns. For example, 'fraternal return' is part of the series pattern of archetypal initiation/passage (specifically for initiation's inherent "death/resurrection" aspect and its expression in the key 'return' instances in *The Dawn Patrol, The Twentieth Century,* and *Air Force).* Similarly, the dismemberment motif is part of the initiation/passage pattern in the sense of "sacrifice/restoration," as the minor binding motif is, in its sense of "initiation/sacrifice."

'Pals' is the principal motif of the series-prevalent ego/shadow pattern—as the anima is a pattern, involving certain motifs. One of these latter, the 'fancy or feminine apparel/item/accouterment' motif, is often one and the same with 'dramatized/transacted object' pattern instances. Both participate in instances of the 'convergence' pattern, which tends to be mandala-Centric (and Self-relevant), in pattern. The 'triangle' motif, as we shall see, is so diverse that it is virtually a pattern. It usually involves a male pair, in and of the pals motif, plus an anima figure (in the anima pattern): hence in an ego/shadow/anima composite. In addition, the triangle motif often involves 'convergence' with a 'dramatized object' of anima (as well as mandala-Centric) aspect, as exemplified in Tom, Matt, Fen/Tess, and the bracelet, in *Red River.* Again, the series patterns and motifs tend to occur together and interrelatedly.

The series patterns, as I have been referring to them, are the recurrent features, both archetypal and mundane, of Hawks-the-auteur's authorship of his films. The archetypal and the mundane very much interrelate, in the series.

(For example, the "mundane" pattern of professionalism/male-supremacy is a function of ego/shadow containment or suppression of the anima factor.)

The expounded series patterns and their motifs are an analytical way of considering Hawks's auteur dimension: an overview concerned with the ways the director repeats himself from film to film. My own project had its inception in the overview of Hawks in Peter Wollen's book *Signs and Meaning in the Cinema.* The Wollen synopsis (derived as well from continental criticism of the time) has proved rather incisive. The Wollen view requires some paraphrasing here, since my own study is a development of the same. What follows will also serve to introduce the fraternal return motif.

The Wollen overview aptly contrasts the Hawks series with that of John Ford (as well as Budd Boetticher). Differing from Ford's essential "nostalgia on the family level of history" (in Andrew Sarris's phrase), Hawks's world tends toward a lack of family-centered society and concerns thereof—except for those which are suppressed, or which, in some heroical (nondomestic) way, are mitigated or, in the series comedy pattern, are denigrated or lampooned. What positive society there is, is that of the adventure dramas, and consists, typically, of a small isolated group focused around a leader who is a peer, the group character being shaped by (a) the requirements of a difficult professional task with its unwritten standards and ethics, and (b) the net result/pattern of the interacting character personalities: of the mostly male bunch who do not reflect very much on what they do, though perhaps designating themselves as "crazy." Female hangers-on are a disruptive influence or are "dangerous" until initiated into the group, and an undercurrent of homosexuality seems to be present.

As Andrew Sarris observes (in *The American Cinema*), the John Ford man "knows why he is doing something even if he doesn't know how. The Hawksian hero knows how to do what he is doing even if he doesn't know why" (p. 120)—hence the Hawksian edict/theme of *professionalism.* A film-viewing friend of mine put the Ford/Hawks comparison rather well (if bluntly and parodically) when he remarked that Ford characters were "clean-cut guys" and decent people, whereas Hawks men were honorable but "rats" in type (in unwitting reference to the shadow preponderance of the series). I believe he was thinking, in particular, of *Only Angels Have Wings,* and the semi-itinerant commercial pilots with nothing much to live for, somehow, but their jobs with the rickety mail service at the edge of the Costa Rican mountains.

This paraphrasing of the Wollen overview, with touches of Sarris and others (and the Wollen overview itself), are necessarily oversimplified and a little parodic. Yet the Wollen view provided this writer with what proved to be a sound introduction to Hawks.

The adventure-dramatic aspect of the overview posits what we would call an "extreme situation," which is background and discursive context for the fraternal return motif—in terms of the latter's earnestness of wish-fulfillment, namely of evading death.

The basic instance of 'return' is in *The Dawn Patrol* (1930, not the 1939 remake by Edmund Goulding). In the film, the airmen come and go between morning missions and evening garrison (in the composite 'odyssey/close-quarters' motif, which originates in this film). The group going out every day with less returning than went is the basic drama and an intense and true-to-life one. About midway in the film, Douglas Fairbanks, Jr./Scott, not having enough time to get into full garb, one morning, takes off still in his pajama shirt—dark, with light polka-dots. That day he is shot down, and so is the German who got him, but the "Hun" is captured, unhurt. Chivalrously, despite his having shot down their comrade, they entertain him, bringing him into their party. In a good humored way, they try to teach him good English pronunciation.

Communal music is used in the film. In one scene, the group, scattered around the room, focuses on a gramophone with which they sing. Their theme-song ("The Dying Airman"), a traditional airmen's ditty, is worth relating in part, for it pertains to the series patterns, and particularly to the 'return' motif. (Other portions of it are sung in *Today We Live.*)

> Forgot by the land that bore us
> Betrayed by the ones we held dear
> The good they have all gone before us
> And only the evil are here.
> So stand to your glasses steady
> This world is a world of lies.
> Here's a toast to those dead already
> And here's to the next man who dies.

At their party, the English airmen entertain the German, managing to generate very good spirits—in festivity of a sort functional for morale amidst the daily life/death circumstances. Nearby, one of the characters sits, the estranged one of the group, a very nervous type, like a man about to crack. Suddenly he rises and interjects in panicky tones that here they all are, about to die, sooner or later, and 'why are you so cheerful, and moreover around this Hun who killed one of us today?'

Haunting the set a little, on the canteen wall (and as I have been able to gather, a typical accouterment of an air garrison then), rests a souvenir German wingtip with the Iron Cross, symbolizing death perhaps. Moreover, it is juxtaposed with the wall roster indicating group survivors and, by crossings-out, those who have "gone before." Richard Barthelmess/Courtney reprimands the frantic man, saying that he has a lot to learn there about air-war chivalry and other things.

As the party continues, who should come barging in but Scott! Supposed to be dead, he has survived intact and 'fraternally returned' on foot, still in his **polka-dotted** pajama shirt (to strong anecdotal effect), and bearing gifts of bottles of wine he has confiscated from somewhere.

They call Courntey's attention to this happy arrival, and as he beholds the 'returnee,' his close friend, he says, "Scotto. You're just in time!"—namely for the party, or the party's zenith, as if his return were not like a miracle but in due order. The German, introduced to his "kill" of the day, greets Scott with pleasure and respect for his good fight earlier. Indeed, the party is on and in good fettle.

The Iron Cross wingtip, though not in view here, might take on a deeper and more complex significance to the reflective viewer now—representing, in its incongruity, a merging of opposites: foes managing a night's conviviality together, and the dead returning.

Scott's sudden "return from the dead" into the midst of the party is the original 'fraternal return' motif instance (barring an earlier instance in one of the scarce or lost films preceding *The Dawn Patrol*). To this writer at least, it has the character of a true tale or account. (Reportedly, Hawks paid John Monk Saunders for the use of his name and story and then independently wrote the screenplay for *The Dawn Patrol*.[16] It is hence possible that the 'return ' account was acquired by Hawks from a more direct, nonliterary source than Saunders.) And yet, Saunders's stories of the original air war contain other real-life-like accounts, and the 'return' incident could as well be his. In either case, it is like unto real-life reportage. Hence 'fraternal return' and its companion motif of 'dismemberment' share a folkloric character, as it happens.

The important feature of the dismemberment and fraternal return motifs is their holistic "restorative/resurrective" dimension, which rectifies the anima-suppressive "hazing" part of the series initiation/passage pattern. The pajama shirt is an early 'fancy apparel' instance of anima aspect—yet an anima representation which rests on a triumphant ("resurrective") pinnacle, more than being subjugated to the typically suppressive 'convergence' pattern. (The latter is absent from the film portion in question.) Other instances of the return motif contain an odd, irruptive element paralleling Scott's pajama shirt (namely the instances in *The Twentieth Century, Ceiling Zero, Air Force, The Big Sky, Monkey Business, Rio Lobo,* and the oblique 'return' instances in *Red River, The Thing [From Another World],* and *Hatari!*). In view of the return motif's holistic "death/resurrection" feature, this incongruous/"surprise" element is particularly mandala-Centric, and a composite expression of the Self.

The dismemberment and return motifs are thus borne of the earnest wish-fulfillment of mayhem restored and the dead returned: that is, they are compensatory within the aforementioned "extreme situation" of Hawksian adventure drama. We can only sympathize.

Next in the series, the fraternal return motif recurs in *The Twentieth Century* (1934), an intense comedy with features in common with the series adventure dramas. The group is a small theater brood numbering five—yet mostly three, as two of them come and go in the story. These latter are Charles Levison/Jacobs and Carole Lombard/Lily, an actress who is early and rather violently initiated into the fold by John Barrymore/Jaffe, and who flees from him on other ventures but is forced back in the end. The story is mainly about their striving to retain her and then getting her back by extreme measures. The other, Max Jacobs, leaves the group in a huff fairly early and becomes (and remains) a rival producer, in later rivalry for Lily's talents.

Yet it is he who "returns' (obliquely), in the manner of Scott in *The Dawn Patrol.* The key sequence here involves a comico-melodramatic scene taking place on the Twentieth Century Limited (the once famous passenger train), in transit from Chicago to New York. In the scene, Lily is lured from her verbal commitment with Jacobs to rejoin the group, coincident with Jaffe's "rising from his deathbed" like a man resurrected. As though in reference to the Iron

50

Cross on the set of *The Dawn Patrol*, where Scott "returns from the dead," there are two x's in the smoking car where the scene takes place, obtrusively sketched on the lampshades, one of them very near Jaffe's "deathbed." (This also reiterates the numerous x's formed, by one means or another, through *Scarface* (1932), particularly in scenes where one or more persons are killed.)

In the sequence on the train, producer-director Jaffe, in the course of some antics with his loaded gun is accidentally wounded, though not seriously. Lily (and Jacobs as well) are on the train and, rising to the opportunity, Jaffe and his cohorts, Webb (Walter Connolly) and O'Malley (Roscoe Karns), set to hoodwink her into signing a new contract to get her back. O'Malley and Webb prepare the scene as Jaffe stretches out in the smoking car to feign dying. Lily, elsewhere on the train, having received word of Jaffe's wound, is expected to come to him once again before he succumbs.

A little earlier, Jacobs reappears in one scene. There, Jaffe is trying to persuade Lily to rejoin him in a new venture. Both are in a peak of hysterics. Like a sunrise—or like the eye of the hurricane which this hubbub is—Jacobs rather suddenly enters the car with the immediate offer of a great role for Lily in a new play he is producing. She quickly accepts (more or less). They embrace, and Jaffe is sadly left in the lurch. This is the first time Jacobs appears again in the film since earlier bolting the group. He wears an expensive-looking coat with a fur collar-lapel, to striking and rich effect.

In the "death scene" which shortly follows in the smoking car, Jaffe and cohorts are in a race against time, as Lily is coming, but Jacobs is sure to be on his way too, to deter her and foil their scheme. In the same sequence, a pair of exotic Passion Players arrive on business with Jaffe, but are excluded. (Jaffe is harboring extravagant plans to produce the Passion Play with them, and with Lily as Mary.) At length, Lily enters and falls in grief and remorse at Jaffe's side, as the latter melodramatically feigns dying. (Here, the four of them parody the Crucifixion, with Jaffe as Christ down from the cross, Webb and O'Malley as disciples, and Lily as Mary.) He makes a last request that she sign the current contract—to be buried with him. Half delirious, she signs the paper. Jaffe recovers instantly, as if from death itself, clutching the new contract (mandala-Centrically, as Webb and O'Malley likewise place their hands upon or near it) as Lily is once again enlisted with Jaffe Productions. Rather simultaneously, Jacobs arrives—not barging into the car but appearing in the entrance, as Jaffe says to him, "You're too late...." Here Jacobs does not wear the coat but only a suit.

In the next scene, the last in the film, the group are at rehearsal once again, with Jaffe now wearing a fur-collared/lapeled coat himself, exactly like Jacobs's in the earlier scene. In one way, it is as if Jaffe has "stolen" it from Jacobs in the same act of hoodwinking Lily away from him—or the luxurious coat is a "trophy" of Jaffe's certain "resurrection" into prosperity again.

This sequence contains Jacobs's 'fraternal return' to the group, although: (1) the instance is split in half between (a) his earlier reappearance in the fur-collared/lapeled coat and (b) the point where he arrives too late at the smoking car, and despite the fact that: (2) on the story level he does not return at all but is thwarted and excluded, and (3) Jaffe, and not he, ostensibly "rises from the dead."

Although it is not a very coherent instance, all the elements of the motif are there. Jacobs's earlier, sudden re-emergence in his abundant coat, like a sunrise, is the crux of the instance, due to the "anomalous"/mandala-Centric element of the coat, important to the motif, and corresponding to Scott's pajama shirt in the *The Dawn Patrol* instance. Yet his likewise sudden arrival at the smoking car later (without the coat) is still in character with the motif in an action-dramatic way. (On one level, he "fraternally" participates with the three Jaffe cohorts in their 'convergence' upon Lily, who becomes 'objectivized' in the mandala-Centric piece of paper containing the Jaffe contract. This anima-suppressive convergence feature is, again, not functional in the *The Dawn Patrol* instance. Here however, it provides Jacobs with a cryptic fraternal element.)

Note the line, "You're too late..." in the smoking car scene. It is opposite from the line "You're just in time," in the *The Dawn Patrol* instance, and probably links to it in a way of reversal. Because of this, and with Jaffe's "death/resurrection" enactment (and, of course, with Jacobs's "fraternal convergence" upon the scene), the smoking-car scene is indeed part of the instance which, in its somewhat garbled way, parallels that of *The Dawn Patrol*.

The 'return' instance in *Air Force* closely reiterates that of *The Twentieth Century*. In the hospital scene, Captain Quincannon dies, and on one level "resurrects" there, by virtue of having hallucinated the restoration of the B-17 with his bedside comrades participating in the same (and who later rebuild the plane and put her into action again). The 'returnee' in the scene is not Quincannon, of course, but Lieutenant Rader who has come from the field to rejoin the group at bedside. Rader bears the motif "surprise" feature of an infantry rifle slung over one shoulder, the object being out of place there. Here Quincannon parallels the "dying" Jaffe and Rader the 'returning' Jacobs, as the *Air Force* 'return' instance features a comparable split, between two characters, of the "death/resurrection" and physical 'return' aspects, with Rader's "anomalous" rifle serving in a mandala-Centric way. Again, the *Air Force* instance importantly combines 'fraternal return' with the similarly holistic dismemberment motif. The instance is discussed in further detail in the section on *Air Force*.

The leonine, fur-collared/lapeled coat is a factor which, on one level, links rivals Jaffe and Jacobs in the *Twentieth Century* return instance, in view, again, of Jaffe's wearing an identical coat in the last scene. By virtue of their coat(s), Jaffe and Jacobs interchange cryptically as one character. In the series, this sort of ego/unconscious unity-in-duality is particularly expressed in the motifs of 'clothing exchange' and 'self-encounter/splitting off.' (These are discussed in later sections and Appendix 1.) In the case of Jaffe, Jacobs, and the coat, we have at least an inkling of these motifs, which develop in later films.

Hence Jaffe, who "resurrects," and Jacobs, who obliquely 'returns,' combine their identities by way of the common mandala-Centric coat to compositely parallel the "resurrecting"/'returning' Scott and his mandala-Centric pajama shirt in *The Dawn Patrol*.

How consciously Hawks did this—or, in what *way* consciously—is difficult to say for certain. It is doubtful that he was conscious of it in a clinical/-

Jungian way (and the same is true for the series patterns in general). Initially, the war anecdote and the return instance with Scott must have brought the Christian death/resurrection mythos to the director's mind in some way. With the heated (Christian, death/resurrection) "Passion Play" business in the smoking car scene of the 1934 comedy, Scott of *The Dawn Patrol* hence became readily associated—specifically in the person of Jacobs, who similarly "returns" to the group on foot, and whom Hawks then crossed with Jaffe, via the coat, to effectively complete the motif, in its second instance in the series here.

The Twentieth Century also follows *The Dawn Patrol* in a major point of scenario. Each film (in common with *The Road to Glory*, 1936) features, near the beginning, a routine speech by the commander orienting the group (the theater group at rehearsal and the respective military groups at first briefing). In each case, the scene is essentially repeated at the end of the film with a partly different group, emphasizing, austerely and professionally, that "the job goes on as before save for replacements." This common framework between *The Dawn Patrol* and *The Twentieth Century* probably associated the films to the extent that Scott's 'return' was readily carried into the 1934 comedy.

In addition to the initiation/passage-"death/resurrection" aspect and the general mandala-Centric expression of the fraternal return motif, the 'returnee' is, in certain instances, an archetypally laden figure in his own part—as in the remarkable instance in *Gentlemen Prefer Blondes*.

This instance involves ego/shadow 'pals' Dorothy and Lorelei, and Pierre, their cab-driving cohort and animus. (Considered within the greater context of the ego/masculine-predominant series patterns, Jane Russell/Dorothy is a shadow-aspected anima figure, while Marilyn Monroe/Lorelei is an anima figure per se and Pierre a shadow type. Yet in the film itself, the girls' relationship to him is as to an unconscious figure of the opposite sex, and hence their animus.)

In the film, the two showgirls make friends with Pierre, a blond, brown-moustached, dark-clad cab driver. He speaks little English and so talks rather little. They make a fraternal cohort of him as he chauffeurs them around their Paris shopping tour like a close comrade, a "fellow soldier" of sorts.

This is series-characteristic. Minor characters sometimes function in close relationship to the main group or pair—as is notable in the sundry cafe crowd joining in with the girls' song number later. (In *Ball of Fire*, the briefly appearing traffic cop, instead of giving the professors a ticket for long out of date registration on their antique automobile, quickly assists them in their cross-country odyssey in instant, comradely rapport.)

After their shopping spree, the pair go through their blues-cathartic "When Love Goes Wrong (Nothin' Goes Right)" song number in the evening sidewalk-cafe scene. Near the end of the song, with everyone having joined in in full-voiced assurance, we hear a little string of honks. As the girls look in his direction, Pierre comes rolling up in his cab to fetch them, on schedule. Dorothy's lines to him (spoken, not sung) are: "Pierre! You're just in time!"—almost exactly as in *The Dawn Patrol*. It is none other than a 'fraternal return' instance. Indirectly, or on an inspirational or creative level, it is one reason why the scene is a very good one.

In the series, we frequently encounter a female character between or amongst two or more men as a "shared" anima. Here, in reversal of this, we have Pierre with the two girls and hence, correspondingly, a psychic figment of them in turn. In the series 'triangle' motif, a pair share an anima/animus figure in this way due, ultimately, to their all constituting ego/shadow/anima-or-animus portions of a common psyche in the pattern.

Pierre is an ethereal figure—like Lotta in *Come and Get It*, and Tess in *Red River*, who are, on one level, figments of the male characters (ref. the sections on those films). His relatively silent, dark-clad (shadowy) countenance lends to this archetyping. He is even something of a "ghost." In a brief scene during their shopping tour, with Pierre in the forefront of the shot, cheerily though silently chauffeuring them as they talk in the back seat, one of the girls remarks, "It's the first time I've been shopping without a man along!" The remark is, I think, very significant. Pierre's eminent, yet *designatedly nonexistent*, presence there alludes to his ethereal (psychic, or archetypal-unconscious) character. He is even cryptically indicated as being spectral or "dead"—thence "resurrected" (in the way of the return motif) in his 'fraternal return' in the cafe scene, shortly.

In general, Pierre is an appropriate 'returnee' because of his archetypal profundity (i.e., in his approach to the Self): a proper Centric figure in a motif expressing death/resurrection and hence the holistic Self.

The general treatment of Bruce Cabot/Indian, the older member of the animal-catching group in *Hatari!*, has a touch of 'fraternal return' and includes something of the ethereal Pierre. Hospitalized and away from the job for part of the film, and incapacitated throughout the story (with a gradual return to the field), Indian is effectively present yet absent as a character. (At the hospital, Gerard Blain/Chips abruptly enters the film, a little as Indian's shadowy "double" and, as it happens, like a traditional specter, as if he were Indian "returning from the dead." Ref. the section on *Hatari!*.) The victim of a rhinocerous, Indian becomes the focus of the group's overcoming the "rhino" jinx upon them (the "jinx" being a concretization of his understandable new fear and pessimism regarding rhinos). He is special—even "precious"—because of this, and for other features, namely his more advanced age and job seniority, his certain presence-yet-absence aura, and his recovery from a critical condition (in "death/resurrection," on one level).

He may be said to be the *group circle unbroken*, in common with Tom's return and reinstatement at the end of *Red River* and Lily's in *The Twentieth Century*. Tom and Lily may bear some relation to 'fraternal return,' but they lack important features common to the motif—*irruptive surprise* for one. Indian, in his oblique 'return' in the latter part of the film, lacks irruptive surprise, though his walking stick (an object of some negative connotation) serves as the anomalous feature. Thus (with his other features considered as well) he seems indeed to 'fraternally return' as he climbs out of the truck and hobbles over to preside over the hog-tied rhino and the mended jinx, finally.

In the Hawks series, age-exceptional characters, both old and young, tend to receive special treatment. Children are anima-linked, like those in *Monkey Business*, or are precocious, like Matt as a boy in *Red River*. The two street boys in Dorothy and Lorelei's "When Love Goes Wrong" scene interject with an able precociousness, as though knowing what the song is all about and hence as age (or song) peers. Hawks has expressed that he dislikes children in films. Thus, when required to include them, he tends to make them adventuresome or mature beyond their age (as "adults") or to render them in a negative way, as tricksterish, anima-linked figures. (J.B. of *The Ransom of Red Chief* is both.)

Old characters often die in action. Witness Manuel in *Tiger Shark* and Papa Laroche in *The Road to Glory*. Otherwise, older men are injured, infirm, or anima-aspected and comedic.

Briefly stated, the "ego" of the Hawks series tends to favor people old and young enough to be usefully employed.

The mostly elderly professors (who are "squirrely cherubs") in *Ball of Fire*, are gainfully employed, but are still rendered comically—like senior executive Oxly in *Monkey Business* and the lame Stumpy in *Rio Bravo*. Eddie, in *To Have and Have Not*, an incompetent and comic old alcholoholic, is a shadowy 'pal' to Harry, and like the brain-damaged ex-pilot in *Ceiling Zero*, was a good professional at one time and is retained on that account.

Such "ego rejections" are subject to psychic repression on one level, and are thus lent to archeypal aspect in the series, like the old and infirm Indian in *Hatari!*. The baby, clutching (old) Oxly's gold watch amidst the song session in *Monkey Business*, is "properly" comedic yet mandala-Centric there. He reiterates old Papa Laroche mystically clinging to the antique bugle in *The Road to Glory*.

Dutchy, in *Only Angels Have Wings*, is old but able-bodied, alive, and a productive member of the group. Yet he is comedic, "soft," and anima-linked. Further, he has a royally archetypal moment in the film, as we shall see.

As related in section II, the late-arriving churchman in *Sergeant York*—one of the oldest members of the community—properly renders comedy as he comes to the meeting in his new squeaky shoes (a derogatory 'fancy apparel' instance, since they are button-shoes). Yet he is a cryptic (and hence a profound) part of the archetypal irruption from York and his pals outside—where York's initials, nearly shot in a tree-trunk, are mandala-Centrically featured.

Most spectacular however, is the archetypal aspect (or "honor) bestowed upon General Sternwood, early in *The Big Sleep*. Significantly, he is the most agedly decrepit character in the series.

Next, we examine the films chronologically, and through the unfolding process of the their career as a series. What follows will not in all cases be comprehensive film reviews but will cover all points of interest to the present purpose and in sufficient story-dramatic context. In the majority of cases this amounts to a comprehensive review, since the series patterns and motifs are themselves incisive and comprehensive.

The reader may wish to refer ahead to the Summary and Description of Series Motifs and Patterns in Appendix 1. A short glossary of dramatic and cinematic terms is provided behind the Selected Bibliography.

PART TWO: THE FILMS

Red Line 7000 (1965)
The homicidal Mike Marsh, a negative shadow figure.

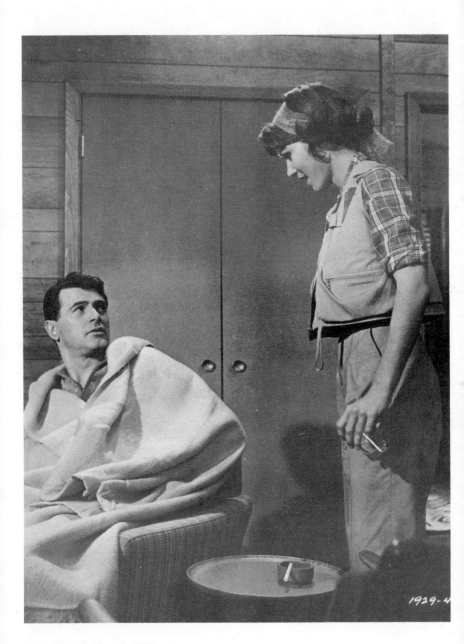

Man's Favorite Sport? (1963)
Roger and Abigail: the assertive anima.

The Crowd Roars (1932)
Joe and Lee: the assertive anima.

Land of the Pharaohs (1955)
Hamar, the high priests, and Princess Nelipher. Ego-masculine retaliation against the assertive/recalcitrant anima.

Bringing Up Baby (1938)
Susan and David. ("Oh, you tore your coat.")

The Thing (From Another World) (1951)
Captain Hendrey, members of the group, and Nikki. Woman as ego-masculine peer (the "initiated" anima).

Hatari! (1962)
Sean, and Dallas the alienated anima (linked to the animal kingdom).

Hatari! (1962)
Pockets, Sean, and Luis. The animal-compound group invades town society to recover Dallas, using her baby elephants as "bloodhounds."

Tiger Shark (1932)
The Hawksian triangle: Mike, Quita, and Pipes.

I Was a Male War Bride (1949)
The Hawksian triangle: Kitty (Catherine's meddling shadow, on one level) reluctantly interrupts Catherine and Henri on their wedding night.

Bringing Up Baby (1938)
The irruptive anima: David forced to wear a feminine garment (juxtaposing with Aunt Elizabeth in her more masculine dress).

Rio Bravo (1959)
Dude and Stumpy confiscating Feathers's tights. Ego-masculine 'convergence' upon the irruptive anima in the form of a feminine garment.

The Big Sky (1952)
Pals Jim and Boone: ego, and shadow with anima aspect.

Gentlemen Prefer Blondes (1953)
Pals Dorothy and Lorelei: anima with shadow aspect, and anima.

Gentlemen Prefer Blondes (1953)
Dorothy, Piggy, and the positive ego figure Watson. Close-knit ensemble dramatics with the *sense* of touch.

Ceiling Zero (1935)
Tex, Dizzy, and Jake. Close-knit ensemble dramatics with the *sense* of touch.

Scarface (1932)
Opposition as relationship. Violent 'object transaction' as Tony defiantly strikes a match on Guarino's badge, leading to a brief fisticuff.

Viva Villa! (1934)
Pals Villa and Sierra, with grim 'object transaction.' (Elsewhere, the owner of the boots is being tortured to death.)

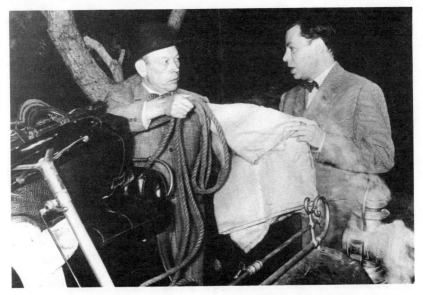

The Ransom of Red Chief (episode from *O. Henry's Full House*) (1952)
Pals Sam and Bill in practical 'object transaction,' with unobtrusively occupied foreground.

Corvette K-225 (1943)
The chart-room scene and convoy briefing: spacial dramatics, professionalism.

Ball of Fire (1941)
Bertram Potts and his professor colleagues: the Hawksian group of professional peers.

The Twentieth Century (1934)
Theater cohorts Jaffe, Webb (with 'odd hat' motif), and O'Malley.

The Road to Glory (1936)
Humorous, Centric 'object transaction,' intensive tactile activity (shaving), with an erotic note (in the racy magazine).

Sergeant York (1941)
Alvin York wins the community shooting match: congenial masculine transaction/'convergence.' The Hawks hero as group peer.

Barbary Coast (1935)
The vigilante group lynching Knuckles: violent masculine transaction/'convergence.'

Come and Get It (1936)
The sleight-of-hand operator, Swan, Lotta, and Barney in 'close quarters.' ("Swan, make room for the lady.")

Corvette K-225 (1943)
Serious horse play in the engine room, as two pals threaten one who would intervene in their fight. Medium lighting.

Only Angels Have Wings (1939)
Dutchy, Les, Bonnie, and·Joe: characters as projected psychic functions (Self with
anima aspect; anima; and contending ego and shadow).

Land of the Pharaohs (1955)
Pharaoh slays Nelipher's personal slave, in a minor Hawksian 'triangle.' Medium-low
lighting, the set adorned with the film's recurrent leopardskin feature.

The Big Sleep (1946)
Vivian Sternwood/Rutledge and Phillip Marlowe, with 'binding' motif.

Man's Favorite Sport? (1963)
Initiation/passage: Abigail and Isolde (with 'odd hat' motif) 'converge' upon Cadwalader after an inconvenient dousing, all of which leads him to the manly triumph of temporarily discarding his toupee.

To Have and Have Not (1944)
Initiation/passage: Harry and Eddie contra Mr. Johnson (who is due for serious comeuppance for his poor sport fishing and cheap character).

The Big Sky (1952)
Poor Devil, Teal Eye, and the keelboat group, in 'object transaction' with the film's mandala-Centric liquor jug. Medium low lighting.

His Girl Friday (1940)
Earl Williams and Hildy Johnson. Cigarette transaction carrying shadow/anima relationship.

Red Line 7000 (1965)
Dan and Gabby. ("Are we still friends?")

Red River (1948)
Buster, Matt, Cherry, Tom, and Groot, with shadow figure Dan Latimer recessed in the frame.

Howard Hawks with Kirk Douglas on the set of **The Big Sky** (1952).

FIG LEAVES
(1926)

In this early Hawks film there are a few points of interest pertaining to subsequent series patterns.

Early, a snake—among many other spectacular things—is featured in the Keatonesque prehistoric sequence. As the film shifts to modern times, Olive Borden/Eve's conniving neighbor directly assumes the snakes's part. She is hence the series' first posited link between Woman and the animal kingdom. She schemes to get Eve into the high-fashion kingdom of Josef Andre (Andre de Bersanger) and away from home and husband Adam Smith (George O'Brien). This is thwarted, and Eve returns home in the end.

Adam and his partner Eddie McSwiggen (Heinie Conklin) have a plumbing establishment and are good pals. At one point, the motif of 'pals' in its 'triangle' aspect seems to appear. To instruct Adam in handling his wife forcefully, Eddie has him play out a socio-drama, with Eddie playing the wife, donning a makeshift skirt and waxing effeminate. Adam then plays the husband part as advised. Eve enters and, not noticing the skirted pal (off to one side), begins to upbraid Adam for being away and late for something. Behind her the pal gestures in earnest pantomime for Adam to "get tough" and stand up to her.

Here, seemingly, is the first series instance of a character playing a protagonist's archetypal shadow with anima aspect, through the pal's slipping into the unusual playacting in the makeshift female garb. This archetyping is perhaps augmented by his being (to Eve) an invisible ("ethereal") party in the confrontation.

Next, there occurs the series' first instance of 'fraternal encounter/pre-encounter.' Prototypically here, the motif consists of a dramatic and fateful crossing of paths leading to a subsequent principal association. (As regards the motif in general, the relationship may be indicated a little ahead of time in an oblique way—or the clash may be prematurely intimate, in some way.) In this instance, Josef Andre in his car simply bumps into Eve in a crosswalk and stops to help her back to normal, from which encounter she subsequently joins his fashion kingdom (with certain assistance from her neighbor, a Josef Andre accomplice). It is a strange and sumptuous realm, almost a never-never land, as palatial as it is imprisoning. One striking scene has a bunch of the veteran girls roughly, coercively undressing and then redressing Eve in high-fashion to go to work properly—this in the Hawks manner of initiatory "hazing" concerned with professionalism.

The two plumbing buddies come to the highbrow fashion show (which they will discover, to their surprise, includes Eve) and set to cutting up boisterously, in an instance of 'pals'/group tricksterism.

In one sequence, a saxophone becomes an object of some focus, as a potentially "live" and 'dramatized/transacted object,' although it does not function in an integral series-pattern way (i.e., is too loosely a part of the dramatic context).

Hawks is credited with the story.

59

A GIRL IN EVERY PORT
(1928)

Here and still early, the series patterns are forcefully introduced, as the important 'pals' and 'triangle' motifs are definitively presented. The story, by Hawks, is mainly ingenious.

Central to the film is its drawn out 'fraternal encounter/pre-encounter' motif instance, a broad story-dramatic device underlying the entire story and film. The story is of two merchant sailors who do not know each other, though who move along the same trade routes. They veer in one another's direction to cross paths, violently and fatefully, whereafter they become firm friends. The end portion of the film reiterates this encounter within fresh crisis circumstances and with German Expressionist touches, hence sealing it as both a story of a friendship and a story of Fate.

The trade routes contain a certain feature which sailors Spike (Victor McLaglen) and Bill (Robert Armstrong) share and which eventually causes them to collide, namely the available girls of the ports, certain of whom they both encounter (by more than chance). Indeed, Spike begins to discover his girlfriends, far and wide, bearing a common insignia, an anchor within a heart, in a trinket or tattoo. These are personalized mementos bestowed by Bill, whose amatory trademark thus poses the rivalry of some other sailor somewhere moving in on Spike's "skirts." Spike, in an accumulating slow burn, vows to punish this fellow when he runs onto him. Thus he 'fraternally *pre*-encounters' Bill.

Also to his frustration, Spike finds more and more of the girls to be marrying off.

It is the old triangle afoot, or developing, among Spike, Bill, and the girls, and later with Tessie (Louise Brooks). As it will turn out, it is a special sort of triangle, and becomes the classic instance of the peculiar 'triangle' of the series patterns. The heart/anchor insignia is thus imbued with an erotic violence. It is also the initial and perhaps the chief instance of an object becoming transactionally "live," like the bracelet in *Red River*.

The two men happen into a South American cantina at the same time. Here an intuitive sequence is played out, a little humorously, as Spike senses an uncanny something about one fellow near at hand—as their 'fraternal encounter' commences. Presently, they chance to get into a fight over a girl, but join forces together against the police who come.

They both land in jail, occupying adjacent cells. As Spike shaves in the mirror he gets the surprise of his life. He finds the heart/anchor symbol engraved, not on a girlfriend this time, but in a bruise on his own chin! In a moment, he is able to notice its source—Bill's signet ring, engraved with it like a seal. Here indeed, in a blatant way, Spike confronts his irrupting shadow in Bill, and something else as well, a closely-associated anima-imbued feature in the heart/anchor insignia—both of which can be said to have been psychically creeping up on him over the years.

Prior to settling this "old dispute" of Spike's, they team up in another fight, outside the jail, which brings them instead to shaking hands afterward in new friendship. As noted earlier, they promptly lure a cop onto a pier and shove him off, as if in a toast to being pals now.

Thereafter they brawl frequently with outsiders. Bill, when in a jam, hollers "Spike!"—the signal for him to intervene in needed assistance—at times in annoying interruption of Spike's picking up a girl. These days Spike still chases "skirts," but somehow Bill does not. On one level, as it will ultimately transpire, such interruptions for brawling are to lure Spike away from "skirts" and into their own vortex of fist-frays: a kind of "morass," of greater unconsciousness personified in Bill.

Herethrough, two minor series items surface. After a fracas, Spike, in warm fraternal gesture each time, tugs Bill's knuckles to normal, a sensation-functional feature, like the fisticuffs themselves, and of course like their earlier fight with each other (and not least, Spike's terrible clobbering of Bill at the end of the film). The other item, a proper series motif (since it occurs in three or more films of the series), is a physical gesture of Spike's when ordering their drinks. He holds up two fingers, signifying (1) two drinks, one for each of them, and (2) metaphorically, their being pals, a comradely twosome. This little action—a sensation- or tactile-functional action as well, for its body "sign language"—will appear a few times in other films of the series, indicative of close relationship; and the post-brawl tugging of a pal's fingers is used again with Jim and Boone in *The Big Sky*.

At this point the pals seem not to go to sea anymore. At least they are little separated. Then Spike falls in love with Tessie, a carnival high diver, brunette, sultry, toughish—a Hawks heroine type who will recur a few times in the series. Bill knows her from the past, and knows her to be a tramp. She wears his heart/anchor trademark in a hidden tattoo. She warms up to him anew, but he says no, and refrains from telling Spike because Spike is so head over heels in love. At one point, Spike buffs her shoes, indicating his having succumbed fatally. (Such, in later films, posits a point of male character-failure or doom.)

In one scene, a "crossroads of fate" is cinematographically drawn.* Spike sits on a stool, giddily daydreaming of settling down on a farm, to hearth, home, and marital bliss with Tessie. Behind him is an almost white background, aptly, as though stressing his innocence. Elsewhere in the room Bill coolly tries to dissuade him from it all, but still not letting on the truth about her. In the frame composition with Bill is, contrastingly, a darker or shadowy pattern of things, somewhat like a vortex or morass, of which portent he is a part, as Spike's pressing unconscious half. This partial cinematographic morass seems to become expressionistically operant in the film's final sequence, which is as follows.

Spike discovers Tessie having evidently been betraying him with another fellow, observing her mussed bed. Although it was not Bill, but someone else, he discovers Bill's heart/anchor tattooed on her. Unaware that it is from the distant past, he assumes the worst. His old vow to pulverize the sailor who has been moving in on his "skirts" all the time is once again aflame, but like never before. The scene is medium-dark shadowy and, as he tosses Tessie aside and

*This was pointed out by Fred Camper, via Ron Haver's program notes on the film, at the Howard Hawks retrospective at the Los Angeles County Art Museum in 1974.

charges out after his pal, he casts a large shadow on the door—the door bearing a stark, diamond-shaped pattern in turn. The "Expressionistic sequence" is thus afoot, in added suspense, as well as a sense of fatalism.

As he races down the street after Bill, whose hours or minutes may be numbered, *couples*, arm in arm, adorn the scene in contrived visual comment. (It is in stark contrast, representing the life he will not have after all—as well as echoing, perhaps, Spike's earlier finding his seaport girlfriends to be gradually marrying off, augmenting the frustrating awareness of his sailor rival somewhere in the world.)

Suddenly he hears the old familiar cry "Spike!" hollered from someplace. It is Bill in a cellar saloon with two toughs moving in on him in serious assault. Spike is transfixed—as here the story-dramatic forces indeed come to head. In the crisis, Spike whirls about, as in a vortex, trying to detect where Bill's cry for help is coming from, as the shots take in poster images behind him, which include an anchor and a girl.

He bounds down the stairs into the cellar saloon, where he and Bill quickly overcome the two assailants. Then, with Bill already badly beaten up, Spike renders him a severe blow. He then lies bloodied and unconsicous on the floor for a long time, as Spike broods sourly.

Spike goes to the bar and makes to signal for a single drink—with one finger—but then climactically holds up two, indicating their twosome again, or still. He gets down on the floor and nurses his pal back with the second drink. Somewhat melodramatically they make amends, as Bill, horribly gored up, groggily but happily relates the truth about Tessie now, and they both vow never to let a "skirt" come between them again. Nearer the end, Spike once again tugs Bill's knuckles out, the medium close-up on it taking in the heart/anchor symbol on his ring.

Thus ends the film Hawks referred to, genre-wise, as a "love story between two men."

Thus, the film broaches the 'fraternal (pre-)encounter,' 'pals,' and 'triangle' motifs of the series, in their ego/unconscious dynamics of shadow and anima emergence.

The girls in the ports, and Tessie, are the anima factor(s) around which the Spike-and-Bill ego/shadow contention (1) irrupts and eventually (2) egotizes in at least partial resolution. This certain resolution/egotization looms compositely in the eros/anima-associated heart/anchor symbol, which is importantly shown again near the end of the film on Bill's ring. An ostensive enough mandala, the monogram even seems to function a little beyond space and time. It readily suggest being a composite representation of the Self (along with being anima-connected and considerably out of the shadowy "morass" associated with Bill). Altogether, the little object is transcendent-functional in the general Spike/Bill/Tessie contention, for which it seems to present a psychic or symbolic "solution."

The triangle among Spike, Bill, the girls and the Louise Brooks character is the prototypical series 'triangle' motif instance. Closely involved with 'pals,' the motif's main emphasis is an ego/shadow one, concerned with the relationship between the male protagonists involved. Here and elsewhere in the series, the ego/shadow protagonists come to some special essence as the woman, one way or another, fades away or fades to the background—at times to unrealistic effect or story dramatic flaw, as we will see particularly in the case of Lotta in *Come and Get It*. In this case, and in the prototypical instance in *A Girl in Every Port*, she becomes 'objectivized,' remaining behind in a mandala-Centric 'dramatized/transacted object' between the ego/shadow protagonists like a minted coin (i.e., in the serving-tray keepsake in *Come and Get It*, and the heart/anchor monogram in *A Girl in Every Port*.

It has been suggested more than once by writers that the film and its many reiterations throughout the series contain an undercurrent of homosexuality. There is something to this, I think. However, the series pattern in question is a complex one to interpret.

In Hawks films, characters tend to be projected representations of close-knit psychic processes. In general, the pressing archetypal factors of shadow, anima, and Self bend the more conventional dramatic and cinematic factors into an odd sub-drama which is like a graceful tendency toward myth. In the 1928 film, Spike encounters himself—his own shadow aspect in Robert Armstrong/Bill, a different type than the husky, moderately brutish McLaglen character—relatively ectomorphic and passive, and easily enough an alter-ego. This ego/shadow contrast and dramatic contention, closely-knit with an erotic/anima factor, can, when played out, have a "homosexual" look here and in its variations at subsequent points of the series. (Concerning the overall series pattern of 'homosexual allusion'-'homosexual joke,' note again the dream presented and commented on by Campbell and Stekel at the end of section IV, where a dreamt sexual change in a prostitute is attributed to an ordinary bisexuality in unconscious life.)

In slipping into the "low life" of their particular palhood at the end, however, Spike and Bill resolutely spurn the mature-heterosexual side of adult love, marriage, and so on. Herewith is a "homosexual" condition in a qualified sense, and one which, I think, is borne out by the series patterns in general. It is a condition of erotic limbo; namely that of child-Eros' stage of *passage* by way of masculine peerage and the latter's part in weaning the male psyche from mother and family. In this regard, the series patterns describe or indicate an archetypally-related "homosexuality" in the qualified and mainly covert sense of male-adolescent initiation/passage. (This is complete, in the film, with the adolescent accouterment of "skirts," the view of women as sexual objects. The anima here, in the scattered girlfriends and the "cheap" Louise Brooks character is, in one respect, a special male-adolescent view of Woman. A few of the heroines in the series make reference to this 'tramp stigma,' defensively protesting its real or imagined insinuation by a male protagonist, as in *Ball of Fire, To Have and Have Not*, and *Red River*.)

In fewer words, the series pattern of 'homosexual allusion/undercurrent' is an archetypal aspect of the series-pattern sociological and psycho-social circumstances (particularly those of the adventure dramas). Not unnaturally, these same predominantly male circumstances may harbor a covert taboo on homosexuality. This is suggested at points, I think, in the instances of lampooning jibes against it in a few of the comedies (in the subpattern of 'homosexual joke').

Even so, the violence between the pair in the 1928 film—particularly in the last sequence, with its Expressionistic embellishments, and the way the battered and unconscious Bill is visually dwelt on—holds an erotic element, in a way of erotic subsitution and what would be termed *repressed homosexuality*. This also may be interpreted of the series in general, and seems to be a fairly common feature of one or more older generations of men in our culture.

As regards the series pattern of 'homosexual joke'-'homosexual allusion/undercurrent,' the present study emphasizes the archetypal basics of projected ego/shadow/anima dynamics in a context of fixated male-adolescent initiation/passage. (Ref. the subsection on the latter.)

Also, the not-infrequent 'triangle' accouterment of the 'dramatized/transacted object'—in its functioning in the cryptic 'objectivization' of the woman or of anima/eros—suggests to me a stoical homoerotic chastity, a sublimation and transcendent-functional restoration of the erotic/anima factor in a composite expression of the Self. One is reminded of old knights and the similarly stoical ideal/objectivization of the Grail: a chalice-like symbol of anima aspect. alluding to optimal masculine Self-realization. In a way of speaking, the 'dramatized/transacted object' pattern in Hawks is the "poor man's Holy Grail" (sans religiosity).

More mundanely, we may infer that the 1928 sailor pair opt for their special pal-hood because it is the best resolution a couple of "stiffs" like them might come to. In their situation, their pal-hood may well be worth more than even trying to better themselves with a "skirt."

Flesh and the Devil (1927), directed by Clarence Brown (from the novel *The Undying Past* by Hermann Sudermann), resembles *A Girl in Every Port* in ways that invite some comparison here. Was this prominent film a precedent or model for the Hawks film?

Comparing them, *Flesh and the Devil* (a kind of "Freudian morality play") carries considerable (conservative) social comment whereas *A Girl in Every Port* has almost no social dimension in itself. The Brown film's overall point is, I think, one of male friendship as the cornerstone of society's, or life's (or flesh's) stability and viability.

Early in the story, two upper-middle-class boys on their special island in the middle of a lake perform the age-old blood-brotherhood ritual. There they exchange blood, assisted by the one's sister who is the "second" for both of them. Later however, a woman comes *between* them instead as, in the course of the story, a certain beautiful woman gets involved with them both. Eventually, the two estranged friends set out to duel over her—on their old island where they once pledged and sealed eternal friendship in blood. The pious, prayerful sister of the one persuades the beautiful woman to hurry out to the island (frozen over now in winter) to stop the two men before it is too late, but on the way there she falls through the ice and perishes. Even so, the pair cannot bring themselves to duel and so are friends again because of this.

The film ends with the two friends united around the one's mother and family, including the pious sister in whom the friend now expresses an interest. (She had earlier indicated an interest in him.) All is sensible, domestic, and less passionate, with the romantic other woman out of the way.

Hence we have the Brown/Sudermann "triangle-of-one-flesh" in the two blood-bonded friends and the one's sister who is ritually between them and moreover (suggestedly) destined to marry his friend—all in all, as close as can be gotten to incest and still being short of it.

In common with *A Girl in Every Port* and the Hawks 'triangle,' the Brown/-Sudermann triangle is principally concerned with the two comrades, the girl being secondary—once Eros is out of the way in the form of the other, problematic woman. Otherwise, despite the common dramatic structure, the triangle functions to contrary meanings in the two films—the one familial and the other more or less asocial.

As noted in the subsection on the shadow, the Hawks film seems, in its own way, to utilize the literary, dramatic, and cinematic motif of the "double" (*die doppelgänger*), with Bill, on one level, a reflection of Spike. More generally, the 1928 film is patterned after German cinema, a mode which will, at most, play a less ostensive part in Hawks's subsequent film making—excepting perhaps for his apparent use of the old "full moon" entity in the 'triangle' scene in *Tiger Shark*. Faintly, Mike Mascarenas of that film, and his prototype in Tony of *Scarface*, are Expressionist-type "martyrs," ultimately stemming from the martyred man in Georg Buchner's 19th century play *Wozzeck*.

THE DAWN PATROL
(1930)

In section V, the prototypical instance of the important 'fraternal return' motif (occurring in this film) is examined.

As Hawks's first sound film, *The Dawn Patrol* is in many ways competent, but more cinematically nondescript where the series patterns are concerned. Markedly, the film is weak in ensemble dramatics (very opposite from the 'merged dramatics/dialogue' pattern that will unfold in the series), and is with little physical contact or tactile transaction.

There are nevertheless the incidents with the athletic medal and the boots of deceased pilots. In the scene where Douglas Fairbanks, Jr./Scott's younger brother (played by William Janney) arrives and talks with flight commander Courtney (Richard Barthelmess), a lighted candle burns near them in the low-lighted room; and the younger, newly-arrived man gives Courtney an athletic medal to pass along to his brother (Scott), should he perish the next day. Perish the kid does—and, as Courtney had said to him, "None of us will leave here. We'll all die sooner or later." Subsequently, Courtney goes on a suicide mission in place of Scott, in part to make up for sending the latter's brother out to his death. Here the object, earlier paired with the lighted candle, takes on more dramatic life when Courtney takes the medal from his pocket (which he neglected to pass along to Scott for the kid) and regards it in the moments before death as he plummets downward. Here, as with the heart/anchor token in *A Girl in Every Port*, an object acquires a particular cinematic function for having passed between the two of them, or by certain extension, three of them, in a tactile-functional note.

The medal is of course a consciously employed symbol in the film. Another conscious symbol—one not unlike the medal—is in one of the supporting characters, namely Phipps (Edmund Breon), the clerical man of the air unit, a spectacled, older, less soldierly fellow who processes the paperwork of the pilots in their arriving, coming, going, dying-off, and getting replaced. At one point, he soft-spokenly mutters a philosophical something about the individual men coming and going but the group going on. He is a reflective point in the film, and will have certain counterparts later in the series, each in his different way—more concrete, *shadowy* ways than the relatively contrived, idealistic Phipps. Archetypal values are projected in these characters (among them, Sparks in *Only Angels Have Wings*, Bensiger in *His Girl Friday*, and Zeke in *Sergeant York*).

These two symbols lend something more to Scott and his 'fraternal return' by their presence in the film. More concretely and corporeally symbolic are the boots of downed and deceased pilots, chivalrously dropped and delivered back to the group garrison by respectful German emissaries. They are objects of some life, serving to focus on the perished owner. This we will see recurring in a variety of ways in the series, in the archetypal 'meager last possessions' motif.

THE CRIMINAL CODE
(1931)

I found this the least significant film of the series, for the purposes of this study. There is little of the series patterns to be observed, and it is not a very good film, except in places.

The early police headquarters scene is striking. In the police station, a character saunters up to another (police) character's desk and sits on it, talking with him and another man in an office-convivial way. The occupational, man-to-man contact and transaction here is good, and in the special manner of Hawks cinema, in which the sensation-function obtains, even sans physical contact.(Two outstanding examples of the same are the business meeting among Marlowe and General Sternwood in the greenhouse, and the Marlowe/Eddie Mars meeting in the latter's office, in *The Big Sleep*.)

Shortly, an ambulance has arrived at the scene of an assault, amidst gathered onlookers, displaying its dark cross insignia in a very corporeal manner, signifying death, as the police arrive and then leave with the suspect. It is cinematically strong.

THE CROWD ROARS
(1932)

The Crowd Roars is an early film of interest, as the series patterns begin to develop. Hawks is credited with the story.

Initially, before race driver Joe Greer (James Cagney) leaves the train to return home for a visit, his brunette girlfriend Lee Merrick (Ann Dvorak) removes, rearranges, and replaces his vest pocket handkerchief in interpersonal and tactile-functional transaction with an object. It is "motherly" as well, and suggestively, his departure from the train to an all-male conclave is, on one level, an "escape" from her in this aspect. (Ref. the subsection on rites of passage, and discussion of the "enveloping" anima early in section IV.) She must stay on the train as he departs because she is considered "not good enough for his family." She weeps over this in the privacy of the train.

The masculine pair shoving Woman away at the end of *A Girl in Every Port* comes to mind, as Joe's "family" conclave consists of Joe returning, Joe's younger brother Eddie, Dad Greer, and a male cohort or two in the older man's commercial garage, where they are soon gathered around a race car. (So this is what Lee is not good enough for! One thinks offhand that if she knew, she might not have wept.)

As they arrive at the garage, manually rolling Joe's race car in, having taken it from the train, Joe asks for a drink, and Dad Greer (Guy Kibbee) replies, "Sure," rather softly and in some shared intimacy regarding the same. Soon a half-pint bottle is warming them, as Dad Greer's previous, cryptic-like tone of utterance now seems to amount to: "Sure. A nice convivial drink around, just like always," although effectively focusing on the bottle as a transactional object and a point of mandala-Centricity. Grail-like, it is a projected symbol, ultimately, of masculine Self-realization (ref. the heart/anchor symbol as the "poor man's Holy Grail," in *A Girl in Every Port*). In an augmenting way, moments earlier (as they enter the garage with the race car), a hanging light bulb passes very near the camera—rather "corporeally" linking with the bottle now in their midst, like the candle flame echoing the kid's medal in *The Dawn Patrol*. It is an early instance of the series compositional pattern (of 'foreground object/action') which thrusts an object or an action into the foreground of the frame to *tactile*-functional, and in some instances more symbolic reference (such as here).

There it is unveiled that Eddie Greer (Eric Linden) has begun racing too, since Joe was last home. Joe promptly tries to talk him out of it, but Eddie is clearly "hooked." As Eddie refuses to be dissuaded and demonstrates that he is as crazy as Joe in the matter of cars and racing, Joe's attitude abruptly shifts. Joe makes a fairly dramatic about-face with him—normal "exoteric" becomes fraternal "esoteric," as Eddie is sympathetically "in," in a manner of initiation/passage on the spot. Right there, Joe begins *coaching* his brother!

Subsequently, Joe draws further away from Lee who becomes very lovelorn, since Eddie has "replaced" her. Her friend Ann (Joan Blondell), who is hostile to men, brings her comfort as she and Lee confide together.

Next, Ann tries to seduce young Eddie, but Joe retaliates, intent on keeping his brother "away from booze and women." Ann succeeds however, and she and Eddie begin going together, thence marrying. Losing Eddie, Joe hits the skids, becoming a virtual derelict. Later, he and Lee get back together, marking his recovery. She confesses that she vindictively encouraged Ann to hustle Eddie away from Joe "to make him know what it was like to lose someone he loved"—that is, to know what it was like for her to lose him (Joe). This "cross-sexual" comparison touches *A Girl in Every Port*, and is an early note of the series 'blurred sexual distinctions' pattern (and hence the irrupting *anima*).

Brothers ('pals') Joe and Eddie are soon partners again and win the Indy 500 as a team, their car catching fire near the end and cracking up across the finish line. The last shot in the film of the girls, cheering away in the stands, seems indeed to stress their aloofness from the reality down on the track—the danger and trouble their fellows are in—as though Lee and Ann are merely part of the proverbial crowd that roars. (One suspects that this juxtaposition of Lee and Ann cheering with Joe and Eddie in trouble is faulty editing; but it may still be significant on the auteur level.) Through the film, the scenes with the girls together as commiserating friends suggest their closeness in a manner estranged from the men. In this, the film, to a considerable extent, includes the woman's viewpoint.

For their "crazy" part, Joe and Eddie "pair off" as well in the end. In the last little sequence following their Indy 500 victory, they are being toted away in an ambulance, crudely bandaged from their wreck. With more than minor injuries, they are still in high spirits, and compel their driver to race with another ambulance (carrying two other drivers who cracked up). This larkish ending, with the banged-up brothers/'pals' separate from Lee and Ann, reiterates the end of *A Girl in Every Port*—inclusive of physical injury. All in all, tensions and estrangement between the fellows and the girls are left unresolved. Hawks's other racing film, *Red Line 7000* (1965) concludes rather oppositely, as though in a series-pattern mellowing over the years.

SCARFACE
(1930, RELEASED IN 1932)

Produced by Howard Hughes and Hawks, scripted by Ben Hecht and others, *Scarface* is probably the most praised and noted film of Hawks's career. Also, it seems to have been Hawks's favorite.

I feel that, in many ways, it is nearly as accomplished as we have been led to expect, and certainly by way of Hawks's own visual and dramatic style, which is present in its basics, often powerfully. And yet, remarkable as the film is for its time, it is not a mature work in terms of Hawks's ensemble acting, its pacing, and the other behavioral-dramatic ways in which his direction comes fully into its own in *The Twentieth Century* (1934) and beyond. In this sense, my own long-delayed viewing of *Scarface* (which had been unavailable for many years) was disappointing.

For the same reason, I would begrudge rating it as Hawks's best film. The series patterns are there, but in important ways, they fail to work as pivotally and integrally as they do later. The "Poppy," "organ grinder," and "bean shooter" scenes are well couched in the series patterns and motifs (inclusive of 'object transaction' and 'triangle') but, as ensemble dramatics, they fail to jell or "catch fire" as they might have (if *Scarface* had, say, followed *The Twentieth Century* and enjoyed the precedence of that Hawksian-behavioral milestone). If the auteur approach to a director's career may reveal good work which would normally or isolatedly seem nondescript, then the same approach and dimension may cut other, previously recognized works down a notch or two. I contend that this is the case with *Scarface* (excellent though it remains).

The project was very well founded, with Hughes, and (not least perhaps) Ben Hecht, and Paul Muni. These people figured inordinately in the result, providing a major part of the project for Hawks to shape in turn.

Scarface centers on a particular character study with a psychoanalytic turn. This latter is the fateful incestuous trap that emerges with Tony Camonte (Paul Muni) and Cesca Camonte (Ann Dvorak). *Bringing Up Baby*, one of the most important and influential films of the series, moves on and from a "psychoanalytic" point of scenario as well. This is not in terms of an individual character study, but as a thematic dictum, namely, "the love impulse in man initially expresses itself in conflict." Functioning well with the series patterns, this is repeated, more or less, in *I Was A Male War Bride* and *Hatari!*, and is part of the series 'friend/foe'-'affection/violence' and 'fraternal encounter' dramatics stemming ultimately from *A Girl in Every Port*.

As for Tony's character, it is, for our purposes, importantly indicated by way of his 'fancy apparel/item' instance(s). The same is reiterated in the quasi-heroes of *Tiger Shark*, *Viva Villa!* and *Land of the Pharaohs*—films similarly featuring a fatal shadow/anima preponderance in or upon the main protagonist. Tony's shadowy yet protagonistic character is hence a major enough contribution to the series patterns—not least for its reiteration in Pharaoh (twenty-five years later and in an important film). Tony is specifically echoed in a number of supporting characters throughout the series: in Louis Chamalis of *Barbary Coast*, Dan in *Red River*, the alien in *The Thing (From Another*

World), Poor Devil in *The Big Sky*, J.B. of *The Ransom of Red Chief,* and more. He is also reflected in Mother York of *Sergeant York.*

In a way less able to be pinpointed, I feel that Tony is an important shadow-archetypal inspiration for many subsequent performances of the series. He seems to be vaguely present, like a directorial "ghost" (i.e., shadow) in ego-figures John Barrymore/Jaffe in *The Twentieth Century,* John Wayne/Tom of *Red River,* and others. Although it is difficult to illustrate, the arch-shadowy Paul Muni/Tony Camonte may well be Hawks's most vital and seminal inspiration.

Ben Hecht is said to be largely responsible for the playful use of the x's physically or cinematographically formed one way or another in death scenes (for "x marks the spot where the body lay"). These enjoy reiteration elsewhere in the series, though they are less typical of the series patterns in their rather expressionistic semiology, and in being symbols mainly apart from, more than part of, dramatic transaction/context. (The *Hatari!* instance is an exception.)

In dramatic terms, the director's style is rather well realized in certain of the police, the C. Henry Gordon character for one. To me at least. they are more interesting than the gangsters, in their particular professionalism (as a dramatic vehicle): probably a more familiar and easier thing to portray at the time, and in being more positive. Note the interesting technical coolness of the (uniformed) policemen, first at the station, and then a few minutes later at the shootout with Tony at his apartment—not so much a brutal coldness as, again, *professionalism,* and in pointed contrast to the sordid murderousness of Tony.

Early, Tony and the oppositely fierce cop, Ben Guarino (C. Henry Gordon), are set off in special opposition when Tony defiantly strikes a match on his badge to light up a cigarette. Here, in the barbershop scene, with the police arrived to take Tony and Guino Rinaldo (George Raft) in for questioning, Tony Camonte is fully introduced as a character, and a tough and fearful one.* Hence when Guarino, after a pregnant pause, strikes Tony for the indignity and disrespect, it is a dramatic moment. (Tony's act is echoed in *The Twentieth Century,* when Webb, anima-suppressively, tries to strike a match across the Joan of Arc poster of the leading lady who did not fare too well.)

The mostly silent, coin-flipping George Raft/Guino is an effective portrayal despite Raft's novice stature as an actor. It is he who is reiterated in shadow figures Sierra in *Viva Villa!,* and Isolde/"Easy" and, to a degree, John Screaming Eagle in *Man's Favorite Sport?,* and others.

Karen Morley's low-keyed portrayal of the toughishly sophisticated Poppy anticipates, to a degree, Lauren Bacall/Slim in *To Have and Have Not.*

The "incestuous" note in the film accrues in the 'triangular' entanglement among Tony, Guino, and Tony's sister Cesca, an earnest eighteen-year-old breaking loose from her brother's protectiveness. Tony's desperation, in his threats and bribery, to keep her away from fellows, is echoed in Joe's resolve to keep his brother away from booze and women in *The Crowd Roars.* Tony

---

*In his makeup here, he seems modeled directly after the eminent turn-of-the-century New York gangster Monk Eastman, surely one of the most fearfully ugly men ever photographed. Ref. Herbert Asbury, *The Gangs of New York* (New York & London: Alfred A. Knopf, Inc., 1928), p. 263.

71

and Cesca conclude in the way Spike and Bill do in *A Girl in Every Port*.

Cesca comes to kill Tony for his jealously having killed Guino, his best friend, and her husband for a very short time. She cannot go through with it when she beholds Tony's regressed, childish condition now. She arrives at his apartment/fortress with a handgun, dressed in blackest mourning, and in general, in a totally reversed demeanor from her former self. She is virtually a different character. She tells him that she cannot kill him because "you're me and I'm you. It's always been that way." Although for her part, this has too little basis in the story-dramatic development thus far, she is yet Tony's anima/shadow and certain "double" here, as Bill is to Spike in *A Girl in Every Port*. As the police converge on the apartment (to arrest Tony for killing Guino), Tony and Cesca are plunged into a great psychic dependence on one another. In a pinnacle of unreason, Tony proclaims that they do not need anybody but each other, that they can rule the town alone. His new consciousness (an awareness of his incestuously motivated wrongdoing in killing his pal Guino over Cesca), coupled with the stress of the showdown at hand, has unhinged him. When Cesca is killed by a police bullet, he comes apart almost completely—not in the shock of grief, but in the abject manner of a shattered ego. He dies trying to escape.

Again, Cesca's treatment in the scene is somewhat wrenched from the rest of the film. It suggests a motivated plunge on the director's part, namely to redo the end of *A Girl in Every Port* in its aspect of the "double" and that of Spike and Bill's resolution of unmitigated friendship. (Or is the discontinuity a result of original footage being cut? *Scarface* underwent a number of deletions and additions by censors.) In any case, the 'triangular' aspect of Tony, Guino, and Cesca stresses the brother and sister relationship.

Tony and Guino—and even Tony and Guarino, the relentless cop—likewise pattern after Spike and Bill of *A Girl in Every Port*, in the way of ego/shadow relationship and contention, and the 'friend/foe' pattern.

In the 'triangular' "organ grinder" scene, Cesca, having received some heavy cash from Tony as an inducement to "no more fellas," is up in her room putting it away, when music from an organ grinder sounds from the street. Guino is down there, waiting for Tony. Cesca tosses him a coin for the organ grinder and monkey there. As the organ grinder pauses in his music, Guino pointedly keeps her coin and tosses one of his own into the cup, smiling up at her as he begins tossing her fifty-cent piece up and down (as he habitually does with a coin). The organ grinder resumes his music and, thanking her, moves along his way. She smiles down at Guino through the ironwork on the balcony, part of which forms an *x*, juxtaposing with her. (Later he will be gunned down on her account, as she, indirectly, will die on his.)

Hawks had George Raft toss a coin this way, at points throughout the film, as a tension release to assist his uneasy acting. This went very well and was probably a boon to his generally good portrayal. It seems to be part of the same (sensation-functional) dramatic method in which Hawks so often has players doing something or exchanging an object as they interact—or, in the striking example in *Corvette K-225*, getting jostled about by the ship together in rough weather as they carry out an important sequence. Similarly, major or minor interruptions are characteristic of scenes.

In one scene, Tony tries out a confiscated Tommy gun and heads out on a job with it. Just before he and some henchmen exit, Poppy interrupts him for a moment as she tosses him his pistol, adding that he ought to retain it in case the new "bean shooter" fails. (It is an 'object-transaction' of small dramatic moment or communication however, compared to those to come later in the series.) Earlier, in the 'triangle' scene with Johnny Lovo (Osgood Perkins), Tony first meets Poppy, whom he will later seduce away from Johnny, mainly by killing him, and confiscating his entire domain. Here, a female statuette is featured in the foreground, juxtaposing with Poppy in the background (though not to the integral compositional effect of later 'foreground objects' in the series). In the same ("Poppy") scene, a cigar ('object') transaction, and a 'fancy apparel' instance are featured, the latter as Tony touches and admires Johnny Lovo's silk housecoat.

Later, Guino kills a member of a rival gang, a florist, who, in the derogatory 'fancy or feminine item/accouterment' motif, is denigrated for this occupation. Guino returns to Tony wearing a rose, signifying the mission's accomplishment. Next, Tony gives it (momentarily) to Poppy. This anticipates the transacted dog in *Air Force* and the bracelet in *Red River* (though as an object-transaction it lacks the depth and import of those later to come).

More effective—more ahead of its time (of 1930)—is the "spaghetti" transaction in the restaurant scene where Tony, Guino, and Angelo (Vince Barnett) enter and come to a table where a few of the gang are dining. The scene is briskly paced, which helps it and its content. The three reach the table just as the waiter brings a plate of spaghetti. Tony accosts him, smells it approvingly, and tells the waiter to get him a plate of the same. In a minute, after some transaction with a newspaper (hastily obtained from a vendor outside) Tony, Guino, and Angelo must head out on some brief, violent business—just as the waiter brings up the new serving. Tony orders him to keep it warm for him. As they hurry out, Angelo steals a taste from it. For our purposes, it is a very important scene.

We find this sort of involved 'object transaction' later in the series, to important effect. Too, the *coincidence* of the first plate coming to the table just as Tony and the others arrive there, echoes the coincidence/clash factor of many 'fraternal encounter' instances of the series (the scene being modeled on the motif). The plate of spaghetti is of Centric/anima aspect. (See below.) As such, it action-dramatically echoes the Centric "anomalous/surprise" factor of important 'fraternal return' instances. (The transaction with the second-arriving plate reiterates that of the first in terms of the same elements—save that the three comrades are leaving instead of arriving, and one of them tastes, rather than smells it.)

Initially, Tony compliments the heavy garlic content of the spaghetti sauce, in the same manner of his expressed fondness for "effeminate" fanciness and gaudiness in clothes, jewelry, and his apartment decor, in other scenes. Hence it participates with his anima-aspected 'fancy apparel/item' motif instances—again, which forbode his doom, in the frequent way of the motif. Relatedly, Tony and Guino (designatedly a "tomcat") are ladies' men. Women seem always to chase after them and their booty, and Poppy remarks facetiously to Tony that he will "drive all the women wild" with his fancy, gaudy wardrobe.

In general, women are metaphorically juxtaposed with objects and animals, in the film. In one of the restaurant scenes, Poppy suggests sardonically that she might "go well with salad dressing." Witness too, Mabel with her feathery stole and the birds and goldfish in her home, Poppy and the female statuette in her introductory scene, and Cesca 'objectivized' in her own fifty-cent piece in Guino's hand. Late in the film, Cesca is juxtaposed with a bird statuette, as she wears imitation-leopardskin cuffs and collar, in the scene with Guino cutting out female paper dolls. (She says of the identical cutouts, "The one on the end is cute.")

Further, Tony, of shadow/anima aspect, is early introduced as an ape-like shadow amidst shadows of potted palms. Even so, his character is replete with the heroic traits of fearlessness, martial competence, and personal power, prior to his becoming more *reflective* (ref. his interest in the W. Somerset Maugham play *Rain*, for one thing), and prior to Cesca's "dying on him" as if she were Mother abandoning him at the very doorstep of Her womb. Whence Guarino and the police triumph.

TIGER SHARK
(1932)

Prior to seeing *Scarface* (well-touted, but little-available), I learned certain things about it by seeing *Tiger Shark*. It derives from *Scarface*, though to a greater extent from *A Girl in Every Port*. In place of the gangsters, professionally, are men of the Pacific fishing trade. Descended from Tony is Mike Mascarenas (Edward G. Robinson), who is not so negative a character, being heroic, but flawed—in which fateful way he is like a German Expressionist protagonist-martyr; of shadow aspect, and folk-heroically tricksterish in his somewhat comic demeanor.

The film opens with a scene pertaining to the series initiation/passage pattern in its combination of (1) ordeal, and (2) comeuppance for selfish cowardice by way of sacrifice, in which carnage (3) Mike's hand is lost as well. Mike and a fellow fisherman are adrift in the open sea in a lifeboat. His comrade there is drawn as a weak, selfish one, adamant on having more water than can be his share. Mike, in sturdier posture, defends the water flask for the sake of both their lives. In a scuffle over it, the fellow goes overboard to the hovering sharks, the "white-bellied devils" as Mike has been calling them. Though he did not intend to throw him to them, Mike nevertheless revels in the man getting devoured alive. The most minor of characters, the fellow anticipates the important Johnson in *To Have and Have Not*.

From this exertion, and the excitement of rescuers approaching, Mike faints, his hand dangling in the water. A shark gets it. The rescuers reach him in time to save him, though the limb is gone to one of the despised predators, who "decide everything" in Mike's obsession—and in fact, as it will turn out. The sharks, as a fateful problem, both psychologically and as frequent marauders of an otherwise abundant tuna-catch in the story, seem to replace Tony's incestuous trap in *Scarface*.

Next, the shot is in medium close-up on Mike's new hook in the act of scratching Richard Arlen/Pipes's upper back, which is always itching but out of Pipes's reach. Through the film, this is a (sensation-functional) feature of relationship between the two pals, and similar to Spike's tugging of Bill's fingers to set his knuckles right in *A Girl in Every Port*. Mike jests, in his braggartly way, that his blunt hook does this little recurring favor better than his hand could, hence implying no complaint of losing the latter. Pipes is a handsome ego type, whereas Mike, though the main character, is again a vigorous shadow type.

The film thus features the prototypical instance of 'dismemberment.' The motif is treated in detail in section IV. Here it revolves around the death and sea burial of the old fisherman, Manuel, and his idea of needing to be physically whole to enter heaven. (Mike thinks of himself as an exception for being such a good fisherman and hence on the good side of ex-fisherman "Saint Pete," the gatekeeper.) (Also ref. section I and Appendix 1.) As Mike returns the deceased Manuel's sea bag and a few things to his surviving daughter, Quita (Zita Johann), we have an early instance of another motif, which may be called the 'meager last possessions' motif. Occurring several times in the

75

series, it is introduced in the chivalric dropping of a downed enemy pilot's boots into the deceased's garrison area, in *The Dawn Patrol*. Mike goes into Quita's waterfront abode, gauchely plunks down Manuel's sea bag, and lays a few coins and a crucifix on the table, thus announcing her father's death. In instances to come, the motif pointedly relays the wry and stoical message of 'so little to leave behind' or 'not much to show for all those years.' It is given to projection of an archetypal-heroic kind. By contrast, in the series patterns, gaudy abundance and related fanciness are unheroic as, on one level, they represent the thwarting, irruptive anima and her morass of greater unconsciousness. Like his counterpart in Tony, Mike will perish partly for this, as well as through his fatalism towards "the sharks, who decide everything," and who are the same anima-rampant unconsciousness within.

The 'meager last possessions' motif and its opposite in fancy or gaudily-abundant doom (the ignoble way to go) are two modes of objects acquiring "live" dramatic force in the series patterns, as exemplified in the highly developed case of the bracelet in *Red River*.

Mike, a great fisherman, does not do well with the girls, unlike Pipes, as it will turn out, and particularly Fishbone (Vince Barnett), who is not a fisherman but the boat engineer, a ladies' man whom Mike bullyingly joshes regarding his girlfriends. Significantly, he is an unheroic, comic type whereas Mike is a blustering, quasi-comic yet heroic type. Once or twice Mike kicks him for no good reason, as Villa now and then kicks the silent, undefensive Sierra in *Viva Villa!* (or as Spike floors Bill to unconscious passivity at the end of *A Girl in Every Port*). In this, Fishbone is rather Mike's shadow.

Mike sets off to marry Quita, sans any courtship to speak of. He dons some cologne, which Pipes ribs him about for its being "effeminate." Mike in high spirits answers, "Yeah! That's me—female!", echoing Tony in *Scarface*.

Mike wears an earring (though this is masculine for a Portugese sailor and fisherman). Early and late in the film, part of his working garb is a knit shirt with a pattern of wavy stripes across the chest (though which is more stark than gaudy). It is for his wedding that he will get fatally dolled up in the extreme and get drunk on top of it.

Quita, in financially poor straits due to her father's passing, and being very young, is forced toward the beginning stages of prostitution (it is suggested). Hence she readily enough accepts Mike's sudden and blunt offer of marriage. Here, she takes a cigarette in hand and says, "Got a match, Mike?"—meaning yes.

This is Hawks-exemplary, her answer of "yes" being not in words so much as an action, namely the object-transactional (tactile-functional) item of cigarette-lighting. Cigarettes, their lighting and exchanging, are a prominent device in the series and, like much else, are transactive or functional in both amatory and comradely relationship.

Next, Mike gets all spruced up for his wedding. He is very proud, as Quita is a beautiful girl, and it rectifies his past failures with the ladies. In the barbershop he orders and receives the works, including a manicure and his hook getting buffed. The working girls in the barbershop later come to the wedding party, and are pointedly included among the basic fishing group and neighborhood. This detail is interesting in its illustration of the series' ways of peer-group dynamics—sometimes emphasized by way of persons who would be outsiders being brought into the fold in some way (like, for certain examples, Clark in *The Twentieth Century* and Williams in *His Girl Friday*). The barbershop girls are a part because of their preparation of Mike for the occasion.

At the wedding party he is in his gaudy attire, and in this way is in the part of Tony of *Scarface*. Since he is not one for dancing, he has Pipes dance with Quita, adding that if he could dance he would be able to quit fishing and become a gigolo. This stoical/heroic remark implies a rather extreme masculine/feminine dichotomy. Linking dancing so flatly with the "effeminately" undignified trade of gigolo reflects, in the implied polemic, considerable ego/anima strife—which condition is as though "effeminately" (compensatorially) seething out in Mike's foppish getup! And dangerously so, as may be inferred, in portending ill for him. In this dichotomy he anticipates the alien in *The Thing (From Another World)*, who is an ultra-stoical figure, yet in a compensatory way, rampant as an irruptive anima expression. (Ref. discussion of the "shaving" scene in that film in section IV.)

Just earlier is the wedding ceremony, of a sort which Hawks will repeat a few times. Once again, the predominance of the masculine peer group is notable (in terms of male-adolescent passage, ultimately). The fishing boat crew are clustered behind and near the wedding couple, in an extension of Mike and hence the couple, thus mitigating the marriage on one level. This 'group-mitigated wedding ceremony' motif is rendered in different ways in its instances in *Today We Live, Ball of Fire, I Was a Male War Bride,* and *Gentlemen Prefer Blondes*. Otherwise in the series, marriage is generally absent, derogated, drawn as unfortunate, or as in *Monkey Business*, rendered in the manner of the 'pals' motif.

The scene begins with a medium close-up on Mike's hook, the wedding ring looped over it (in a profane touch perhaps, echoing Manuel's profane sea burial, treated in section IV). The camera draws slowly up and back to take in the scene with Mike's crew assembled and with Pipes as best man. (Also, the late Manuel of the group was her father, and may be said to be involved as well. Later, in anger at Quita for having taken up with Pipes, Mike says of the sharks, "They took my hand away and gave me this. They took away your father and gave me you!") The hook and ring function, in the foreground, in the mandala-Centric way of many 'dramatized (foreground) objects' in the series. The cermony in progress, Pipes's upper back begins itching once again. Mike reaches up with his good hand and scratches it again for him. Climaxing the little scene, it is a tactile-functional transaction bringing Pipes almost into the marriage itself—or portending of the 'triangle' to come, one of the principal series instances of the motif.

At the wedding party, Mike in his irruptive shadow/anima demeanor gets too drunk and has to be put to bed, clothes and all. Pipes sets to assist him as Quita intervenes, saying, "No, Pipes. That's my job now." Implying a similiarity in their roles, it is in the 'blurred sexual distinctions' pattern, which works in strong dramatic device at times in the series. Similarly, later, as Pipes is being doctored for an injury, Mike paces the floor back and forth entirely like the stereotypical expectant father! with Pipes as the mother-to-be.

One scene is particularly pleasing in its characteristically Hawksian group-dynamical dramatic action. Here Mike, a touch whimsically, is slowly hoisted on a winch into his boat and into the midst of the crew as they all move about hurriedly and willingly to his sharp yet good-natured commands, tending to things, preparing to ship out. Mike is entirely the skipper, yet in-amongst and one of the crew, a peer in it. Such is the Hawks hero in general.

Soon Quita is unable to stand Mike any longer, and having fallen in love with Pipes, starts to take up with him. Pipes, for the sake of his pal, prepares to end the affair by shipping out for other parts and leaving them. As fate has it, he has his accident (with a fish-hook) and is laid up, unable to flee as planned.

The film's climax and conclusion come when the three are at sea together on the fishing boat, with the rest of the crew. (Quita asked to come, to Pipes's apprehension but to Mike's great approval. Innocently, Mike has dubbed the three of them "just one big happy family.") Mike is on the bridge, rifle in hand, ragefully, frantically shooting sharks, his obsession with them running at its zenith. All comes apart in this sequence—which, on another level, irrupts in another, archetypal order of things. Pipes and Quita are below deck in an anxious love scene when, the shooting having stopped outside, Mike suddenly looms in the doorway and slowly enters the cabin in the celebrated shot in which he gradually fills the frame with his enraged image. He knocks Pipes unconscious and locks Quita in a compartment, tosses Pipes into a lifeboat lowered among the sharks, then punctures the bottom with a harpoon.

Here, a little font of water wells up in the boat from the hole made by the harpoon. It is very symbolic (in effect, at least), as though mandala-Centric to the general irruptive ego/shadow/anima drama at hand.

In the heated course of things here, Mike falls into the sea as well, and is himself mortally maimed by the sharks, who once again "decide everything"—from maurading a tuna catch to the parting of friends and spouses. Pipes is saved. The death scene on deck, with the crew around (as at the wedding) and Quita and Pipes close on either side of Mike, is comparable to the conclusion of *A Girl in Every Port* and *The Crowd Roars*. Mike gives Pipes and Quita his blessing, opining that it is better this way, and adding that he is "the best bait in the Pacific Ocean. Mike no go to heaven. Saint Peter come and get Mike." Quita starts to cry hysterically and Mike silences her. He then turns to talk with Pipes on his right, giving her no more attention there for the rest of the scene, as she is in effect shoved aside. His principal communication there is with Pipes, and just before dying he scratches the latter's upper back once again, in the usual way, though with his good hand. (The recurring act is even like a 'dramatized object' in the film.) As his hand then falls away in death, the film ends. We are left with a general homoerotic impression.

Indeed, on one level, the point is: the relationship of the two men somehow culminated via the girl, in the irrupting violence over her who is but a go-between. As a principal 'pals' and 'triangle' instance, it again refers to *A Girl in Every Port*. Like the mandala-Centric heart/anchor insignia of the earlier film, the little font of water in the punctured boat is, in effect, like some deeper truth obtaining amidst the strange, violent drama (of Mike, Pipes, Quita, and the sharks). It is all myth-like, with the mystery which attends the mythic—or a mystery of ego, shadow, and anima, as wielded by the greater Self.

In the little outdoor camping sequence, midway in the film, the full moon is featured. This is an unusual thing for a Hawks film. The lunar orb is linked, perhaps, with the story's irrupting 'triangle,' as Pipes and Quita begin their affair more or less in Mike's presence there, to his unawareness (as he repeats his designation of their threesome as "just one big happy family"). Other key 'triangle' scenes in the series contain expressionistic features stemming from the morass/"vortex" around Bill in the scene of Spike's daydreaming of marriage with Tessie in *A Girl in Every Port*. Corresponding features may be noted in 'triangle' scenes in *The Road to Glory, Come and Get It, Only Angels Have Wings*, and other films.

The full moon in *Tiger Shark* may be another Hawks borrowing from German Expressionism, where it is an old motif (stemming majorly from the eminent moon in George Buchner's early nineteenth-century play, *Wozzeck*). To the best of my knowledge, there is not another moon, full or otherwise, to be found in the Hawks series. Even so, the orb may figure as an archetypal/irruptive feature of the Mike/Pipes/Quita 'triangle'—or quadrangle, if the sharks are included.

TODAY WE LIVE
(1933)

Set in World War I, this somewhat melodramatic work is in basic ways a sibling film to *The Road To Glory*. Comparing *Today We Live* and *The Road To Glory* (1936), and then contrasting them with the rest of the series, we can observe screen writer William Faulkner's influence in both films. It is basic to both and collaborates well with Hawks and the series patterns. They made a good team.

Concerning Hawks's visual/dramatic style, and particularly in terms of medium-low lighting and busy, tactile-functional close contact among players, *Today We Live* is as important as *The Road To Glory*, is advanced over *Scarface*, and amply leads into *The Twentieth Century*.

It is evidently by way of the Faulkner-based script (over, say, directorial improvisation) that the film's 'triangle' motif instance is employed in the unusually refined and dramatically involved way that it is. The film pivots, more or less, on its triangle instance and its heroine Diana (Joan Crawford). She is centered among: Claude (Robert Young), her abiding childhood sweetheart; newcomer Bogard (Gary Cooper); and with her brother Ronnie (Franchot Tone) figuring as well, resulting in a quadrangular 'triangle,' a largely nonviolent one.

Her role, in its involvement with the three men simultaneously, each in his way, is rendered with coherence and realism. Further, Crawford/Diana carries approximately two roles in one: that of a landed Englishwoman and the bearing that goes with it, and—rising to her ambulance-service part in the Great War—that of khaki-clad comrade and pal with the others. Claude treats her concurrently as a sweetheart and like a man. Twice or more he is stern with her in her faltering nerves as he might be to a male comrade. He indicates "Good girl" to her when she pulls herself together. The epithet recurs somewhat thematically, and it and Diana in general introduce the series role-type of Woman-as-soldierly-companion ("initiated" from the status of troublesome, recalcitrant anima). Diana is altogether supportive and companionable to the men—maternally so in one important scene, as Claude (this time) gives in to nerves and must take momentary refuge in her arms with his head upon her breast. This mode of embrace/attitude is repeated a few times in the series, recalling Diana here (and in general) and expressing a maternal aspect of the series anima pattern.

Diana recurs in June Lang/Monique in *The Road to Glory*, who is a different type from Crawford and portrays her role accordingly. She is likewise dressed in a uniform with a prominent red cross insignia, like an identity—clothes they each fill in a stately, professional way.

Early in the film, Bogard comes to Diana's family estate to purchase it, just as it has been learned that her father has died in action. To the other householders she begs not to be excused but meets the guest, striving mightily to remain poised. He does not react to what seems an aloof curtness on her part as she shows him around. At one point she offers him a cigarette from a coffee table container of them. In this series-characteristic object-transaction, the action and shot suddenly come alive in the Hawks manner (the sequence having been dramatically mediocre and nondescript thus far, its upper-class, indoor setting not being given to Hawks's style). In the moment, as she is fighting to retain composure, she seems to seize upon the cigarette transaction to covertly warm up to him, it being the only means at hand of venting feeling, in lieu of, say, breaking down and weeping on the newcomer's shoulder.

Though it may be more accidental than by design on the part of Crawford/Hawks—since the shot and action "leap out" of the otherwise ordinary sequence—it is an excellent moment, and perhaps part of a Faulkner/Hawks scene strategy for her.

Eventually she comes apart and must excuse herself. It has the appearance or takes the form of a gross rejection of Bogard, who is then informed that it is due to the news of her father's death received minutes earlier.

Next is the reunion scene with Claude, her brother Ronnie, and a pastor: moments of hugging, kissing, and a handshake for the clergyman, as she is finally in tactile relationship with all three at once, each man related to more or less differently, and according to character relationship to her.

Then, in mellow 'triangle,' Claude, Ronnie, and she go strolling arm in arm, and the war being on and separations imminent, they exchange rings three ways, in the object-transaction pattern, though less curtly than in other instances in the series—indeed, more in the drawn-out manner of such an event in a novel.

This scene, taking place at a little bridge over a brook running through the estate, is repeated at the end of the film, only with Claude and Ronnie having fallen in battle and Diana wearing their rings with her own, shown in close-up. She walks with Bogard, purchaser of the estate and with whom she is now united—the estate thus retained for her. As I recall, the shot of the three rings (on her thumb) includes a wedding ring on her third finger. In any case, it is an oblique instance of 'group-mitigated wedding ceremony,' like those in *Tiger Shark*, *I Was a Male War Bride*, and *Gentlemen Prefer Blondes*, for the other characters being brought in, in a manner of group inclusion.

Just earlier, she and Bogard stand by the family memorial with her brother Ronnie's name added below her father's. (Is Claude's name there too?) On her blouse is a decorative row of stark x's in the motif of the x's accompanying the deceased in *Scarface*.

In the early reunion sequence, with the departures of Ronnie and Claude for France only a short time away, another object transaction is employed, likewise in a novelistic, scenario-involved way more than a curtly actorial, Hawks way. Diana takes a handkerchief from one of the men to dry her weeping eyes, and subsequently leaves it with the family duchess for the same, who next returns it to the men on a tray serving them tea in their room. In a literary/dramatic way, it becomes a symbol of the subdued emotion at hand (over the father's passing and the boys being on their way to the front soon), as composure is yet maintained. More novelesque than tactile-functionally Hawksian, it yet anticipates the cigarette-smoking/exchanges in *Only Angels Have*

Wings, which are likewise pointedly functional for keeping emotions in check. (In the 1939 case, it is to ward off despair and panic.)

Next, Diana goes to a town near the front with the ambulance service, where the three are united again, this time clad as soldiers on the wet night. The narrow causeway is crowded with war vehicles and other soldiers, all tactile-functionally imposing, and participatory in the friends' close contact (not given to refined verbal communication due to the noise and bustle). All is cinematically opposite from the earlier sequence at the estate. They go to Diana's austere quarters, and playfully chase and capture a cockroach to keep for informal sport—the mode here being one of momentarily regained childhood and its (tactile-functional) sense of play. A lone candle in the dingy place accompanies a subsequent private talk between Diana and Ronnie. Dramatized (Centrically) even here, it becomes more so as Ronnie uses it to relight his pipe—which he smokes in an upside-down position through the film, a corporeal, Hawksian sort of character touch, though featured in the Faulkner short story *Turnabout,* upon which the film is based, in part.

Shortly Bogard enters the story again, as Diana's wooer, whom she loves in return. Missing in action and reported dead, he turns up. (Since he does not suddenly arrive on a scene, it is not properly a 'fraternal return' instance, though as a "return from the dead" it may be said to relate to the motif.) His renewed courting of Diana is upsetting to their friendly 'triangle,' and Ronnie at one point expresses brief animosity to Bogard (the 'quadrangular' intruder thus), though it readily passes.

In jealously however, Bogard takes his rival suitor Claude on a bombing mission as front gunner. Bogard's purpose is to get him killed, his front gunners having been killed off readily, and with Claude naively anxious to go up with him and his copilot McGinnis (Roscoe Karns). Claude instead performs brilliantly, downing some "Huns," saving their lives, and surviving well, his combined beginner's luck and naive fearlessness serving them very adequately.

Subsequently, (sailors) Claude and Ronnie take Bogard out in their torpedo boat—on a mission, as it turns out, and in similar mischief towards him (sans intentions to get him killed). The mission succeeds and they all return, but with Claude blinded. Unwilling to go through life thus, and decently releasing Diana for Bogard (whom she loves most), Claude, with Ronnie, usurp a suicide mission of Bogard's (by torpedo boat in lieu of his plane) before Bogard and McGinnis can intercept them.

Just before Claude and Ronnie leave on the mission, they peek in for a last look at Diana asleep. Blind Claude has Ronnie look in, as he thence "looks" at her via Ronnie. He says, "Are you looking at her, Ronnie? Look at her while I'm touching you." It is a richly tactile ego/shadow devising of course. The two men are as one, and are one via anima/pal Diana between them (and, of course, in their impending suicide mission together). Before they depart, they leave their rings for Diana (who will soon wear them in the last sequence of the film): hence the mandala-Centric 'object' factor, completing this important 'triangle' scene. In its gentle way, it looks ahead to the extravagant ego/shadow dramatics and devisings of *Ceiling Zero.* It seems to me to combine Hawks and Faulkner about equally.

In certain juxtaposition to Bogard, Claude, and Ronnie is the supporting character, Roscoe Karns/McGinnis, a humorous type though hard and professional, contra their romantic role types in the film. Considerably more a Hawks type, it is he who sings "The Dying Airman" in the saloon scenes and displays the best horse sense in combat. The old air corps ditty runs, in part, as follows.

A poor aviator lay dying
At the end of a bright summer's day.
And his comrades were gathered around him
To carry his fragments away.
He spat out a valve and a gasket
As he stirred in the wreck where he lay.
With his comrades all gathered around him
These were the last words he did say:
Take the crank shaft out of my liver
Take the manifold out of my brain.
Take the piston rods out of my lung, boys
And assemble the engine again.
Forgot by the land that bore us
Betrayed by the ones we held dear,
The good they have all gone before us
And only the evil are here.
So stand to your glasses steady
This world is a world of lies.
Here's a toast to those dead already
And here's to the next man who dies.

VIVA VILLA!
(1934)

Hawks directed about half of this film before being replaced by Jack Conway.

The outdoor scenes, with the Mexican rebels arming and massing, loading the trains, and so on, with the women ably assisting as group *compadres*, are generally excellent or brilliant. The boisterous cantina victory-revels are with richer qualities than most directors would instill in such scenes. One or more of the outdoor scenes compare with the outstanding panning shot in *Land of the Pharaohs* (1955), of the pyramid in progress with its strewn groups of workers, craftsmen, and foremen engrossed in the details of their respective tasks throughout the panoramic shot, all in the ever-important series theme of job, work, and professionalism. (Here indeed, Hawks realized the Cinemascope medium he was encumbered with, and as such the scene is a high point of his later period.) One or two of the mass scenes in *Viva Villa!* are as excellent and as humanly detailed. In these, Hawks had a way of humanizing a crowd, as though it were a smaller group—perhaps by instilling each *section* of the mass with an intimate sense of their specific task or activity and/or what they were about.

Other early scenes in *Viva Villa!* are competently done, but they are more expressionistic and dramatically "isometric," lacking the Hawksian *ensemble* qualities, although wrought in good medium-shadow cinematography. Touches of Sergi Eisenstein are evident. Hawks's fuller "behavioral" style (introduced in some part in *Scarface*) emerges in 1934 in the heated businesses among Jaffe, Lily, Webb, O'Malley, Jacobs, and others, in *The Twentieth Century*.

Early, Pancho Villa (Wallace Beery) is having a scribe write a love letter for him, demanding that a signifying bull be drawn on it. The scribe refuses, insisting on having a pair of doves kissing. Villa also wants the scribe to refer to him as her (the woman's) "desert pansy." On the wall behind them, pigeons or doves are painted. All this portends fatally for him in the way that the 'fancy/gaudy apparel/item' instances do for the heroes of *Scarface* and *Tiger Shark* whom, again, Beery/Villa takes after. In the end, where Villa is assassinated, he carries a woman's bathrobe (in an instance of the 'feminine apparel' motif), and pigeons or doves in cages are present! (This part of the film was clearly Jack Conway's but must have been planned as such from the film's initial, Hawks days.) These "bird" scenes touch the anima-relevant 'animal' motif, which emerges fully in *Bringing Up Baby* (1938).

There is the scene where the dudish, pith-helmeted *Saturday Evening Post* writer comes on the scene of the Mexican Revolution, an agape amateur amidst the more solid newsmen there ahead of him, as a bit of fun is poked at him, he being a group outsider. (Ref. Johnson in *To Have and Have Not*, in terms of garb as well as exclusion.) This may belong to writer Ben Hecht, an ex-newspaperman, or Hecht/Hawks from the early days of the project; the scene seems to be Conway's.

Early, Villa and the bandits conduct great violence, highlighted by the mock-trial of offending landed gentry, with peasant corpses for a jury.

An interesting aspect of the film is Sierra, the Leo Carrillo character. Beery/Villa is a shadow type of hero-protagonist, yet Sierra is a meaningful shadow behind him in turn. Carrillo is known for his loquacious roles later, but in *Viva Villa!* he is rather taciturn—one of those Hawks characters who say relatively little yet are important in the cinematic whole. He is the willing butt of Villa's petty irritations, as Villa abuses him (along with others), kicking him and telling him "Shut up!" Importantly here, Sierra retains dignity and character-purpose other than that of a comic butt who receives abuse—a not untypical Hawksian altering of role type.

Sierra early confiscates a fancy jeweled mirror from the landed class, which becomes somewhat dramatized as an object in the anima/mandala-Centric way that we find in the series (as he dandyishly primps in the mirror). Yet it stays mainly with him, is not passed along to speak of, unlike the dog in *Air Force,* the bracelet in *Red River,* and the tiara in *Gentlemen Prefer Blondes.* In his relative silence-with-heavier-presence, he stems from Guino in *Scarface,* and is like Pierre the cabby in *Gentlemen Prefer Blondes* (who is discussed near the end of section V), and others in the series including Sparks in *Only Angels Have Wings,* Mother York in *Sergeant York* (in fair part), the mute priests in *Land of the Pharaohs,* and Isolde/ "Easy" in *Man's Favorite Sport?* All these figures are of major shadow aspect.

THE TWENTIETH CENTURY
(1934)

Twentieth Century's important 'fraternal return' instance is discussed in section V.

The Twentieth Century is an awesome film, with an intense and dark drama moving under the surface of a correspondingly energetic and fast-paced comedy. This is one film of the series in which the initiation/passage pattern is predominant, being the deeper and more violent milieu or framework of its peculiar comedy drama. It also one of the finest films of the series, and important in that it is with *The Twentieth Century* (more than *Scarface*) that Hawks debuts in full flower—although John Barrymore/Oscar Jaffe owes something to Tony of the earlier film in the dynamic way that he (not unviolently) *fills* the sets and scenes of this comedy with his histrionic presence. Too, he and Lily (Carole Lombard) considerably anticipate Walter and Hildy of *His Girl Friday* as a professional yet amorous and sex-antagonistic team. As an ensemble-dramatic duo, they are generally brilliant.

Andrew Sarris agreeably tagged *The Twentieth Century* the best American film of 1934 (over Capra's *It Happened One Night*) and observes that it is "the first comedy in which sexually attractive, sophisticated stars indulged in their own [low comedy] instead of delegating it to their inferiors"—another example of the Hawksian pattern of role-altering/reversal.

It begins with the medium-lighted rehearsal scene in a New York theatre. Light sources we can see are an upright bulb at one end of the stage and a desk lamp over the script on a table in front, the lamp and script a rich image figuring powerfully in the scene, repeatedly retained in the shifting frame, at times passing or lingering near the camera. A cinematic "hub," it is potently mandala-Centric in the scene (with precedence in *Tiger Shark*, in the opening medium close-up on Mike's hook with the ring in the wedding scene).

There in the rehearsal, two of the group confer off to one side, quietly though hotly, and close together (sensation-functionally, the contact well-nigh physical). Here Jacobs and Webb are not fighting, but are concerned with the serious acting ineptitude of producer-director Jaffe's new leading lady. Jacobs, in charge of the rehearsal at this point, exudes a quiet fury over her. O'Malley is also present.

Among the three—Oliver Webb (Walter Connolly), Owen O'Malley (Roscoe Karns), and Max Jocobs (Charles Levison)—one senses some deep and special oppression for the poor girl. Soon Jaffe grandly enters the rehearsal premises, the lighted script to the foreground. After a speech to the troupe, he begins working coolly and patiently with the players, and particularly the new girl—whose name has been changed from Mildred Plotka to Lily Garland, in the beginnings of her initiation/passage this night. He sits at the lighted script table. Soon he gets up, moves into their midst (the camera lingering on the lighted script), and at this point or very shortly, begins chalking lines on the stage to direct Lily's movements. As this grows more involved, the stage—after a little flash-forward—is covered with chalkings for her. This is comedic, of course. In realistic terms, such would be more a hindrance (or an effective hazing) than an assistance. Instead of being guidelines, they are a labyrinth. On one level, this harsh floor-defacing is a psychic irruption (and the initial series instance of the minor 'floor marking[s]' motif).

Presently, Lily breaks down and tearfully, desperately wants release. She has in fact never "acted" until that evening, having been fondly snatched from Woolworth's that day by Jaffe, who at points in the film is something of a Svengali parody. She puts on her overcoat, readying to leave, as a bright gardenia, pinned to it, comes to our attention. Jaffe calms her, removes her coat, and sets to continue rehearsing with her. Surreptitiously, he removes the hatpin fastening the gardenia to her overcoat, the camera in close-up on the mandala image. All in all, the scene's eminent lighted script and the gardenia form a "corporeal correspondence," like the transactional bottle and light-bulb in *The Crowd Roars*.

He has awakened Webb, who dozed off (the rehearsal with Lily having gone into the wee hours now). Jaffe has been trying to get her to scream appropriately for a sudden, tragic moment in the play. He instructs Webb to go to a seat high in the balcony, which he does, sitting down and beginning to doze off again. At the point in the script where she is supposed to scream, Jaffe jabs her with the hatpin, and she screams, loudly and clearly.

This is contiguous with a shot of Webb in the balcony—from the rear, where we do not have the impression of his dozing, but instead of his looking "overseeingly" down at them onstage. The dynamic of this has the effect of Webb's overseeing participation in Lily's getting jabbed with the pin. (Earlier in the rehearsal sequence, Webb similarly looms rather eminently, in the rear of the stage area, in much the same 'convergence' dynamic upon Lily.) In confirmation of her loud scream, Jaffe, onstage, claps for her. Webb then claps sleepily, as the two of them clapping thus complete the 'convergence' upon her. The scene cuts to opening night and the applause of the entire house, as Lily takes her bows onstage. Delivery boys jog to the front with bouquets of flowers from wooers (echoing, a little, the earlier gardenia image). As she bows, with the most professional grace now, the shot moves upward to rest on Jaffe, who is sitting high on the spiral stairway backstage. In black garb, Svengali-like, he looks coolly down upon her as though in triumph of his own—in much the same "overseeing" manner of his cohort Webb in the balcony, just earlier.

This feature of character contact or relationship over a distance of ground (or other dramatization of space) is encountered a number of times in the series. It is, in general, a function of the close-knit/close-contactual character of relationships in Hawks films (the deeper pattern of which is 'characters as portions of one psyche'). Spike and Bill of *A Girl in Every Port* set a precedent in their fated 'fraternal encounter' via the girls of the world's far-flung ports. As it happens, Jaffe, Webb, and Lily comprise a certain 'triangle' instance (a minor one). In the film, Webb is Jaffe's shadow, and of anima aspect in (1) his being married, (2) in being a certain go-between for Jaffe and Lily, and (3) in the important dramatic business around his derby hat. (The latter is discussed below.)

From her beginnings with the hatpin, Lily Garland (formerly Mildred Plotka) is now a professional actress and a star, and the sequence has thus been one of harrowing initiation/passage. Yet this first initiatory phase of the film is not quite over. The essence of the rehearsal sequence is repeated backstage when Jaffe goes to her bouquet-laden dressing room. As he touches one of the flowers, a bit sadly, we feel that he is temporarily humbled. She is reflected in her stage mirror with a circle of lights bordering it, which will shortly contain Jaffe as well, as he brings her his congratulations and fond tidings. Lily shows him the "initiatory" hatpin placed ornately on a little cushion now, as a tender keepsake to always remind her of all he did for her (as the object accumulates drama—here and later in the film). Jaffe waxes humble, and soon she is in his arms and destined for future Jaffe productions. He coolly nudges the door shut with his foot, as the scene fades out on the gilded star on her door, which Jaffe earlier instructed a stagehand associate to nail up. Indeed, Lily is once again converged upon by two men and an object! Jaffe and the stagehand (his comrade-by-sex) thus "seal" the business of Lily with the object, which becomes a symbol like the heart/anchor emblem in *A Girl in Every Port,* which "seals" the pals' solution to the Woman problem (anticipating the pyramid and the entombed priests jointly sealing up the incorrigible Nelipher in *Land of the Pharaohs*).

Lily is hence the anima jointly initiated and suppressedly contained by the personified forces of ego/shadow. This pattern is repeated in ways throughout the film.

Lily, greatly rebellious at Jaffe's tyrannical confinement of her activities, prepares to leave her palatial penthouse and go out on the town on her own. Jaffe's cohorts are obliged to talk her out of it. (They intercede for the pair, especially the more sympathetic, genteel Webb.) They enter the sumptuous place, with Jaffe on his way too.

On one level, it is a violent "invasion" of her femininely luxuriant quarters. O'Malley stretches out on her gondola-like bed, obscenely: hat, shoes, trenchcoat, and all. This gauche invasion of her bed, in its unusual contrast with him in his gritty, wet-weather garb, is part of the same general ego/shadow 'convergence' upon her. Heavy drinker that he is, he commences to nap. Webb, in his gentler way, starts to beseech her. Spiritedly she affirms, "I'm no Trilby!"

The shot cuts instantly to—Jaffe, in his dark garb, fully the visual affirmation of Svengali! He has entered unnoticed until now, and moves broodingly in and toward her. In effect, it is: "Wrong! You *are* Trilby!"

Here we have another Hawks device, namely, 'verbal/action simultaneity,' which introduces the important 'merged dramatics/dialogue' pattern (not to be confused with the famous 'overlapping dialogue' device, which will be treated in the section on *His Girl Friday,* and subsequently). Ultimately, 'merged dramatics/dialogue' is a function of 'characters as portions of one psyche.' In this typical instance of 'verbal/action simultaneity,' Lily's spoken line is quickly combined with a physical event (Jaffe's entrance) which, in effect, answers her statement in characteristic sensation-functional action over words. (Note the "bottle/George" scene in *Come and Get It,* which features a comparable instance, and utilizing an odd instance of 'fraternal return.') The 'merged dramatics/dialogue' pattern will be further discussed by way of its examples as we encounter them.

As Jaffe thus closes in, the convergence upon Lily is once again complete for the moment. Jaffe orders the pair outside and goes into an excellent scene with her, feigning suicidal intentions. It is a fairly lengthy ordeal and quarrel, with Barrymore and Lombard at their best, the boys having to wait outside in the rain.

At one point, the scene cuts to a brief shot of Webb and O'Malley outside, sitting under a common umbrella, their backs three-quarters to the camera, O'Malley with a pipe in his mouth. Webb (who is rather Jaffe's shadow, on one level) glances around toward where Jaffe and Lily are and shakes his head in misgiving. The shot is *A Girl in Every Port* compressed into about five seconds. Webb's mute shake of the head indicates the graveness of the Woman problem, which is relegated to the lavish apartment, away from the nobler (austere) outdoor wet. The slightly anomalous, comedic touch here is the obtrusive umbrella they are under. (The contraption is like an anima irruption, and hence an object in certain 'triangle' there with 'pals' Webb and O'Malley.)

Next, Jaffe commandeers his private detective, McGonigle (Edward Kennedy), to trail her, in further masculine 'convergence.' In one excellent shot he talks to Jaffe on the phone with his feet and lower legs on his desk toward the foreground of the shot, very coarsely.

Shortly, he informs Jaffe that Lily has skipped town for adventure and fortune in Hollywood. Jaffe goes into a fitful tirade, staggers down the stairs, throwing his shadow on the wall, his cohorts trailing helplessly along with him. Below, he violently drenches newly-made posters of Lily with great swaths of black paint at hand.

Here Max Jacobs quits and leaves them. Recovering cool and courage, Jaffe starts anew, designating another actress in the cast for the part—a brunette, who comes forth coolly but smiling at her chance to play Joan of Arc. Next, in Chicago, the play flops, and the three emerge from the theater discussing it. Webb, as he remarks of the woman's failure to be good enough in the part, strikes a match across her poster image there, leaving perhaps a mark (the match breaking), not so much a complex 'convergence' action as an "obliteration," like the earlier paint-throwing on Lily's posters.

They have to escape creditors and jail. In flight on the Twentieth Century Limited, the fun begins as the film's acute shadow figure emerges. A very significant character/figure, he is Matthew J. Clark (Etienne Giradot), a little religious fanatic who goes about the train putting up circular evangelical stickers. Here, psychically speaking, the cat is out of the bag as, moreover, the combination of the lunatic and his stickers link with Woman and the recalcitrant anima problem. This is indicated when a shot through the train window has one or two of the white, round stickers on the pane (in the relative foreground thus) juxtaposing with—Lily. She is on the platform in one of the stations, back from Hollywood, amidst local fans. In a moment she has entered the train, wearing a leopardskin coat (in a touch of the animal/Woman connection), and carrying a bouquet, which she holds like a shield, displaying its roundness. This echoes the earlier gardenia, and particularly Clark's round, lunatic religious stickers of a moment ago. Thus she and Clark link on one level.

Clark is supposed to be a millionaire, but his checks bounce. The uniformed train conductors move about in hot pursuit of him, exhibiting some earnest professionalism (in the series theme). However, one of the conductors unknowingly gets a "Repent" sticker on his own back. Webb gets one plastered on his derby hat and is unable to remove it entirely. Jaffe tells Webb that he ought to burn the hat. In part, this is a jibe at the odd hat itself, as Webb clings to it, saying at one point that he prefers a derby. This is the prototypical instance of the 'odd hat' motif, with instances later in *Red River, Gentlemen Prefer Blondes* (obliquely), *El Dorado* importantly, and minorly in *Rio Lobo*. The combination of Webb and his shadow character, and the emphasis on his odd hat bearing the sticker originating with the rampant shadow/anima figure of Clark (plus the tie-in with Lily), make Webb's hat an important point of the series archetypal patterns.

Webb continually picks at the hat's sticker, eventually resigning himself to its permanence. On one level, this is a handshake with the "dark brother within"—namely with Mr. Clark, the greater shadow of the Jaffe/Webb/Lily/O'Malley group. They in fact bring Clark a little into their fold.

Believing that he is an eccentric millionaire, they woo his "investment" in their otherwise dim future—to contract Lily again and go into business out of the red and free of jail. Clark hence becomes one of the group for a while. This anticipates the rapport between Williams and Hildy (and to a degree, or by certain extension, the other journalists) in *His Girl Friday*. Williams goes berserk with a pistol—quite as Mr. Clark wounds Jaffe with the latter's gun. Bonnie, who accidentally wounds Geoff with his gun in *Only Angels Have Wings*, is linked as well.

Hence, in the series archetypal patterns, we have a linking of Woman/anima, animals, the shadow, 'gun lunatics,' and (as we will see, in later films) children: all of a piece.

On the train, Jaffe and Lily visit, and their old relationship re-emerges briefly, portending their getting back together shortly. They fall into a catfight, as of old. Hereabouts, Lily, alone, muses over the original hatpin, set in velvet within a little frame, this time, a thoroughly dramatized object now. As such, it is contiguous with other mandala-Centrism associated with her: the original gardenia, her dressing-room mirror, and her bouquet on the train (coupled with the round evangelical stickers).

Finally there is the new contract which, through a deception, they get her to sign, as the piece of paper, 'converged' upon by Jaffe and cohorts, is thus mandala-Centrically featured. (Ref. the smoking car scene, treated in section V.) Here, as the hands of Jaffe and his cohorts Centrically clutch at the new contract, it reiterates an earlier dramatic business in which Webb and O'Malley each hold to Jaffe's hand which clasps his revolver, as they restrain him from possible suicide. Mandala-Centric as well, it is of course a metaphor of fraternity—and of "the three musketeers," as they dub themselves in the film. Jacobs's sudden descent upon the smoking car scene, in oblique 'fraternal return,' is hence like a final mandala-Centric "capping" of the film's general ego/shadow 'convergence' upon the anima in Lily (who, in her Centrism, connects with the Self). (Again, ref. section V.)

All in all, *The Twentieth Century* is as much in the initiation/passage pattern as the drama around Bat's grueling reinstatement among the pilots in *Only Angels Have Wings.*

In addition, Jaffe and Webb wrestle (somewhat) in one scene, like the Biblical Jacob and his shadow in the form of an angel. Trying to calm the hysterical Jaffe, Webb implores him: "I know you won't believe me, but I'm the best friend you've got!"—like the shadow pressing the unwary ego who needs to be receptive to the unconscious.

BARBARY COAST
(1935)

Barbary Coast is one of the two or three gross failures of the series, torn against itself by the contrary forces of Hawks and (we suppose) the Goldwyn studios. (Later, in *Come and Get It* and particularly *Ball of Fire*, he will work well with the same producers.) Yet there are some noteworthy things in the film, and the vigilante sequence is important in the series patterns.

In Slocum (Harry Carey, Sr.) and his several cronies who become the core of the vigilantes we have an exemplary, though tricksterish instance of the Hawks-type group around a peer leader: in this case, a kind of sheriff without a badge. They contend successfully with Louis Chamalis (Edward G. Robinson) and his town hall mob, who up till then rule San Francisco themselves. Louis (pronounced "Louie"), the fancily-clad boss, reiterates Tony and Mike of the series and, characteristically, is subject to emotional problems around (himself via) Woman in Mary "Swan" Rutledge (Miriam Hopkins), which prove his undoing, though not precisely his death. This seems to be cryptically evaded in the last scene of the film (as we will examine, below).

When the poetic James Carmichael (Joel McCrea) encounters Swan, as she visits his outlying prospector's abode to get out of the rain, an undergarment of hers is soon hanging near the fire to dry out, in the manner of spelling feminine peril, though it is a minor instance, being of little dramatic consequence or reference in this particular film. Also between them is a book of Shelly's poems he lends her. As her employer and boyfriend Louie comes upon it and has a jealous fit over it, it becomes more dramatized, and corporeally focuses their minor 'triangle' in the manner of the heart/anchor insignia in *A Girl in Every Port*.

Early, upon landing in San Francisco, Swan expresses an odd rapture for the fog. Thus begins the series fog-or-rain/Woman connection, which recurs later with series heroines Bonnie and Tess, and in more minor and oblique ways elsewhere. "Goldwyn Girl" Miriam Hopkins does not work well as a "Hawks heroine." She is too romantic, unlike, variously, Louise Brooks, Joan Crawford, Karen Morley, Ann Dvorak, Carole Lombard, June Lang, Frances Farmer, Jean Arthur, Rosalind Russell, Jane Russell, Ella Raines, Lauren Bacall, Margaret Sheridan, Angie Dickenson, Charlene Holt, and Jennifer O'Neil, of the series yet she gives a fine performance. Unfortunately, her performance is for naught, due to the film's general failure.

The vigilante insurrection in the latter part of the film emerges/irrupts by way of a shadowy combination of things which impart the overthrow and disintegration of Louie's regime. It begins outside the office of the *Clarion* newspaper with the irate McTavish (Donald Meek). McTavish's pal Sandy was murdered earlier by Knuckles (Brian Donlevy) of Louie's gang—news which the *Clarion* covered up due to mob terror upon the newspaper's amiable but unheroic editor. Outside the *Clarion* office is a display case with some posted clippings. Casting an initial, ominous shadow upon it, McTavish tacks up a piece of paper of his own, declaring suppressed town news and accusing

Knuckles of murdering Sandy. This "folk edition" of the *Clarion* is uglily scrawled, in large letters and bad spelling, by the semiliterate (and perhaps heroically anti-thinking-functional) McTavish. Very much a primitivistic scourge upon the literate, "dandyish" newspaper and its high-toned editor, it is an object and irruption of shadow aspect, and of considerable dramatic transaction. McTavish and the editor, who comes out, are next gunned down by Knuckles who then snatches the scrawled page from the display case. The editor, having fatally opposed Knuckles there, rallies in sudden inspiration from McTavish's "folk edition," renounces his weak ways before dying, and pleads for integrity to his assistant and to all present.

Slocum and his boys quickly converge on the newspaper office and, with the young assistant editor, print an edition of their own denouncing Louie and his rule, and generally indicate their intentions to take over. Armed, they storm the town, distributing their own special edition.

Thus, the town insurgence is elicited from, or "born of" the corporeal, shadow-irruptive semiliterate page: a deep prime mover. The scrawled page is hence an important item in the series archetypal patterns—as the vigilante uprising is an important group shadow/tricksterish expression. Significantly, the vigilante insurgence gives rise to a new series motif: the 'group-delineative/"circular" montage' device. In a loose form here, it is employed in the grim but excellent scene of Slocum and his gang apprehending Knuckles and lynching him. The vigilantes accost him and tramp along the muddy nighttime street, giving him a mock trial as they go. The shots move back and forth among the group as they talk and as Knuckles protests—the resulting montage sequence, in effect, delineating their close-knit group character (hence the term "circular" in the sense of self-contained). Patterned a little after Sierra in *Viva Villa!* in his little-spokenness, Knuckles now bursts his habitual cool, realizing that the end is at hand. Hanging him to a lamp post, they all pull together as an ardent, single-minded gang. The shot of them all, here, functions Centrically or unifyingly with respect to the preceding montage portions. (The first really pronounced instance of the device/motif is in *His Girl Friday,* in the scene of Williams's capture.)

The subsequent little (night) scene of Louie and his forces contemplating Knuckles dangling from the lamp post, is similarly strong. The fancily-clad Louie mutters "Cut him down" in a preoccupied tone, as though he were more lost in thought than on top of things. His line reiterates the same from Beery/Villa, in *Viva Villa!* rendered differently, though as quietly, in the scene where he and his band arrive too late at the disciplinary peasant hanging.

Another strong scene is the brief one of the townsmen in line and filing through for vigilante rifles. It is a good example of Hawksian economy. One man asks. "Who are we fightin'?" Slocum utters Louie's name; the man drawls "That's okay by me" and takes a rifle. So much for swearing-in and indoctrination.

As for Carmichael and Swan, they take the opportunity to elope. Here Louie fatally—as his "fatal fancy clothing" stigma foreshadows—steers a few of his remaining forces after Swan instead of working at securing the town. Even so, Louie will become the MGM "bad guy with the heart of gold" as he lets her go with the man she loves, a little prior to his capture. (Here, he also reiterates

Mike of *Tiger Shark*.)

As Swan and Carmichael are apprehended by Louie and his men, she promises to remain with Louie and love him if he will just spare Carmichael and let her send him away on an outbound ship at hand. (Carmichael is wounded and nearly unconscious there.) Shortly, his henchmen having fled, Louie hovers reflectively over them, as she and one of the ship's officers attend to Carmichael in his delirious state. In his cocky way, Louie bids her to leave with Carmichael, saying in effect that he cannot be bothered with a dame like her (who will not love him of her own free will) when he has "big things to do in this town."

Slocum and his vigilantes suddenly arrive for Louie, keeping a polite distance for the moment. Then, as the lovers prepare to embark for east-coast civilization, Louie turns to the vigilantes and says, "Let's go!", and strides off a little ahead of them, even as if he were leading the small group.

On one level, Louie *joins* them, more as a comrade than as a condemned prisoner, with Slocum and his group having abruptly, fraternally 'returned' for one of their own! It is a somewhat more cryptic instance of return than that of Jacobs in *The Twentieth Century*, as in a way of reversal, the group rather 'returns' to the 'returnee' in the dandydish Louie, who is of archetypal shadow/anima aspect. His cryptically joining them instead of being lynched by them, gives a touch of "death/resurrection"—all proper to a 'returnee.' It is also a union of foes/friends in the pattern.

The above is also like the ending of *A Girl in Every Port*, where Spike rejoins Bill to the exclusion of "skirts"—as Louie joins certain riotous peers and excludes the maudlin, romantic "MGM" likes of Swan and Carmichael!

Excepting these richer points, *Barbary Coast* remains a poor product. In spite of Ben Hecht and Charles MacArthur's writing credits, it is bad on and from the script level, and the film illustrates Hawks's inability to work well with a fixed scenario and contrary screenplay (notwithstanding the apt subject and setting). It would of course seem that Hecht and MacArthur were constrained by studio forces as well. Parts of the film, however, obviously belong to Hawks.

The early scene with the ship arriving, with voiced communication through the fog—poor, contrived hyperbole about the gold rush at hand—is nonetheless precedent to the superb river/fog scene in *The Big Sky* (1952).

In section IV, *Barbary Coast*'s instance of the important 'dismemberment' motif is examined.

CEILING ZERO
(1935)

Among the most exemplary of Hawks films, *Ceiling Zero* is a film to discuss more synoptically than in detail due to its quantity of relevant points. *Ceiling Zero* (scripted by Frank Wead, from his play) comes forth so voluminously and so fast as to require a small book if we were to deal with it in the piecemeal way in which we are able to treat the others films of the Hawks series.

This aviation film is probably the best of James Cagney/Pat O'Brien adventure dramas from Warner Bros. Almost throughout, it is a fair "choreography" of Hawksian action dramatics in their inter-player situations of close, essentially physical contact, and attendent devices of the sort which constitute an important part of the series behaviorism. These are played to the hilt, and the pace at times is too fast for a viewer to easily follow. In these respects, *Ceiling Zero* is a Hawksian self-satire, with features exaggerated as if for pedagogic display. As with Faulkner, Hecht and MacArthur, and Billy Wilder in the series, Hawks made a good team with Frank Wead as regards scripting.

The film's intertwining (ensemble) dramatics of the peer group in action together fully introduce the 'merged dramatics/dialogue' pattern (as anticipated in the "spaghetti" scene in *Scarface*, Claude and Ronnie's 'triangular' farewell to Diana in *Today We Live*, and the "Trilby" scene in *The Twentieth Century*).

Yet the film is "precocious" in all this—rather ahead of its time career-wise—which testifies to the aptness and creativity of the director's collaboration with Frank Wead. In a like manner, *His Girl Friday* (1940) is as important as it is, dramatically, through Hawks's affinity with the Hecht/MacArthur dialogue in *The Front Page* (which play, of course, readily became *His Girl Friday*). *Ceiling Zero* is very companionable with the 1940 film in terms of rapid pacing ("speed") and attendant dramatics.

Dizzy Davis (James Cagney), after some regulation-violating acrobatics over the airport, lands his airplane and is boisterously greeted in reunion with old comrades there (fellow mail pilots). In his initial rough-housing embrace with pal Jake Lee (Pat O'Brien) he exclaims, "Lover boy!" to him, since, as we soon learn, there is a particular woman between them, who broke with Dizzy for Jake—thus in a 'pals'/'triangle' instance.

Quickly Dizzy is shoved from friend to friend in the manner of a team upon a player who has saved the day for them. Finally he tumbles giddily to the airfield—and at a pair of fancily-shod feet. These belong to a somewhat gaudily-dressed Federal man who has just sauntered up on brief business with Dizzy. This sort of man or agency will eventually deprive him of his license, and indirectly his life—for bureaucratic reasons, more or less. The sudden, dandyish Fed is hence a "fatal fancy foreboding" upon him, quite as the doves and the flower are to Villa early in *Viva Villa!* (Dizzy is an ego-heroic type though on the other hand given to recklessness and extensive womanizing in the shadow/anima-rampant pattern.)

In this, his reunion, there is a minor 'fraternal return' instance. Dizzy of course 'returns,' yet the visiting Federal agent enters the scene, action-dramatically, like a 'returnee' (ref. the split-in-half return instance with Jaffe and Jacobs in *The Twentieth Century*). The agent's 'fancy apparel' instance serves as the "irruptive surprise" factor, which, in its anima aspect, also serves in the 'triangle' reference among Dizzy, Jake, and the woman between them. Further, Dizzy's encounter with the Fed this way is an early series anticipation of the 'self-encounter/splitting off' motif. (The latter is discussed in the section on *The Big Sleep*.)

A strong dramatic point in the film is that of the brain-damaged ex-pilot, who is nearly useless but is kept around polishing door plates and other brass in deference to his previous service. Not having seen him since before his accident, Dizzy cheerily greets him as one old cohort to another, finding out his case the hard way, as the man only gapes idiotically. Juxtaposed with the (solar-like) metal work which he constantly polishes, the fellow is the more a sacrificial hero, given to archetypal projection (as in the case of a "resurrected" 'returnee' or a restored 'dismemberment' case) as a symbol of the Self, on one level. On a dramatic and perhaps archetypal level, he is foreshadowed in Phipps in *The Dawn Patrol*, and echoed in the alcoholic Eddie in *To Have and Have Not*, and thence the lame Stumpy (and even the alcoholic Dude) in *Rio Bravo*. Again, the too-old, the too-young, the injured, the infirm, and the dead—as "ego rejections"—are lent to "archetypal honors" in the series.

Tex Clark (Stuart Irwin) is a skilled and brave pilot, but severely henpecked in the manner of the hero coming under his wife's slipper. (Ref. discussion of the anima in the subsection on the same, and in section IV.) As he is on the phone with her and intimidated, he magically gains the courage to talk back merely as, shadow-like, a cohort comes beside him to listen in and be close to him in his minor plight, their two-against-one stature proving a match for the harridan/anima at the other end of the line. Like Dizzy, Tex subsequently dies heroically.

Jokes and banter in the 'blurred sexual distinctions' pattern abound, with female characters in government uniforms in and about. At one point Dizzy says to one of the girls, "That's a cute outfit"—it being mainly similar to his and his male comrades' own. Hence she is in the fold with them, in her initiatory "common cloth." Something similar obtains with Diana and Monique of *Today We Live* and *The Road to Glory*, respectively, and with Catherine and her Army fatigues in her cross-country trek with Capt. Henri Rochard in *I Was a Male War Bride*.

Again, the film is a fabulous display, a "Hawksian circus," if lacking in the director's effective and important *low*-keyed dramatics (of which we have more in *The Twentieth Century*, for all its intensity).

THE ROAD TO GLORY
(1936)

This World War I drama is a very good job from every aspect. Like its companion film, *Today We Live*, it is special in its collaborative basis on the script level over such action-dramatics as we know to originate on or close to the Hawks set. An exceptional scene is one obviously improvised: with Lt. Michel Denet (Fredrich March) shaving, as he and another soldier conduct a humorous 'object transaction' with a racy magazine. It is a somewhat glaring (and very sensation-functional) interlude, with a 'triangle' aspect.

Hawks collaborated well with screenwriter William Faulkner, who is responsible for much of the result. At times the film runs like a play—as we note, for example, the dramatically implosive scene of the enemy demolition being audibly planted near the French dugout (exploding minutes after the unit moves out and others move in).

The little scene of Monique (June Lang) praying in the cathedral for her soldier companions is virtually the only unmitigated religious scene in the Hawks series. She is yet a real "Hawks heroine" in the 'triangle' instance with Michel and Paul Laroche (Warner Baxter) who both love her. Harmoniously, she refuses to commit herself to either of them, with the war on and all. As, having indicated this, she walks away from Michel, he reflects to himself in quizzical admiration (for "their" girl). Then, as he exits, the shadowy-baroque background is lingered on for a brief moment. This reiterates, a little, the morass/vortex of sorts around Bill in the portending 'triangle' scene in *A Girl in Every Port*, as well as, perhaps, the full moon in the parallel scene in *Tiger Shark*. Here the triangle is in variation from the prototypical instance(s), for Monique's essential gallantry in lieu of troublesomely coming between the two comrades in arms.

Lionel Barrymore realizes a good vehicle in Papa Laroche, who retains an old bugle in patriotic fetish. Hawks employs it as a Centrically dramatized object. Near the end he has his son Paul blow it as they are about to die in a suicidal mission in behalf of their unit. (Hence Paul—who, like Claude in *Today We Live*, has become blind—does not "get the girl," but his pal Michel does instead.) Juxtaposed there—in a version of the "poor man's Holy Grail," ultimately symbolizing masculine Self-realization—is the spoked wheel of a farm implement, recalling the similarly idealistic candle/athletic medal pairing in *The Dawn Patrol* (as well as, ultimately, the heart/anchor symbol of *A Girl in Every Port*).

'Fraternal suicide mission' is a story-level motif, with instances in *The Dawn Patrol, Today We Live, Ceiling Zero,* and *The Road to Glory,* with oblique instances in Kid Dabb in *Only Angels Have Wings* and the priests and Nelipher in *Land of the Pharaohs.*

COME AND GET IT
(1936)

In general this was a good film for Hawks, working with Samuel Goldwyn (William Wyler directing most of the last few hundred feet). In points of style, and in certain production factors, we find the hand of the MGM studios over that of the director. Yet in spite of this, and despite the film's relative adherence to plot/story (over the more series-characteristic development of characters in relation to one another and to their situation), *Come and Get It* is laden with series-pattern material. Hawksian dramatics and archetyping are at work, scene after scene.

In the early sequence in Iron Ridge and the North woods logging camp, Barney Glasgow (Edward Arnold) is introduced as an ambitious boss, though in good rapport with his men, being more or less their peer, for he is a champion logger himself. All this is in the series pattern of the *occupational group*. The loggers have energy, prowess, and fairly good morale in meeting his escalating demands. Since he seems to feed them well and their camp conditions are visibly decent, he and they are hence in the "best tradition" of the labor heroism of the early lumber woods.

In the cookshack/mess hall, he reprimands one of the men for having liquor there. He does not fire him, neither then nor shortly when he and a pal fight with Barney, but brusquely confiscates the bottle, and blames drinking for the group's falling behind schedule. Next, in the mess hall scene, the cook's young assistant spills coffee on one of the same pair. As one of them starts to assault the lad, Barney intervenes, in a firm but rough-housingly friendly way still, but as the pals set to attack him, he knocks them both to the floor, semi-unconscious.

Suddenly Barney's pal, Swan Bostrom (Walter Brennan) enters, and as they have not seen each other in some time, Swan delivers his special long-time-no-see greeting, which is to jump up on Barney as though onto a horse, only straddling his chest. It is sensation-functionally comparable to Spike's frequent, fraternal tugging of Bill's knuckles in *A Girl in Every Port*. Indeed, Swan then shoves one of the recovering loggers back to the floor with his foot—not even having seen the fight or knowing anything about it. Having thus kicked the fellow on trust, he says, "That'll teach you to fool with Barney Glasgow!"—which is to say, 'Any floored antagonist of Barney's is one of mine.' Here of course is a strong note of 'pals' solidarity, emphatic here in its ego/shadow function (as Swan, on one level, is an extension of Barney, in the latter's fight with the unruly men).

In the subsequent logging sequence, one of these floored men is shown on good working terms with Barney again, as the latter is in the field supervising and pushing the pace. In retrospect thus, the fight, like Swan's contactual, rough-house greeting, becomes a point of group-dynamical relationship, in the affection/violence pattern of the series.

Although they are very minor characters in the logging camp sequence, the cook ("Cookie") and his young assistant are focused on in an archetypal way. As Barney confiscates the whiskey bottle from the logger, he tosses it to the cook, telling him to get rid of it. But Cookie indicates pleasure in getting it, and we guess that he will soon be guzzling the stuff himself. The booze is anima-linked, in view of Barney's blaming it there for the crew's falling behind schedule—and particularly in view of subsequent irruption concerning the boozy Cookie. Later in the film, Swan remarks, "That fool Cookie, he set fire to the camp and she burn down." In this, Cookie corresponds to the shadow/anima-relevant 'gun-lunatics' Clark in *The Twentieth Century*, Williams in *His Girl Friday* and, prototypically, the trigger-happy Tony of *Scarface*. Like the alien in *The Thing (From Another World)*, Cookie also functions like the commotion-causing nurse on the island of soldiers noted in the latter film. (Ref. discussion in section IV.) (Swan's remark about Cookie burning down the camp takes place years after the initial logging camp sequence, and the original Cookie and the later "incendiary" one are not likely to be the same man. Yet I would maintain that the verbal/occupational identity between them identifies them as one figure.)

All in all, the cook's helper and the shadow/anima figure of Cookie are extensions of one another. Early the boy helper is featured in the immediate background (a little in the way of a significant background figure and minor character), and behind Barney and Swan, in one scene, like the third (anima) figure of a very minor 'triangle' instance.

Subsequent to the logging sequence in the field, the pals are in a boxed steam bath. There Barney, for amusement, has the attendant pour more water over Swan, raising more steam than Swan can comfortably take, in the ever-important tactile way of relationship, in the series, and here in the way of slapstick.

Next is the office scene amongst the two pals and a businessman friend of Barney's, who hints strongly that Barney should opt to marry his daughter and merge Barney's up-and-coming fortune with his own. As agreement becomes tacit, the businessman friend produces a cigar for Barney, and then, as the pals are leaving, he halts Swan briefly with one for him too, at which point the cigars become emphatic (as well as a little humorous), and sweepingly encompassing them all as a small group.

Such occurs a number of times in the series, with an object or an event dramatically "popping up" or otherwise brought to brief focus, transactionally among two or more characters. The scenes would not be the same at all without this focal, Centric, and essentially corporeal emergence. Related is the 'verbal/action-simultaneity' of Lily's saying that she is not a Trilby just as (Centrically) the Svengali-like Jaffe enters (irrupts), in *The Twentieth Century*. Such popping up tends to be mandala-Centric and a composite representation of the Self. Yet always we note its tactile/shadow or tactile/anima import. The "spaghetti" scene in *Scarface* is another example (where the waiter with the platter of pasta pops up to 'fraternally encounter' Tony just as he comes up to a table of cohorts), like the "bottle/George" scene in *Come and Get It* (discussed below), where an object pops up as an oblique 'fraternal returnee.'

At the profitable season's end, Barney treats his loggers to a "jamboree" in Iron Ridge—as the archetypally rich saloon sequence commences. Here Barney and Swan meet saloon employee Lotta Morgan (Frances Farmer), commencing a Hawks-type 'triangle' (though it is ever friendly among the pals, in this instance). Barney meets her at the table where he outwits the shell-and-pea manipulator for five hundred dollars.

There, Barney says, "Swan, make room for the lady," and Lotta literally (physically) comes between them, as Spike, Tessie, and Bill of *A Girl in Every Port* are briefly synopsized. He says to her, "Are you gonna bring me luck?" She says, "If I do, it'll be the first time," as herewith, a female character is given a 'tramp stigma' in the motif.

Barney proposes to bet the large amount on the game. The sleight-of-hand man says that he does not have that much. Almost instantly the saloon boss pops through the crowd with enough to cover the bet (the word having carried very fast that *Barney Glasgow* was preparing to bet, and with it, the reasonable assumption that he would bet a lot). This logical, though unusually prompt, emergence by the saloon boss at just the right moment is a 'word/action-simultaneity' instance, in being a sudden emergence (irruption) relating to something just remarked in dialogue (an ego/unconscious dynamic, on one level, and part of the 'characters as portions of one psyche' pattern). This particular 'simultaneity' instance compares with the "Trilby" instance in *The Twentieth Century*, although the "saloon" instance inobtrusively merges with other dramatic action, whereas the "Trilby" instance comes forth like a punch line, to dark-humorous and violent effect.

Clever Barney is allowed to win, due to the boss's wishing to avoid exposure of the crooked game, and in fear of his loggers who are still present. Aside, Lotta asks the boss if he wants her to get the money back. She assures him with few words (and in the manner of saloon professionalism) that she will if she can have something to put in his drink.

As she in fact helped Barney to play the game his way—in an "instant camaraderie" akin to 'fraternal encounter'—she does not go through with doping him and robbing him of his winnings. But before this, she is on for a song number, "Aura Lee," backed by a pianist and a singing waiter quartet.

Here, deep-voiced Lotta is rendered in a moderate pastiche of Marlene Dietrich. Barney begins falling for her, Swan exuding misgivings in the 'triangular' way. A trace of shadow from her parasol falls upon her face, in a "brunette" and obliquely, a 'rain/fog' note. (This motif seems to denote initiation, in the series patterns. Ref. discussion in the section on *Only Angels Have Wings*.) Such shadowy touches, as well as the "Dietrich" touch, are imported from the genteel expressionism of Sternberg.

In the scene, Lotta and her song create an intensive anima focusing—particularly as she renders an encore from the mezzanine (where she has joined the pals at a table just before the encore is requested of her). She thus establishes herself and her song in two places, over a distance of ground. In emphasis of this dramatized space, the waiter quartet rush, convergingly, from elsewhere in the room to a position just below her, to accompany her encore. Effectively in turn, one waiter scurries up a bit late (verily in a minor 'fraternal return'), indicating his having come from a more distant point in the room (and the piano is of course some distance away now). Juxtaposed with her on the mezzanine, at points, is a gas flame and a picture on the wall of a woman; and the camera at one point is in an up-shot of her, past the quartet holding one or more trays of beers, their heads quaintly, tactilely together in close harmony.

Her intense, songful image, established thus between the two parts of the room creates a dramatic (cinematic) space, and her encore portion effectively forms the Center of a cinematic mandala composed of (1) both parts of the song number, as well as (2) the room in general, via the converged space of the waiters rushing from points in the room to convene below Lotta to accompany her encore. Indeed, it is from this mezzanine Center (and "source"), and through this certain, resulting "created space" of Lotta's, that the brawl will transpire, even as if through a created medium. Such is the overall effect.

As the loggers all leave to get something to eat elsewhere, and Lotta quickly comes into cahoots with Barney, who is refusing to give up his rightful winnings, the brawl ensues. It begins as Barney and Swan repell saloon employees who charge up the stairs to extract his five hundred dollars. Thereafter, it is a one-way fight, with Barney, Swan, and Lotta sailing serving trays at hand at the saloon men, smashing mirrors and the hanging lamps.

The brawl serves to establish their friendly 'triangle' (as such establishes Spike and Bill's friendship in *A Girl in Every Port*). Archetypally, it is: ego (Barney)/ shadow(Swan)/ anima(Lotta) and Self(the trays). The latter indication comes to light as Barney and Swan, later in the film, reunite around one of the trays (mandala-Centrically), retained as a keepsake, and which rather "replaces" or 'objectivizes' the deceased Lotta. (See below.) At the brawl's end, they leave merrily together with Lotta rolling one of the trays along like a hoop, and Barney knocking out a last intact mirror with one as he laughingly hollers, "Timberrrrrr!"

Appropriately, the archetypal Swan (who is Barney's shadow with anima aspect) initially discovers the stack of trays at hand. He is somewhat taken back by it (or by himself) after inadvertently picking one up and bashing an attacking waiter, the tray as though an irruption from out of himself. Here, Barney says to him, "Swan, you've found a gold mine!," referring to the stock of tray-weaponry there.

This is an interesting line, seemingly paralleled elsewhere in the series, and probably pertaining to the Self. One of the parallels is in a scene which links with the saloon brawl sequence. This is in the comedy *Monkey Business*, where the board meeting turns to uproar with the arrival of the two regressed adults and the ape (a 'triangular' 'fraternal return' instance, as it happens). As the trio play havoc there, Oxly exclaims, "We're on the brink of a new world."—the youth vitamin manifestly successful and the conquest of aging at hand. The other striking remark is in *The Twentieth Century*, in the ('triangular') scene where Jaffe "captures" Lily in her dressing-room, the Centric, "sealing" star tacked to the door (the scene, again, in certain reiteration of the preceding 'initiatory' rehearsal). There he says to her, "You're at the foot of a golden stairway"—her career now.

Apart from Jaffe's high-flown language in general, in *The Twentieth Century*, and the maudlin acclamations about the gold rush at the beginning of *Barbary Coast* (as well as the fancy language of a few characters in the latter film), this sort of hyperbole is little-heard and rather unimportant in Hawks cinema. Yet the hyperbolic remarks in the three scenes—two scenes of which are, again, related—may well pertain to the Self, which is operant in the scenes, in the first place, in terms of their *transcendent-functional concentra-*

tion. Hence again, Barney (ego)/Swan (shadow)/Lotta (anima)/ the trays (Self), and with the Self echoed in Barney's hyperbolic remark.

Lotta and her song/encore mandala will be further discussed, with regard to the 'anima-ego' motif, in the section on *Red Line 7000* and in Appendix 1.

'Dramatized/converged space,'—player to player contact over some distance—is a significant series device and pattern. Though not used too often, it is a corporeal extension of Hawks's predominant close-contactual dramatics. It is initially seen to real effect in Webb's certain "vector" upon the rehearsal from the balcony, in *The Twentieth Century*. It is anticipated in *Scarface*, where Cesca tosses Guino a coin for the organ-grinder. In *Red Line 7000* there is the simple, common-sensical, yet exemplary instance where Gabby, out on the dance floor, tosses her hat back to Dan at their table, she and he thus "filling" the space concerned, as well as emphasizing the good standing of their relationship despite her rocking and rolling with others.

Come and Get It features two unfavorably foreboding 'feminine apparel' instances. Early, Barney brings Lotta gifts, saying, "This'll show you I know something about women's clothes." This is repeated later with the deceased Lotta's daughter, whom Barney will woo at one point by helping her with her shoe. Significantly, he ends up a humiliated, partly defeated character in the film.

Yet in the same early "clothes" scene, he suggest to Lotta, "Ever try wearing your hair without those thingamajigs?" referring to her little curls in front—like frills to be stoically eliminated in the series way of anima suppression.

Next, there is the remarkable "shirt" scene with Barney and Swan.

It comes to pass that Barney must carry through with the earlier arranged business-marriage, and leave Iron Ridge and Swan, and Lotta. In the medium-lighted scene in Barney's hotel room he prepares to depart, asking Swan to say goodbye to her for him. In the next scene, Swan will do so, and successfully propose to her himself, hence bringing their 'triangle' to a head—though again, they have been a comfortable threesome all along. Later as well, Swan will write to Barney, "You and Lotta were the people I always loved best in all the world."

In keeping with such pivotal 'triangle' scenes, the "shirt" scene features a certain "morass," a Centric emergence of sorts, like the parallel scene in *The Road to Glory*, and the *"X"* scene in *Only Angels Have Wings* (to be discussed).

These, again, reiterate and story-dramatically parallel the scene in *A Girl in Every Port*, where Spike, musing fondly on his prospective married life, juxtaposes with Bill who is darkly and fatalistically in cinematographic morass/vortex. Correspondingly, Swan-and-Lotta ("Bill") are the stoical, honorable "woods" life Barney is forsaking, not untragically as it will turn out, for the wealthier but emptier city life. In their case, the commenting "vortexture"/morass is the oddly-lighted figure of Swan himself, as he listens sadly to Barney's tale of parting.

The lighting on Swan is such that his shirt, of a very small check, stands out in subtly pronounced *relief*. Swan is made symbolic in a 'fancy apparel' instance, thus becoming 'objectivized' via his cinematographically overpronounced shirt! (This is one scene lighted more by Hawks than MGM.)

As Barney's shadow, Swan is anima-related in this 'fancy apparel' instance. Too, he subsequently marries Lotta and, moreover, has a daughter by her whom Barney will later try to court for his mistress. Further (as we will see below), Swan is cross-identified with Barney's daughter Evvie. The film's 'triangle' instance is hence a very involved one, though ever-harmonious on the story-dramatic level.

On one level, such archetypal features of pivotal 'triangle' scenes—such as Swan's emergent shirt, the "baroque morass" behind Michel and Monique in the instance in *The Road to Glory*, and seemingly the full moon in the camping scene in *Tiger Shark*—are like a would-be "anchoring" resource of the transcendent function amidst ego/shadow/anima upheaval and conflict. Below, we will note how the serving-tray keepsake transcendently (as well as mandala-Centrically) focuses their 'triangle'—in a more compactly egotized and story-developed way than Swan's eerily emergent shirt.

Soon it is years hence, and Barney the lumber baron is "settled down" in urban Society in a mainly empty marriage, though with the companionship of his daughter Evvie (Andrea Leeds), a brunette "Hawks heroine" type who empathizes with the Barney of days gone by. At the breakfast table they chide the staunch mother, as Barney privately makes the 'twosome sign' to Evvie, with two fingers (borrowed from Spike and Bill of *A Girl in Every Port*).

On one level, and in one scene, Evvie is, again, identified with Swan. In this scene she reads a letter to Barney from Swan, expertly imitating the latter's Swedish brogue. (Evidently learned from Barney over the years, her Swan imitation is, I think, too adept for realism—a significant point on the auteur level. Dramatically, it is very effective.) In view of other cross-identifications in the series (including those of the 'self-encounter/splitting off' kind), the example of Evvie/Swan seems to meaningfully obtain as a 'double' instance. (Ref. 'double/doppelgänger' (c), in Appendix 1. The 'self-encounter/splitting off' motif is discussed in the section on *The Big Sleep*.)

In reading Swan's letter to Barney, Evvie tries to get her father back to Iron Ridge for a needed vacation, he being somewhat out of sorts. As she succeeds in talking him into the fishing vacation with Swan, Barney calls Thomas the servant in to "pack a bag for..." as he absent-mindedly hesitates. "Fishing, sir?" the servant smilingly fills in for him. Thomas, at Evvie's instigation, has already packed the things for Barney. Outwardly mundane, this is, on one level, the unconscious working ahead of, and predetermining a course for, the unwary ego (Barney), with the servant as shadow, though Evvie as well, and Swan, absent though he is. Since Evvie knew he would make the trip, it is an early series instance of 'second-guessing.' Along with 'verbal-' and 'verbal/action-simultaneity,' 'second-guessing' is a prominent expression of the important 'merged dramatics/dialogue' pattern, in which characters share or participate within one another's private psychological or behavioral space (thus partaking, in turn, of the 'characters as portions of one psyche' pattern).

It is a dramatic mode of characters who are close-knit, and is thus part of the series group/ensemble dramatics in general. One is reminded of the simple, common-sensical but exemplary bit of merging dialogue/drama in *Red Line 7000*, in the scene where Dan and Gabby break up.

> She: Are we still friends?
> He (smiling): What are you doing for dinner tomorrow night?
> She (smiling): I'm having dinner with a friend.
> He: See you tomorrow night.

The interinvolved fatalism of Spike and Bill in *A Girl in Every Port* anticipates 'merged dramatics' though in a scenario more than a dramatic way.

As the pals reunite in Iron Ridge, Swan is not as strong as he once was and so cannot jump up on Barney as of old. It is here that we learn—with no adequate explanation—that Lotta has died. The pals regard the serving-tray keepsake, taking it down from the wall in happy reminiscence of the saloon brawl and of the three of them that night. They talk of each of their chip-off-the-old-block daughters, in such a way as to express affection for each other: namely, *through* their daughters, in the 'triangular' way. Too, on one level, the tray has "replaced," or is and even was, Lotta. Hence is She now an 'objectivized' "appendage" of the pals, quite as with Spike and Bill and the mandala-Centric heart/anchor insignia between them with Tessie otherwise purged. It is a little grim here, as if Lotta never quite existed, save symbolically (as their, or the ego/shadow's anima). Hence Lotta's flawed, too-abrupt purge from the story (though significant or meaningful on the auteur level).

Her surviving daughter, Lotta Bostrom is played by Frances Farmer as a blonde. Swan's niece, Karie (Mady Christians), lives with Swan and his daughter. Barney, very taken by young Lotta, has the three of them come to Chicago for a visit. He then hires Swan in one of his mills and gets them a home, thus inducing them to stay.

Previous to this is the important 'song session' scene with Barney and Swan's family in close-contactual relationship. It is the finest and most exemplary scene in the film, at once "pure Hawks" in its peer-group dramatics and "pure Goldwyn" in its familial, musical Americana (two differing twains meeting, via Hawks the resourceful auteur). If we had to choose a few scenes to represent the entire Hawks series, this, the "accordian" scene, would be one of them.

Richly in the tactile-functional pattern of 'foreground object/action,' the "accordian" scene begins with a medium close-up on the dinner table, now empty save for an empty glass upon it. Karie removes the center leaf and closes the table, as Swan, with his foot, pulls the table nearer to him and puts both feet up on it. Dinner is over, and schnapps is, in general, flowing in the scene, the initial empty glass being Swan's.

In the scene, Swan plays "Aura Lee" on the accordian as the daughter sings it the way her mother used to. As she does this, Swan becomes apprehensive at Barney's evident, painful reminiscence now of all he once left behind. While Barney listens, the part of him facing her is bathed in light, and the side toward Swan shadowed, the composition echoing the idyllic Spike and the shadowy Bill in the pivotal 'triangle' scene in *A Girl in Every Port*.

Barney becomes very upset at the old memories returned, yelling, "Stop it!

Stop it!'' as he gets up from his rocking chair, which bounces up and down in his absence. (Twice in the scene, the spring-rocker continues bouncing this way after his getting up, in strong, corporeal, Centric action which participates in the dramatic context.) Swan quickly proposes a lively tune, "Nellie's Hat," to cheer Barney up. Promptly taking this hint, the daughter urges Barney to sing it. Coming out of his gloomy state a little, he agrees to, if she will give him a kiss. Euphorically, Swan interjects that they will each and all give him one! Barney, and the others as well, sing some of "Nellie's Hat" before he kisses the daughter—heavily, to Swan's disconcertedness.

As he gets up to manually induce the shy Karie to kiss Barney, Swan gets a painful kink in his back. This is 'triangular' on one level, in its interruption of the kissing business (echoing Bill's distracting of Spike from amorous pursuit in *A Girl in Every Port*). They manually help Swan with his back. Then—and in close dramatic connection with (a) the kiss, and (b) Swan's ailment and their quick attention to it—Barney, suddenly in soaring spirits (from kissing the daughter), broaches the idea of their all coming to Chicago with him for a visit. As this finds contagious agreement (more or less—they are a little taken aback by its suddenness), they all finish the song, celebratively, with gusto and heightened togetherness, concluding in a close circle (the shot of them here a very fine one). As the song ends, Swan comments on a faulty accordian key—which stuck disharmoniously, and which Karie reached over and mechanically assisted him with. "By George, I gotta get that thing fixed." he says. The others laugh heartily and the scene fades out.

The scene is a very Hawksian intertwining of persons, actions, and things, in its characteristically tactile, group-dynamical contiguity—and mandala-Centricity, in more ways than one (in Barney's rocking-chair, the anomalous accordian note, and their song-circle itself, particularly at the end). Each of these, alone in a scene, would tend to be Centric. Note the faulty accordian key's retroactive emphasis in Swan's concluding remark, making it a dramatically unifying detail and Center. The faulty key corresponds to the cigars—the initial one, and the second, more emphatic one popping up, in the early office scene. After the disconcerting "Aura Lee" solo, the *shared* music's part in healing Barney's disturbance and hence restoring the group's harmony, anticipates the famous "steak" scene and "psychotherapeutic" jam-session in *Only Angels Have Wings*.

The intriguing "bottle/George" scene in the Chicago restaurant where the four of them go, is a companion to the "cigar" and "accordian" scenes. As they enter, George the head waiter, of Barney's acquaintence, seats them. Barney says aside to him, "George, take this lamp away, will you?" which he does. As a stoical-like elimination of "superfluity," this corresponds to Barney's earlier suggesting that Lotta wear her hair without "thingamajigs," and is hence a similar point of anima suppression. Complexly, the removed lamp "pops up" again in the form of a champagne bottle, in reemphasis, thus of the initially stressed anima/Center of the lamp. This occurs just as Barney finishes, to their (mixed) acceptance, his further proposal that they stay and become part of his company and life there. Here he adds, "Well, we were talking about having a good time. Well, *good,*" just as a waiter brings up a bottle of champagne, which Barney pats approximately on the word "good."

The initial lamp, and the concluding 'verbal/action simultaneity' with the bottle, serve as corporeal factors participant with dramatic action and development—like the cigars, in the early office scene, and the bouncing rocker, the faulty accordian key and Swan's back ailment in the "accordian" scene. The "bottle/George" scene touches 'fraternal return,' as the suddenly emerging and Centrically stressed bottle is, on one level, the suppressed lamp returning (even as in "death/resurrection")! The scene anticipates the brief but important lab scene with the scientists in *Monkey Business*, with Dr. Bruner's bald head in place of the 'returning' lamp/bottle. (Ref. the section on the film.)

Later, there is the masculine business with the paper cup, a promising invention around which Barney, his son Richard (Joel McCrea), and Tony Schwerke (Frank Shields) convene in capitalist venture.

Tony Schwerke, an ordinary worker whose idea it largely is, wants to marry Evvie and vice-versa. Barney brings him into his office to discuss her and the paper cup (the projected wealth from which Schwerke hopes to be able to support her). Schwerke trips over the doorway floor partition—just as Barney does whenever entering his office. As a shared corporeal contingency thus, it functions fraternally between them, and echoes the faulty accordian note earlier (which was "tripped" over as well). It even combines with the dramatized paper cup over which they confer, and for which Barney gradually comes around to share the optimism of the others, as the object becomes very Centric.

Familially here, Barney's son Richard will marry Swan's daughter—whom Barney, a little tragically, will fail to make his mistress—as Schwerke is to marry Barney's daughter, Evvie/"Swan." As the three men focus around the cup in turn, it recalls Spike, Bill, the girls, and the heart/anchor object and Center in *A Girl in Every Port*.

Talking with Barney, Evvie relates that she fell in love with Schwerke when he was changing her tire in the rain (in a touch of the 'rain/fog' motif), there in the mud and wet, "so dumb and sweet, like a bug turned upside-down." In advance of *Bringing Up Baby* and later comedies, it is the initial striking instance of the series-comedic, shadow/anima-irruptive mode of hero-humiliation at the hands of Woman, and with a touch of the 'animal' motif.

The courting scene with Richard and Swan's daughter around, in, and through the spilled taffy is of course very tactile-functional. Along with the "accordian" scene, a few scenes initially focus on something in the foreground, in the manner of Mike's hook-with-ring in *Tiger Shark*, though more casually. These include: Swan's daughter's iron at work; the little anchor weight dropped to stay Barney's horses and carriage; and, as the scene opens on Richard giving his conservation talk in a living room, Richard's ring—his right hand with a ring on—is in the foreground. This rather couples with Barney and the anchor weight as he arrives outside for the same meeting.

In either a specific (semiological) or quasi-symbolic (moodful) way, 'foreground objects/actions' provide a corporeal reference to the dramatic action at hand, and often introduce a scene. The technique is seen to strong effect in the script table and lamp repeatedly to the foreground of, and Centric to, the rehearsal sequence in *The Twentieth Century*, masterful in its

106

casualness yet strength. Powerfully as well, in *Air Force*, foliage rises in the foreground as the "green kid" parachutes to the ground, having been machine-gunned by an enemy fighter while still in the air.

The company party sequence on the grounds of Barney's mansion home is William Wyler's, except for the 'triangle' scene in a bedroom inside the mansion.* Here and in certain of the adjacent footage, Hawks cinema is indicated, as Barney and Richard come to crisis and physical conflict over Swan's daughter, who is anxiously present. In the the course of the dramatic action there, she rejects Barney for the son. Medium-low lighted, the scene is exemplary in its understated violence (its relative low key), and carries an effective cinematographic density (lent in considerable part by the soft curtains, very close at hand). Next to the "accordian" scene, the "curtains" scene is the best in the film.

Walter Brennan received an award for his performance. Edward Arnold/Barney's performance is among the most memorable of the series, and Andrea Leeds/Evvie/"Swan" is a minor but intensive Hawks heroine.

---

*Certain sources claim that William Wyler did not direct on this sequence, despite his directorial credit.

BRINGING UP BABY
(1938)

Bringing Up Baby, the series' principal comedy, seems well-based in the story via Dudley Nichols and Hager Wilde, though evidently given to considerable improvisation. It was suited to the Hawks mode of ego/shadow/anima strife, being the particular psychological comedy that it is, with Woman and animals as fairly explicit forces preying upon a trapped, repressed academic fellow (if finally assisting his normalcy and presumably his greater happiness). It was aptly chosen as a project, bringing to form, expression, and series-precedence the "Hawks comedy" as generally considered. The subsequent series comedies, excepting *His Girl Friday* and *Gentlemen Prefer Blondes,* six in all, take after it (including *The Ransom of Red Chief*).

As Hawks remarked critically in an interview, no character in the film is very sane, not even the psychiatrist, though it is he who proffers a major maxim or truism, namely "The love impulse in man initially expresses itself in conflict." This is thematic for the film and the series patterns more generally, in their recurrent 'affection/violence,' 'friend/foe' patterning.

In the film, Susan Vance (Katharine Hepburn), a madcap of great proportions, involves David Huxley (Cary Grant) in a chain of calamitous, nonsensical capers in and about the well-to-do New England countryside which ultimately sever him from his impending marriage to Alice Swallow (Virginia Walker), a woman of belittlingly staid propriety. Even so, Miss Swallow says to him early, "I see our marriage as a dedication to your work," and is for this part an "initiated" Hawks heroine—like Diana and Monique of *Today We Live* and *The Road to Glory,* and particularly Edwina in *Monkey Business,* who in terms of professionalism, are masculine-supportive instead of comedically anima-recalcitrant. Significantly, Miss Swallow is brunette and dark-clad (in vague reference to "initiatory" 'fog/rain'), in contrast to Susan's less austere and, at points, rather bizarre costuming. Yet Susan serves David (indeed, in the way of initiation/passage) as Bill serves the amorously headstrong Spike in *A Girl in Every Port,* namely as a peer and a 'pal' on one level, in her special variation of the motif. At the same time she is the series recalcitrant anima in an extreme form, yet with "masculine" features as well, namely her golf playing and her uncommon assertiveness. (Again, the series patterns contain odd mixtures, occassionally odd cross-referencings, and reversals. These are not inconsistencies as much as they are probes, and of course "natural" in lieu of conceptual contrivance. 'Reversal' is a series device and pattern in its own right. An important example is Hildy, a man's role but played by a woman, in *His Girl Friday.*)

The ensuing rambles of Susan and David strike a chord of the eventful cattle drive in *Red River* a decade later. The pair initially meet and clash on a golf course, a setting of more than one memorable comedy sequence in American film. They then go through an automobile bout in the parking lot. Susan, earlier the golf athlete, is now very much the "woman driver," yet undauntedly so, which is the difference. Here she begins to be a manner of "Ulysses," one of physical and other mishap at cost to others than she, particularly to David, who is almost ruined professionally, due to the caper.

Next, in wholesale 'fraternal encounter' (again) she clashes with him in the country club lounge. Susan, friends with the bartender, is learning a trick from him—one of tossing an olive into the air and catching it in the mouth. It is a little outlandish for eastern Society but a sensation-functional point, of dexterous skill (like Pipes's cigarette tricks in *Tiger Shark*, by the way). One olive goes astray on the floor, and who should come toddling along to slip on it and fall but David. Unlike two ordinary people just earlier gone their separate ways, they are ego/shadow/anima in "teleological" cluster and collision. As David says there, "I might have known it was you. I had a feeling as soon as I hit the floor."

In a little while, the psychiatrist, Dr. Lehmann (Fritz Feld), on hand with his wife, picks up the olive trick, or begins attempting it, as it is thus passed along like an object, like the medal in *The Dawn Patrol*. Such transaction in the series ranges from common physical action on a vague center to a more explicitly mandala-Centric object shared and dramatized (like the serving-tray and then the paper cup in *Come and Get It*, and particularly the dog mascot in *Air Force* and the epical bracelet in *Red River*). Too, Susan inadvertently takes the psychiatrist's wife's purse, but has David return it, in another such instance. However, as David is troublesomely stuck and embarrassed with it for a while, he is hence nabbed by a 'feminine item' in the motif—for which he will not eventually get killed, though it portends the moderate hell he will go through in the film.

In the country club lounge, and particularly in one of their apartments, large, round bas-reliefs in the decor juxtapose with David and Susan. In the former setting, one is prominently behind them at a point when Susan is beginning to glean, the 'love impulse in-of their conflict.' It is a touch like the serving-tray keepsake between the pals in *Come and Get It*.

Subsequently, David is at home and bickering on the phone with his fiancee. A delivery man in a uniform like that of a gas station attendant arrives with an important package for him. As he waits a little impatiently for David to get off the phone, he looks him over as if in mild disdain for his better or dudish clothes. As David quarrels with Miss Swallow, this shady delivery man provides moderate encouragement. At one point David says to him, "I'm getting married tomorrow," to which he curtly replies, "Don't let it throw you, buddy." A minor but stark shadow figure, he is an adventure-dramatic note, under the circumstances, and a reiteration of Bill seeking to dissuade Spike from women and Tessie in *A Girl in Every Port*. Again, Susan is "Bill" as well in the film.

David signs for the package, which is a dinosaur clavicle arrived to complete the skeleton he, as a paleontologist, is completing. The ultra-masculine delivery man, like the (comparably shadowily-clad) Miss Swallow, is hence linked to David's professional concerns. Later, Susan's dog will steal the clavicle, dogs liking bones as they do. The little fellow then romps off with and buries it, to great havoc as they follow "George" about the estate in search of it, trying to get him to dig it up. In this sequence, Susan impetuously sends their clothes away for laundering. Dressed in her bathrobe with a chevron-like *SV* (her initials), she momentarily puts on his hat, in allusion, on one level, of confused identity (namely, David's confused identity). In and of the same ego/ shadow/anima crisis here, on one level, they both make do with odds and ends of clothing found at hand to go chasing the dog and bone. Susan's getup, significantly, is all of a piece (an Oriental outfit), but David must don sundry togs resulting in a funny costume, in a clown/shadow manner, if with "appropriate" hunting items, for the bone chase. Just earlier, David had on her fuzzy, ultra-feminine nightgown—the first major series instance of this particular anima irruption in a character—as he sarcastically remarks to the intruding Aunt Elizabeth (May Robson) that he has "gone gay all of a sudden." At a few points in the series, homosexuality is jibed at, like something on the shadow side of the hero, or a special taboo. (Ref. the section on *A Girl in Every Port*, and Appendix 1.) In amusing contrast to David forced into the feminine garment is Aunt Elizabeth's rather "mannish" outfit.

On the level of the Nichols-Wilde script, the clavicle is a phallic symbol, and perhaps one of castration. In terms of the series patterns it becomes a transacted, dramatized object. At the end of the film, Susan returns the clavicle her dog ran off with (and has finally dug up again). David is on the scaffolding at the summit of his dinosaur skeleton, and as she heedlessly climbs the ladder to hand it to him, they both hold to the clavicle as the skeleton collapses in a heap below them. "Oh, well," he says as they embrace, and the film ends with his professional/dinosaur work in shambles. (Should he have gone with Miss Swallow instead? a viewer may ask.)

Susan is temporarily minding a pet leopard, Baby, with whom David initially clashes in her apartment. Previous to going up there and running into the animal, he argues with Susan as she sits in her car by the curb (a "masculine" station-wagon). In the course of his altercation/tantrum, he exclaims that he must be rid of her, since he is going to be married very soon. With this, the shot changes to an indeed beautiful (interspersed) shot of her, as she laughs at this statement of his—simply laughing in the mirth of a gadfly. A brief but pivotal point it is, partly for its cinematic beauty, a moment of Hawks at his visual-dramatic best. Here she is Bill of *A Girl in Every Port*, in the combination of her medium-lighted cinematography and enigmatic scorn at the idea of David's getting married to someone. She is of course Bill, in terms of the further capers they will be off on, as David is pulled along in a fatalistic manner.

Shortly, in her apartment, he encounters the leopard and hastens out and down the street. Here the leopard follows closely as Susan drives alongside of him elated by the situation, talking chidingly to him. He is thus converged between them, she and Baby moving as one creature. This is akin to Jaffe and, from the distance, Webb, 'converging' upon Lily in the rehearsal scene in *The Twentieth Century*, only here it is David who is to be the initiated one in the course of the odyssey of capers led by Susan, the "feminine trickster."

Shortly, Susan and the leopard play a trick on the funny constable. In a little town, she parks by a fire hydrant and Constable Slocum (Walter Catlett), out for duty and arrest, argues with her over the hydrant. The hydrant is a considerable transactional object/Center there, between Susan, the constable, and the cat, which he doesn't notice hopping from her car into the adjacently parked one. She then asserts that the car by the hydrant is not hers, but that the next one over is, and she and the cat then easily skip town in the stolen car. It is a fine little scene, Centered on the hydrant as it is, and with joint ego/shadow dramatic action in the cat's swift move like a creative cognition on her own part. Thus the hydrant and the players form another instance of mandala-Centrism/patterning. Soon discovering the trick, the vociferous but bungling constable, hot on the job, is off on Susan's trail.

Late that night, circumstances bring Susan and David to the slumbering Dr. Lehmann's home where they—and her dog and leopard as well—do a serenade in the dramatic motif of 'song session.' The song (the theme song of the film) rendered by man, woman, cat, and dog is, of course, "I Can't Give You Anything But Love, Baby," elsewhere sung to quiet the leopard. Later, she and David are lost in the woods, the dog and cat off on their own. The leopard and dog are 'pals.' Susan earlier stresses that they like each other, as they fight playfully. She and David crawl through brush in their once-elegant clothes. Rudely, the ever-exasperated David lets a branch fly back in her face, as she struggles through on all fours. Here she is rendered as a cat herself, in the 'animal/Woman' connection, an eminent feature in this film, and hand in hand with "female tricksterism." The shots of her here, in the wooded shadows, are cinematographically superb, as it happens.

In jail finally, she goes into an act to beguile the jibbering constable into her plan of escape. Changing character completely—echoing Evvie/"Swan" in *Come and Get It*—Susan the lively socialite becomes the moll of a principal gang. Here Katharine Hepburn pulls out all the stops. In general, her performance as Susan is spectacular, but this sudden "underworldly" change of demeanor contributes something in addition to establish her and her symbolism at the heart of the series patterns.

The preposterous Walter Catlett/Constable Slocum, the funniest one in one of the funniest of all films, is easily led along to think that he is getting the hottest of tips on great unfinished police business with regional gangs. Released from her cell and into an interrogation chair, she takes the constable's cigar, who takes it back as the psychiatrist (who is present) gives her a cigarette—a prominent, twofold 'object-transaction' of some grace and flair on her part. Carrying forth this way as "Swingin' Door Suzie," Susan is able to escape through a window to go and look for Baby and the dog, who are rambling the countryside unattended.

In the events of the night, another leopard has entered the action, a vicious one from the circus, which gets confused with her tame one by two or more disconcerted characters.

Finally, circumstances conspire so that nearly everyone in the film—every principal and supporting character and animal—is either present at or descends upon the jail more or less at once: a collossal 'convergence' (hinting at being a mass 'fraternal return'). Susan, out after her animals (which 'return' independently of her), returns, tugging along the now-intimidated circus cat, believing him to be Baby. The anomaly/extremity of *everyone's* more or less simultaneous convergence there is in accord with this, the American cinema's foremost "crazy comedy."

Most agree that *Bringing Up Baby* is the funniest of the Hawks comedies. Its chief feature is one of *odyssey,* one of the fundamental patterns of oral and written literature. Odyssey has an archetypal aspect in its correspondence to the inner journey, the rocky road of individuation and Self-realization: the teleological "path," wrought with shadow, anima/animus, and much else of difficulty, finally leading to the Grail (Self). In this particular film, the Hawksian "poor man's Holy Grail" is of course the dinosaur clavicle between the pair in the last scene. On the level of the Nichols-Wilde script, the object represents sexuality achieved, for David, by way of Susan, who is a kind of muse (despite her "Ulysses" qualities).

Thus, 'odyssey' might be expected to be a series motif or pattern. *Bringing Up Baby* and its comedic descendents *Ball of Fire, I Was a Male War Bride,* and *The Ransom of Red Chief,* and the adventure-dramatic *Air Force, Red River,* and *The Big Sky,* are the chief series 'odysseys,' concerned, in significant part, with a physical journey. More obliquely, there are the instances of *Monkey Business* in its rampant predicament of the mind-altering vitamin B-4 and "regained youth," *Land of the Pharaohs* in its stationary but mighty and lengthy building task, and *Hatari!* in its great running in circles after animals.

Hatari! like *The Dawn Patrol, Ball of Fire,* and *Only Angels Have Wings,* alternates between 'close quarters' and an opposite sense of 'odyssey' in its scenario structure. Elsewhere in the series, 'close quarters' is featured in its own part, in *To Have and Have Not, The Thing (From Another World),* and *Rio Bravo,* and at other points.

ONLY ANGELS HAVE WINGS
(1939)

Along with *Scarface* and *Rio Bravo, Only Angels Have Wings* is one of Hawks's most praised films. This is not undeserved, as it is an outstanding and essential work, with great and detailed dramatic depth and a particularly excellent performance in Thomas Mitchell/Kid Dabb. Like *The Twentieth Century* and *Bringing Up Baby*, it is couched in an initiation/passage pattern. A fair portion of the film focuses around Bat Kilgalen, alias McPherson (Richard Barthelmess), a pilot blackballed and shunned for a one-time act of cowardice involving the death of a comrade. Through the latter part of the film he gruelingly reinstates himself, having come in need of a job to the professionally elite Geoff Carter, who in turn gives him difficult assignments (wanting to give him a chance to reinstate himself).

This is much the case with other characters, who undergo passages of their own. Bonnie Lee (Jean Arthur) learns how to be a part of Geoff's (and hence the group's) life. Kid Dabb undergoes the passage of dying heroically—if horribly, through a melodramatic scene. Judith McPherson (Rita Hayworth) is "shaped up" as a more loyal and supportive wife to Bat, and Geoff Carter (Cary Grant), the hard-nosed professional, is made to weep in the end.

The story and drama of *Only Angels Have Wings* are, more simply, the advantageous comeuppance of its main characters—including Kid. Kid is sadly washed up as a mail pilot because of failing eyesight: an incapacitation which—in the world of these wilderness aviators, where job and personal identity are one—is well enough served by one last, sacrificial job. (In the motif of 'fraternal suicide mission' here, Kid reiterates Paul in *The Road to Glory,* and others in the series.) The story is by Hawks who, as usual, worked on the script uncredited, teaming with his frequent colleague Jules Furthman. Hawks's testimony as to the real-life derivation of the story and its characters is well known.

The film begins in a foggy Costa Rican seaport, busy with maritime and dock activity, a shadowy but bustling setting. As a boat comes in, an officer on the bridge turns to give a hand signal to the helmsman, a tiny but strong bit of footage. (See further notes on this in the portion of the 'twosome sign' motif in Appendix 1.) There on mail business with the docked boat are Joe Souther (Noah Beery, Jr.) and Les Peters (Allyn Joslyn), two of the commercial pilots with Dutchy and Geoff's rickety little mountain/jungle mail service on the edge of town. Bonnie disembarks from the boat. Playfully the pair follows her as, tourist-like and something of a babe in the woods, she begins excitedly taking in the interesting sights. Accosting her, one lifts up the other's hat in a how-do-you-do, like one man, in the ego/shadow 'pals' manner, and reminiscent of similar dramatics in *Ceiling Zero*. She is not immediately interested, as these fellows seem a little shady.

Peeking inside a dingy honky-tonk where a combo and dancers are performing, she interjects from where she is, chanting with the call-and-response arrangement to the cheerful notice of the musicians and dancers, who acknowledge her as an extemporaneous combo member. The distance across

113

the room is spanned with the instant rapport, in the 'dramatized/converged space' pattern. Here we might guess that she has been a professional musician. Since some of the musicians there, as it happens, will drop by the hotel/ headquarters of the pilot group for informal music later, where Bonnie will have gravitated as well, it is a 'fraternal pre-encounter' instance. Bonnie's spatial transaction, and her "spearheading" of the (very mobile) banana port sequence in general, derive some from Lotta's spatial-dramatic eminence through the saloon in *Come and Get It.*

As the pilot pair continue to bother her, Bonnie grabs a sword (somehow at hand, at what seems to be a dockside blacksmith shop) and brandishes it in their faces—a fierce, recalcitrant anima figure now, staying them completely. This act is the pinnacle/Center of the sequence as, nearby, sits a little structure with a container of molten metal over a fire, in mandala-Centric emphasis as well.

Here, when it becomes explicit that the pair are Americans, she says in a changed tone, "Americans? Well, why didn't you say so!" From there they are off arm in arm in extemporaneous camraderie. Thus, via the series-typical violence/friendship pattern, the three of them are brought to a convivial 'pals'/'triangle' condition.

Hereabouts too, "Brooklyn" is mentioned in conversation, and instantly a little vehicle on tracks toots its horn like a New York taxi and barges through, making them dodge it—a 'verbal/action-simultaneity' instance, popping up like the wine bottle at Barney's restaurant table in *Come and Get It.*

The film is off in very good fettle indeed, as they head away together.

Bonnie winds up with them at the semi-rural hotel and headquarters, each fellow in friendly competition for a date with her. Dutchy (Sig Ruman), the hotel proprietor and businessman for the little mail service, enters to serve them, and a friendly altercation ensues over who will buy the drinks. Abruptly (interruptingly) the shot changes from this little hubbub of dialogue to the amiable Dutchy holding up one hand and saying, "Drinks on the house." (Actually, this is part of an interspersed shot.) Silence ensues.

In the sudden quiet shot, he is bathed in a subtle complex of light and shadow—a Center, in close combination with his words, which brings the minor dispute to a head and a simple solution. It is a dramatically simple yet high moment. Immediately, in certain echo of this dramatic/cinematic Center, the pair clasp hands (the shot having returned to the table again), the argument nicely settled for them, (perhaps via their instigation, namely to take advantage of the pliable Dutchy). Here, not least for the odd cinematography on Dutchy, is an irruption, a cinematic "popping up" like a sunrise, as it is all a dramatic/cinematic mandala. Dutchy, here, considerably parallels the earlier port sequence's irrupting pinnacle/Center in Bonnie brandishing the sword near the fiery rig of molten metal.

Bonnie begins getting acquainted with the place, still the agog tourist off the beaten track. Joe Souther, of their threesome, has gained the date with her, but first is called on a brief mail run. The weather is not good.

Geoff is on the radio with Tex. In the room, Geoff talks with one or two others about the fog situation, then returns to the radio and to relate the same to him, but Tex adds that he is already briefed, since he heard their conversation over the radio. This is in the series pattern, compositely, of (1) the close-knit group of one professional mind, and (2) 'merged dramatics/dialogue'—the radio business with Tex being related to the numerous series instances of 'second-guessing,' as earlier broached in the "fishing" scene in *Come and Get It*. Also, (3) 'merged dramatics' relates to an ego/unconscious dynamic, of characters tending to work as aspects of a common psyche (outwardly mundane though the Geoff/Tex business is).

Next, an evident *x* instance reminiscent of those of *Scarface* is rather starkly rendered. As Joe heads out to his job, a Latin girl, one of the various hangers-on of the group, waits for him. As she moves anxiously toward him, she brings to our full visibility a crucifix around her neck—emerging rather sharply and semiologically. Indeed, Joe will perish this wet night. He tries to allay her anxiety over weather conditions and next takes off through the shoddy airfield with its great puddles.

It is soon decided that he must circle back and land, since the pass has quickly become a pea-soup fog. Moreover, Joe becomes stranded over the airfield, where even their searchlight is blotted from his visibility. Here ensues the excellent and tense scene of their trying unsuccessfully to guide him in, Geoff at the radio at the edge of the field, Kid Dabb having a smoke there, his face wrought with a veteran's anxiety. More of this sequence shortly.

Just earlier, Dutchy comes forward with the news that dinner is ready and Joe can come in for his steak and his date with Bonnie as soon as he lands. Bonnie is beside Dutchy, likewise unaware of what is really going on. The cheerful two are well-lighted in blissful effect. Geoff, before heading outside, throws them a dark look (turning about three-quarter to his rear). Here, on the rearward side of his face—toward the "blissfully ignorant" pair—he is more lighted than on the side of him toward the outside, where Joe is in fatal trouble, and where job, duty, danger, fate, and the great outside are. This considerably defines the characters and the situation in the film. Cinematographically, the basic variant of this is, of course, the pivotal 'triangle' scene in *A Girl in Every Port*, with blissful, marriage-minded Spike juxtaposed with the shadowed morass on Bill's side. It is archetypally similar in the 1939 film as well, in terms of ego (Geoff), shadow (Joe outside), and anima (Bonnie/Dutchy).

Earlier, Bonnie and Dutchy were paired off this way ahead of time, as they both have "fancier" Scotch while Joe and Les, the pilot pair, each have bourbon, in significant character reference. (Something similar occurs between Cricket and Slim in *To Have and Have Not*, and with the ex-soldiers in *Rio Lobo*, who emphatically refuse the fancy rum and order whiskey.) At one or more points in the film, Bonnie is well-lighted in meaningful contrast to Geoff and/or the Kid in shadow. Similarly, in *Red River*, Tess in her entry into the story, though out of doors, is cinematographically like a spiritedly feminine flame amidst the masculine others—with Matt, moveover, in deep shadow at one point, as he encounters her there. These are points of the anima-as-though-"rising." In the "blissful innocence" shot with Bonnie, Dutchy is given stark anima import. At one point in the film, as he goes upstairs to retire for an evening, he takes a bird, perched on the stairway railing, and totes it up with him, an evident pet, in the 'anima/animal' connection. As a character he is older,

115

funny, plump, and a little panicky at Geoff's joking suggestion of sending him up with mail as well. Appropriately, it is Dutchy who early posits Geoff's character as a "hard man." To this, Geoff replies, in an anxious little speech, that he does not run things differently than any other airline he every worked for. Yet he exudes misgivings (over sending Joe out to his death); and Bonnie ultimately gets to the "softer" side of him.

Geoff himself is a good flier, going out on jobs too dangerous for the others to undertake, and is thus a group peer.

Joe crash-lands due to his being in too great a hurry to get back to Bonnie. This is in keeping with the danger-that-is-Woman theme of the series, though on the story level Bonnie is not blamed. (The blame, such as it is, is laid to Joe's being "just not good enough" to have the patience, as ordered, to circle until the fog lifted.) Near the end of the film, Bonnie is careless with Geoff's gun. It goes off, wounding him, thus linking her with the series shadow/anima-rampant gun-lunatics in Clark of *The Twentieth Century* and Williams of *His Girl Friday*. Hence on one level, Bonnie is a little dangerous throughout.

The famous "steak" scene follows Joe's death, where his steak dinner, sans its taker, is simply passed along. Bonnie becomes upset at this, for which Geoff and others are a little rough on her. The steak, a principal 'dramatized object' of the series, thus focuses Bonnie's guilt feelings and what seems to her to be the group's callousness. Correspondingly, as Joe's wristband is given to one of the female hangers-on, she receives it in an outburst of mourning and object-fetishism.

The "steak" sequence, an early stage in Bonnie's initiation into the group, rudely imparts to her a beginning understanding of the mail pilots. After the "hard knock" over the steak, the pendulum swings Bonnie's (and Woman's) way when the group shortly gathers for some communal music—functionally to exorcise the gloom of Joe's death (which gloom and anxiety Bonnie has, of course, helped bring to the surface there). The honky-tonk musicians on hand now, she takes the lead very competently at the piano, and thus undercuts Geoff (who nonetheless sings out nicely on "The Peanut Vendor"). In the story, she relates to his warmer "better half" and helps him to revise his misogyny.

The next day she continues on her way, leaving to catch the boat for home, but (in the manner of fate, and because of her deep plunge into the group already) she returns, remarking to the effect that, "one of me is on the boat home, and the other of me somehow had to come back." This is of course an initiatory step, an archetypally imbued one, in its blatant ego/shadow irruption personified in two. In this archetyping, she has a touch of 'fraternal return,' but anticipates the 'self-encounter/splitting off' motif, which is alluded to a number of times in the series previous to its occurrence in full flower in *The Big Sleep*.

In one scene, there is an outstanding, archetypally-imbued 'object transaction'—a cigarette exchange between the Kid and Geoff. The Kid often lights a cigarette for Geoff, but is seemingly lighting one for himself at one point. As Geoff comes hastily in, he takes it for himself, as the Kid, after a pause, breathes out the smoke. In its ego/shadow, 'merged dramatics' way, it take after the rollicking ensemble work of *Ceiling Zero*. In general, cigarettes, their lighting and exchanging, are employed in a dramatically deeper way than usual in *Only Angels Have Wings*, as an antidote for the tension the pilots are under, a means of suppressing despair and panic.

Geoff, the Kid, and Bonnie, in their way, form a 'triangle' instance. She eventually reaches Geoff partly through his pal, the Kid, and rather takes Kid's place in a symbolic way after his death, all in the series-frequent ego/shadow/anima dynamic. Significantly, the Kid interrupts a love scene between them, which scene involved him in the conversation.

Bonnie: "I'll be like the Kid" (not bother you), as Geoff replies, "He drives me nuts" (as he kisses her).

At this point the Kid comes in. He apologizes for interrupting, but is overjoyed that Geoff and Bonnie are obviously hitting it off well, and that Geoff, despite bitter past experience, is not lost to women.

Later, there is the scene where Bonnie and the Kid are discussing their respective love for Geoff with the pattern of wiring behind them forming a rough X: like a transcendent-functional emergence, a raw symbol-formation amidst the 'triangular' irruption and complexity. The little scene corresponds with the comparable 'triangle' scenes in *The Road to Glory* and *Come and Get It*. Here, Bonnie begins to "replace" the Kid. The Kid is Geoff's shadow with anima aspect—is part of Geoff on one level (this being as important as the certain homoerotic allusion).

Near the end of the film, Geoff playfully wrestles with the Kid to have a look at the coin he always tosses with, finding that it has two heads. After the Kid's death, Geoff weeps over the former's little pile of belongings, all that remains of him, in this principal series instance of the perished hero's 'meager last possessions.' They include the (semiological) two-headed coin, which he handles—the coin which, shortly, he tosses with Bonnie to decide for her if she stays or leaves, thus assuring that she will stay! This is to her joy, of course, when she discovers the biased coin. The object is Centric to a 'triangle'-type transaction thus, and on one level functions as did the earlier x-shaped pattern of wiring behind her and the Kid (whom, again, she symbolically replaces). The earlier x may be associated with death, like those of *Scarface*. Further, the Kid is 'objectivized' in the mandala-Centric coin in the manner of Lotta and the serving-tray keepsake between the pals in *Come and Get It*.

Geoff has just rushed out with Les to take the mail up again, as the fog is being rained away. (Principal in the story and drama is the group's ongoing struggle to meet performance standards to qualify for long-contract subsidies for better, life-saving equipment, planes and so on.) Bonnie waves to him happily from the doorway, the shot of her through a curtain of rain, in the not-unfamiliar Hawks touch, whether with fog, rain, shadow, or a comparable embellishment, brought to Woman. In view of Diana and Monique of the series (in their soldierly, wet-weather garb), and now Bonnie-with-rain replacing Kid, 'fog/rain' seems to symbolize initiation (or would-be initiation), as Woman is perhaps "graduated" to the status of a "Bill" who, in *A Girl in Every Port*, is associated with shadow and anima thus, the crossing of which is very common in the series (including in male "candidates" for initiation/passage, such as Boone in *The Big Sky*, Dude in *Rio Bravo*, and Mike in *Red Line 7000*). Again, shadow figures usually display the irruptive anima, in

117

Hawks films.

Geoff, getting into the mail plane with his copilot, does not wave back (is not looking Bonnie's way). Just before they go outside, Les says to Geoff, "You and me?" ("Am I assigned to go up with you?"), recalling the lines between 'pals'/ 'doubles' Tony and Cesca in the last-shootout scene in *Scarface*. Hence the ending resembles that of *A Girl in Every Port* and *The Crowd Roars*: two comrades alone; and in the supremacy of male camraderie, with Woman/anima, one way or another, put aside.

Another shadow figure in the situation—who is rather the shadow of the entire group—is the interesting character in Sparks (Victor Killian). The radio engineer of the group, he is a little reminiscent of Phipps in *The Dawn Patrol*, being a relative background figure, though important. A very dark brunet, he is taciturn, ratty-looking, even moronic-seeming. We find in the course of the film that he speaks Spanish well, and knows Shakespeare: an anima touch in its higher ("fancier") culture and implied introspection amidst the austerity. Kid Dabb's 'meager last possessions' are assembled by Sparks as Geoff reflectively comments, "Not much to show for twenty-two years," thus rendering the series note of austerity/gloom in-and-of the perished hero's Spartan dearth of material.

Near the end, Sparks functions very importantly. As Bonnie is making to leave, with Geoff not ready to extend himself to have her stay or to even say goodbye, Sparks suggests to her, soft-spokenly, that she ought to say goodbye to him (or on another level, ought to go in and have him get her to stay, which Geoff does). It is there that she discovers him weeping over the Kid. Like Kid Dabb, Sparks is a go-between, even a prime mover: one, again, of shadow creativity intervening for the emerging anima (of which he is a part as well). He has a parallel in Sierra in *Viva Villa!* (in the latter's relative silence), in Dorothy and Lorelei's Parisian cabby "animus" in *Gentlemen Prefer Blondes*, and, as we will examine, in the negative character Bensiger in *His Girl Friday*.

Much of the story is around Bat Kilgalen (alias McPherson) and his reinstatement after once bailing out on his mechanic. The mechanic having been close to the Kid, the Kid particularly hates Bat, yet it is Kid who will go up with Bat on a dangerous mission. The Kid's eyesight is below standard now. Each goes for his own reason. For the (grounded) Kid it is his last likely mission, and his end. A condor comes through the windshield, breaking his neck. Despite other trouble, Bat brings them both in, getting severely burned in a fire that starts. Before the Kid dies, he vouches for Bat anew, and Bat is reinstated. The men drink with him again.

Concurrently there is the grisly death scene with the Kid, a lone lantern burning, Geoff there saying goodbye, and thunder and lightning outside like Valhalla beckoning. This is a form of passage as well: a chief one of the series, as the death scenes in *Air Force* and (in its feigned way) *The Twentieth Century* make more explicit, and in the light of connections between the deceased Johnson and (the alive but "death-resurrected") Mme. de Bursak in *To Have and Have Not* (and Johnson's connection, in turn, with the dying and "resurrecting" Captain Quincannon of *Air Force*).

Judith (Rita Hayworth), glamorous wife of Bat and former girlfriend of Geoff's—the one he would like to forget—is not supportive of her husband and newly plays up to Geoff. Behind the bar is a pitcher of water which Geoff often uses to cool off his head. He gives Judith this same treatment, ruining her hairdo. Subsequently, she comes around as though from the experience of the water alone, and becomes more of a comrade or 'pal' to the (in turn) reinitiated Bat. It is an important initiation/passage instance, recurring in *To Have and Have Not, Gentlemen Prefer Blondes,* and *Man's Favorite Sport?*

One feels that the film's special success is in part linked with the more sympathetic interplay of ego, shadow, and anima aspects: as the "dark brother" and the "recalcitrant female" within are, to a good extent, redeemingly embraced, the resulting holism a cinematic boon. Man-the-measurer-of-all-things reflects more upon himself, via Bonnie and, for that matter, Sparks. Like *Red Line 7000* later, *Only Angels Have Wings* displays a psychic mellowing this way.

At the same time, the film is lent to certain melodramatic excess at points. Too, Cary Grant, I think, is somewhat miscast as Geoff. He performs well, but is too dashingly glib in the part. Yet the film is a contender for Hawks's best film because of the way its comprehensive *drama* works well with Hawks *cinema* (i.e., with the Hawksian behavioral and cinematographic features). In this additional dramatic depth, it is beholden to the more literary-dramatic Hawks/Faulkner projects *Today We Live* and *The Road to Glory*, and particularly in terms of Bonnie's derivation from Diana and Monique of those films, both of whom richly combine the soldierly/comradely and the maternal.

HIS GIRL FRIDAY
(1940)

His Girl Friday is almost certainly Hawks's finest comedy, and a contender for his finest film as well. As a Hawksian remake of Hecht and MacArthur's *The Front Page* (1931, directed by Lewis Milestone), it blends "crazy comedy" and drama in a rich way. As a film, it is as nearly flawless as it is complex and involved in its dramatic technique. Cary Grant and Rosalind Russell are beautifully cast and give outstanding performances. Their "sex-antagonistic"/ 'pals' pairing has precedence in Jaffe and Lily of (Hawks, Hecht, and Mac-Arthur's) *The Twentieth Century*, and *His Girl Friday's* rapid pacing and close-knit group dramatics are beholden to Hawks and Frank Wead's *Ceiling Zero* (another film of frequent, racing vocal hubbub amidst emergency situations). The latter two films, at least, represent unusually close collaborations between director and script.

His Girl Friday, in particular, is noted for its use of 'overlapping dialogue' technique, famously associated with Hawks cinema in general, although it is not encountered as often as Hawks's other major contribution to cinematic technique: the device of 'merged dramatics/dialogue.' (The latter is a separate method, and more profound in its more varied applications to dramatic action and character relationship.) 'Overlapping dialogue,' or "speed," as Hawks usually called it, basically consists of a player hurriedly beginning a line before another player's line is fully delivered, so that part of the time, two (or more) characters are talking at once—with the result engineered so that important words and dialogue content still emerge on the sound track. As players thus "step on each other's lines," they are, in turn, paced a little faster than would otherwise be workable, dramatically. (Importantly, dialogue "padding" or inessential words are at the beginning and at the end of lines.) In terms of the series patterns, the technique (which I categorize as a motif) is a function of close-knit character interaction. In variation, different characters' lines may not quite overlap but "run into each other," as in the dramatically strong but low-keyed talk among the card-playing newsmen in the early pressroom sequence in *His Girl Friday*. By contrast, (overlapping) "speed" serves as a vehicle for agitation, excitement, or altercation. In its resemblance to real-life conversation, it is a "naturalistic" technique, easily deriving from the "realism/ naturalism" of the Hecht-MacArthur play *(The Front Page)*, and readily applying to the practical/functional dialogue in the aerodrome in Wead's *Ceiling Zero*.

The opening portions of *His Girl Friday* are particularly excellent. Also, they are mainly apart from or added to the *Front Page* part of the scenario. As Rich Thompson writes in his program notes on the film, "[Hawks, and writers Ben Hecht and Charles MacArthur] wove *The Front Page* into the pattern of male-female antagonism courtship that runs through Hawks comedies as a major theme. The first two sequences of *His Girl Friday* are original in so far as situations and character development are concerned. We do not even get to *The Front Page* for twenty minutes, and by that time we are so absorbed in the characters of Walter and Hildy and the performances of Grant and Russell that the newsroom patter seems like a bonus." Along with other departures from story and script per se, this testifies to Hawks's penchant and talent for reworking the screenplay on or near the set and through the actors.

In this early sequence, Hildy Johnson (Rosalind Russell) returns to the newspaper for a last goodbye with her ex-editor/husband Walter Burns (Cary Grant), as she is through with journalism and will soon marry an insurance man and lead a more normal life (or so she thinks!). As she enters his office, her equanimity (from cheerfully greeting old cohorts in the cityroom, just earlier) changes to a visible readiness for a lovers' quarrel with Walter. Barging in thus, she initially comes eye to eye—not with Walter, who is facing the other way, but with his funny, shadowy underworld contact/cohort Diamond Louie (Abner Biberman), who is there helping him shave—holding a mirror for him and directing his use of an electric shaver. Here, briefly, is an ego/shadow/anima "triad," with Walter and Louie in tactile-functional exchange and Hildy (anima) aptly contacting the shadow in Louie previous to Walter (ego), who is slow to respond to her bold entry and is a little surprised to see her.

In the rich scene which ensues between the recently divorced pair, Walter says to her, "Divorce means nothing these days. We've got something between us nothing can change,"—namely journalism and their experience together in it, much more primary than marriage was for them. In the story, Walter skillfully conspires and works to bring her back. She is easily in demand there, being an outstanding reporter. Comedy notwithstanding, *His Girl Friday*, like *The Twentieth Century*, and as much as any film of the series, is concerned with professionalism.

This is part of the adventure-dramatic pattern. Yet richly, the comedy pattern of anima recalcitrance/domination and connected hero (ego) failure/humiliation prevails as well. The professionalism of the film is that of an elite amidst a comedic hubbub of corrupt bunglers in the case of the political officials and bureaucrats, and third-raters in the case of the criminal-court reporters. The 'pals' elite are Walter and, not least, Hildy, a woman, although Walter repeatedly refers to her as a "newspaperman." The other newsmen, who more than once display their lesser competence, are referred to by Hildy as "gossiping old ladies," and Bensiger, among them, is indicated as a potential "bridesmaid" at her imminent wedding. Journalist Sweeny, who is good at "sob sister" work at his paper, is jibed at as being in the throes of "having twins," and moreover is married (his wife being the actual twin-bearer). In the course of things, Sweeny goes off the important Earl Williams story as Hildy returns to the paper to take it on. In general, the anima factor dominates.

Hildy is maternally protective toward her contrastingly mild-mannered fiance, Bruce Baldwin (Ralph Bellamy), who in a like manner is overly attached to his formidable mother (Alma Kruger). Further, in the pattern of recalcitrant-anima domination, Hildy and Molly Malloy (Helen Mack) are companionable as the latter invades the pressroom and upbraids and shames the newsmen for their poor standards. (As she is doing this, Hildy comes into the room and pauses before going around her to her desk, as Molly pauses in turn in her tirade, sensing someone behind her. It is an apt 'fraternal encounter' instance, as subsequently, Hildy sides with her against the other reporters. Earlier, while interviewing Williams in jail, Hildy 'pre-encounters' Molly in a photo of her in the condemned man's cell, which Hildy asks him about.) In a minor way, Molly is Hildy's shadow.

Hildy of *The Front Page* was a man. Hawks, in an instance of his 'reversal' mode and method, has a woman play the part. Early, this certain 'sex role-reversal' is focused in a brief, larkish bout between Hildy and Walter over male courtesy, which she jestingly opts for in holding a gate open for him. Roz Russell is altogether realistic in the part, and with Paul Muni of *Scarface*, renders the series' finest performance of a leading role. As for Walter of their journalistic twosome, he is a considerable Hawks hero, being a competent (if excessively ruthless) professional—though, in a more shadowy way, he falls into certain comedic indignity in the 'triangular' course of things with Bruce, Hildy's fiance, who is, after all, Walter's shadow, on one level.

Hence it is very much a Hawks comedy, yet with an adventure drama working hand in hand with it. (*His Girl Friday*, via the older Hecht-MacArthur play, is the only film of the series to concern itself with deeper social issues, in its plugging the La Guardia government in New York City and lampooning machine politics, demagogic anticommunism, and antinegro racism. The censorial preaching added to *Scarface* under pressure, and the wartime propaganda of *Sergeant York* and *Air Force*, are insignificant series exceptions. When once asked about broader social issues, Hawks replied, "I don't stick my nose into that.")

Early, as Hildy returns to say goodbye to Walter Burns, she alludes to semi-unconsciously seeking to become ensnared again with Walter and the vortex of the *Morning Post*. Here she is the unwitting Spike of *A Girl in Every Port*, as Walter Burns parallels the pressing, shadowy Bill. She also recalls Bonnie mysteriously lured back to the mail-service fray in *Only Angles Have Wings*, the latter indicating, "One of me is on the boat home and the other of me had to come back."

The early sequence features an excellent trucking shot of Hildy entering and walking through the cityroom, in full prestige, intercut with employees and newspeople saying hello to her again, from her own eye-level, camerawise. Here she echoes Bonnie (in her initial, "banana port" sequence), and Lotta and Susan, of the series, who move very *consequentially* through a cinematic space, and in Susan's case through a goodly portion of the film (*Bringing Up Baby*), like a manner of feminine Genesis. (See discussion of Lotta in the saloon sequence, in the section on *Come and Get It.*)

In Walter's office, Diamond Louie, who will figure in the action and mischief to come, helps him shave, a little in the tactile-functional way of Kid Dabb's tending and bandaging Geoff's gunshot wound in *Only Angels Have Wings*. As Walter and Hildy are alone in the office, a fine session of dialogue ensues as the story and characters are beautifully launched. The scene is punctuated by a cigarette exchange between them, taking a few seconds (the finest such instance in the series). Their lovers' quarreling (in 'overlapping dialogue,' at times) subsides as Hildy (tactile-functionally in lieu of words) thrusts her engagement ring in Walter's face to indicate her plans to marry Bruce within twenty-four hours. Here, Walter worrisomely puts a dark flower in his lapel, fondling the lapel as though scheming (as he faces away from Hildy, in the moment). It is to woo her. She notices it, and is affected. The flower may say, "I'm carrying a torch for my old pal/colleague Hildy, and here it is." On one level, it seems to be an irruptive morass/vortex in and of the irrupting 'triangle' scenes in earlier films (as in *Tiger Shark*, with its full moon accompanying Mike, Quita, and Pipes). In any case, it is a Centric object.

Walter, Hildy, and Bruce, the insurance-selling homebody with a mother-attachment, go out to lunch. Walter wants to meet Bruce-the-paragon, saying, "I'm particular about who my wife marries." In the restaurant, Walter and Hildy smoke and have a spot of rum in their coffees, but not Bruce, significantly—the cigarettes and rum being dramatically meaningful objects. These and the earlier cigarette exchange are part of her connection and eventual return to the paper, like deep, portending psychic movements. There, in a shadowy way, Gus the waiter silently but physically interweaves the conversation with his lunch service, like an extra member of the party. A cohort of Walter's, Gus shortly helps him conspire against Bruce. (Throughout the film, Bruce is the butt of things to the point of persecution. The film is a little cruel in this, though Bruce holds his dignity pretty well through it.)

Walter and Bruce are of course adversaries, in competition for Hildy. Both early and later, Bruce's umbrella, a somewhat "effeminate" object in its own right (or within the particular ego-masculine context of the series patterns), is suggestively, fussily transacted between him and Walter, as though in a mocking homoerotic allusion, in derogation of the home-fellow (though of Walter too, as he slips to the comedic indignity). In general, he behaves toward Bruce in a manner either "fairyish," or dotingly, as if to a small child—in either case insultingly, though mild-mannered Bruce does not take it as anything unusual.

In their 'triangle' instance, Bruce stands between Walter and Hildy, and as things develop, Hildy provides for this deeper ego/shadow communication between Walter and Bruce (which incidentally is very funny). In the early office scene, in response to Hildy's description of the man she is going to marry, Walter nastily quips, "Sounds more like a guy *I* ought to marry."

In the early criminal-court pressroom scene with the other reporters, Hildy obliquely derogates Bruce herself, as fun is poked at her future family life. Entirely "one of the boys" there, she speaks of it as a good break for her, however, adding that she will no longer be "like you chumps," stuck in a crazy, unlucrative profession. Teased along by Walter, her own addiction to news reporting will surface again with dramatic developments in the Earl Williams story, namely his breaking jail.

Bruce, an opposite type from Walter, is sufficiently his shadow. Yet Williams (John Qualen) is the colossal shadow figure of the film with whom Hildy forms a special communication. Both in terms of character and, on one level, his eerie relationship to the protagonists, he reitereates the lunatic Clark of *The Twentieth Century*. More of Williams below.

In the early restaurant scene—excellent in its close-contactual, low-key dramatics—Walter succeeds in getting Hildy to do one last story, the Williams case. Just earlier, Walter has Gus the waiter call him to the phone, although there is no call for him. Instead, Walter calls the paper and has Sweeny taken off the Williams story and sent on vacation, adding—'second-guessingly'—that Hildy, although she does not know it yet, will very soon be on the story (and hence back to the *Morning Post* for good). With Williams's culminating jail break, she returns to journalism hook, line, and sinker. As for Bruce, he is finally, literally rendered into the arms of his formidable mother. (Late in the film, as the interfering woman is induced to flee the pressroom, it is into Bruce's arms where, in the moment, they are like reunited lovers.)

Next door to the pressroom the gallows are being noisily tested for Williams. (In one shot, the apparatus is fatalistically shown with the looming shadows of the police there.) As Molly Malloy comes in and chews out the newsmen for their callous approach to the Williams case, she says, "It's a wonder lightning don't strike you all dead"—as we instantly hear the gallows going bump next door, in 'verbal-action simultaneity.' (As it happens, this instance is borrowed, intact, from the 1931 film of *The Front Page*.)

A couple of nicely low-keyed scenes with near-overlapping (or 'end-to-end') dialogue take place in the pressroom among the mainly card-playing newsmen. Again, most of these reporters are progressively drawn in a bad light, as they act trivially and less effectively when subsequent events and stories break—unlike the elite Walter and Hildy.

In one important scene, Hildy goes to the murky jail to interview Williams (who had gone berserk with a gun and killed a cop). As Rich Thompson observes, Williams is more like an animal in a cage than a man in a cell. In the 'animal/anima' connection, his place of confinement is a birdcage-like affair, and anima-relevantly, with a vase of flowers and a picture of Molly who had befriended him when down and out. There, Hildy lights a cigarette for him and hands it to him through the screen. After a moment he hands it back, saying, "I don't smoke." Hence they are in contactual rapport, in the pattern. Here, as well as later, a certain relationship obtains, one between shadow (with anima aspect) and anima. It is also one of minor 'triangle' amongst Hildy, Williams, and Molly (in her picture there, and) via the 'fraternal encounter' between the two women in the pressroom later (reiterating Spike and Bill in *A Girl in Every Port*), and their dual ('pals') part in shaming the other newsman in regard to Williams.

Instead of reprieving Williams at the bequest of the state governor, the city machine is contriving to hang him, despite his evident insanity. (He shot a negro policeman, and the regime needs the black vote.) Williams's shadow/anima "underside" manner of partnership with journalism is by virtue of his key part in Hildy's and Walter's journalistic triumph—in ultimately ruining the politicos of the town, including the sheriff, who in their incompetent, crooked course of business with Williams, undo themselves at the pair's journalistic hands. Williams (an alleged Red) breaks loose with the sheriff's gun, causing police, politicians, minor bureaucrats, and newsman to run hither and thither in uproar as the manhunt and its reportage proceed farcically, except for Hildy and Walter's part.

As the manhunt is getting nowhere outside, who should come through the pressroom window but Williams, gun in hand. As luck would have it, he and Hildy are alone there. She greets him with nerve and fair rapport. As the window shade, which he disturbed, springs up, he whirls and wildly fires his last round. Schemingly, she and Walter hide him in a roll-top desk at hand, where (as in the 1931 film) he will lie curled up while a hubbub of action and dramatic farce unfold in the room.

This desk, in its sense of antiquated physical encumbrance, and in being an abode for the rampant shadow/anima likes of Williams, belongs appropriately to Roy Bensiger (Ernst Truex), the semiostracized "sissy" of the newsroom. (Bensiger does not play cards with the others, is a would-be poet and literateur, speaks a little French, and was earlier joshed as a potential bridesmaid for Hildy's wedding. In the original play, he is mainly a hypochondriac and a food faddist.) He echoes Sparks in *Only Angels Have Wings* and Phipps in *The Dawn Patrol* as a relative background figure of archetypal importance. In an oblique way, he participates with Molly and Hildy in their earlier upbraiding of the newsmen. As Molly bawls them out, they laugh at her at first—while Hildy, contrarily, takes notes for a story, exuding a compassionate attitude (as good journalism would, under the circumstances). Molly, significantly, rests one hand on the back of Bensiger's chair, in apt contact thus with him and his anima portion there, as he sits in a mute, sorrowful attitude. (Elsewhere, it is indicated that he wrote compassionately about Williams.) Later, Molly sits in Bensiger's chair, helping to hide the fugitive Williams.

Williams is hence kept aside, pursuant to Walter and Hildy's plans to deliver him up at the right moment, so that their paper may take credit for his capture, with the governor let in on the credit—to the ruin of the town machine. Thus in the end, when the pair are under arrest and handcuffed together for harboring a fugitive from justice, it is not for long.

Williams, huddled within the huge desk, is the hub of it all, as he is the political and journalistic football, and finally the culprit again (albeit reprieved). At one point Bensiger toddles in and goes toward his desk (and Williams). Walter quickly accosts him and fraudulently hires him on the spot to write for them, promising him a better salary and sending him over to their offices, thus diverting him—adding, to Hildy, that it served him right for quitting his paper without proper notice. So much for Bensiger's professional standing, although through Molly and Hildy he links to a creative anima function.

At a key point, when most of the principal characters are in the room, it is revealed that Williams is hiding in the desk (like a "mock turtle," as Walter earlier puts it). Sheriff Hartwell and a few police are there. Bruce's mother fearfully rushes out of the room and into Bruce's arms; one of the policemen then closes the door and stands in front of it with his gun drawn. As all focus on the desk and Williams, a 'group-delineative/"circular" montage' sequence ensues, involving the sheriff, the newsmen (sans Bensiger), and—mandala-Centrically—the shadow/anima figure, Williams. It runs as follows.

(1) As Sheriff Hartwell and two detectives are converged around the desk, a series of brief shots alternates back and forth between the babbling sheriff and the gibbering reporters on the phones, the repetitive shots of Hartwell being sandwiched with individual shots of the reporters. At the sheriff's count of three, he and the police open the desk and shove their guns into Williams's

face, as the latter, on camera now, says, "Go ahead and shoot me!" In the last montage shot, one of the reporters announces the moment of capture to his editor at the other end of the line.

(2) Quickly, this rapid montage sequence is reiterated in a different form when the police remove Williams from the desk and take him out of the room. As they pass the reporters, in what is basically a single moving shot, each newsman utters something else on the phone at the moment of Williams's being carted past him. Next, Walter grabs the *Morning Post* phone and tells his city editor of Williams's being "captured by the *Morning Post*," before Sheriff Hartwell takes the phone from him. (End of sequence.)

The sequence functions as a mandala-Centric 'convergence' upon the shadow/anima-rampant Williams, and prefigures that of the priests around and upon Nelipher inside the pyramid in *Land of the Pharoahs*. The latter example employs 'group-delineative/"circular" montage' as well. Although deriving from *The Front Page* (1931), the newsroom montage/'convergence' is anticipated in *Barbary Coast* and serves as the precedent for several group-delineative/"circular" montage sequences in later Hawks films (particularly the instance of the B-17 crewmen in *Air Force*, with Williams paralleled by the mandala-Centric airman doll/good-luck piece). Since Hecht and MacArthur also worked on *Barbary Coast*, it is likely that the instance (with Knuckles and the vigilantes) in that film derives from *The Front Page* as well. (In *His Girl Friday*, the montage of Williams's capture is preceded by another montage sequence—also deriving from *The Front Page*. At the point of Williams's breaking jail, quick shots of the reporters on the phones are sandwiched with a few shots of Hildy, who stands aghast. Here, amidst the effective whirlwind of new activity, thus, Hildy succumbs to her old addiction to reporting once again and, in place of leaving the paper, jumps on the story.) The Hecht/MacArthur/Milestone influence on Hawksian montage is further discussed below.

At a late point, Walter and Hildy excitedly prepare their Morning Post-captures-Williams story, as the "mock turtle" lies curled up in the desk hoping for the best (which eventually comes, with his reprieve). The other reporters are elsewhere. While she is extremely busy composing and typing her story, Bruce comes in and tries to get Hildy to leave with him on the nine o'clock train to Albany. As he beseeches her with these words, she unintentionally and exasperatedly puts "leaving on the nine o'clock train" in her copy. This is, of course, in the 'merged dramatical' pattern (of two or more private spaces dramatically interchanging, one way or another).

Similarly, Walter, talking on the phone with his city editor, utters a loud "No!" to the latter, regarding something, just as Bruce finishes saying to Hildy, "You don't want to come with me, do you?" Bruce looks quizzically over at Walter, as though the "No!" were directed at him. This is a 'verbal-simultaneity' instance (of the same pattern). Shortly, amidst the hubbub there (consisting of Bruce and Hildy arguing, Hildy typing, and Walter arguing with his city editor on the phone), Bruce laments to Hildy (as she is trying to concentrate on her story), "I'll keep! I'm like something in the icebox, aren't I?" Immediately, the frame shifts to Walter, who momentarily looks away from the phone and toward Bruce, saying, "Yeah!"—an intended insertion this time. Hence, the scene intricately combines very rapid pacing, 'overlapping dialogue,' and these 'merged dramatics/dialogue' instances.

In the end, Walter successfully comes between Hildy and Bruce, and she returns to him, Walter and the newspaper profession winning out over marriage to Bruce, who returns home with his mother. Indeed, as Walter and Hildy plan to quickly marry again and take a honeymoon furlough at Niagara Falls, a strike in Albany (Bruce's town) promises to deter the journalistic pair, in keeping with the series' negative attitude toward marriage. Walter says wryly, "Maybe Bruce can put us up," and the film ends on this 'triangular' note.

Lewis Milestone's 1931 film of *The Front Page* features both major similarities and important differences with the Hawks remake. Much of the dialogue is identical.

In place of Bruce is Pat O'Brien/Hildy's fiancee, a girl from a respectable family. Instead of a cynical but highly professional journalist, Walter Burns (Adolph Menjou) is drawn as a dapper, arrogant boss, with Hildy as his mediocre, dominated, and rather mesmerized sycophant. Burns is a wholly negative character, a virtual gangster, and the relationship between him and Hildy is an almost totally negative one. In all ways, the newspaper-professional factor is utterly lampooned. In the Milestone film Williams is not a shadowy lunatic but a persecuted and weary, yet idealistic and defiant radical, ready to die in the name of humanity.

The rapid montage sequences in *His Girl Friday* are rendered almost exactly as in the 1931 film. Milestone, and writers Ben Hecht and Charles MacArthur, are hence authors of the 'convergence' upon Williams (and the likely source of the 1935 *Barbary Coast* montage instance), ahead of Hawks's influence. Yet the Milestone/Hecht/MacArthur-authored montage sequences in the 1935 and 1940 Hawks films are significant in terms of the series patterns, due to Hawks's own applications of this montage to later films. This is in terms of Hawks's various 'group-delineative/"circular" montage' usage to the effect of 'convergence'/Centrism. Important instances of the device and motif will be noted in the sections on *Sergeant York, Ball of Fire, Air Force, Red River, A Song is Born, The Big Sky, Land of the Pharaohs,* and *Hatari!*

Again, Hawks selects and utilizes the material of others within his own directorial context and auteur dimension.

SERGEANT YORK
(1941)

The first half of this celebrated film contains a number of excellent or outstanding sequences linked by other scenes ranging from ordinary to trite or poor. All things considered, if the second part of the film were comparable in quality and kind with the first, *Sergeant York* might rate among the three or four outstanding films of Hawks's career. As it is, it drops off at the point of Alvin C. York's leaving his rural Tennessee home to enter the Army.

The film's second half is mainly nondescript where both the series patterns and cinematic quality are concerned, although the battle scenes are very competent, in the Hawksian way of sensation-functional action drama. The homecoming scenes in New York City (set mainly indoors at the Waldorf-Astoria) are peculiarly mediocre, in terms of Hawks's more usual sense of camera placement and frame composition. These scenes, combined with other odd features of the "homecoming" sequence such as newsreel clips and the use of super-imposed news-headlines, suggest to this viewer that the New York portion was directed by someone other than Hawks. In any case, the film seems, to a good extent, out of Hawks's hands after Alvin York (Gary Cooper) and his younger brother George (Dickie Moore) climb aboard the mule to ride to where Alvin is to leave for training and thence overseas. The film of course had to follow York's biography on many points, and was hence less given to project improvisation (always a practical source for the series patterns and motifs as previous series material is remade).

Sergeant York is untypical of the series in the film's thematic religiosity and sense of tradition. Yet these are gracefully handled by Hawks, and in ways which are part of the series patterns. In a key way, this is due, I think, to the post-pioneer Appalachian community's stoical material circumstances and attendant heroic (post-pioneer) values, a foil to anima-aspected opulence (as denigratively featured in Pharaoh and his wealthy, theocratic encumbrance in *Land of the Pharaohs*). Witness, particularly, the early general store scene with the ego-masculine/community rejection of the out-of-town ladies' garment salesman (discussed below).

Regarding the biographically essential religious theme, the community's folkish religion has a down-to-earth communitarian function in its peer-congenial, close-contactual informality over, say, a grandiose piety. (It is not basically different from the fishing crew catching the shark to recover Manuel's eaten-off legs to thence give him a holistic sea-burial—inclusive of Mike's colloquial service to "Saint Pete"—in *Tiger Shark*.)Archetypally there is, of course, the pentecostal-irruptive feature, which is group involved and tactile-functional in the scene of York's conversion.

Further, in the early church scene, Pastor Pile's sermon (by no means an excessively pious one) is made rude sport of as he is interrupted several times (in the pattern of suppressive 'convergence'): first, by latecomer Zeke and his noisy shoes; then by another man, who sneezes (at the precise moment of

Zeke's sitting beside him, in significant association); and then by Alvin York, Ike Botkin (Ward Bond), and Buck Lipscomb (Noah Beery, Jr.) shooting their guns outside. As Pastor Pile (Walter Brennan) must end the meeting early, he in effect bids any man who wants to, to go and get the hell-raisers, who are likened to the Devil knocking at the door of a house of worship. Violently as well, Nate Tompkins (Erville Alderson), the business shark of the community and a church deacon, threatens at one point to "lay Alvin out in two pieces" with a large wrench. Piety thus runs thin enough in the first half of the film.

The sequence of York's conversion at a night-time church meeting functions via the 'fraternal return' motif. York, drunk, is up for revenge one stormy evening against Nate Tompkins, who went back on a deal with him over a piece of land. In a fantastical manner, lightning, as if from Jehovah himself, strikes Alvin (i.e., his rifle), stunning him and his mule. As it happens, it is near the meeting house from which the strains of congregational singing are heard (in the group 'song session' motif, as in the earlier church scene). Naturally impressed by the coincidence of things, and barred from an act of murder by the proverbial lightning bolt, he goes to the meeting, stumbling in bewilderedly. A prominent image outside is a wagon wheel (an image which seems to be given conscious repetition through the first part of the film). Without interrupting their singing—although it is an extraordinary event for Alvin to come to meeting—they manually (tactilely) assist him to the pulpit area where Pastor Pile leads on in the singing, in humorous concert with the lightning flashes outside, like Divine Retribution at hand. York, assisted to the front by the group, is singing with them himself now ("That Old Time Religion"). The pastor, in great gesture, has him kneel. He then simply shakes hands with Alvin, in a down-to-earth, common-sensical, Hawksian note.

The 'return' motif accrues in terms of the pentecostal irruption here, yet more simply via the emergence of York's sudden, unexpected attendence. It is of course a very ostensive initiation/passage. Does he also "return from the dead" on one level, in view of his lightning accident? So it would seem! Too, it seems to reiterate old Zeke's clamorous late arrival at the earlier church meeting. (The latter is archetypal in its part in the general 'convergence' from York and his noisy pals outside—where York shoots his initials in a tree, in a monogrammic, mandala-Centric note.)

With his conversion/'return,' his friendship with Pastor Pile solidifies. In the story, it is here that York changes his ways from rowdiness to religion, and exchanges homicide and the gallows for national heroism, ultimately, since his religion and conscientious objection eventually come to the service of the Army at war, by way of his conclusion that fighting well will save more lives in the long run. ("The Lord sure do work in strange ways," as the film's slogan goes.) Herewith, religion converts to professionalism.

Earlier, York, always a great one with a rifle where game is concerned, is out hunting with his brother George and a few hounds. As they cross the Williams property, he pauses in the chase to speak to Gracie Williams (Joan Leslie), who has grown up since they last saw each other. Here she is rather beautifully introduced in terms of three series motifs. These are 'fog/rain/shadow,' 'anima/animal,' and 'fraternal pre-encounter.'

On her front porch, as she intermittently combs her hair in the scene, her

129

brunette countenance is overlaid with subtle shadows, from the house and particularly from nearby foliage, in the way of ("initiatory") 'fog/rain/shadow' (with Hawks at his cinematographic best here). In her initial lines, she earnestly directs Alvin and George to where the dogs went in pursuit of the fox, briefly pointing in the direction. In their subsequent conversation, she shows familiarity with dogs and hunting, thus relating to him in his own ego-masculine terms—yet in the 'anima/animal' connection too. The connection is emphasized when she mentions a frog as well. Too, on one level, she "replaces" the fox of their chase! At her initial directive regarding the fox, York himself points to where the fox and hounds went, readying to continue the chase with George, but he remains transfixed for a moment in this pointing position as he stares at Gracie now grown up. The fox and she are of course one. (Indeed, this fox/Gracie identity or "split" is anticipated in York's earlier lines to George to the effect that he is not sure if it is a red or a grey fox they are chasing. Since it later turns out to be red, Gracie might be said to have assumed the grey!)

"I figured it was you out a-huntin', " she says to Alvin. "No mistakin' the voices of them there hound dogs." (She then mentions frog croaking at moonrise, in the course of a little display of Appalachian expression as part of her character introduction.) Knowing Alvin in advance by the sound of his dogs, she 'pre-encounters' him thus, in the way of an unconscious entity's rumblings before irruption. In a like manner, Alvin pre-encounters his anima in Gracie—as the same ego/unconscious dual personification is prefigured in Gracie—via the early red/grey fox duality.

Significantly, Joan Leslie/Gracie is cinematically different in her introductory scene than subsequently in the film (where she displays hairdos, hats, fancier dress, and a bubbly girlishness). In *Scarface*, Cesca is similarly, *shadowily* different in the final-shootout scene, where she is rather explicitly drawn as Tony's 'double.' This prefigures Gracie's introduction in the "hounds" sequence with Alvin. Both sequences look forward to the 'self-encounter/splitting off' motif, initially occuring in *The Big Sleep*.

Alvin is subsequently resolved to marry Gracie. This is broached in the family circle, in the medium-lighted York cabin. The scene opens with Alvin combing his hair (with some difficulty) in a mirror—in continuation from Gracie's doing so, just earlier, as the last shot of her rather fades/ "bleeds" into his. Mother York (Margaret Wycherly) works at her spinning wheel, she and it being juxtaposed with the fire in one outstanding shot (the film's wheel motif principally occuring in this scene). In the scene too, she sews up a rip in Alvin's coveralls, as he stands still for it. George cleans a rifle and the younger sister seems to be working at something in her lap—all variously corporeal, in the pattern. Midway in the scene, George interjects in the dialogue between Alvin and his mother by aiming and testing the rifle (sans ammunition, of course), as the mother turns and respectfully tells him not to do this.

Alvin leaves, having related his notion of "settin' up" with Gracie. The frame changes to the shot of Mother York, her spinning wheel, and the fire behind her, as, to herself, she shakes her head in some misgiving. Just earlier in the scene, George, a little in the background, does the same, as Alvin reveals that he wants Gracie. These reiterate the shot of O'Malley and Webb under the umbrella as the latter gestures in the same way toward Jaffe and Lily in her penthouse in *The Twentieth Century*, which of course stems from the pivotal 'triangle' scene with Bill concerned about Spike's nuptial expectations, in *A Girl in Every Port*. (Further, there is Susan laughing at David's marriage plans in *Bringing Up Baby*, and Groot's mutely expressed concern about Tom and Fen in *Red River*.) In reference to these expressed misgivings in the series, we have thus a 'mutely or wordlessly expressed concern at a pal's amorous involvement and/or nuptial plans' motif (closely linked with the 'triangle' motif). As it happens, Mother York is not so much a mother to Alvin as a 'pal,' in the motif of Spike and Bill in the 1928 film, and of Barney and Swan in *Come and Get It*. (Mother York is further discussed below.)

As Alvin comes courting Gracie, the involved "porch" scene ensues, moving powerfully via the 'triangle' motif among York, his rival Zeb Andrews (Robert Porterfield), and Gracie—with her Uncle Lige (Tully Marshall) present and effective as a background figure. Zeb is there ahead of Alvin, at twilight. A little humiliated (in the comedic pattern of the hero under Woman's heel), Zeb holds a loop of Gracie's yarn as she knits: a tactile-functional Center among the three of them and the uncle nearby. As Alvin chides Zeb for it, Gracie rather obligingly takes the yarn herself. (Later, Alvin will briefly fall under Woman's heel in a little slapstick interlude where Gracie, angry, shakes a kitchen knife at him causing him to tumble from his seat with her pail of peeled potatoes spilling over him. Significantly perhaps, she more or less accepts his ongoing proposal of marriage in this scene, the nuptial prospect being thus denigrated, or unfavorably stigmatized, in the pattern.)

Upon Alvin's arrival at Gracie's, his presence is foreboded a little by the gate creaking loudly (in minor 'pre-encounter') as Gracie then turns toward him. He takes a position between Gracie, who is in the right rear of the frame, and Zeb who is seated on the porch against a post and to the left foreground. There, through part of the scene, Zeb's jealous irritation is very focused. "Knittin', Zeb?" York chides him. There in the medium-shadow, Zeb flashes angry glances Alvin's way as the men commence quarreling. After sending Gracie inside to bring him a drink, York comes around the post and, more or less from behind, grabs Zeb as though to pummel him thoroughly. In this act, York's reaching arm, and his yanking of Zeb to his feet and out of the frame, leap abruptly yet naturally into medium close-up. Immediately, the frame cuts to Gracie inside and, next, her returning with two cups of "nippin' cider" (in the 'shared drinks in common' motif, Centric between the pair and a factor in Zeb's exclusion). Zeb's hurrying away in the distance easily implies his having been quickly, physically forced to leave, though the clash was not fully shown. Gracie, initially, cannot understand why he should leave in such a hurry.

An important aspect of the scene is rendered by Gracie's old, moderately senile Uncle Lige. Sitting a little away from the trio in his rocker, between two resting hounds, he reads the Bible and talks to himself, loudly at points, thus interrupting the dialogue among Alvin, Zeb, and Gracie with phrases from the scriptures. These enter the conversation mostly at appropriate or ironic points and in effective comment, in the manner of 'verbal-simultaneity' (like Walter's inadvertent "No!" popping up and effectively addressing Bruce's remark, in *His Girl Friday*). With animosity beginning to heat up between Alvin and Zeb, Uncle Lige chances to interject with, " ... biteth like a serpent and stingeth like an adder." As Gracie begins to go inside, and York readies to pulverize Zeb, the uncle says (at a point when Gracie passes close to him and the hounds), "And the lion shall lie down with the lamb."

As Gracie is wondering why Zeb is fleeing in the distance, the uncle says, "Whatsoever thy hand findeth to do, do it with thy might." This cues Gracie as to what happened, particularly as she perceives Alvin's guilty look here. In his 'merged dramatical/dialogistic' way, the aged uncle is a shadow to the scene. Yet Mother York is as well. When Alvin comes out with his intentions to marry Gracie, Gracie reveals that she has already learned about it from Alvin's mother! Not unexpectedly, Hawks flies in the face of ordinary courtship, with such as a minor 'triangle' of son, mother ('pal'), and fiancee-to-be.

York has the mistaken idea that Gracie prefers Zeb because he owns some bottomland, and so is out to obtain a piece of this choice land himself, working extraordinarily hard and long at odd jobs to raise the money. He finally raises the full amount by winning the beef prize at a community shooting match—a good scene in terms of its series-characteristic group banter among the match participants. This sense of the *group* is underscored, midway in the scene, by a 'group-delineative/"circular" montage' sequence of each of the contestants firing. (These shots are sandwiched with shots of their respective target-hits, which Centrically compliment the group/"circular" aspect.) Nate reveals that he has broken his agreement with Alvin and sold the land to Zeb just prior to Alvin's winning the shooting match (stressing that the agreement with Alvin to extend his time on the deal was not a written one). Hence, Alvin takes leave of his drinking pals that night to go after Nate with a gun, but after his conversion comes to make peace instead. After this, he goes to the Andrews farm to make amends with Zeb. The latter, admitting his own vengeful motives in the matter, gives Alvin the opportunity to obtain the land by working it for a couple of seasons. (Hence, "the Lord sure do work in mysterious ways.")

In this scene, Zeb is feeding stalks of cane into his mule-driven sugar-cane press as he sits near the hub of the turning windlass. In talking with him, Alvin has to duck the spokes of the turning windlass a couple of times before getting out of their path by sitting down near the hub—this of course in humorous, tactile addition to the otherwise verbal communication. As he sits down with Zeb he lends a tokenistic hand to the work, shoving a stalk of cane into the press. Such stems in considerable part from George Raft's coin tossing as a dramatic aid, in *Scarface*. As object impositions and transactions, they bring the sensation-function to the dramatic fore. The "cane press" scene is exemplary here—somewhat more so than the earlier, semicomical trading of various items and goods among York and Nate Tompkins.

Earlier is the first of the two tavern scenes. It is the strongest scene in the film, in its medium-lighted and generally low-keyed but seething dramatic action: rather naturally erupting in a brawl. Essentially a humorous scene, it is Hawks direction at its epitome in terms of archetypally-imbued action (via the tricksterish shadow). With great directorial feeling for the heavy horseplay, the brawl participants are filmed in frequent medium close-up. Although their playful yet rough fighting cannot be termed choreographic, the two couples dancing in the background to the player piano prior to the brawl meaningfully juxtapose with the subsequent fracas among the three pairs (or "couples") of opponents. Thus the ongoing music plays a metaphoric role in the fight. So much the more does it become an activity of *relationship* in the 'affection/violence' pattern when aptly, at one point, Ike misses his opponent and roundly clobbers Alvin by mistake. It is from such, in the series, that one gleans an odd homoerotic factor in Hawks cinema, which I think may be viewed in three related ways. In order of importance here, these are: (1) Projected cognitive relationship of ego, shadow, and anima, the anima represented in the dancers and in the brawl's allusion to couple-dancing. (2) An expression of repressed homosexuality. (3) Possibly a representation of Eros' functioning in ways other than the strictly sexual. (Ref. the two nude friends wrestling by the fireside, in philosophic emphasis of (3), in Ken Russell's film of D. H. Lawrence's *Women in Love*.) These psychic twains of course meet and merge.

Alvin, Ike, and Buck come in, soon to start getting drunk together, passing a single bottle back and forth, a commonplace thing, but squarely in the deeper 'object-transaction' pattern of the series. The tavern is on the Tennessee-Kentucky state line, the former state being dry and the latter wet, with the state line painted across the floor. Some heavily spoken humor is made around Alvin and his pals needing to step over the line in order to buy. This they do, with the camera in medium close-up on the painted line and their traversing feet—a little in the manner of 'dramatized/converged space' since, as in *Come and Get It*, the brawl will presently ensue through the same space. The 'object-transactive' state-line business also echoes the chalking of the stage floor which functioned strongly in the violent rehearsal scene in *The Twentieth Century*. This minor motif of 'floor marking(s)' is repeated in the dance diagram chalked on the rug in *Ball of Fire*.

As they buy a bottle on the Tennessee side, Alvin sticks his hand out. His pals put their coins in it and he then puts it all in the bartender's hand, all very tactile/group-functionally. His comrades go to a Kentucky table. York, in a giddy mood, pauses for a moment, his back to the bar, as a woman at a Tennessee table smiles at him. This is to the annoyance of one of the card-players there, who angrily throws his cards down, glaring at York. York then disregards her (and him), and steps across the line again (the camera in medium close-up on his feet doing so), going to the midst of his pals at their table—a little as though to safety or haven from this siren-that-is-Woman, in the pattern, yet away from trouble with her obvious man-friend, or both, as these link in the series 'triangle' motif. Indeed, the fight will shortly be between York and this man (and thence the others of both groups), sparked by Alvin and the woman.

Before the fight, Alvin's little brother comes in with a rifle to fetch him home, pointing the gun at him, then pressing him with its fearful muzzle, corporeally enough. As George enters the saloon (the muzzle of the old-fashioned gun preceding him through the door), he is initially seen by Ike, of the group, who pauses in his drinking to stare at him, thus calling Alvin's attention to his brother (recalling the shadowy Diamond Louie coming face to face with Hildy before Walter does, in *His Girl Friday*). More directly than the business of stepping back and forth over the state line on the floor, George's humorous coercing of Alvin with the traditional long rifle sets the mood for the fight about to irrupt.

"Ma wants you," York's little brother explains, curtly but listlessly. As Alvin complies, the irate man at the poker table laughs at the same, implying that York is a "Mama's boy." George holds Alvin's coat as Alvin orders the man to his feet and then clobbers him, leading the two groups into their fond fracas (combining boxing and wrestling). George is not appalled at it, but relaxes with his gun, yawning. It might be a routine matter.

The brawl replaces the dancers, who rightly cower against the wall and around the piano. As one opponent is knocked against the piano, the pace of "Oh You Beautiful Doll" increases beyond ragtime tempo. Shortly, a young man seated at the player piano (an evident music lover) has the anxious woman there move aside a few inches so that he can move the (earlier-shoved) lever from "fast" back to "slow" (the camera in close-up on it), the music subsiding accordingly.

Here we see clearly that the piano is a mechanical one—earlier suggested when the one brawler, shoved against it, raised the musical tempo. (Also, the piano roll was visible.) But the close-up on the fast/slow lever sharply emphasizes the fact, and thus pops up as a Center. The tune slows down just as York pounces upon his supine opponent (reminiscent of Swan's affectionate hopping upon Barney's chest, in *Come and Get It*), and bangs his head against the floor to the man's submission.

The sequence features four 'mandala-Centric' points: (1) the traversed state line on the floor; (2) the close-knit negotiation of the small change for (3) the bottle—an eminent "Grail"-like thing amongst the shadowy comrades at their table; and (4) the piano, and particularly the fast/slow lever shown in close-up. The dancers and, to a considerable extent, the intrusive George, figure in the shadow/anima background.

As York gets up from his subdued opponent, Ike inadvertently clouts the former who tumbles across the room and lands upside-down against the door. Here, a brief montage exchange ensues between York, upside-down, and his brother who is standing, looking down at him and calmly repeating the summons, "Ma wants you, Alvin." This is followed by a shot of both of them in these opposite positions, the brother to the foreground and side of the frame, as York says, "Comin' George," and curls down from the door to get to his feet. In a summarial ego/shadow way, this montage exchange between Alvin and George, and the two-shot of them, are as though patterned after jacks on a playing card, the one upright and his conjoined partner upside-down. (Also ref. the two-headed coin in *Only Angels Have Wings.)*

Back home "at gunpoint," Mother York greets Alvin in a mainly silent, dramatically excellent mixture of apprehension, maternal authority, and empathy, as Alvin displays child-like embarrassment. As with the earlier George/Alvin montage, the mother, within the cabin, is in natural, "authoritarian" upshot from his eye level below the front step. In a voice more kindly than is expressed in her demeanor, in the moment, she has George fetch her a bucket of water. Alvin pulls his coat around him, in preparation for the (tactile-functional) dousing which she renders—suggestedly as a routine matter—in two splashes. Rosie York (June Lockhart) brings him a towel, and smiles as he enters the cabin.

134

Earlier, he was absent from supper when George was sent for him. In minor dualistic or 'reversal' effect, breakfast is now at hand. The family sits at the table as the mother says grace, all heads bowed, though Alvin, agitatedly and less piously, looks up in minor interruption of what would otherwise be a comprehensive or ideal familial image. This potential ideal image is disturbed or fragmented in turn as the boyish Alvin occupies the (paternal) armchair of the circle and table. Like Pastor Pile's early sermon, Mother York's prayer has a secular aspect, as she says, "The Lord bless these vittles we done got, and help us to be beholden to nobody. Amen."

Next, the familial image is further put aside as, in the scene's final shots—each a two-shot of Alvin and the mother alone—she smilingly passes a bag of salt to him for his pone, as he happily enough receives it in a way of personal restitution for his last night's dissipation.

The bag of salt—earlier purchased at Pile's store—is hence a focus of normalcy restored. The scene's Center, hereof, is askew from the family circle at table and concentrated in the 'object-transaction' between (Pile and the mother, earlier, and now) the mother and Alvin. (See the "general store" scene, discussed below.) Partly in common with the "family" of cowboys and cattle in *Red River* (discussed in section IV) the scene is, on one level, a detraction from family—taking its Hawksian slant via the 'pals' motif.

Margaret Wycherly/Mother York renders an excellent portrayal. Her lines are relatively few and spare. Like a matriarchal symbol in one way, she is yet a peer to Alvin and has a stoical, androgynous aspect (in the 'blurred sexual distinctions' pattern). Too, her and Pastor Pile's respective makeup have common touches, as though to cryptically merge the two characters, who are both York's 'pals' in the story. Sage-like, she alludes to the Self, in her shadowy way. She is indeed an archetypally-imbued figure—even anticipating the hermaphroditic alien in *The Thing (From Another World)*, and thence J.B. of *The Ransom of Red Chief,* in the latter's "androgynous" prepuberty.

Early, she soft-spokenly, though irately and effectively, defends her son in the face of his community hell-raising (previous to his conversion). As the church folk examine his initials shot neatly in the tree outside the church and remark that "it's that Alvin York and his pals in their liquor again," Mother York regards the initials in the tree trunk and says, "Mighty good shootin' for a man in his liquor, ain't it?" and walks on, as George and Rosie follow after. (Again, the initials are mandala-Centrically featured in the sequence, here and during the earlier gun-play.)

Next, she is further introduced in the exemplary scene in Pastor Pile's general store. This is an apt Hawks situation as, in the shadowy to medium-lighted 'close quarters' of the congested store, some men of the community (most of the main supporting players of the film's first half) sit around in colloquial banter and gossip. Luke has arrived by mule-back with the mail.

A traveling salesman, a wholesaler from foreign parts, tries vainly to get Pile to stock some newer items in women's apparel: a flowery hat, and fancy bloomers which the salesman displays to all present. He urges Pile to try to create a demand for the nonindigenous things. Misgivings pervade the room. He is of course an emissary of the irruptive anima in this major 'fancy apparel' instance. Rather short, he is dudishly dressed, and with his own quaint hat, he seems modeled upon Bensiger of *His Girl Friday*.

Pile cuts him off to distribute some mail—tossing a newspaper across to Lem (Howard da Silva), and handing letters to two others on either side of the now-disconcerted salesman, as these actions effectively "surround" him, in terms of the resulting dramatized space. In the scene, Clem Bevans/Zeke (the man with the tricksterish squeaky shoes at the church meeting) discreetly taunts the newcomer, curtly correcting his mention of "Jamestown" to "Jim-town." As the urban fellow mentions the war in Europe, Zeke expresses their general indifference to such. ("Tain't in our corner nohow.") Then one young man says, "If you're hankerin' for trouble, mister, it ain't scarce right here in these mountains." Thus, the anima-irruptive fellow is well 'converged' upon, in the pattern. (Other prints of the film, as I recall, feature an alternate "general store" scene, in which this general 'convergence' is more pronounced.)

Mother York enters the store, a basket on her arm, humbly dressed. Behind her, visible through the doorway and in stark juxtaposition with her, is the spoked wheel of the salesman's automobile—a clear predecessor of the strong image, shortly, of her spinning wheel by the home fire (and thence others, including the wagon wheel in the scene of York's 'return'/conversion). As she is entering, Luke the mail carrier is passing some gossip of how Alvin raised such a fight in the jail at Jimtown that they had to release him. (One is inclined to link the eruptive Alvin, here, with the irrupting anima represented by the salesman in ther midst. Also ref. the ultra-stoical yet anima-rampant alien in *The Thing [From Another World].*)

The general Alvin York gossip stops short at Zeke's signal, and all are hushed and intimidated as Mother York enters. In bemused curiosity, she handles the strange hat on the counter, as the salesman perks up at this renewed prospect of marketing it. She trades a few eggs with Pile for a can of baking powder and the bag of salt. The latter, a stark white object, is somewhat stressed in their dialogue—is focal here, as in the "supper/breakfast" scene shortly, where its transaction is completed with Alvin. In its stoical juxtaposition with the wholesaler's fancy items, it becomes still more symbolic.

Before leaving, she asks Pastor Pile to minister to hell-bent Alvin. There, Pile indicates respect for Alvin, who works hard on the poor, rocky York land, and cannot be blamed for "bustin' loose, now and again." As she leaves, she passes the salesman, who sadly folds his unsold bloomers.

The second half of the film carries little interest for our purposes. The early half was, in part, filmed in backwoods Tennessee where Hawks utilized some of the local people. Max Steiner's musical score, utilizing a number of folk songs and familiar melodies, is elaborate and excellent without being overly obtrusive. In the film, Hawks successfully blends a *pictorial* factor with his usual, less contrived visual style. This feature derives in part from paintings of rural American life (such as those of Thomas Hart Benton).

Gary Cooper received an Oscar for Best Actor, and Hawks was nominated for Best Direction.

136

BALL OF FIRE
(1941)

This principal Hawks comedy is, again, a successful collaboration among Hawks, screenwriter Billy Wilder, and producer Samuel Goldwyn. Wilder and probably Goldwyn had a considerable effect on the result. In ways which could be discussed at length, it is cinematically "watered down" for Hawks; yet it is a favorite of this writer for its special qualities of levity over intensity. The film contains two portions which are unsurpassed in their series-pattern relevance. These are the "D.A.'s office" scene and, particularly, the very musical nightclub sequence.

The situation is that of a fairly characteristic Hawks group, save for the intellectual factor (which serves as a shadow/anima feature). There is a team of professors at work on an encyclopedia, living in a house owned by the foundation backing the project. In addition, there is Miss Bragg (Kathleen Howard), their formidable head-of-household, who is the recalcitrant anima triumphant, entrenched, and stratified. In the pattern, they are all the hero-under-Her-heel, and in other 'reversal,' she is the authoritarian schoolmarm and the professors her obsequious pupils! When they come in from their morning walk, each says, "Good Morning, Miss Bragg," as they file past her to assemble for an address from her. In her positioning here, she figures as a Center, much the way a stack of books and, subsequently, a glass of milk in the hand of Bertram Potts (Gary Cooper) are later 'converged' upon by the boys. In the early scene, however, the matron stands on top of them, as it were, and is Centric in that way.

Miss Totten (Mary Field) of the foundation, who has a girlish crush on Potts, addresses the group on business. When Potts exchanges angry words with her, Professor Gurkakoff (Oscar Homolka) runs a hand up Potts's back—reminiscent of Mike scratching Pipes's upper back in *Tiger Shark*, in tactile-functional transaction thus. Afterwards Potts says to him, "Professor Gurkakoff, that maneuver up my spine was unnecessary." To which he replies, "Was it, my dear Potts?" Potts was unduly rankled and/or seemed about to fall astray with Miss Totten, in deviation from their stoical, not to say monkish task there. Aptly, the psychoanalytic Gurkakoff renders insight into the 'affection/violence' matter.

Gurkakoff, pipe-smoking, brunet, Russian, and with bushy eyebrows, is rather taciturn, yet with strong presence as a character, like Mother York and others of the series. His tasks on the encyclopedia include the psychology portion. He is something of a 'pal' to Potts, as Oddly (Richard Haydn) will also be (the latter in terms of the 'triangle' motif)—yet the entire group of them are 'pals.' Put another way, the professors form a collective character, though Potts, Oddly, and more subtly Gurkakoff, are in the foreground or attain more focus. Gurkakoff recalls Sparks in *Only Angels Have Wings* in his little-spoken prominence, and as Potts's and the group's shadow. Later, in the ego/shadow/anima dynamic, he will assist Potts to get together once and for all with Sugarpuss (Barbara Stanwyck), as Sparks assisted Geoff and Bonnie in the earlier film.

Potts goes to work outside their cloistered confines to study slang and popular speech—in the field, a radical step for him and for them. Contact and adventure with the outside, which invades their academic haven in turn, will constitute the drama, as in the case of paleontologist David's racing around with Susan in *Bringing Up Baby*.

From this ensues the nightclub sequence around Sugarpass O'Shea, jazz vocalist with the Gene Krupa band, an outstanding and epitomal sequence in its acted-out complex of ego/shadow/anima and Self.

In the club, Potts scribbles overheard slang in a pad, while loosely position-ed between two girls in a way of their 'convergence' around him, in the pattern of Man's irrupting anima. Although the instance is casual in itself, it is more significant in terms of the entire sequence in which he is somewhat overwhelm-ed by Her. The band onstage begins "Drum Boogie." It commences with a shot of Sugarpuss's index finger outside the curtain (in clasping it) beating time with the orchestra, just before she emerges to sing—this in the pattern of a 'foreground object/action' focused upon, often prior to frame expansion into the scene, a corporeal Centering. During the song number, the band members, in a relaxed montage sequence, are in easy, natural communication with one another as, after all, a Hawksian peer group. The subsequent, informal 'song session' runs through the same sort of relaxed montage in a very "circular" and group-delineative way.

Potts indeed wants to talk to Sugarpuss, as she is obviously a great source of current jive jargon.

After the number, Krupa and Sugarpuss do their informal bit off to the side with a bunch of fans. Brilliantly, this little portion—juxtaposing as it does with the formal show-business just completed—exemplifies the *shadow* in terms of something off to the side of or on the underside of the ego. The other archetypal features figure too, in the same dramatic action and imagery. The little portion is epitomal both in terms of its American musical-comedy style of cinema and our more recondite series patterns. (Sadly, it is missing from cer-tain prints.)

Gene Krupa yanks the tablecloth from a table and sits down. He takes two wooden matches in hand, and has the close circle of fans there chant part of the song, "Drum Boogie," over and over in soft tones as he scratches out the rhythm on the matchbox. Sugarpuss, close at hand in her shimmering gown, and at one point reflected in the mirror-like tabletop adjacent to Krupa's lively match-work, softly sings the encore for and with the private party (and essen-tial group) there. As it ends, Krupa strikes both matches, holding them together in a large flame, a mandala-Center, and, after a few silent beats, he and Sugarpuss blow it out with a great, combined *whoosh.*"

Commonplace as it all is (likely improvised by Hawks and Krupa on the set), the series patterns seldom concentrate so strongly.

Again, it has a shadow aspect as an informal, "primitive" or "folk" encore away from the ego of the show biz spotlight (somewhat in the manner of "after hours"). In addition to the anima in Sugarpuss (particularly via her reflection in the tabletop), the intensive, montage-rendered mandala-patterning of it all

138

and the culminating match-flame, express the Self. It is, of course, not without the sensation-function in its close communion. As a two-part song number it is precedented in that of the saloon sequence and brawl in *Come and Get It*, where Lotta's encore portion is likewise intensively group-involved and archetypically Centric.

Like the "accordian" scene in *Come and Get It*, the tavern brawl in *Sergeant York*, the "rough weather" sequence in *Corvette K-225*, the long exchange around the liquor bottle in *To Have and Have Not*, the Marlowe/Sternwood interview in *The Big Sleep*, the river/fog sequence in *The Big Sky*, the "When Love Goes Wrong" song number in *Gentlemen Prefer Blondes*, and the panoramic panning shot of the pyramid-building in *Land of the Pharaohs*, the "after-hours" song encore in *Ball of Fire* is among the best and most exemplary sequences of Hawks's career.

Backstage, Sugarpuss learns that she is to be summoned as a material witness against her boyfriend, Joe Lilac (Dana Andrews), and so rushes away from Potts to escape with a couple of gangster cohorts, though Potts leaves his card with her, inviting her to come by the Totten House to help him research.

Potts is then almost knocked down by six girls rushing to go onstage. He is left with a feather from one of their costumes, does not know what to do with it in the moment (like David stuck with the purse in *Bringing Up Baby*), then gives it to the watchman there at the desk. As Potts hurriedly leaves, a couple of policemen (pursuing Sugarpuss) descend on the watchman who (in much the same penal manner as the cops) steers them after her.

In its 'animal/Woman' connection (with the girls as "birds"), it is an irruption and threefold suppression of the anima: respectively in (1) Pott's being overwhelmed by the girls and stuck with the feather, (2) which like a hot potato he puts on the watchman, as (3) it and he are summarily pounced on by the police—whom the old fellow (4) vehemently sends after Her. It recalls the entire film *The Twentieth Century*, with Jaffe and his cohorts perpetually converged upon Lily.

For that matter, it is like the boys saying to Sugarpuss, later, upon the occasion of what seems to be her engagement to Potts, "We feel as though you're marrying all of us, a little," as one by one they file through and render their affections—echoing Mike's entire crew at his wedding in *Tiger Shark*.

Reciprocally, Sugarpuss later says to the professors, with love, "I'd like to keep you all (you 'squirrelly cherubs') in a locket always," in essential 'reversal' and 'convergence' on her part.

As Sugarpuss and the gangsters contemplate a hideout for her, they suggest a waterfront warehouse they know. She objects because of the rats there. The solution seems to be for her to take Potts up on his invitation to come to the Totten House to help him do research, since the police will never look there.

However, the "rats"—or the "mice," let us say—are there also. Upon arrival, she is met by Potts, as the boys shyly hide in the Victorian woodwork as it were, peeking out from places, moving gradually forward in a bunch. (They are of course not used to the likes of her around there.) As she and Potts run into Oddly behind a door, he excuses himself and timidly darts off. Sugarpuss

139

asks Potts, "Are there any more of them?" (rodents, suggestively, or "church mice").

Eventually all the boys have crept forward to where they are clustered with Potts and Sugarpuss. They conceal her from Miss Bragg for a while, until one morning when Miss Bragg produces a nylon stocking. With renewed life (via Sugarpuss) they stand up to Miss Bragg and overrule her in the name of research, and Sugarpuss stays. Others from different walks of life meet there with Potts to help him with his slang project. Sugarpuss, in her glittering belt, in one scene gets the boys into a line doing the conga to one of their newly purchased pop phonograph records and a chalked dance diagram on the rug (echoing the dramatic floor markings in *The Twentieth Century* and *Sergeant York*).

Earlier is the excellent "D.A.'s office" scene. In the office, an item of evidence is being brought against Joe Lilac, a set of fancy pajamas given by Sugarpuss. A 'fancy apparel' instance, the pajamas are bringing trouble to Lilac, and characteristically by way of Woman/anima. The scene begins with a medium close-up on his monographed initials on the shirt, and expands to include the D.A. and a few gang members in transaction around (and in 'convergence' upon) it. The crooks are rigging a lie to the effect that the pajamas belong to another fellow there—who tries on the shirt which is too big for him, as he lamely explains away this and other questionable points.

In the pattern of 'friends/foes,' a certain ambiguity is present there, I think—a dim sense that the crooks and the D.A. are less than enemies, on one level. Yet the D.A. is scornful of Lilac's lawyer, who arrives on the scene and proffers a gloved hand, in mock friendliness, as if to say, "You're not so clean yourself." This sudden object/comment/joke pops up in an emergent Centering, like the second cigar in the office scene in *Come and Get It*. Another Center in the room and scene is the desk lamp, which is alight and, in one shot, to the foreground—even though the set/room is well-lighted. This is somewhat repeated in the scene at the inn later, also a fine scene and involving a warm, song-filled confab among the professorial group—which Sugarpuss underscores by exiting early, remarking that it is their party and girls ought to leave. The light from the fireplace, visibly emitting reflections, effectively "accompanies" the boys as the curiously lighted lamp does the crooks and D.A. in their particular confab. Like some curious masculine "hearth" in each case, they echo the serving-tray/"Grail" reminisced upon by the pals in *Come and Get It*, and of course the lamp and script in the rehearsal scene in *The Twentieth Century*.

Lilac orders Sugarpuss to play along with Potts's wanting to marry her. The professors' (first) cross-country 'odyssey,' stopping over at the inn, is supposedly to travel to her father's home for the marriage but it only allows Lilac and the gang to intercept them at the inn.

Sugarpuss loves Bertram Potts (and the rest of them as well) by now. There, Lilac and Potts have a physical confrontation.

Potts, crushed by her bolting from him with the gang, does not realize that she loves him until later when Gurkakoff observes that in returning the wrong ring to him (one Lilac gave her), and keeping Potts's engagement ring, she indicates her true affections via the 'dramatized objects.'

Lilac intends to force Sugarpuss to marry him so that she will not be able to testify against him in court. His men intrude upon the professors, Miss Totten, and one or two of Potts's slang-project helpers and hold them at gunpoint in the Totten house to avert any interference. The gangsters are then foiled and taken captive by means of brain (applied science) over brawn, and the boys make a second cross-country 'odyssey' to foil the forced marriage, all riding in the one-ton truck of one of Potts's slang informants.

Very tactile-functionally too, one of the bound gangsters inside the rough vehicle is "tortured" by tickling as the route to the wedding is extracted from him, bit by bit. In the same pattern, Potts, who in the inn sequence was struck by Lilac, now prepares to get him in kind as he studies an old boxing manual to learn the craft by the time of their arrival. There he beats Lilac at fisticuffs, thus in a little 'triangle' around Sugarpuss.

All has become physical adventure. En route, Miss Totten, hanging onto the back of the truck, exclaims, "I never had so much fun in all my life!"—essentially David's words to Susan at the end of their 'odyssey' in *Bringing Up Baby*. Their journey to and interception of the marriage ceremony recalls the end of that film, where every character is converged upon the jail. Also, it is a little in 'fraternal return' that the justice of the peace is interrupted by the approaching song of the boys in march time and Latin, as they arrive, armed with the Tommy guns of their gangster captives, in time to save Sugarpuss. On one level, their 'return' functions in a trickterish, marriage-denigrating way—like Sugarpuss's earlier punctuations of the marriage ceremony with bitter wisecracks against Lilac, her husband-to-be. (Further, the justice of the peace is an old, deaf, and dodderingly negative character.)

Just before the boys physically arrive, Sugarpuss happily recognizes their approaching song (earlier sung at the inn confab), in this Hawksian touch of 'pre-encounter' and contact-over-a-distance ('dramatized/converged space').

In the inn sequence, we have the major 'triangle' instance among Potts, Sugarpuss, and Oddly. As Sugarpuss excuses herself from the conclave of camaraderie and songs around Potts and his engagement, she retires to her room—room nine. As she closes the door, the number, loose at the top, slides around to make a six. Back in the lounge, botanist Oddly, a widower, gives Potts some fatherly advice on his bride to be, using botanical metaphors and reminiscing over his lost wife, with whom he never got beyond a platonic stage before she died. As Gurkakoff aptly strikes up "Sweet Genevieve" among them, Oddly excuses himself and hurriedly retires also.

Potts, irked at Oddly's counsel being too timorous for a man in love such as he (Potts) is, goes to Oddly's room—room six—to tell him so. Due to the dislocated number on her door, a "six" now, Potts mistakenly enters Sugarpuss's room and begins having it out with her as if she were Oddly. She and Oddly thus "merge," in a shadow/anima way. She does not let on that she is not Oddly and hears him out. A shot of her eyes in the dark gives the striking effect of their being those of an animal such as a cat. (Reportedly, her face was blackened for the scene.) It is here that Sugarpuss falls fully in love with him, with crucial results for the story. (See Appendix 3 for Hawks's own comment on the scene).

It is the only dark or shadowy scene in the film. The pivotal 'triangle' jumble

141

amongst Potts, Sugarpuss, and Oddly seems to include the shifting number on the door and, mainly, the shot of her eyes in the dark as a transcedent-functional irruption (a figurative morass/vortex) in the way of pivotal 'triangle' scenes (as in the "shirt" scene in *Come and Get It*).

Earlier, in the boys' and Sugarpuss's cross-country 'odyssey' to the inn, Potts, Sugarpuss, and Oddly sit close together in the back, rather pointedly in their threesome-to-come. Significantly here (although her purpose is to travel disguised, the law being on her trail), she wears a veil of black lace, in the anima-initiatory 'rain/fog' note.

In Potts's petty quarrel with Oddly, we have an instance of Hawks-style character exchange and development, namely the unfolding of drama via more or less intense character exchange around an emotional, sometimes minor pretext (as exemplified in the long exchange over trifles between Harry and Slim in *To Have and Have Not*). This important dramatic feature of the series expresses the feeling-function, and the anima. It often concerns 'the love impulse expressing itself in conflict,' as broached in *Bringing Up Baby*, and links with the 'friend/foe-affection/violence' pattern.

Remaining points of interest are: the 'fraternal encounter'/'group contagion' instance in the policeman stopping the group in their journey (noted in section V), and the ego/shadow business in the uniformed garbage man (Alan Jenkins) coming into the Totten House to seek answers to a published "Quizola" contest. (He will later join Potts's slang project.) As Miss Bragg complains of his intrusion, the boys stand up to her, "shooing" her out of the room. This reiterates Tex standing up to his wife on the phone, morally supported by a pal's presence, in *Ceiling Zero*, and the shadowy delivery man bolstering David in *Bringing Up Baby*. In the same ego/shadow/anima dynamic, the khaki-clad garbage man is "Bill," the professors "Spike," and Miss Bragg "Tessie" of *A Girl in Every Port*.

THE OUTLAW
(1940, RELEASED IN 1943)

Hawks completed about thirty-five minutes of *The Outlaw* and quit when the opportunity to direct *Sergeant York* arose. The film was inadequately completed by Howard Hughes, who signed it as director.

The Outlaw relates a fanciful tale of frontier figures Doc Holliday (Walter Huston), Billy the Kid (Jack Buetel), and Pat Garrett (Thomas Mitchell). Figuring more peripherally are Doc's (and subsequently Billy's) girlfriend, Rio MacDonald (Jane Russell), and a horse over which Doc and Billy contend. Minorly but significantly, Doc and Billy contend over and transact Doc's bag of cigarette tobacco.

The far-fetched scenario was the most Hawksian of vehicles in terms of 'character interaction/development as story.' In view of its generally excellent first half-hour, it is regrettable that Hawks failed to complete the project. Here, as in *Scarface*, Hughes and Hawks were a very good producer-director team.

In addition to the Doc/Billy/horse/Rio contention, Doc, Pat, and Billy act out a masculine 'triangle,' in which newcomer Billy comes between best-of-friends Doc and Pat. Doc sides with Billy, whom Pat, as sheriff, is after for striking him (Pat) as well as for stealing Doc's excellent roan horse. Aside from protecting the sympathetic character of Billy from the generally unreasonable Pat Garrett, Doc sticks with the Kid pursuant to thieving or finagling the horse back (which Doc stole from someone before Billy stole it from Doc).

Herewith, Doc and Billy contend over the brightly colored little horse, and to some extent later, over Doc's girlfriend Rio. In the course of this, the two gunmen become better friends (in the ego/shadow/'animal'/anima dynamic). This is to Pat's increased ire and mortification as he, again pursues Billy for revenge for personal insult, now complicated by his jealousy over Doc. Doc sides with Billy the more against Pat's (unprofessional) hot-headedness and because Billy—though in ways a more expert gunman even than Doc—needs Doc's help in the face of Pat's hired guns and underhanded trickery. Vaguely, Pat Garrett echoes the tragicomical politician/sheriff Peter B. Hartwell (Gene Lockhart) of *His Girl Friday*.

Ultimately, Doc and Billy do not fight, since Billy cannot bring himself to draw on "the only partner (he) ever had." In the Hawks way of 'violence/affection,' Doc only nicks Billy's hand and ears with the hot lead, and the scene is concluded by an exchange of tobacco, symbolizing their full 'pal-hood.' Similarly, Doc freezes in the act of shooting Pat (having wished only to deter him), as Pat, in character, guns his old friend down (though it is due to his unskilled over-reaction more than an intention to kill him). "Doc!" he pleads, "Why didn't you shoot? You had me beat a mile! You had me cold," to which Doc replies, "Maybe I don't like cold meat, Pat," as he expires.

At Doc's graveside, Pat says to Billy, "It sure is funny how two or three trails can cross and get all tangled up," which serves basically as a thematic statement for the film. Succinctly if not curtly, Billy's words over Doc in the way of a "service" are, "So long, Doc." In the last scene, Billy rides away with Doc's horse and Rio.

Scripted by Hawks's old colleague Jules Furthman and Hawks himself, the latter uncredited, as usual, the project had the makings of an epitomal Hawks drama, as well as an ideal Western (or one of satirical bent, perhaps). The novice performances of Jack Buetel and Jane Russell were perhaps bound to clash with the veteran talents of Huston and Mitchell, however.

As a very corporeally realistic Western town, "Lincoln, New Mexico" (in its old-adobe New Mexican-Territory character) surpasses the frontier towns in *Red River, The Big Sky*, and Hawks's other Westerns. (Credit probably goes to producer Hughes for bringing the company to this authentic setting.) Unusually for Hawks, the film opens with an elevated panning shot of the stagecoach entering the town, thus displaying the latter from the air. Even so, the next shot is from a balcony, from behind two men, one sitting on the railing, smoking, the other nearly off camera with his feet on the railing—overlooking the stage-coach arrival from their high angle, as the more usual eye-level factor in Hawksian camera-placement is gracefully recovered (by way of a very minor 'pals' motif instance).

Having arrived on the stagecoach, Doc is washing in the W.C. at the rear of the saloon. Past Doc, and through the long barroom, we see Pat enter the swinging doors in front, looking around and saying, "Mike, where's Doc Holliday?" Doc quickly recognizes Pat's voice, leans out of the open door and says, "In here, Pat," all in deft contact over a distance, in the 'dramatized/converged space' pattern.

Doc has paused in his hand washing as, very tactile-functionally, he affectionately clasps Pat's shoulders before drying his hands. Doc is in town looking for his stolen horse, seen up that way (the strawberry roan). In addition, he broaches a business deal with Pat, who says that he will let Doc have some money but adds that if the deal is anything like their last one, not to tell him about it. Here Pat reveals the sheriff's badge on his belt. Doc bends down and looks at it, quizzically, denigratively, and asks, "Where did you get that thing?"

In response to Doc's saying, "Pat, you're the last man I thought I'd see so easily satisfied," Pat says, "A man's gotta settle down sometime." Herethrough is our first suggestion of Pat's "decline" (from a less law-abiding life).

In the W.C. scene, Mike the waiter brings Doc's bottle into their midst, as Doc asks Pat what he will have. Pat has not yet ordered, but in the ego/shadow 'pals' dynamic, he says to both Doc and Mike, "Well, I started with rye. I don't see no cause to change." Mike smiles understandingly, and takes the tray and bottle to a table in the backroom area. Shortly, Mike is able to relate where Doc's stolen horse is, having seen the flashy little roan before coming on duty. Mike says little in the early saloon scenes in the film, but he is very expressive, both actorially and directorially, being thus a significant, shadowy supporting/background character in the pattern. He in fact steers Doc to the little horse.

As Doc and Pat momentarily team up against Billy, 'converging' upon him

144

in the barn to recover the coveted horse, Billy scornfully says, "The great Doc Holliday ... getting someone to help him, and a policeman at that." Here, Doc frowns, and goes back on Pat, to the latter's consternation. "I'd never hear the end of this," Doc explains (i.e., if he teamed up with a lawman against Billy). Doc returns Billy's guns to him.

In general, Doc and Billy, who are by no means models of law-abiding scrupulousness are drawn as heroic figures—as Pat Garrett steadily indicates the opposite of himself, in his poor actions (costly in terms of the lives of his hired deputies) and a temperamental ineffectuality in the situation. A lesser gunman, and physically soft, he compensates with trickery and underhanded moves (though with fair success in his sheriff's job).

The growing twosome of Doc and Billy is stressed in the "poker" scene, which opens with a close-up on a dish of Doc's cigarette remains. He is flicking another ash into the plate which, with its knife and fork placed neatly together, obviously held his dinner much earlier. Still in fair close-up, the camera moves between his and Billy's hands manipulating chips and cards. Doc is shown winning the hand. Their sitting at less than right angles to one another, and the large amount of chips in the "pot," suggest that there are other card players off-camera. Billy quits the game, getting up as, following him, the camera rises and pans left to reveal a third, rather nondescript man at the table, next to Doc. In the far background, just earlier, a man was slumped at a table as though dozing or drunk, or both. Doc asks the third poker player to cash in his chips for him, which he does—this, as Billy takes Doc aside where he accuses him of cheating on the last hand. Doc does not deny this, but it is kept between them. Here, juxtaposed between them, is a picture of a cowboy on the barroom wall. The third man brings Doc his winnings and departs with a disgruntled vocal expression. As Doc and Billy leave, Doc gestures back toward the table, saying, "Good night, gents, and thanks," indicating others at the table, who then say good night from off-camera.

Although it has important structural differences, the scene is a predecessor to the important "supper/breakfast" scene in *Sergeant York*, where Alvin and Mother York (and their 'object-transaction' with the bag of salt) are Centrically focused to the discreet de-emphasis of the rest of the family at table, who parallel the off-camera poker players and the rather servile third man. The latter are more or less linked with the sleeping man in the background, as the 'pals' twosome are juxtaposed with the more heroic cowboy picture.

Concerned that Doc may try to steal his horse again, Billy prepares to sleep in the barn with Red. Here, in the second "barn" scene, Jane Russell is introduced to the American cinema, in her famous, violent roll in the hay with Jack Buetel/Billy. A formidable, recalcitrant anima figure, she is very brunette, dark-clad, sultry, and spiritedly hateful and homicidal, being there to ambush Billy for once killing her brother over a girl. Initially, her effectively cat-like eyes peer at him from the darkness and from behind a wheel (as, mandala-Centrically, the wheels of a buggy there are subtly featured in the heavily-shadowed scene). Her eyes thus anticipate those of Sugarpuss in the dark 'triangle' scene in *Ball of Fire*. As her assassin's bullet misses the kid, a bout of stealth ensues within the dark barn. Wrestling in the hay with Billy,

Rio tries to impale him with a pitchfork. Sex and violence mingle in the scene in the Hawks way. Later in the film, she will nurse him back from a near-fatal gunshot wound from Garrett (who caught him off-guard at one point), as Billy's and her relationship develops.

In the "barn" scene, Jane Russell/Rio delivers an interesting and strong portrayal (though less so, later in the film). In most ways, Jim, Boone, and Teal Eye of *The Big Sky* derive from Doc, Billy, and Rio. In positive aspect, Pat Garrett is a certain predecessor for John Chance of *Rio Bravo* and Cole Thornton of *El Dorado,* in the latters' trickery and advantages assumed in professionalistic compensation for their lesser forces, lesser competence, and handicapping injury in the face of adversaries. Rio, in the "barn" scene, influences the demeanor of Princess Nelipher in *Land of the Pharaohs,* and is an instance of the shadow/anima-rampant motif of 'gun lunacy/carelessness.'

AIR FORCE
(1943)

In this film, the first of Hawks's three contributions to the war effort, the B-17 crew undergoes an initiation/passage like that of Bonnie in *Only Angels Have Wings*. This occurs in the first half, in the group's four-step process of introduction to the hard, momentous fact of sudden war in the Pacific. In the film, there is much drama around the real-life historical shock of the Pearl Harbor raid, treated on one level as certain 'initiation.' This, along with other points of initiation/passage, did much to bring home an awareness of this important pattern of the series to me—seeing *Air Force* for the fourth or fifth time.

Early, the assigned crew, who partly know each other already, convene in the group pattern around the B-17 *Mary Ann*, her name prominently, corporeally visible behind them. All is in readiness for the entire air unit's transfer from San Francisco to Hawaii. In the course of things to come, Sgt. John B. Winocki (John Garfield), at first the rebellious one anxious to get out of the Army, largely "shapes up" with the stark fact of Pearl Harbor and the Pacific war before him, which at this point in the film is only hours away.

In addition, and more significantly for our purposes, there is the initiation/passage around fighter pilot Lt. T.A. Rader (James Brown) who, out of professional pride in his own realm, is not particularly enamored of their B-17 and makes mild fun of it as he later hitches a ride with them. Chancing to return a few times to action or reunion with the group, he eventually becomes convinced of the value of their machine, marking his final initiation into the group. This is an involved, archetypal process, as we will see.

Before their flight group leaves San Francisco, some goodbyes are said. John Ridgely/Capt. Michael A. Quincannon's wife asks to stow away, like a true Hawks heroine, and his son gives him a good luck token, a little airman doll on an elastic band to hang in the cockpit. This object becomes dramatized and virtually a character in its own right. It is shown in close-up three times through this early sequence of their flight and 'odyssey' of cumulative encounters with the new Pacific war (the first two of which are 'pre-encounters').

The first step of their introduction to the imminent war is in hearing Japanese conversation on the radio with attendant sounds of gunfire. The next taste of it comes when they stop on an outer island and skirmish with some fifth columnists—Winocki wanting to pursue them into the foliage with his hand gun. Taking off successfully, there is a shot of the airman doll bouncing on its rubber band—its luck still holding for them.

Later (skipping over to stage four of their initiation) Commander-in-chief Roosevelt, on the radio, relates the facts of Pearl Harbor and their country's being in a state of war with Japan. As the famous speech proceeds, there is a 'group-delineative/"circular" montage' sequence of the crew members at their various stations around the aircraft, attentive to the President's speech—unto a final shot of the airman doll, the object hence like one of the crew, and mandala-Centric to the group (in its anomaly, and in its occurring last in the

147

montage sequence). Shortly, it and its function will be replaced and extended by the dog mascot.

Previously (at stage three of their initiation into the war) they land at devastated Hickham Field. It is nighttime, and the field, in flames, is viewed from the air prior to their coming in. Emerging from the plane, they are in shock at it all, like agape boys. They confer with a colonel, who reprimands Quincannon for leaving the outer island and not remaining there as ordered (though it is quickly made clear that they had to, for good reasons).

Just earlier, a shot of the ruined airfield is punctuated by a wingtip with a circled star being hurriedly carried across the foreground, in manner and function like the lighted script in the rehearsal scene in *The Twentieth Century* and other Centric and/or foreground objects in the series. At Manila later, two shots at different times feature the shadow of a particular tree in the foreground, to similar effect and function. Comparably, in the scene of the "green kid" being machine-gunned in the air as he parachutes, some foliage rises in the foreground as he descends to earth—quite as the shot of Joe's crash-landing uses emerging terrain in the foreground, in *Only Angels Have Wings*. Such is a means of bringing the tactile-function to bear in a scene, and may render semiological or more vague symbolic effect as well.

In the early sequence and first leg of the *Mary Ann*'s 'odyssey,' there is the effective use of fires: first in the flares on the San Francisco airstrip (in the foreground as well), which rather anticipate or 'pre-encounter' the fires of bombed-out Hickham Field. Shortly again, there are fires marking the runway on Wake Island, where they land for refueling (having been ordered to proceed to Manila, due to a change of plans). Once again, an object—the separate but similar fires—functions to link dramatic action in greater contiguity, like the cigars in the early office scene in *Come and Get It*.

At Hickham, they pick up Lieutenant Rader, the pursuit pilot, who is also to go to Manila. A stranger to the group, he is yet group-connected in the Hawks way, in having been on a date with one crew member's sister when the attack came. Because she was injured, there is angry suspicion of negligence and/or cowardice on his part. Although it is soon dispelled, with their apologies, a stigma, on one level (i.e., in no dramatically overt way) is upon Rader, who is all the more a candidate for the 'initiation' he will acquire (in finally acknowledging the worthiness of the B-17). This side issue concerning the crewman's sister is an effective pretext for a Hawksian-dramatic character exchange, like that between Potts and Oddly in *Ball of Fire* and Harry and Slim early in *To Have and Have Not*. (In the examples of this pattern, the subject of contention tends to be dramatically secondary to the contention/relationship in itself: namely, as emotional contact between the characters is effectively in the forefront.)

At Wake Island they acquire the little terrier named "Tripoli," as the doomed marines there send him along with the crew to Manila. It is against regulations to have the dog aboard, and when he is discovered, Winocki cockily proffers responsibility for sneaking him on the plane, although he is not the guilty party. He does this mainly out of pugnacity, yet becomes a fuller comrade in doing so, as though in the course of an unconscious group dynamic at work. In the resulting confusion which Winocki creates (over who actually brought the dog aboard) the Captain ultimately allows the fuzzy terrier to stay. With nobody blamed for his stowing away, the responsibility is thus assumed by the entire group (as rules/formalities are transcended, in the group-dynamical pattern). It is a point of passage, particularly for Winocki, who joins the group more by effecting the positive, creative group-dynamic. The dog, a Center and a transcendent-functional entity in the process, will continue as such at Manila.

They intend to pass the dog on to his fellow marines at Manila. There he becomes a 'dramatized object' among several parties. Initially, he is passed along to a marine named Callahan (Edward S. Brophy), who later, and significantly, returns to help the group with their disabled plane, he and his fellow marines bringing fuel. Once again the dog comes aboard, with Callahan now linked to the group as he takes off with them too.

The dog is pivotal (not least for his archetypal aspect, combining 'animal'/anima and Self). Earlier, he figures in the progressing initiation/passage of Lieutenant Rader. Trained to bark and bite at the mention of Japanese commanders like Tojo and Moto, he is loaned to the pursuit pilot at one point, without Rader's being told about this tricksterish penchant. Rader gets nipped now and again without knowing why. When Callahan chances to inform him as to why, Rader smiles in wry appreciation of the joke on him, as he looks yonder to where the (hence more endeared) group are pursuing their crazy, moderately insubordinate plan of rebuilding the *Mary Ann*.

Here the pursuit pilot is preemptively consecrated into the group (i.e., some time before he is in fact). His full 'initiation' obtains at one point when he is aboard their B-17 as it/she is performing well at the height of the Coral Sea battle. He is asked, "What do you think of our plane now?" Rather unprecedentedly he answers, "Boy, I'll take her for mine!"

In its playful (sensation-functional) violence, the group's little trick with the biting dog recalls Lily's initiation to acting through Jaffe's wielded hatpin in *The Twentieth Century*. It also looks ahead to the plans for Tom's finger amputation in *Red River*, which, had it been used, would have similarly consecrated Tom to the group, in its quasi-ritual touch.

Hence, the dog functions importantly in Rader's initiation/passage. As a symbolic-tending transactional object, the dog is rivaled, in the series, only by the epical bracelet and its interpersonal path in *Red River*.

Introduced to the film in group-dynamical terms, the dog is totem-like (as mascots are, in Western culture). In general, the dog is interpersonally-connective (in his group-Centric way), as though, on some level, to make a more primary group of far-flung and numerous troops. In general, in *Air Force*, a good deal is made of characters, far and wide, knowing each other or having common contacts, friends, and relatives, in the series pattern of the (extended) group.

Just after the *Mary Ann* arrives at Manila, they have to take off again on an emergency mission, subsequently having to crash-land, resulting in damage deemed beyond repair. In the air battle here, Quincannon receives wounds which shortly prove fatal. Next is the famous death scene of Quincannon in the medium-lighted hospital. An important and pivotal scene, it also hosts a major 'fraternal return' instance and, considered with the scene's aftermath in the rebuilding of the *Mary Ann*, alludes to 'dismemberment/restoration.'

During his fatal mission, Quincannon had everyone bail out, while he and the insubordinate Winocki stayed with the plane, crash-landing her and (as it will turn out) not damaging her beyond repair. At the beginning of the death scene, the nurse (a tough brunette, and "Hawks"-type of female player) gives Quincannon a sedative, the setting-in of which sends him into hallucinations of their all being aboard the *Mary Ann* again, which Crew Chief Sgt. R.L. White (Harry Carey, Sr.) has said is repairable, humoring him. Quincannon gives commands to the bedside group as if they were all at their stations, as they play along with him in his last minutes there. At his life's end, he says that they are all "heading right into the sunrise" (toward the bombing of Japan). He expires, and the shot shifts to a point from behind the bed. The nurse—who, like a member of the group, has remained closely in their midst through the scene—looks up, and in so doing comes into more light, in the "emerging anima" way. She quickly summons the doctor, who comes over and, likewise in considerable light, checks the patient. In a curt, fatalistic Hawks way, he says, "That's all, boys." The nurse (having shown professional competence throughout) then covers Quincannon's face. The "emergent" nurse and doctor echo, of course, the well-lighted, anima-relevant Bonnie and Dutchy in their pairing in *Only Angels Have Wings.*

The 'returnee' to the scene is Rader the pursuit pilot. Although he has parted ways with the group and is stationed elsewhere in the vicinity, he shows up at Quincannon's bedside, as a ground trooper for the time being. He totes a rifle over one shoulder. This anomalous feature—jestingly referred to there by Quincannon—corresponds with the special feature of Scott's pajama shirt in the basic 'return' instance in *The Dawn Patrol.*

Just after their initial landing at Manila, the crew chief gets news of his son dying in action. He is handed a very small bundle of 'meager last possessions' and remarks, after a moment, "Not much to show for twenty years." It is similar with Quincannon in the effective "rite" of the field-hospital scene, as he invests special import in the plane, as though it were an extension of himself in which he subsequently lives on (through his having stuck with her through the crash-landing and all). Herein lies the allusion to 'dismemberment' and attendant "restoration." (Ref. discussion in section IV, and in Appendix 1.) Thus, the crewmen act out the captain's and their hallucinatory, mystic-like "resurrection/restoration" allusion in performing the near impossibility of getting the plane into the air again and away from the advancing Japanese in the nick of time. They then turn around and help defeat them in the Battle of the Coral Sea—where Rader irrupts with, "Boy, I'll take her for mine!" (i.e., the *Mary Ann*), in certain passage of his own.

The "death/resurrection" (and/or 'dismemberment/restoration') mode of the hospital scene properly accompanies the 'return' instance, as it does in the instances in *The Dawn Patrol, The Twentieth Century,* and obliquely, *Gentlemen Prefer Blondes* (with Pierre as a "ghost"). Too, the group's spontaneous follow-through with Quincannon's "resurrection" cue there is a prize instance of 'group contagion' (which is usually involved in dismemberment/restoration instances). The scene and its aftermath compare with the "dog stowaway" scene around Winocki and the mandala-Centric terrier, who

150

effect a certain group-transformation as well.

In the twilight scene of their final race against time to repair the *Mary Ann* before the Japanese arrive, the arrival of the marines and soldiers with gasoline is strong in such a way as to suggest 'fraternal return' inspiration as well—leading into the famous "bucket brigade" scene of refueling her.

In the last scene, where the entire unit receive orders that will send them towards Tokyo, the unit, at leisure, is interrupted by the commander who, aside, orders that someone turn off the radio across the room—echoing Barney and the table lamp in the "bottle/George" scene in *Come and Get it*, in the pattern of focusing on something corporeal in a scene (and which, again, may take on additional, symbolic import).

In an earlier briefing scene, two men have a question to ask the commander. It turns out to be the same question—the second man having his answered when the first receives an answer, thus in an average group-dynamical, ego/shadow, 'merged dramatics/second-guessing' instance.

I am made to understand that the film was contemporaneous with a general public-relations/propaganda effort to push the B-17s in the American war effort. If *Air Force* was part of the same, then it nonetheless took its Hawksian slant in the recondite, archetypal ways of Quincannon, the *Mary Ann*, the airman doll, the dog, Rader, and more.

CORVETTE K-225
(1943)

In this wartime tribute to the corvettes of the Canadian navy, Hawks is credited as producer and Richard Rosson as director. Yet Hawks's visual and dramatic style prevails in more than half of the film. The scenes variously below deck, and particularly the rough-weather sequence, could have been authored by no one else.

Corvette K-225 is a significant film of the series, if only for the storm sequence. Here the ship is riding roughly, tossing things and men about, with a depth charge loose and rolling about the deck, and at one point a cupboard door opening and closing behind the foreground drama, all in tactile-functional contingency and facilitation of character transaction (ultimately recalling George Raft's dramatically useful coin-tossing in *Scarface*). In addition, the storm sequence ably hosts a vital initiation/passage rendering.

Through the storm, night, and medium to medium-low lighting, the corvette commander (Randolph Scott) and other officers, with varying force, sternness, and would-be leniency, bring an unruly young officer around to co-operation, duty, and profession. The sequence cinematically flowers, in contrast to other parts of the film, both in quality (although it is a little overdone at points) and in the familiar ways of Hawks direction.

The sequence seems to have a 'triangle' aspect in that the young officer's sister (Ella Raines) and the commander are slightly more than friends on shore. The commander earlier returned a totem-pole trinket to her which belonged to her older brother, perished at sea while serving under him (in a touch of 'meager last possessions' along with the 'object-transaction/dramatization'). As though in place of her, in the 'initiatory' rough-weather sequence, is the steward, who is juxtaposed there in the course of the commander's rough " shaping up" of her younger brother. The steward initially practices jitterbug steps, holding to a post for balance as the ship tosses, a phonograph providing the hot music. In this, he is of shadow/anima significance, and probably for his "feminine" job of serving. He anticipates Cricket in *To Have and Have Not* and recalls Bensiger in *His Girl Friday*. He is in close rapport with the commander and officers. Archetypally, he seems again to function in lieu of the Ella Raines character, to bring the 'triangle' motif into the dramatics, in the hence ego/shadow/anima-dynamical sequence of "hazing." The sequence and he are a high point in the series archetyping.

As the young officer "shapes up"—redeeming himself mainly by successfully taking charge of the loose depth charge on deck—the corvette commander, in new camaraderie, hosts him to a game of cribbage: tactile-transactionally in turn.

Otherwise, aboard the corvette, the crewman sing "Bless 'Em All," in the group 'song session' motif, and, in similar communion, converge upon the mandala-Centric kettle of grog for their ration. Among the crewmen who file past the mustering officers in the early scene of character introductions are a couple of fine, Hawksian items. Not least is the bearded sailor off to sea again to escape troublesome matrimony, a beautiful little creation/portrayal. Then there are the 'pals' pair (played by Andy Devine and another) who constantly fight, yet are as inseparable as Laurel and Hardy. In one of the medium-lighted engine room scenes, the pair momentarily leave one another alone to suddenly threaten a third man, there intervening in their precious fighting. (Naturally, he exits topside as quickly as he is able! No pair could be in better practice for assault.) Their turning upon him is an abrupt dramatic "joke," a sudden or irruptive emergence. The brawling pair are of course directly out of *A Girl in Every Port*.

One sailor (Fuzzy Knight) tries to smuggle aboard the same little dog used in *Air Force*, and is allowed to retain him in function of the 'group-dynamical/contagious' overruling of rules in a positive, group-enhancing way (as in *Air Force*).

A fine and series-exemplary scene is that of the general briefing among the convoy officers in the shoreside chartroom where the route and procedures of the convoy of cargo ships and corvette escorts are perused. Early, there is low keyed, near-overlapping dialogue and close-knit dramatics in the joking and shop-talk among everyone—as among the card-playing newsmen in *His Girl Friday*. An old skipper named Smith, a pal of the Randolph Scott character, borrows a cigarette from him, in the 'pals' manner. Later, this old seaman and his cargo ship *The Star of India* are sunk by a U-boat as his 'pal' the corvette commander, in heart-and-gut-felt revenge, is then out to sink the German submarine, and does—like the sailors in Bacon and Lawson's *Action in the North Atlantic*, and as Marlowe will pursue the slayers of his pal/shadow Jones, in Hawks's *The Big Sleep*.

In the chartroom scene, the admiral, seated in an armchair, is an encompassing and unifying feature as he is moved along tracks over the long table by two sailor attendants, thus traversing it and the group as he follows, with a pointer, the route and its details for all present around the lengthy chart. A natural or "functional" situation and scene, it is nonetheless a function of the series ego/shadow archetyping and peer-group dynamics—very tangibly and corporeally, as nearly always in the series.

This and other scenes in the film are pure Hawks. When asked (by this writer) if he directed at all on *Corvette K-225*, Hawks answered evasively, though admitting that he "supervised" and worked on the script. In any case, his hand is often present. Parts of the film—particularly the scenes of Randolph Scott on the bridge during the sea battle—are stylistically contrary to Hawks: more idealized, and probably belonging to Rosson. The tavern scene in which the Barry Fitzgerald character and cronies muse over whether or not a glass of beer has a soul like that of a ship, combines both directorial styles, like other portions.

TO HAVE AND HAVE NOT
(1944)

With its title borrowed from Ernest Hemmingway's short novel, *To Have and Have Not* is to some extent a redoing of Curtiz's *Casablanca*, the model providing a sufficient, if not outstanding vehicle for Hawks.

A few maintain that it is Hawks's best film. This is a view one can respect, at least, due to the dramatic excellence of so much of it, such as in the early drawn-out interchange between Harry Morgan (Humphrey Bogart) and Marie Browning/"Slim" (Lauren Bacall), also in the performance of Walter Brennan/Eddie, and the sequence of the early Vichy interrogation via the effective Captain Renard (Dan Seymour).

Early in the film, set on the Vichy-ruled island of Martinique, we encounter the interesting and important supporting character in Johnson (Walter Sande). Johnson is a probing enactment and focus of the series initiation/passage pattern. He has some precedence in the "green kid" gunned down in the air while parachuting in *Air Force,* and in Joe the headstrong pilot in *Only Angels Have Wings.* They retroactively take on archetypal character through the excellent, profound Johnson.

On the fat side, and touristically light-clad and pith-helmeted, he hires Harry and his boat for sport fishing. He carelessly loses a rod and reel, and is pettily arrogant toward Eddie and generally unsportsmanlike. Further, he is preparing to skip town without paying Harry for services and equipment-loss. Significantly, he gets killed.

The death is incidental, in a chance Vichy-Resistance skirmish in the saloon where he catches a stray bullet. Yet on one level, he is killed for his poor sportsmanship and cheap character.* Discernibly, this links in the initiation/passage pattern as a quick, rough "shaping up"—notwithstanding that he dies from it. The example of Mme. Helene de Bursak (Dolores Moran), who undergoes a very ostensive 'initiation' in the film and at the same time figuratively "dies," throws light on Johnson, and vice versa. (She is discussed below.)

Johnson infuses the deaths of other flawed male characters of the series with the same pattern significance—in the case of Tony, Mike Mascarenas, Kid Dabb (in his failing eyesight), the "green kid" in *Air Force,* Pharaoh, and others. It is by way of the character and figure of Johnson that the initiation/passage aspect of death emerges more fully or clearly in the Hawks series (again, importantly informed by the curious initiation/"death" of Mme. de Bursak in the same film).

Both the "green kid" and Johnson die by happenstance, yet with a stigma upon them—that of greenness and poor sportsmanship respectively. In the instance of the kid being gunned down in the air, it is happenstansical in that it

---

*Also, he is lent a (derogatory) anima stigma, when it is early suggested that he may be "lucky with women" (i.e., be a ladies' man).

154

could happen to any parachuting soldier. But his being tagged "green" is significant. As we shall see, he and Johnson anticipate Dan and Fen in *Red River*, at which point we may coin another motif for the four of them; a cruel one of 'significant happenstansical death.'

Significantly, much drama and the launching of the story turn on Johnson, both alive and dead. He is a principal character in this sense, and is treated with certain directorial affection. Harry first gets acquainted with Marie/"Slim" when he notices her lifting Johnson's wallet (which the latter has simply dropped, like a boob) and then goes after her and the wallet in private, since he has a stake in Johnson's ability to pay him. Here he discovers a ticket for an early flight out of Martinique indicating Johnson's plans to skip away without paying. Approximately here, Slim becomes a 'pal.' They go down to confront Johnson with this incriminating discovery, Slim doing so willingly enough, having come to dislike him and his attentions anyway.

Their cornering him is ruthless but righteous. At one point, Slim strikes a match for Harry's cigarette, bringing the point of her camaraderie in the matter fully home to Harry as well as Johnson. It is a dramatic point, stressing their pairing off against Johnson, in the act and 'object-transaction' (which irruptively pops up, in the mandala-Centric way). Next, gunfire errupts and Johnson is killed before he can be made to pay off in traveler's checks (subsequently found on him). Harry and Slim are taken to Vichy headquarters for possessing the accidentally-killed man's wallet, which the Vichy confiscate in turn. At the headquarters, the wallet and its monetary contents are considerably dwelt on, among all present.

All in all, the object is well-transacted and dramatized—in a touch of the 'meager last possessions' motif. In time, the wallet, as trivial a business as it is, becomes linked with Johnson a little as the wrecked B-17 is to Quincannon in *Air Force*. Johnson and wallet partake of the "death/resurrection" and/or 'dismemberment/restoration' aspect of Quincannon and airplane. Both examples relate to Mme. de Bursak's initiation/"death"—wherein she renders a mock 'deceased's meager last possessions' instance as well. (See below.) Johnson is, of course, a thorough shadow figure, as compared to the ego figure of Captain Quincannon and the recalcitrant anima figure in Mme. de Bursak.

Later, on a dare, Slim finagles a bottle of liquor, which is transacted at least three times back and forth between her and Harry's hotel rooms (above the saloon) as they become closer in the course of moderate altercation over it. In terms of purer dramatics, this character-unfolding interchange of such triviality yet of such depth and performance is probably the chief sequence of the Hawks series. At one point, Harry says of the bottle, "Getting to be quite a problem, isn't it?" Initially she left it with him to make him feel cheap (for inducing her to finagle it). Again, the sequence is exemplary in its development of relationship "in itself" (on an emotional and physical level) with the issue of contention being secondary. (In this case, the "issue" of the bottle of rum or brandy is all but nonsensical, like the Vichy concern over Johnson's wallet, which is in the pattern as well).

Even so, the most interesting 'object-transaction' in the film, and one of the most interesting of the series, is a purely verbal one. The "object" is the film's "dead bee" joke, which is recurrently made by Harry's alcoholic 'pal' Eddie in an absurd little routine to test people. A candidate's response to the worse-than-bad joke indicates, one way or another, whether he or she is "all right" (or may be initiated into their informal group [Eddie, Harry, Slim, and Frenchy] in terms of a vague fraternity of the "all right").

Further, an instance of its employment partakes of the 'double/*doppel-gänger*' mode, in the latter's foreshadowing of the 'self-encounter/splitting off' motif, which fully emerges with Marlowe and Jones in *The Big Sleep*. Near the end of the film, Eddie, forgetting that Slim has already heard the "dead bee" joke, starts to pull it on her. She surprises him by delivering its lines to him instead, at which he exclaims in some alarm that it is as if he were talking to himself.

In addition to Johnson, Cricket (Hoagy Carmichael) is a character of special interest, as an important background figure, though he is of course spotlighted for song numbers at the piano with his combo and has more lines than, for example, Sparks in *Only Angels Have Wings*, and Bensiger in *His Girl Friday*. Again, he is anticipated in the musical steward in *Corvette K-225* and is of the same shadow/anima import, for his own musicality, and his color-ful shirt—and his relationship with Slim, as they become partners in the saloon's entertainment, in the familiar series pattern of professional relation-ship.

Pointedly, in one scene, as they prepare to go over some song material, he asks her what she will have from the bar, and with her reply of "scotch and soda," he tells the bartender that he will have "the same," essentially in a manner of 'object-transaction' (albeit 'shared drinks in common'), recalling the same between Dutchy and Bonnie, and thence Joe and Les, in *Only Angels Have Wings*, Hildy and Walter in *His Girl Friday*, Pat and Doc in *The Outlaw*, and looking ahead to Mike and Gabby convening, Centrically, around identical drinks in their "Pepsi" scene in *Red Line 7000*. The pair's introduction to one another is worked, in a similar way, with an object. Early, the opening shot of Cricket at the piano pans from Slim, seated in the foreground at a table, over to Cricket (as he is a few yards to the background), the shot and frame now tak-ing in the burning candle on another table, close in the foreground. In a mo-ment she steps over to the piano to join him in his song, uninvited but welcome, as it will turn out. This derives from the rehearsal scene in *The Twen-tieth Century*, with its Centric, cinematically pivotal script and lamp in the foreground at times, and from which Jaffe moves back and forth.

Cricket, though largely a background figure, is shown to be in intimate touch with things, namely with Harry's business. Early, just after the shooting in the saloon, he flies into a hot, ragtime piano piece to retain business or atmospheric normalcy—but then, noticing Johnson felled, he lapses into "Rockabye Baby" (actually more sardonically or cruelly than would be realistic, though it works well), at which Harry says, "Cut it out, Cricket!", smiling a little, sharing the joke. To our surprise (at this point in the film), Cricket irrupts thus into the story foreground—demonstrating his awareness of Johnson and his poor character. Cricket and Harry are hence as one man, in the ego/shadow pattern. In the story, he is also interposed with Harry and Slim in a strong 'pals/'triangle instance (a friendly, harmonious one).

156

The end of the film is, verily, rendered at Cricket's hands. Supporting character that he is—like Phipps, Sparks, and Bensiger of the series—he is yet posited as a deep prime-moving force here, befitting an unconscious figure. The Vichy police foiled, Harry, Eddie, and Slim exit—to join the Resistance finally. Cricket festively strikes up a few moments of rhumba, and they dance out and away. As Cricket ends the little piece, the camera focusing on him as he strikes the last note, it literally ends the film.

Cricket, as Harry's shadow with anima aspect, is a major archetypal figure of the series, like ego/anima Hildy, shadow/anima Mother York, and the shadow/anima/Self figure of J.B. in *The Ransom of Red Chief.*

Regarding other characters: Eddie is a 'pal' to Harry; and one of the Vichy thugs, who talks but once in the film, is violently paired-off with Harry as the latter repeatedly taunts him for being so silent. This is preparatory to the later showdown in which this thug is the first to be assaulted by Harry: which is, on one level, out of the "relationship" formed, relationship opening a path not for friendship or association, but for the bullet. It recalls Tony and Guino in *Scarface*, and compares with the major 'friend/foe' instance in Cole Thornton and Nelse McLeod in *El Dorado.*

In addition to Johnson, a major and very expressive instance of the initiation/passage pattern is, again, in Mme. de Bursak, wife of Resistance leader Paul de Bursak (Walter Molnar). As they secretly arrive on Martinique for business, Paul de Bursak is denigrated for having his wife along with him. Notwithstanding that it is for a good reason (to keep her from being taken hostage in Europe), his wife accompanies him, on one level, as a recalcitrant anima figure, in the Hawks-comedic pattern. Relatedly, a point is made of his being a lesser soldier than Harry would be, and when he is finally incapacitated, he urges Harry to join the Resistance in his place.

Not particularly faithful to her husband (for she makes a subtle pass at Harry), the wife and her initiatory comeuppance reiterate Judith in *Only Angels Have Wings*. Her initiation/passage occurs in the saloon cellar scene, where Harry operates on Paul de Bursak to remove a bullet, in the medium-low lighting and "dugout conditions." There, the troublesome Mme. de Bursak—whose earlier behavior contributed to her husband's getting wounded—serves as a nurse, but faints at the gore, spilling most of the chloroform. Subsequently however, "Nursie," as she is dubbed, comes around to a more soldierly and supportive attitude. Lastly, before she and her incapacitated husband leave, she brings forth her heirlooms, a handful of jewelery, "all she owns," for safekeeping, and if need be for the cause.

Indeed, on one level, she (1) dies (in fainting in the cellar) and (2) subsequently bequeathes her handful of 'last possessions,' in the motif (i.e., one nearly always involved with death, in the series). As an 'initiate' herethrough, who "dies," she links with Johnson hence. (See also, the "toupee" and "pill" scenes in *Man's Favorite Sport?* in connection with Judith and Mme. de Bursak.)

In the film, Lauren Bacall debuts outstandingly, modeled after Marlene Dietrich, yet in a very fresh characterization and portrayal. William Faulkner scripted on the film, which shows in the celler sequence, which takes after comparable scenes and settings in *The Road to Glory.*

157

The figure of Harry Morgan provides a focus for the series 'edict'—that of professionalism as an omni-inclusive value. Harry becomes gradually involved with the Free French not through dawning idealism but through a chain of events which, in a businesslike way, enlarge the sphere of his occupational concerns. Early, the Vichy police are the cause of Johnson's ultimate failure to pay Harry for services rendered. They also impound Harry's money and passport. Broke, he takes the available job of bringing Paul de Bursak to Martinique. As for Slim, she is broke as well, but ends up taking a job with Cricket instead of accepting a handout from Harry (and hence does not leave the island as Harry wishes her to at the time). All in all, Harry is a better and more resourceful soldier than Paul de Bursak, all via the course of "minding his own business" with his boat. Herewith, he joins the right side of the fight—namely, with people who pay him.

THE BIG SLEEP
(1946)

The credit sequence for *The Big Sleep*, Hawks's only mystery-thriller, is in front of two lighted cigarettes, initially placed on an ash tray by silhouettes of Bogart and Bacall (after a brief shadow-play of Bogart lighting her and then his cigarette), in effective tribute to this notable 'object-transaction' feature, of cigarettes (used prominently in *Only Angels Have Wings*). Too, it is in tribute to Hollywood's new pair.

Also prominent, throughout, the film is the tactile-functional relationship between private detective Phillip Marlowe (Humphrey Bogart) and his car. An unattractive coupe of the time, it is shown off as a sturdy machine which gets the job done, as reliable transportation, as a hiding place for stakeouts, as carrier for a small arsenal of revolvers, as a shield for gun battles, and even useful as a ruse (when Marlowe, at one point, runs it off the road and lets the air out of a tire as solid pretext to enter a gang garage after hours).

The vehicle is a rather striking 'objectivization' of his shadow. The anima is often rendered in object form in the series, and occasionally the shadow is also, as here (and as in McTavish's scrawled "folk edition" of the town newspaper, in *Barbary Coast*). As Bogart/Marlowe's short stature is emphasized in the film, the "sawed-off" coupe is all the more his "double." This (highly directorial) feature of the car-as-friend is particularly emphatic due to the *loneliness* of the Chandler character Marlowe. He and his car reiterate Captain Quincannon and his B-17 in *Air Force*. In the latter film, the Captain is more married to the *Mary Ann* than to his wife back home, and in a lonely way, sacrifices his life for the plane.

In its involved mystery plot, *The Big Sleep* is untypical of the series. The story is, to my mind, very inadequately rendered; yet the film succeeds in dramatic ways and contributes importantly to the series patterns at a number of points. (In section IV, the film's dual 'binding' instance and its linking with the "Northern European" mythic parallel in *The Thing [From Another World]* are discussed.)

In the early sequence in the Sternwood mansion, Marlowe's short stature is emphasized, as Carmen Sternwood (Martha Vickers) chides him about it. Marlowe has arrived for a business interview with General Sternwood (Charles Waldron)—a scene which comes off exceptionally well, in its professional man-to-man transaction which at the same time contains some warmth. It is the best scene in the film, one of the most memorable of the series, and rich in series-pattern material.

The scene opens with a mossy bough in the foreground, as the interview commences in the Sternwood greenhouse, in the presence of rich foliage, orchids, and seemingly rare plants. Tactile-functionally as well, Marlowe sweats profusely there (the stimulating greenhouse conditions recalling the ship's tossing in the storm in *Corvette K-225*, both of which are dramatically facilitating). The aged Sternwood seems to be comfortable there, however, as if he were a plant himself. Infirm, blanketed, and wheel-chair-ridden, he cannot drink, and so vicariously enjoys the tall brandy served Marlowe, which accrues as an 'object-transaction.' (Later thanked for the drink, the general replies, "I enjoyed your drink as much as you did, sir.") The conversation in part concerns a one Sean Regan, who has disappeared and who, as it happens, is an old friend of Marlowe's. The latter reminisces on their having alternately drunk together and shot at one another in rum-running times, in the 'friend/foe'-'affection/violence' pattern. Later, Regan chauffered for the Sternwoods and was very well-liked by the old man. Here is a basis for Marlowe and Sternwood's ready, close communication, as they (the three of them) form a group. (It is significant that, in the Raymond Chandler novel, Marlowe did not know the missing Regan, though in the film both men do, as a result of Hawks's script intervention.)

Further, the three men have a 'triangle' aspect, with Marlowe and Regan as 'pals' and the General as the anima figure (in the 'blurred sexual distinctions' pattern). He is anima-relevant in being decrepit from "a very gaudy life," replete with fancy and potent alcoholic beverages, as he describes, and in comparing himself with a common spider. Also, his having two wild daughters (in "having wrongly indulged in parenthood at his age") seems to render him the nonentity that he is: namely a 'triangular' "animus" between the sisters, like the "ghostly" Pierre amongst Dorothy and Lorelei in *Gentlemen Prefer Blondes*. (Ref. discussion of Pierre in section V.) He vicariously enjoyed Regan's drinking as he now does Marlowe's—and as Marlowe even sweats for him in the greenhouse humidity, Marlowe being a man contrastingly "with blood in his veins," as the general notes.

If General Sternwood is "vampirous" in all this, he is akin to Indian receiving blood/life from young Chips in *Hatari!*, and to the vampirous alien in *The Thing (From Another World)*. Pointedly, in the latter film, the vegetable hermaphrodite is drawn to and takes up residence in the North Pole laboratory/station's greenhouse (where the vampirous murders take place, where it plants seedlings of itself, and adjacent to where Dr. Carrington secretly plants alien seedlings fed by blood plasma). Insofar as there is nothing like the hermaphroditic, vegetable, greenhouse business in the science-fiction novelette by John W. Campbell, Jr., General Sternwood seems indeed to be the alien's immediate predecessor!

Though more a creation of the Chandler novel than Hawks-the-auteur, the infirm general realizes a special, archetypal place in the series patterns. Like other characters, figures, and features (e.g., the Hecht/MacArthur/Milestone montage of *The Front Page*, utilized by Hawks in his own 'group-delineative/"circular" montage' motif), Sternwood was seized and projected upon as series-pattern material. In this, the general, in his oblique way, founds the series 'blood' motif, subsequently occurring in *Red River, The Thing (From Another World), Rio Bravo, Hatari!*, and elsewhere.

The scene with Marlowe and Eddie Mars (John Ridgely) in the latter's office at his gambling resort, features things in common with the early Marlowe/Sternwood scene. Racketeer Mars and Marlowe are essentially enemies. At least, Marlowe will eventually deal Mars his death. Yet they have some mutual respect, in the 'friend/foe' pattern of which this scene is exemplary. Marlowe in general calls him "Eddie." In the office—in lieu of greenhouse plants—are pictures of hunting dogs and game birds, a statuette of a horse, one of a Scots terrier, and a mirror reflection of one of the hunting dog pictures! This dense 'animal/anima' foliage in their midst functions *transactionally,* as the men confer in a friendly enough way.

The scene is very different from that in the Chandler novel, remade in the series archetypal patterns as it is. It reflects the 'triangular' scene in *Scarface.* There, Tony and Johnny Lovo are in conference, with Poppy very glamorously present and given some attention by Tony, but more to the background, or "shoved aside," with the nude-female statuette to the foreground instead. Though very much in the viewer's attention, she is rather inessential there, save as certain context for the two men—like the effectively semiological statuette. In the Marlowe/Mars scene in *The Big Sleep,* the ('animal/anima') objects function in Woman's stead entirely, with the strong 'triangle' dramatics retained—as in the Marlowe/Sternwood scene (and, comparably, as in the "rough weather" sequence, with the musical steward "replacing" the Ella Raines character, in *Corvette K-225*).

As Marlowe is leaving, he asks Mars if he is having him followed, to which Mars facetiously replies, "I don't like you *that* much," seemingly in echo of Spike 'triangularly' trailing after his future pal Bill, from port to port, in *A Girl in Every Port.*

Earlier, Mars's rather comedic bodyguards searched Marlowe for weapons, and upon leaving the office, he offers himself to a second frisking, in jest there—all in tactile "conversation" among professionals (though they be on opposite sides of the law). Later, Marlowe will steer Mars into the very bullets of these, his own 'gun-lunatic' henchmen.

In the same gambling-resort sequence is an extended, transactive business around Vivian Sternwood (played by Lauren Bacall, and called "Mrs. Rutledge" in the film). Marlowe accosts her at the roulette table (where she will win a large sum of money), as Mars, from another angle, moves promptly in to back up her huge bet. Then, in the parking lot, one of the Mars gang holds her up for it, but is bashed by Marlowe who waylays him in expectation of the holdup, and retrieves her laden purse. Very shortly, the businesslike Marlowe corners Vivian with the accusation that she and Mars are in cahoots, and that all the preceding was staged to give a contrary impression. This is stock action drama (as well as being taken fairly directly from the novel). Yet in its directorial treatment, Vivian throughout is summarily 'converged upon,' in the pattern of the boys upon the anima in Lily, in *The Twentieth Century.* Hawks thus repeats himself, and projects the series archetypal patterns into many kinds of dramatic situations.

In minor yet "classic" ways, there are other transactions between the pair of eventual lovers. In the cocktail bar he holds out his hand for hers, and she rejectingly gives him her glove which, after a few moments of conversation, he returns to her. Early, in his office, as he is somewhat interrogating her, she nervously fondles her knee, after some moments of which Marlowe curtly bids her to "go ahead and scratch" ('object-transactionally,' more or less), which she does with annoyance. Then they do some mischief on the phone with someone at the police station, recollective of the tricksterish Susan in *Bringing Up*

Baby.

Notable in a special way is the slight but involved business between Marlowe and the waitress in the lunch-counter scene (as Rich Thompson noticed and unveiled in his program notes on the film). Marlowe sits with a coffee. thinking over the Sternwood case. Tactile-functionally, he pushes a few coins around on the counter like checkers—as the scene begins in medium close-up on the same, in the pattern of 'foreground object/action.' The camera recedes/rises to take in the entire scene, as—simultaneous with his (gesturingly) getting an idea—the waitress in the background switches on a light, juxtaposing with him in a cryptic visual joke. A "transaction," in the manner of an 'action-simultaneity' instance, it recalls the antics of *Ceiling Zero,* and that film's fluid ego/shadow partnership in corporeal ways. Further, as Marlowe immediately gets up, goes to the pay phone and makes a call—with one of the Centric, "solitary-transactional" coins—he asks the waitress for a match for his cigarette. She promptly brings a light for him, rather in continuity with his and her earlier idea/light "transaction."

Toward the end of the film, we encounter the series' first fully-manifested instance of what may be called the 'self-encounter splitting off' motif—with Marlowe and Harry Jones (Elisha Cook, Jr.), who is his shadow run into.

It may be significant that both men are small. Though they are less opposites, in the ego/shadow way, they are, on the other hand, more like "doubles."

Jones is tailing Marlowe for business reasons of his own, to sell information to the detective. Members of the Mars gang follow Marlowe too, and give him a severe beating with a warning to abandon the Sternwood case. Prior to getting mugged Marlowe looks inside a parked car which was earlier following him, noting its registration (shown in close-up). Hence he knows that "Harry Jones" is tailing him, and knows his name, as he thus encounters him ahead-of-time, in the way of 'pre-encounter' with an emerging unconscious entity (Jones). As Marlowe recovers in the alley, he is being helped to his feet by someone. He looks up and, regaining his senses, he sees Jones there. Jones has leaned him against a garbage can, which is fairly shiny and rather well-lighted in the scene (in a mandala-Centric way). In general here, Marlowe is in considerable shadow while Jones is fairly well-lighted, in the way of a cinematically-emerging unconscious entity, or like a new plant from out of its own darker soil, Jones being the differentiated personification of Marlowe's other half, arisen in this moment of physical crisis.

He picks up Marlowe's hat for him at the latter's request, the detective being little able to do so in the moment. Almost at once, he hits it off unusually well with Jones. There and subsequently, Jones "has brains," "is right," and so on—these being the tough Marlowe's first real accolades to another in the film.

Up in Marlowe's office, Jones coolly regards Marlowe coddling his aches and pains from the beating. Marlowe is washing at a sink and partly behind a curtain, in shade, with Jones near the center of the room and well-lighted, as in the alley. Physically, Jones (short as he is) looms over Marlowe, in the sequence, as Marlowe is either lying or sitting much of the time, hugging his injuries. Thus

Jones's "emergence" is augmented in addition to its aspect in lighting. In their persistence, Marlowe's aches and pains constitute a connective or "interpersonal" sensation-functional feature (very much like his sweating in the greenhouse scene with Sternwood, earlier). Jones is even a personification of Marlowe's injuries, the way Cole Thornton's recurring gun-hand paralysis seems linked with his horse (as well as with two or three characters) in *El Dorado*. In this and a subsequent scene, whenever Marlowe presses a hand to the injury in his right kidney area, Jones is generally either positioned in its direction, or is speaking, or both.

In the 'self-encounter/splitting off' motif, a character encounters or transacts with another character in a way suggestive of his encountering himself in the other character (who is his shadow, mainly, or shadow/anima). A feature of the motif is the ego-protagonist somehow being taken by surprise.

'Self-encounter' is related to, though distinguished from, 'fraternal encounter/pre-encounter,' and the 'double' motif, as well as the instances of a 'character impersonating a fellow character or leaping into a radical character change.' The difference between these and 'self-encounter' is the latter's more intensive *cinematic explicitness* with regard to ego/unconscious personification. Marlowe and Jones constitute a model example, like Jim and Boone in *The Big Sky,* though the instance with Sean and Dallas in *Hatari!* seems even to be psychoanalytically self-conscious, as we shall see.

Subsequently, Jones's murder sets Marlowe into such angry motion that he singlehandedly defeats the Mars gang. In this, Marlowe comments that Jones was "a funny little guy. Harmless. I liked him."

Jones was out to get money pursuant to marrying Agnes Lowzier (Sonia Darrin). Like Jones, she is an opportunist in the story, and indirectly she gets him killed. Earlier Marlowe says, "She's too big for you." Jones retorts, "That's a dirty crack, brother," and Marlowe replies, "You're right," acquiescing again to his shadow in Jones.

Much earlier, in the undercover pornographic bookstore, Agnes is briefly juxtaposed with an Oriental-like statue. She also wears a small Oriental deity there, on her blouse, and at a later point, Marlowe describes her (in his policeman-like way) as "brunette; green eyes—rather slanted," which seems to link her further to the three Oriental figures in the film. The third figure is the prominent Oriental head (concealing a pornographically-used camera) in Geiger's shadowy, pseudo-oriental house interior—a rather "anima-malignant" den of evil and the setting for much of the film.

In Marlowe's final showdown there with Mars, he threateningly smashes the ceramic, feminine Oriental head with a round from his pistol, in anima-suppression on one level (although it is precedented by a more mundane smashing of something in Harry's showdown scene with the Vichy police in *To Have and Have Not*). In its prominence in several scenes, the Oriental head is structurally (Centrically) utilized each time, like the script and lamp in the rehearsal scene in *The Twentieth Century*. On the dramatic level, the ceramic object, in its persistence through the film, seems to represent the case unsolved. When smashed in the final scene, it effectively alludes to the story's culmination, as Mars, the most guilty man in the film, is destroyed in the scene as well. Also, the smashing of the Oriental head probably alludes to its 'objectivization' of Her/Agnes, who had a part in the death of Marlowe's 'pal' Jones. Indeed, as Marlowe is threatening Eddie Mars there, having smashed the ceramic head, he upbraids him about Jones. (Next, he forces Mars outside where, in the dark and haze, he is gunned down by his own men, who mistake him for Marlowe.)

In view of the earlier 'triangular' office scene with Marlowe and Mars, Marlowe's act with the ceramic head would seem to have a 'triangular' aspect, with him, Mars, and it in violent, anima-suppressive ego/shadow relationship, on one level.

The early sequence in which Marlowe visits two bookstores carries a fine juxtaposition of two poles of the world of Howard Hawks, each in reverse of the other, as in a Yin-Yang dichotomy. It anticipates the (ego)jail/(anima)hotel polarity of *Rio Bravo*.

Marlowe is first introduced to Agnes in Geiger's store. He effects a disguise as he goes into the store, shadowily playacting an "effeminate professorial type" in search of collector's items in the ostensive antique bookstore—to see what he can see of the people under suspicion there in the "Yin" place. He and the evasive Agnes have a mild row, but he manages to gain some information.

Leaving this "malignant anima" realm, doffing his professorial disguise and returning to his ego-masculine self, he goes into another bookstore across the way, as thunder sounds and a storm commences. The second, "Yang" bookstore is an "adventure-dramatic" place, in contrast to Geiger's, where he comedically played the "fairy." He hits it off well with the genuine and knowledgeable bookstore clerk there (Dorothy Malone), who is able to confirm with him that the girl (Agnes) in Geiger's store is no professional peer of hers (i.e., knows little or nothing about rare books). Marlowe is thus supported in his surmise that the other store is a front.

Asked about Geiger, she renders a description of him, adding that he "affects a knowledge of antiques: hasn't any." Marlowe replies, "You'd make a good cop." For that she says, "Thanks." Professionalistic rapport is thus created, as they then prepare to split a bottle of rye and become cozier. She closes the front door, displaying the "Closed" sign (the rain will deter any customers), and smilingly pulls down the door-shade with her back to it, in action-dramatic emphasis. It its way of 'close quarters,' it somewhat anticipates the deputies preparing to board up in the jail in *Rio Bravo*.

Marlowe's earlier disguise in Geiger's store (derived from the novel) is echoed here as the anonymous bookstore girl takes off her glasses and lets her hair down in a mild change of character, as they share Marlowe's rye. Rather symmetrically, he in the "Yin" store and she in the "Yang" place respectively touch 'double/*doppelgänger*' in the motif's sense of a 'character impersonating a fellow character or leaping into a radical character change.' Shortly, the Dorothy Malone character helps Marlowe, pointing out Geiger and his henchman as the latter appear across the street—this rather in the way of the familiar "helpful shadow figure" of folktales. Later, Jones functions in a similar way when he (1) irrupts in 'self-encounter,' and (2) helps Marlowe by steering him to an important gang hideout.

RED RIVER
(1948)

Concerning the Hawks Westerns, this writer must vouch for *Red River* as the chief Western of the series and one of the chief representatives of the genre itself. Both it and *The Big Sky* rate above the celebrated *Rio Bravo,* both in themselves and in their auteur dimension (that is, as members of the Hawks series). It is difficult to see how certain informed writers and viewers value *Rio Bravo* over *Red River* and *The Big Sky.*

To a considerable extent, *Red River* is couched in the Cecil B. DeMille pattern in terms of the latter's historical-panoramic dimension, inclusive of the sort of underscored details—cultural symbols—which the "film epic" tends to impose. (Such details and character typology are likewise notable in the MGM-influenced *Barbary Coast* and *Come and Get It,* in their glaring features of Americana, more turgidly renderd than the picturesque same in *Sergeant York.*) One of these features, in *Red River,* is (in its own way) the 'transacted/dramatized object' of the bracelet, in its "epical" import, as distinguished from its less formal predecessor in the transacted dog in *Air Force.* Another item is Tom Dunson's Bible-reading over perished men which, perfunctory as it is (in the series 'irreligion' pattern), nearly clashes with the otherwise Hawksian character.

Yet the "epical" dimension readily stresses the cowboy-as-professional, as trail-blazing stockman and opener of the Chisholm Trail, which is the subject of the screenplay. Too, the film's historical/epical dimension does not overshadow the more finite circle or Centricity of the peer group and its characters. All in all, the "DeMille/epic" aspects impose rather little on the excellent result (even though Hawks seemed to be trying to equal DeMille in the latter's terms). This is a tribute to the director's resourcefulness.

Scarcely a film in the series is richer in the series patterns on every level.

In addition to Tom Dunson's curtly listless Bible reading in *Red River,* the important series points of religion/'irreligion' are as follows.

The most important and archetypally probing 'irreligion' instance is Mike's colloquial, "folk" approach to Saint Peter around the 'dismemberment/restoration' motif in *Tiger Shark* (reiterated in the Indian-religious yet 'group-dynamical' variant in *The Big Sky*). More peripheral yet notable religious points are: Jaffe's comedic "Passion Play" business in association with the archetypal 'fraternal return' motif in *The Twentieth Century,* and Monique's praying in the cathedral for her soldier companions in *The Road to Glory* (an isolated instance of unmitigated religiosity). Elsewhere there is the pentecostal revivalism in *Sergeant York,* jibed at early, though otherwise 'group-dynamical' and closely knit with the backwoods community with which Hawks identified in a general way. In *Land of the Pharaohs,* there is Pharaoh's soldierly "ceremony for the honored dead," and other theocratic features of 'sacrifice/passage' aspect—which are importantly juxtaposed with the heroic

Vashtar's disbelief in the Afterlife. The French-Catholic touches in *The Big Sky* very gracefully form part of the shadow/anima import of Jourdonnais and the Frenchmen—juxtaposing with the unemotional, colloquial joking of the Anglo-buckskin types to the effect that "the Lord made mosquitoes to show man that he ain't so biggety." The brief but respectful funeral service in *Red Line 7000* is soon 'reversed' when the escapist rock and roll music is posited as "[serving] some people better than a hymn." Lastly, there is the destructive gun battle through the church in *El Dorado*. All in all, religion (like the anima and the unconscious in general) is given to suppression, or mitigation, in the series patterns.

Dunson's Bible-reading over the dead, like Monique's praying in *The Road to Glory,* is mainly incongruous with the series patterns, though it is not a dramatic flaw. A note of colloquial, Hawksian common sense is brought to the religion matter when Simms (Hank Worden) comments at one point, "Plantin' and readin'. Plantin' and readin'. If you're gonna kill a man, why read the Lord in on the job?"

In section IV, I discuss the idea or the impression of the cowboy group and cattle as a "family" via the 'fraternal encounter' of Tom and Matt. In Walter Brennan/Groot Nadine's words, the whole business, the ranch and the Chisholm Trail opening, emanates from "the meeting of a man and a boy" and whence the beginning of a great herd. Matt contributes his cow—though Tom instructs him to "tie him up short" to the wagon, as though she were a bull and to be thus tied away from Tom's cow or cows. Though apparently a script flaw, it may be significant in terms of the 'blurred sexual distinctions' pattern, in view of its seeming reiteration in the cow/bull confusion in the dialogue in *I Was a Male War Bride* and thence in the sex-confusions over the animals in *Hatari!*

Brennan/Groot colloquially talks on the sound track, as though in folk-transmission of the tale to a circle of cronies.* Though an epical touch, it yet mitigates the "De Mille" scope of the film via its peer-group centeredness by way of the familiar character. The device of a narrating character is also used in *Land of the Pharaohs* and superiorly in *The Big Sky*.

The opening sequence, of Tom Dunson (John Wayne) and Groot pulling out of a wagon train to go their own way to stake out land for a herd and ranch, features a rich instance of character communication/consciousnes over a distance, in the pattern of 'dramatized/converged space.' This occurs as the trail boss, two trail hands, and then Fen, 'converge' upon Tom from two directions and over a considerable distance of ground. As Tom's wagon pulls out near the middle of the train, the trail boss, riding near the front, pauses and, glancing back, notices Tom pulling out (with two of the trail hands confronting him). He canters back to confront him with this violation of their verbal agreement. Tom tells him in a friendly enough, man-to-man way, that he did not sign anything and that neither the trail boss nor his men are good enough gunmen to stop him. During this exchange, Tom glances behind him as though

---

*Again, some prints of the film omit his spoken-word on the sound track and feature close-ups of hand-written "journal" pages—less effectively, to my mind.

looking for someone, and after we see her hastily approaching from the distance, Fen (Coleen Gray) comes up. Their temporary goodbyes ensue. Tom gives his mother's bracelet to Fen, as Groot (in the 'mutely expressed concern' motif) shakes his head, expressing qualms, as though the hero were getting into trouble or even staking something of his essence here. The latter allusion is more explicit in view of the parallel business in *Land of the Pharaohs,* in which Pharaoh's much-treasured jeweled necklace comes fatally within Princess Nelipher's grasp, in a way suggestive of castration.

As Tom and Groot go their way, they see smoke rising from where the wagon train would be and rightly conclude that an Indian raid is upon it. They prepare for the same where they are, beside the wagon and by a river, as evening sets in. Whence the complex "raid" scene commences—a violent sequence featuring an extensive, mandala-Centric cluster of ego/shadow/anima factors.

A slow moving shot of them on the ground, fortified for the raid, passes Groot and a wagon wheel to come to rest on Tom (the wheel of course a powerful image there in the medium-low lighting). At a distance from them, birdcalls ensue as the Indian party prepares to attack. Groot signals to Tom, with one, two, then three or four fingers, indicating the number of raiders yonder—a functionally modified instance of the 'twosome sign,' indicative of a 'pals' twosome in *A Girl in Every Port* and elsewhere, yet not wholly removed from this basis in the "raid" scene, due to the latter's eerie 'friend/foe' content.

Toward the camera soars a flaming arrow—which necessarily or in effect figures as a key image (or Centrically)—and strikes the covered wagon, Groot hastening to put out the fire. (Later, the wagon canvas will carry the burn scar, in an oblique sense of 'object-transaction.') In the skirmish, Tom rolls into the river in a hand-to-hand fight with a warrior, Groot tossing him a knife with which he kills the brave. Then, in close-up, the warrior's hand and wrist float to the surface—wearing the bracelet, obviously taken from a slain Fen.

As Tom emerges from the river with it, Groot, recognizing it, laments for a moment. Tom then hastens out after the last birdcaller, whom he instructs Groot to answer. The scene fades out on Groot rendering the whistling calls as if he were one of the remaining brave's comrades—this in ego/shadow, 'friend/foe' relationship, and anima inclusive, via the 'animal' (bird) factor, and particularly for Fen's association there.

This rich scene, and the rich sequence of which it is part, involve stages of the recalcitrant anima's irruption, suppression, and containment/'objectivization.' These stages are represented in: (1) Fen, whom Tom leaves, she being a "devouring" anima figure (ref. discussion of her and Tom in section IV), and (2) in Tom's recovering his mother's bracelet (his "essence") given to Fen, and doing so by slaying the warrior who (3) murdered Fen and looted it. On one level, she is murdered twice. Further, Matt as well will later wear the bracelet in Fen's (and the warrior's) stead. In the fight, the warrior is Tom's shadow, as Matt is later—and as Fen, by now, is (4) 'objectivized' in the bracelet, in the ego/shadow transcendent-functional way of anima egotization (stemming from Spike, Bill, Tessie, and the heart/anchor object in *A Girl in Every Port*).

Once again, the archetypal parameters of *A Girl in Every Port* and *The Twentieth Century* are rendered in a single sequence, concerned as these films are with the same anima suppression.

After Matt joins Tom and Groot, and Tom has the fight with one of the gunmen of the wealthy rancher Diego, he passes the slain man's gun on to young Matt. They bury the man to Tom's curtly minimal ceremony as, in the foreground (in the pattern), a fire heats a branding iron which Tom, upon finishing his reading, abruptly reaches for to put a brand on their few head of beef—rather nullifying the scene's (already curt) religiosity in favor of the professional and the tactile.

Later, newly hired and gun-oriented Cherry Valance (John Ireland) and Matthew Garth (Montgomery Clift), in rich 'object-transaction,' exchange guns for a shooting match, as Cherry begins to form his playfully grim notion to obtain Matt's fine gun, though they remain comrades throughout the film. (Though the handle has been replaced, it is, storywise, the Diego gun.) They of course reiterate Doc and Billy in *The Outlaw*. In their conversation, the Diego gun is compared with a Swiss watch and "a woman from anywhere," in a faintly 'triangular' focus of dramatic relationship between them. In the campfire scene, after the drive has started, several characters are gathered around Matt as he sketches a map in the dust, discussing the route with them. Buster McGee (Noah Beery, Jr.) asks Cherry why he hired on for the drive, and he answers that he has "kind of taken a liking to Matt's gun." In the background—and like the musical steward in *Corvette K-225*—is blond Dan Latimer (Harry Carey, Jr.), a family man and soon carrying a 'fancy apparel' stigma upon him, for which, on one level, he will perish in the stampede. (This is discussed in section IV.) In the stampede as well as here—thrust to the background as he is—he is part of the same anima suppression/containment that obtains with Tom and Groot in the ego/shadow/anima-involved Indian raid scene and with Matt and Cherry around the fine Diego gun!

Montgomery Clift/Matt enters the film, as Mickey Kuhn/Matt grown up, after a flash forward to a point after the Civil War and his return from it, the herd multiplied and ready to be driven to market. Matt gives Tom a light for his cigarette, at which moment Tom gruffly checks Matt's wrist, revealing, in medium close-up, the bracelet, a token of trust and partnership (still there, not given away—unlike later, when he gives it to Tess). In a moment, Groot signals them to draw on one another for practice, Matt being a little faster than Tom now in this 'friend/foe' transaction augmentative to the 'pals' symbolism of the bracelet, just earlier. In the background, in meaningful juxtaposition, are a few crosses marking the graves of men who tried to take Tom's staked-out land from him. In the conversation that follows, Matt second guesses Tom in thinking ahead on the route to market in Missouri, in the 'merged dramatical' (ego/shadow) way.

Once again, we have *A Girl in Every Port* encapsulated, the bracelet and the attendant, tactile-functional cigarette exchange corresponding with the anima-related heart/anchor symbol stoically between the two pals in the 1928 film.

One night I had a dream which, in its inexplicit but clear way—of specific feeling-tones—referred to this cigarette transaction coupled with the bracelet. That is, while having the dream, I was at the same time very conscious (in the dream) of the "cigarette/bracelet" scene in *Red River*. I consider the inclusion of this personal item to be instructive here, in terms of its close relationship to the film portion, despite its very different ostensive content, as the dream and the film portion link, seemingly, by way of an archetypal common ground.

In the dream, I was riding along in a car with my mother, who was driving. Glancing skyward I saw fine, criss-crossed patterns of clouds. Little lights emerge from these and move along like a haphazard fleet of U.F.O.'s (in some allusion to checkers on a checkerboard). One U.F.O. begins descending toward the highway and us, to my alarm. Approaching, it amelioratively takes the form of two pie tins placed together and wobbling like a bent wheel on its axis. Then, as it lands, it races along the highway on our left—having become a small car with a long-nosed figure for a driver, like a Kilroy (of post-World War II popular lore). He and the Fiat-like car race ahead and, passing under a concrete bridge, become a U.F.O. again which loops back toward us, flying more slowly over the sidewalk on our right. It passes a pedestrian there—who until that moment was entirely unnoticed and, for that matter, who rather appears just then—and who is the same long-nosed Kilroy figure who is supposed to be in the U.F.O.!

The specifying feeling-tone or sense of the dream was to the effect of the *connectedness* of the cigarette-lighting and the bracelet in the film, the two objects being as one—precisely as the Kilroy figure is in two places at once, presumably piloting the U.F.O. and unaccountably appearing on the sidewalk.

A resemblance will be noted between the dream and the Muchukunda myth, as in both, a man splits off from a host like an Eve from Adam's rib. More ostensive, of course, is the comparable hermaphroditic alien who piloted the flying saucer in *The Thing (From Another World)*. (See section IV for discussion of the myth and its association with *Red River* more generally.) Too, the dream might seem to represent stages of passage. These are: (1) seed (the U.F.O.) becoming (2) "boy" (the Kilroy), then severing the U.F.O. tie as (3) "man" (the same Kilroy as a pedestrian), although concurrent with the dreamer yet residing in the automobile, and with his mother chauffering—corresponding, moreover, to Fen and Tess in their "devouring" maternal anima aspect in relation to the heroes, in the film (ref. section IV).

In the bunkhouse the night before the drive, Groot bets his false teeth in poker and loses them to Quo (Chief Yowlatchie). The latter, adamant on keeping them, will give them to Groot each mealtime. ("My name now Two-jaw Quo," he says.) It is a humorous yet no less strong 'object-transaction' instance, and nearly as tactile-functional as might be. In the same sequence is the Irish cowboy with the New York-ish derby hat, who has floored a now-submissive man that made fun of his hat—to whom the Irishman now offers a handshake in helping him back to his feet. In the 'friend/foe' pattern, it minorly reiterates Webb and his pivotal, archetypal hat in *The Twentieth Century*. Tom enters the bunkhouse and makes a speech about the drive, laying down conditions and having everyone sign an agreement to finish. Groot is the first to sign, flourishingly and as if proudly making his illiterate mark. The contract becomes important in the story, as Dunson regards it as justification for his later tyranny. (It is the third and last major instance of the 'written agreement' motif, stemming from the mandala-Centric contract of the "Passion

169

Play"/'fraternal return' sequence in *The Twentieth Century.*)

In the bunkhouse, one anima-encumbered man complains of his wife as a deterrent to his going and is excused with no hard feelings, and with provision for a job for him when the group returns. Next, Dan comes forth displaying his stuttering. As Tom presumptuously excuses him because of his marital status, Dan manages to suppress his stuttering, saying that he wants not to stay but to go. In realistic compensation for his speech malady, he is the "singing cowboy" of the group (reflecting Cricket in *To Have and Have Not*). Later, he calms the cattle at night by singing to them.

Next sunup, the drive to Missouri begins.

In his book, *Howard Hawks, Storyteller* (pp. 313-314), Gerald Mast discusses the epical panning shot preceding the drive's outset. This is preceded in turn by some fairly rapid montage shots of the group and cattle assembled. The epical panning shot begins with Matt, mounted, with others near him, looking with anticipation toward Dunson (from Tom's viewpoint) and slowly moves from right to left through a panoramic view of the herd, cowboys, and chuck wagons poised and ready to start. The long panning shot ends on Dunson, posed as though for a portrait painting (as viewed from Matt's side). As Mast observes, the resulting panoramic curve between the two pals figuratively resembles the curve of the bracelet with the knob (or "head") at each end. Tom bids Matt to start the drive, which he does, with a second-in-command whoop.

With this comprehensive, epical, "circular" positing, there ensues the montage of quick shots of several of the cowboys giving their occupational whoops. This is followed by shots of the group and herd shoving off, culminating in a more lengthy shot of Groot's comic noise-making in starting his supply wagon. The quick-montage of the cowboys lacks an anomalous, dramatically-focal, or otherwise Centric factor (such as that enjoyed by the 'group-delineative/"circular" montage' sequences in *Ball of Fire, Air Force,* and particularly *A Song is Born*). Even so, the juxtaposed "bracelet" panning shot which precedes it is 'pals'-Centric and very "circumferential." It is all very 'group-delineative,' in any case.

As the cowboys, wagons, and cattle are in motion, Matt and Tom exchange a cigarette and comment tersely on the near-impossible task ahead.

Shortly, the initiation/passage instances with Bunk Kenneally (Ivan Parry) and Dan Latimer are rendered in connection with the stampede. Bunk is a sugar-pilferer. This is given anima relevance, as Groot, in charge of the food, remarks to himself, "It's as bad as havin' a whiskey-tongue or likin' a woman." As Bunk raids the chuck wagon for sugar one night, he tips over some pots and pans, causing the cattle to stampede; whence Dan is killed. In addition to the 'fancy apparel' stigma upon Dan as a "reason" for his death (via the red shoes he plans to buy for his wife), Bunk's sweet tooth is a likewise anima-causitory factor in the death.

Bunk's "anima hand" in Dan's death is one of indiscipline with predictably serious consequences, whereas Dan has no character faults, excepting his recalcitrant anima factor, on one level. (In a shadow/anima way, this factor is involved in his stuttering malady—which he had back at the ranch, nearer his wife, but not as much with his comrades on the trail.) Dan's passing is thus a

170

'significant happenstansical death,' recalling the instance of Johnson's chance death/passage (and its connection with Mme. de Bursak's initiation/"death") in *To Have and Have Not*. Again, paralleling Johnson's poor character and incompetent sport fishing are Dan's thoughts on red shoes and his wife—even though these are not shown to be a distraction from his job. Tom and Matt in fact encourage Dan to buy the shoes and afterward plan to send a pair to his wife along with his wages in full (in a touch of the 'meager last possessions' motif).

As for Fen, she similarly dies as if by some hand of fate, for being "devouring." Again, the 'significant happenstansical death' motif is a cruel one, yet particularly symbolic—of the suppression of a psychic trait or a character limitation or fault.

The morning after the stampede, in which a fair number of cattle were lost, Tom orders Bunk to lean against a wagon wheel for whipping. As Bunk resists this disciplining, he is wounded by Matt, who thus saves him from impetuously drawing his gun on the more skilled Dunson, who might kill him rather than merely wound or disarm him. This is Matt's first serious move against his boss. As Bunk is sent back home, the men show compassion.

The designation of a wagon wheel as the whipping rack here, although handy or common-sensical enough, is interesting in terms of its reiteration in the scene in which the surviving victim of another drive, marauded by rustlers, crosses paths with the group. Badly maimed, with his neck broken, he (played by Billy Self) rests against a wagon wheel, a little as in some crucifixion. There he tells his story, of horrors that might lie ahead for Tom's group as well—of rustlers jumping him and his fellow cattle drivers in their sleep, stampeding the cattle, and later crucifying the boss on a wagon wheel and hanging the rest. The maimed fellow, cut down for dead, is the lone survivor, now retreating home. More than the childish Bunk and his informal sentence upon the wagon wheel, however, the wretched lone survivor reminds us of the tragical Dan Latimer, earlier, and the wagon-wheel imagery in the symbol-laden Indian-raid scene is visually echoed.

If this all consciously derives from Prometheus' sentence upon a wheel (which I would venture to guess it does not), it is rendered subtly enough so that the mythos does not turgidly overshadow the more "natural," archetypal effect. In common with both the myth and the film portions is the archetypal factor: one of (a) initiation/sacrifice/passage in terms of physical ordeal and/or death, and (b) in connection with a wheel/cross: a mandala-image of the irrupting Self. Indeed, the hanged fellow considerably "returns from the dead" as well, and hence rides into camp in a touch of 'fraternal return.' (Ref. sections IV and V in general.)

As Tom becomes more tyrannical, not to say deranged, the group mutiny. It is partly caused by his refusal to take a route away from the Missouri border gangs to Abilene—where Cherry, as well as the lone survivor passing through, heard there is a railroad and hence an access to marketing their beef.

The mutiny occurs when Matt refuses to let Tom *hang* a couple of deserters—"quitters" recaptured. This is a reiteration, on Tom's part, of the hanging portion of the story heard from the lone survivor. It echoes Mike's sudden adherence to an unusual idea (the physical wholeness idea) in *Tiger*

Shark, and Jim's adhering to the same in a moment of stress in *The Big Sky*—ideas not previously embraced but only heard tell of, yet spontaneously embraced in an appropriate crisis. This is in the 'group dynamics/contagion' pattern, the basis for suddenly taking up the idea being merely that it was earlier expressed by a group member. In the instance in *Red River,* the idea comes via the lone survivor and his story, yet from an opposing group—the reputed border gang. For this, it partakes of the obliquely communional 'friend/foe' pattern. On the dramatic level, the hanging sentence is of course an indication of Tom's deterioration.

Tom is disarmed and left behind, as Matt takes over and they steer for the hoped-for railroad in Abilene instead of proceeding to Missouri as long planned. Tom promises to catch up with Matt and kill him for this "betrayal." Though following a gamble, Matt is in truth saving the herd and the mission.

The group cross paths with a saloon proprietor en route to Nevada by wagon train with his whole outfit, including employee Tess Millay (Joanne Dru). Word about her precedes Matt's meeting her. This is as Buster returns from scouting up ahead with news of the wagon train and the promise of needed diversions if Matt will call a rest, which he does. Cherry, second-guessing Matt (in the 'merged-dramatical' pattern), stayed with the saloon wagon train. Here, presumptuously in turn, Matt asks, "Is she pretty?" Buster replies, "Oh Matt, do you remember that filly I used to own?..." Significantly or not, in the very next shot, one of their horses looms strikingly to the foreground, echoing this just previous 'anima/animal' designation, in the motif. It recalls the coveted horse vaguely crossed with Doc's girlfriend, in *The Outlaw.*

All this introduces Tess a little prior to her entering the story—rather out of *them,* like Her creation out of their mere words. As such, she is (again) Lily coerced and contained in *The Twentieth Century,* only here it is from the outset. It is also in the 'pre-encounter' motif. As the cowboys go to the wagon train for a party, Indians are attacking, and they join the fray like good neighbors. Tess is initially seen in the background between Matt and Cherry, as she mans a rifle at her niche in the barricade. Significantly, he and Cherry are the two who get closest to her in the story (along with Dunson, later). Thus she is more or less "created" again, in the brief 'triangle' composition. Their earlier object-transaction with Matt's fine gun (which Cherry compared with "a Swiss watch or a woman from anywhere") is perhaps replaced here by Tess herself! In general, she is a little ethereal, unreal as a portrayal and character, partly because she enters the group's concerns *too* quickly, too sympathetically.

In the first minute or so, in her "feminine tricksterish" air, she is dramatically akin to Susan in *Bringing Up Baby.* In one pair of shots here, she is very well-lighted and Matt is in shadow, in the emergent-anima way, as the pair become acquainted. In view of the double/*doppelgänger*' allusion in the "rain" scene shortly, this light/shadow feature of their meeting is all the more in 'self-encounter/splitting off' reference. (See below.) In a matter of seconds, she and Matt are communicating familiarly, in the way of 'fraternal encounter,' as they help ward off the Indian siege. In less than a minute they are in a lovers' quarrel. As she is saying something quarrelsome to him, an arrow lodges in her shoulder, at which moment she pauses and then finishes her remark. (Here, she echoes Lauren Bacall/Slim and her similarly stoical response to an interrogative Vichy slap in *To Have and Have Not*.) Matt removes the arrow and sucks the wound for any poison. "Gonna make you faint?" he asks curtly. She answers that she will not faint, "at least not before I do something I've been wanting to do...." She strikes him, then passes out from the exertion coupled with the stress of being wounded.

Here Hawks has effectively satirized himself in terms of violent 'fraternal encounter' in the 'love/violence' mode, complete with 'blood' (the latter feature alluding ahead to motif instances in *The Thing (From Another World)*, and *Hatari!*).

After the Indians are repelled, the party ensues. Tess, her arm in a black sling from the day's wound, is by now deeply involved with concerns of the cowboys and specifically, as it will soon turn out, with the falling out of Tom and Matt. She has learned things earlier from Cherry, of course; yet our impression is one of premature intimacy in the matter. It is more dramatically effective than flawed, and in terms of general 'fraternal (pre-) encounter,' Tess and the cowboys are an important series instance of the same.

Next is the archetypally laden "fog/rain" scene. In this scene, and more generally, her portrayal is again rather ethereal, even idealized, like someone in a vision. This quality comes close to being a dramatic flaw, yet it is important on the auteur level. The "fog/rain" sequence is a 'triangular' one, and hosts a 'double/*doppelgänger*' (motif) instance mainly akin to that with Tony and Cesca in *Scarface* (though the feature of the mirror reaches back into German Expressionism and folklore). Tess goes to talk with Matt as he stands his watch in the night fog, having relieved Buster (his second in command now). As she comes out to him he, like Buster before him, is very jumpy due to the low visibility and Dunson's vow to return. "You thought I was Dunson," she says significantly ('triangularly'). Shortly one of the cowboys on horseback passes near them, to Matt's renewed alarm—a minor instance of the 'triangular' feature of a pal interrupting a love scene between a hero and heroine (as with Geoff, Bonnie, and Kid Dabb in *Only Angels Have Wings*, and ultimately based in Bill's seeking to steer Spike away from the vamp in *A Girl in Every Port*). Noting Matt's jumpiness, Tess immediately begins advising him on the way to handle fear, namely to talk it out—such as to her, or if she were not there, then "to a mirror," she adds. She gets him to talk; he talks about Tom Dunson and the ranch he built up. "You love him, don't you?" she says. "He must love you. That wouldn't be hard," she adds, and kisses him. As the fog turns to rain there, she seduces him—reiterating Claude easing his war nerves in Diana's arms in *Today We Live*.

This cinematic cluster, of her coming to him in the fog, his talking to her suggestedly as into a mirror and on the subject of Dunson—and not least, her ready insight that Matt and Tom are really inseparably bonded—is indeed a principal ego/shadow/anima complex of the series. The '*doppelgänger*' aspect is, of course, in the significant "mirror" remarks, Tess being alluded to as Matt himself, or the part of him that would be looking back in the reflection. Again, since the 'double' motif relates to 'self-encounter/splitting off', the small instance of the latter in the pair's initial encounter in the "arrow/blood" scene is underscored.

As suggested even before she enters the film, Tess is rather an "appendage"

173

or figment of the heroes, on one level. Then she enters and almost immediately begins to function in the story to bring the two men back together again, in the fashion of the 'triangle' motif which irrupts in the "rain" scene, where she is a little synonymous with Matt himself, and with Tom closely involved—like ego/shadow/anima portions of a common psyche.

Moreover, we shortly see the bracelet retroactively involved in the "rain" scene, mandala-Centric, Self-like.

As Matt and the cowboys continue the drive, Dunson comes through and meets Tess. She surprises him by addressing him by name before they are introduced (in 'fraternal pre-encounter' again). They talk in her tent, a cinematographically excellent scene with two lanterns as light sources—another pivotal 'triangle' scene. Here it is revealed that she is wearing the bracelet, given her by Matt: a Center of the 'triangle' hence, like the heart/anchor symbol in *A Girl in Every Port*. As Dunson gruffly questions her about it, she defiantly replies, "I got it in the rain." This seems to underscore the archetypal importance of the cinematographic, tactile, and vaguely initiatory 'fog/rain' motif, which takes various forms. Wearing the bracelet as she is now, Tess is Fen returned in an 'initiated' form.

Believing, on the surface at least, that he has lost a "son" and heir in Matt, Tom offers her half of what he owns if she will bear him a son. She conditionally agrees, and subsequently accompanies Tom and his new group, of hired gunmen, to Abilene, Tess seeking the pair's reconciliation, Tom seeking his herd and, he thinks, to kill Matt for the mutiny.

The cowboys arrive at the railroad near Abilene, their hopes realized. As they are driving the herd across the tracks a train encounters them. The engineer expresses great pleasure at the arrival of a herd. They approach the town; townsmen race out to greet them (the trainmen having carried the news very fast). This is all in the familiar 'group dynamics/contagion' pattern, in its ready communication and quick friendship. None are more eager for commerce than Melville (Harry Carey, Sr.), there. A beef buyer, he subsequently buys their cattle at a more than fair price, in appreciation of their "finishing a job (they) had to be crazy to start." As though it were part of the same transaction, he quickly becomes a concerned party in the Matt/Tom conflict, as did Tess. Within hours he knows Matt in depth, knowing that he will be incapable of using his gun on Tom when the latter shows up in town.

Upon their arrival near the town, Melville invites them to bring the herd right into town to bed them down in the streets, even though, as Matt cautions, they "aren't exactly housebroken." Here another motif surfaces, and retroactively brings to focus and consideration related things in earlier films. It may be called the 'sans rites-de-sortie' motif (in the pattern of group tricksterism). *Rites de sortie* are warriors' or hunters' reinitiation into ordinary tribal or civilian life after bloody and intense activity rendering them capably aggressive until purged of the same. Hence, *sans* rites-de-sortie may designate the arriving heroes' disorderly or destructive behavior within normal society. The motif and its allusion are clearer in the *Hatari!* instance with the jungle compound group which, as we will see, follows the *Red River* instance closely. As the herd and cowboys enter the town, fancily dressed men and women look on, providing a contrast.

174

The cowboys and their "unhousebroken" cattle "storming" the streets of the town touch this motif, and so do the vigilante uprising in *Barbary Coast* and the saloon brawl in *Come and Get It.* (In the closely related pattern of group tricksterism are: David and Susan's disruptive rambles in *Bringing Up Baby,* the sailor pair's general brawling in *A Girl in Every Port,* Alvin and his cohorts (and Zeke) disrupting the church meeting in *Sergeant York,* Marlowe and Vivian's phone prank in *The Big Sleep,* and much else.)

In town, Tess comes to Matt, informing him that Dunson is camped nearby with his group of hired guns for a showdown, and that he is immovable in his aim to kill Matt despite the drive's success. The next day, the two men end up only having a fistfight. Tess grabs Simms's gun and (in the 'gun-lunacy/carelessness' motif, and the rampant shadow/anima pattern of Clark, Bonnie, and Williams of the series) she shoots wildly, breaking it up, and up-braiding them like an angry and heavy-handed schoolmarm. This is in some comic relief as, moreover, the pair sit in a rubble of chuck wagon gear a little like Laurel and Hardy amidst "another fine mess." She exits in furious disdain of their behaving like boys, throwing the borrowed gun into Simms's stomach, it bending him nearly double with its impact. Here Tom intimates to Matt, "You'd better marry that girl, Matt."

Matt: "Yeah.... Say, when are you going to stop telling people what to do?"

Tom: "Right now" (smiling). "As soon as I tell you one thing more. When we get back to the ranch, I want you to change the brand," indicating the adding of Matt's initial to it, in full partnership now, as Tom sketches the modified brand design in the dust there. "You don't mind that, do you?"

Matt: (in something like feigned nonchalance) "No."

Tom: "You've earned it" (the last line in the film).

Thus the film, like other films of the series, ends like *A Girl in Every Port,* with the two reconciled partners, the insignia between them (in the brand in lieu of the heart/anchor symbol, shown in close-up), and the heroine having exited after functioning to reunite the pair, Tess being, on one level, replaced by the brand insignia in the dust.

More than one important person on the project wanted the film to end with Tom's being killed, such as in a duel with Cherry, the "gunslinger" of the group. (He and Dunson fight, in Abilene, but both are only wounded.) Hawks won the project over to his ending, which is at once dramatically contiguous, series-pattern consistent (in terms of the 'pals' motif), and easily the best ending for the story.

A SONG IS BORN
(1948)

This flat and careless remake of *Ball of Fire* is Hawks's first color film, yet none the better for it. Virginia Mayo is badly miscast as singer/moll Honey Swanson, and the brilliant Danny Kaye is somehow phlegmatic and hamstrung (as Prof. Robert Frisbee). There are a couple of solid contributions to the series patterns in the first scene, which has a strong moment in the prim Miss Totten (Mary Field) flying into whooping glee in the course of her participation in the "Polynesian mating dance."

In the *Ball of Fire* remake, the professors are involved in musical research exclusively. Professor Frisbee initially demonstrates the mating ritual to Miss Totten using Professor Oddly (O.Z. Whitehead) as the "maiden"—anticipating the 'triangular' confusion among him, Oddly, and Honey Swanson in the motel scene later. (Ref. the parallel sequence in *Ball of Fire,* discussed in the section on that film.)

In the early scene in the Totten House, as the professors take up the challenge to include modern American music in their research, there is an outstanding 'group-delineative/"circular" montage' sequence of five of them, plus one of the hipsters who have happened in.

In a quick sequence of five shots, each man utters one of the new musical terms, as follows: "Jive?"/"Swing?"/"Dixie?"/"Blues?"—with the last shot containing two characters, one a hipster and the other a professor, who respectively utter, "Bobobobadeeebobadeeboo!" and "Rebop!" This montage sequence recalls that of *Red River,* and particularly the *Air Force* example, with its mandala-Centric inclusion of the airman doll among the B-17 group.

Early, the hipster janitors (played by the musical team of Buck and Bubbles) mix with the professors, demonstrating some newer music on the piano, doing a song number, and in general broaching the subject of jazz there. One hip musician communicates the term "rebop" to a professor, who utters it once or twice, quizzically or ponderously. As they are together in the last montage shot, their close-knit "Bobobobadeeebobadeeboo!" (hipster) and "Rebop!" (professor) is an effective ego/shadow mandala-Center or "pinnacle" of the sequence—in dramatic content as well as structure. Note that this last professor utters his term as a statement of *affirmation,* as opposed to his four colleagues who, in their respective shots, utter the terms as questions. In so doing, this professor, as much as his scat-talking partner in the shot, pops up with a confirmation of the new area of research. Indeed, when he previously mulled over the strange word *rebop,* he was, on one level, wrestling with his shadow half.

Thus, the janitor pair bring strange musical tidings, terms, slang, and scat-language into the professors' midst, as a pleasant diversion at first, and then as a revelation of new music. As the archetypally relevant airman doll in *Air Force* merges with the crewmen—partly by way of the repeated close-ups on it prior to the montage sequence in which it becomes explicitly Centric—so do the anomalous hipsters conjoin with the professors, and particularly the hipster who becomes the "rebop" professor's shadow. As his involved scat-utterance precedes the professor's "Rebop!" in their montage shot—like a spur from the unconscious to which the professor responds—the elder intellectual and he are as one man, as ego/shadow portions of one psyche, in the pattern.

Although one of Hawks's three worst films, *A Song is Born* has one very good scene, namely the sequence with Louis Armstrong and Lionel Hampton jamming in a Harlem club, in 'close quarters' with a medium-sized group of enthusiastic fans. This scene, in its generally looser way, employs 'group-delineative/"circular" montage' as well. The two jazz soloists, although Centric to the sequence, are positioned a little apart in the room. It is hence the setting for a factor of 'dramatized/converged space' between them, as the montage moves among the crowd, and (Centrically) back and forth between Louis and Hamp exchanging riffs and phrases (in the call-response way), as they render "Flying Home." Here, the two musicians correspond to the (minorly Centric) Sheriff Hartwell, in terms of the likewise repetitious shots of him in the tighter but comparable instance in *His Girl Friday*. The latter example is more explicitly Centric due to its 'convergence' upon the archetypal figure of Williams.

I WAS A MALE WAR BRIDE
(1949)

'Blurred sexual distinctions' (inclusive of 'sex role-reversal') is an important series pattern, occurring very often in the series in ways comedic and dramatic, great and small. In this project, the pattern is couched in the story itself. From its inception in the story by Henri Rochard (the story's hero), *I Was a Male War Bride*, as much or more than *Bringing Up Baby*, was a project ready-made for the series patterns.

Yet the film's main portion, in terms of quality and deeper cinematic statement, is not the 'blurred sexual distinctions' part of it, but the first half which features the pair's cross-country 'odyssey.' It derives from *Bringing Up Baby*, although with Henri and Catherine more explicitly as 'pals.' In reference to this and to the motif, two bike riders in work clothes, each carrying a ladder (or both carrying parts of a single ladder), pass near the camera immediately after the credit sequence, the ladder(s) like a common object between them, in the pattern. At the inn later, Henri and Catherine request two rooms. In response, the proprietor raises two fingers, reiterating the same 'pals'/'twosome' signification as in *A Girl in Every Port* and *Come and Get It*.

Capt. Henri Rochard (Cary Grant) and Lt. Catherine Gates (Ann Sheridan) and their journey are considerably in the adventure-dramatic mode. Significantly, this is previous to their marrying, and correspondingly, the requirement for Henri to be classified as a "bride" out of army and emigration red tape. This is squarely in the Hawks-comedy pattern, of shadow/anima irruption, and sets the stage and theme for the relative farce which follows. (Here the film declines to a fair extent, as Hawks and Grant fail to render Henri's confusions and mild delirium with sufficient dramatic form.)

In the first part of the film, series-characteristic sex-antagonism mellows after a short while, in a strong note of ego/shadow/anima harmony—if characteristically in terms of a masculine peerage—as difficulties on the journey are shared. (The inn sequence is, in considerable part, beholden to the Bogart/Bacall dramatics in the early part of *To Have and Have Not*, in the low-keyed interaction between Henri and Catherine.) Though very much man and woman, they are yet a chief instance of the 'pals' motif, like Walter and Hildy of *His Girl Friday*—and as couples tend to be, in the series, managing well together as peers or fellow professionals but not as man and wife. Again, marriage is not smiled upon in the Hawks series, save perhaps in its 'pals' instance in *Monkey Business,* and there not at all times.

The point is made early that WAC Catherine and French officer Henri undertook previous missions together in post-war occupied Germany, the film's setting. Through their cross-country trek, Henri wears his French Army uniform and Catherine U.S. Army fatigues, in a visual 'pals' note (as, not dissimilarly, Cricket and Slim order the same kind of drink in *To Have and Have Not*). For Catherine's part, it is a 'sex role-reversal' touch, like her driving the motorcycle with Henri in the side-car. In general, the WACs in uniform are cinematically striking. In the early scenes, Catherine's Infantry Sword shoulder-patch contrasts formidably with a lack of anything similarly stark on Henri's uniform.

Initially, Henri enters the army offices and, in search of a particular room and bureau, reads each long set of initials on the doors. He comes to "LADIES" and, taking it for a set of Army initials, begins deciphering them, as a woman in uniform comes out of the same powder room and eyes him quizzically. Here we have a representation of the bureaucratic, peacetime army as Woman, which will nearly undo Henri in the later course of things. With marriage and its army red tape, he will sink from his and Catherine's early 'pals' portion of the 'odyssey' to an opposite acquiescence and an attendant, irruptive anima, as his role-reversal threatens to become complete (even anticipating Norman in Hitchcock's *Psycho*).

In the offices, Henri and Catherine meet again and embark on old conflicts and altercation. Catherine at one point rather explicitly threatens him with castration, shortly after he returns some items of her laundry to her from his briefcase—undergarments, there in full view of everyone, giving an inaccurate impression and material for sensational gossip. (Yet Catherine expresses ambivalence around the 'feminine apparel' exchange, and we guess that she is capably amorous as regards Henri.) As they get under way with their new assignment, Catherine, in fatigues, tosses him her skirt, and shortly he falls into some slapstick in trying to retrieve her dropped lipstick. All of these forbode unfavorably for Henri in the 'feminine apparel/object' motif. Soon they set out on their mission with an issued motorcycle. She must drive, since Army regulations dictate that only U.S. Army personnel may drive U.S. Army vehicles.

Presently there ensue two events smacking of the initiation/passage pattern—which pervades the journey, like David and Susan's 'initiatory' 'odyssey' in *Bringing Up Baby*. First, Henri and Catherine nearly go over a waterfall as they take their motorcycle into a small boat for a stretch of the way. They share the mishap, marking the beginning of their passage from battling couple to 'pals.' Pointedly, *both* exert to pull themselves and the boat to safety as a line is thrown to them.

Next is a cinematically strange and more symbolic initiation/passage allusion, a different sort of contingency upon them, or him rather. Obliquely, the little scene reminds one of the Indian raid on Tom and Groot early in *Red River*. Henri and Catherine come along a back road at night, their headlight beaming. They stop just past a road sign. Henri goes back and climbs up it to strike a match to check on their course to Baden-Auheim (their destination). Thunder sounds; Catherine notes that a rainstorm is on. She looks up as the rain begins falling (in the 'fog/rain' motif), with their vehicle's spare tire on the back of the side-car corporeally, and mandala-Centrically in the foreground of the shot here. After Henri returns down the signpost, which he climbed with difficulty, he has a white smear all down his front, the post being newly painted. He does not realize it at first. (Catherine refrains from telling him, since it is less important, in the moment, than their hurrying on to shelter in Baden-Auheim.)

An irruption, Henri's defacing is like some mark or "scar" of passage. When

179

they arrive at the inn amidst pouring rain, the innkeeper, again, makes the 'twosome sign' to them—in ego/shadow, and 'triangular' involvement of his own, on one level. Here as well, reference is made in the dialogue to a cow/bull 'sex-confusion,' earlier that day, recalling the instance in *Red River* and looking ahead to the similar confusions over the animals in *Hatari!* The next day, Henri dons a suit belonging to the innkeeper while his uniform gets laundered—a Bavarian native costume too small for him—stressing the earlier Henri/Catherine/innkeeper 'triangle.' Though it also serves as a disguise for the mission, it links with or is part of the same, original paint scar of passage—linking in turn with the funny clothing David and Susan put on in lieu of their clothes-in-laundry in *Bringing Up Baby.* All in all, the two-part defacement of Henri relates to the series instances of a male protagonist forced into feminine garb, in acute anima irruption.

In *The Big Sky,* as the keelboatmen pause for some music and dancing at one point, Romaine in a giddy moment dons a kerchief over his head and mimics being a feminine partner to Pascal, who next is shot and killed by an Indian arrow as a raid ensues. This is capably an initiation/passage instance. Although not a 'significant happenstansical death' (since the keelboatmen relaxed their vigilance and paid the consequences), it is yet an instance of the motif-consequences of 'feminine apparel,' notwithstanding that Pascal and not Romaine is killed. It thus links with Dan and his thoughts on his wife and the red shoes before perishing, in *Red River.* (Dan's example is one of 'significant happenstansical death/passage.')

The initiation/passage stages which punctuate Henri and Catherine's journey somewhat parallel those of the B-17 crew in *Air Force.* All in all, the journey gradually becomes one of egalitarian exchange. Catherine's over-reactions to the wee small stages of seduction on Henri's part are mellowly reciprocated with his very non-seductive, comradely tending of her aches and pains in the inn sequence, where he refrains from forcing himself on her.

The next day, Henri, in his funny Bavarian costume, is subjected to one more ordeal when Catherine, for fun, lets him be arrested by American M.P.'s for being on the premises of black market activity. Next—as though in an appropriate end-of-passage—is the excellent interlude with Schindler the lens grinder (Martin Miller). Henri and Catherine's assignment in Baden-Auheim is to locate this outstanding craftsman, who works in the black market, and to persuade him to work for France and the Allied Occupation. Expecting difficulty in tracking him down and persuading him, Catherine instead runs "smack into him" and finds him not difficult to win over but overjoyed to be able to leave the underworld life and live "no longer like a thief in the night." It is a fine little interlude. The film's only totally serious point, it is squarely in the Hawksian theme of professionalism. It seems to me to allude to a general series 'edict': one of professionalism as an end in itself, or as readily *entailing* ethics and morality in its own pragmatic part. That is, professional competence is ultimately "right action" in which abstract morality and/or ethics are not needed or are nonexistent, and hence superfluous and likely to "gum up the works," causing more harm than good. This is suggested in the ruthless-but-right Walter Burns in *His Girl Friday,* and in Doc and Billy in *The Outlaw,* who oppose the "lawful" but less competent Pat Garrett (who is the cause of more harm in the film than the outlaws), and in the probing example of Cole Thornton and Nelse McLeod in *El Dorado*. (This proposed 'edict' is discussed further in the section on the latter film.)

Catherine expressedly comes upon Schindler through a mutual army acquaintance, in the pattern of the (extended) group. Yet it is a 'fraternal encounter' instance in its aspect of Catherine running "smack into him," as her lines have it. As Schindler says goodbye to them, thanking them a second or third time, Catherine says to Henri, "Nice little guy." As a certain end-of-passage on the journey, and as a kind of ego ideal yet an unconscious figure as well, Schindler seems to allude to the Self.

Their mission accomplished, the pair are more leisurely returning. They take a roadside rest, and Catherine broaches the "sex antagonism" paradox (originally in *Bringing Up Baby* as 'the love impulse in man expressing itself in conflict'). She remarks that Henri and she probably like each other simply because they fight so much.

Next is the "haystack" scene, a prize 'self-encounter/splitting off' instance.

Henri dozes in the sidecar of the parked motorcycle, which is left running as Catherine goes into a comfort station. Some children gather around him; one plays with the throttle—all unnoticed by Henri who sits half-asleep or thinks the children are Catherine returned, and the vehicle starts off on its own. His eyes still covered by his hat, he assumes that she is returned and driving, and says, "Catherine, I don't mind being the first to say it. I like you—very much. And if you weren't here, I'd miss you." Unbeknown, he is talking to himself, though Catherine is now chasing the runaway motorcycle, calling after him. He looks up for a moment, the ride having become bumpy as the vehicle races into a field. Seeing a haystack racing toward him, he ducks for the impact.

A large shadow from an adjacent haystack looms across the mound of hay in which Henri is now buried—as Catherine, running up, passes in front of the dark image, in certain juxtaposition or "transaction" with it. Recovering inside the haystack, Henri looks out the hole to see Catherine peering anxiously in after him, and says to her, "How did you get out there?" In the haystack, they come to a point where, in the subsequent scene, they are engaged and making plans for their marriage.

Thus, Henri, in talking to himself as to Catherine, then suddenly crash-landing in the hay and, to his surprise, finding her outside the haystack, encounters her as part of himself having irruptively 'split off' (Catherine being as shadow, through her aspect as 'pal,' though as anima). As we shall see, the motif is as dramatically rendered with Jim and Boone in the opening scene of *The Big Sky*.

Subsequently, we have the significant exchange with the wedding ring at their church ceremony. The priest asks the best man for it, though he does not have it. Catherine happens to have it, gives it to Henri who gives it to the priest, who, as the ceremony begins, gives it to Henri. In the weddings in *Tiger Shark* and *Gentlemen Prefer Blondes*, others than the bride and groom become closely involved in the hence 'group-mitigated wedding' instances. The same motif is rendered here via the unorthodox transacting of the ring—namely, in its reiteration of the group transactions of the Centric dog in *Air Force,* and particularly the epical bracelet passed among five characters in *Red River*.

181

Also, Capt. Jack Rumsey (William Neff), who serves as best man in their church ceremony, had earlier formed a minor 'triangle' with Catherine and Henri. At their *civil* ceremony, Kitty (Marion Marshall) is the maid of honor, and will form a triangle with the couple later in the film. Hence, with the ring business and with 'triangular' personages Jack and Kitty, the Henri/Catherine marriage is considerably 'group-mitigated.'

With Henri's emigration at hand, he and Catherine consult a lawyer, who advises them that the way to proceed is for Henri to fill out the "war bride" forms and become classified as an "alien spouse." In the background looms a picture of an allegoric-like figure (like one on a Tarot card), a boyish, perhaps androgynous figure, like a foreboding of Henri's "transexual" difficulties to come. One of the least of these is his getting billeted with "war brides, babies, dogs, cats, canaries, and one parrot," in the series Woman/animal/children/anima connection.

The most interesting feature in the second half of the film is Catherine's roommate Kitty, a fellow WAC who, in the fashion of Bill in *A Girl in Every Port,* is her pressing shadow. Kitty is the one who more than once is the unwilling agent serving to interrupt Henri and Catherine in their chances to have some time alone together as man and wife. At one point she receives orders which necessitate her sticking close to them for a long stretch of their emigration trek. She, Catherine, and Henri are a strong 'triangle' instance and variant.

Kitty is cinematically pivotal in the strange little scene where Henri and Catherine come to a crowded apartment to stay the night. There, numerous others are crowded in, in makeshift beds, as the pair are once again foiled in their quest to have some time alone together. Kitty lets them in, initially throwing her shadow—something which occasionally goes with an important sequence (stemming from *A Girl in Every Port,* where Spike casts his shadow before racing out the door to attack Bill for seeming to have seduced his fiancee). In the likewise 'triangular' scene here, Kitty passes close to the camera in front of the pair with bedding for Henri (who will sleep in the bathtub). Asleep on a couch is another of Catherine's WAC comrades. Well-lighted, she is placed rather Centrically, "anima-emergently." She lies almost as if deceased and in state.* Catherine shares a bed with Kitty, and quietly weeps over Henri being required to sleep in the tub. With its tactile-functional jumble of people in the 'close quarters,' it might be dubbed the "slumber party" scene.

Aside from various instances of 'blurred sexual distinctions' and humiliating sex-role confusions, two striking points remain in the film's second half. The first is the nervous, markedly unheroic ("effeminate") expectant father pacing the hospital corridor, expressing the hope that it will be a girl (in a 'reversal' of the stereotype). The other is Henri's wig, which for a while he is forced to wear in disguise as a WAC named Florence (in order to board the ship). As they are finally on the boat home, he is able to rid himself of his WAC costume, and addresses the horsehair wig as "Florence" before tossing it/Her

---

*One may wonder if the *Red River* 'triangle/quadrangle,' with the deceased Fen, is not reiterated here!

out the porthole as he and Catherine are at last alone in the 'close quarters' of their cabin.

Here is another example of the series tendency to personify important objects and to 'objectivize' the anima. The film thus ends with Henri, Catherine, and "Florence" echoing Spike, Bill, and the Centric heart/anchor monogram (which may be dubbed "Tessie") in *A Girl in Every Port.*

THE THING
(FROM ANOTHER WORLD)
(1951)

Despite Christian Nyby's directorial credit, Hawks's influence in this film is, again, ubiquitous—from script adaption, to casting, to obvious player rehearsing and general supervision of the production stage. *The Thing (From Another World)* may be his most exemplary film where group and group-ensemble dramatics are concerned.

A very large part of the film moves through an abundance of 'overlapping/end-to-end dialogue' and 'merged dramatics/dialogue,' from the early card game to the group's last busied siege with the alien (played by James Arness). In section IV, I discuss the hermaphroditic alien and his/its 'dismemberment' instance in their archetypal aspect, and the film's parallels in Northern Mythology, all in some relation to portions of *The Big Sleep*. (Also, ref. General Sternwood's precedence to the alien, discussed in the section on that film.)

Initially, we have the sequence with Ned Scott/"Scotty" (Douglas Spencer) entering the officers' club in Anchorage, and joining Lt. Eddie Dykes (James Young), Capt. Patrick Hendrey (Kenneth Tobey), and Lt. "Mac" MacPherson (Robert Nichols) at their table. Scott, a newspaperman after a story, enters the room from sub-zero weather outside and walks directly to one of the card games, where Eddie, of his acquaintance, is playing. After Scott is introduced to Mac and Hendrey there, he pulls up a stool and sits between them, a little higher than the others, emphasizing his tall stature.

The composition here is a rather beautiful one, with the three dark-uniformed men, and the anomalous yet congenial Scott. Close in, he contrasts with them, with his suit, blazer vest, tie, bald head and glasses, juxtaposed in turn with a hanging light a few yards behind him. In this Centrism, coupled with his familiarity there—and (as is later revealed in the story) his being a veteran of El Alamein, Bougainville, and Okinawa (where he might have perished several times over, but returned), he smacks of 'fraternal return.' Augmenting this perhaps, in its ethereal way, is the empty fourth chair at their table, as though belonging to Scotty. When Captain Hendrey is summoned to General Fogarty's office nearby, Scotty leaves his stool and takes Pat's chair and his place in the game, leaving the fourth chair empty (and a little ethereal, still). (In a more or less friendly way, Scott maintains a quarrel with Hendrey, through much of the film, regarding clearance for his news reporting. This is part of an ego/shadow dynamic, amounting in turn to their sharing the same identity, on one level, in the officers' club scene.)

Scotty's 'return' Centrism is underscored in being carried over to that of Dr. Bruner (also played by Douglas Spencer) in *Monkey Business* (1952). (See the section on that film.) It may be significant that Scott's name is identical to that of the original 'returnee' in *The Dawn Patrol.*

At the poker table, the news-hungry Scott refers to General Fogarty (David McMahon) as "nursing his secrets like a June bride," placing a negative, anima stigma upon the character, who, throughout the film, is rendered in a mild burlesque of absentee, high-level incompetence. (Significantly, Fogarty's name is like that of a character in a Hawks comedy.) As Hendrey comes to the general's office, rings, and is ordered inside, the general barks, "Close the door!"—superfluously, as Hendrey was doing so promptly enough.

Still, the cold breeze from the outside raises the (loose-leaf bound) papers on his desk, which seem to corporeally mock him, as Fogarty stands there in excessive rigidity (his demeanor a function of his undue agitation over matters). Hendrey greets the general as "Sir," and another high officer there by his first name. In the short scene, the mostly silent but expressive third man effectively contrasts with the general, helping to focus the latter's petty character. After a petty reprimand, the Captain is ordered to the North Pole on an assignment.

In a running joke through the story, the general's radio-transmitted orders to the polar station come far behind the (albeit rapidly) unfolding events—this in significant 'reversal' of the more 'group-dynamical/merged-dramatical' second-guessing of the series. In contrast to General Fogarty's inept business is the group's more instinctual planning/thinking/acting in their predicament with the dangerous alien. This is exemplified in their getting the idea of using electricity against the tough creature. Early, Nikki's idea of using heat—"cooking" the (vegetable) alien—proves effective but insufficient. She comes by it in a tactile-functional way, in some association with her making a pot of coffee for everyone. Later, the young scientist wearing the varsity sweater suddenly gets the electricity idea (an extension of Nikki's heat idea), as Bob, the tech sergeant (Dewey Martin), quickly adds a practical note to it. Immediately Eddie says, "Sound's good!" Eddie and the others then hop to it without further conference—in series-typical 'merged dramatics/dialogue,' or as though out of one character or one consciousness.

Further, the sled dogs figure in a practical, 'group-dynamical' way. As utilitarian creatures, they are group members in lieu of serving in the series 'animal'/recalcitrant-anima connection. When the alien creature, retained in the storeroom, escapes from its block of ice, the instinctual dogs, outside, are the first to respond (a little in 'pre-encounter' thus). (On the plane, however, the dogs are companionably tactile-functional in the 'close quarters' there, as temporary pets for fondling.) As the group are transporting the frozen alien back to the polar station, a few of the men make fun of a published Department of Defense extract declaring flying saucers to be nonexistent. Significantly, it bears a lengthy numerical designation, recalling the recalictrant-anima-connected bureaucratic detail and encumbrance in *I Was a Male War Bride.*

Hence General Fogarty as a "June bride," since the lengthily-numbered extract is, pointedly, the stuff of his domain. In general, the polar group echo, in a fairly explicit way, the B-17 group's partial defiance of high command and the strategic dimension, in *Air Force.*

Shortly, Corporal Barnes (William Self), the man on watch in the storeroom, is confronted by the alien, escaped from the chunk of ice. He fires his handgun at it, to no effect, and races out to alert everyone. They converge upon him in twos and threes, in his panicky state. Captain Hendrey discreetly disarms him from firing more rounds from his forty-five (in minor reference to 'gun-lunacy/carelessness'), and Dr. Chapman (John Dierkes), in a kindly way, throws a glass of water in his face to calm him. In Hawks films, 'convergence' may ensue from scattered, distant points, or in one place: Centrically upon/around an object or tactile activity or an anima or shadow/anima representation (such as a panicky or otherwise eruptive or irruptive individual). Again, a chief example is that of Lily 'converged' upon by the masculine group in *The Twentieth Century*.

Barnes takes the role of a "softer," less competent group member. In one fight with the alien, he breaks his arm falling over a bed instead of in the actual combat, to his expressed shame. On the plane, he serves as steward with the coffee, in certain anima stigma (as, otherwise, Nikki is importantly associated with coffee serving, in the film). In *Red River*, he (William Self) played the vaguely 'returning,' "crucified-and-ascended" lone survivor of the raided cattle drivers north of Tom's group, as a shadow figure accorded "archetypal honors" (less frequently accorded an ego figure, in the series).

The ultimate 'convergence,' perhaps, includes a lost man descending in 'fraternal return,' who is both Centric and actively 'convergent,' like Scotty, early—and like the alien, in the scene of the group's finding the spacecraft embedded in the ice. As noted in section IV, the alien (James Arness), descended from space, is a 'returning' group member, on one level. Moreover, he/it "resurrects" by surviving within and arising from the chunk of ice. Early, he/it is 'converged' upon by the group in the scene where they form a circle around the frozen vehicle to determine its size and shape. In this oblique 'return' scene, the group of ten men look exactly like participants in a ring game, with their arms extended parallel to the ice surface.

Here, four of them make comments to each other, in a clockwise direction and back again, within a panning shot along the rear of their part of the circle, which then cuts back to a frame including the first man. Each man shows his face, either by turning his head to one side or in being partly faced toward the camera where he is. Their lines are:

Scotty: "Holy cats! Hey...."

Hendrey (breaking his habitual cool): "It's almost..."

Bob: "Yeah. Almost a perfect..."

A scientist (some distance from Bob): "It is. It's round."

Bob: "We've finally got one."

(The frame cuts back to a view including Hendrey and Scotty, again.)

Scotty: "We've found a flying saucer!" (End of sequence.)

The little sequence is dramatically awkward. Although not worked as a quick-montage sequence, it is written like one. I think it would have worked better if montage were used, and consider it to be a latent 'group-delineative/"circular" montage' sequence. Their commenting is in the 'merged dramatics dialogue' pattern, as the four of them deliver parts of what is, to some extent, one man's stammering comment.

They break the circle, talkatively. Shortly, Scotty quarrels with Hendrey about security clearance for reporting the story (although, amidst their altercation, he calls him "Pat"). Pat remains steadfast.

Although an ego figure, and an excellent officer and airman, Captain Hendrey is lent to the Hawks-comedy pattern, as one whom She (or Nikki, at least) seems to get the better of. Early, he delivers a package of hairpins, on order, to Mrs. Chapman (Sally Creighton) at the polar base, in the "demeaning" 'feminine item' connection. Nikki, as well as his men (including the humble Corporal Barnes), josh him about his wild escapades off duty, teasing which he does not take very gracefully. He has trouble remembering at least one of the escapades. All this is opposite in character to his stoical, professional demeanor and courage, throughout the film. Credibly however, he seems to be one who goes a little mad after a few drinks. This faint Jekyll/Hyde indication alludes to the dichotomously stoical yet shadow/anima-rampant alien itself (and recalls the gossip of ego figure Alvin York's eruptive/irruptive breaking out of the Jamestown jail, in *Sergeant York*). *Nikki*, in fact, is indicated as being able to drink more than Pat Hendrey can (i.e., and hold it).

Her teasing account of Hendrey's legs on display and his "making like an octopus" with her in Seattle, recalls partly identical stigmata lent to Henri in *I Was a Male War Bride*. Thus, like the hermaphroditic alien, Hendrey echoes the "transvestite" Henri. As a reflection of Hendrey, in part, the alien is all the more a cryptic member of the group. (Ref. the 'blood' scene in *Rio Bravo*, which pertains to the alien's connection with the polar group.)

Further, as the men discover the alien's severed forearm, it extends from under one of the slain dogs, as if belonging to the latter! (This is somewhat reemphasized when the arm is later noted as having been found "partly under one of [the dogs].") Hence, in addition to the hand "restoratively" coming to life on the lab table, the 'dismemberment' is initially restored upon one of the group's fellow dogs—in further archetypal identity between the alien and the polar group.

At the end of the film, the group cluster around Nikki (Margaret Sheridan) to assist her in getting Hendrey to marry her, Pat being reluctant. This relates to the series instances of 'group-mitigated wedding ceremony,' the 'triangle' motif, as well as, to some extent, group convergence upon/around the anima (Nikki, in this case) as in *The Twentieth Century*. Earlier, Nikki passes the remark that she might propose to him, at a point where she brings him a parka and his hat, wearing the latter (reminiscent of Susan and David in their "identity confusion" business with clothes in *Bringing Up Baby*).

As a few of the group gather around the shortwave radio for Scotty's final reportage to newsmen in Anchorage, Hendrey and Nikki are shown in the background, talking together as though of matrimony. But this accommodating hole through the grouped players is quickly closed again as they form around Scotty broadcasting his story. The film ends on them rather than on the future couple, recalling the ending of *A Girl in Every Port*, once again, with Spike and Bill shoving marriage aside.

The film is an essential one in its thematic rendering of group professionalism. Nikki and Mrs. Chapman fill the part of good assistants. In pointed contrast to the dignified yet agog and eventually deranged Dr. Arthur Carrington (Robert Cornthwaite), the group on the whole remains businesslike, inclusive of good humor and familiar (rather than formal) relationship. In the face of the novelty and spectacle of the extraterrestrial visitor upon them, they keep their heads, scarcely if ever placing the phenomenon above themselves— all very credibly and convincingly, as well as humanistically. Their wisecracking humor is like that of soldiers under fire.

Carrington begins forming a subgroup around him of a few of the scientists. He privately cultivates some of the alien's seeds in his lab adjacent the greenhouse, feeding them confiscated blood plasma, to raise little aliens for science—like his and the subgroup's "progeny." Soon these scientists break with Carrington, after two are killed and vampirized in the greenhouse (the alien's haunt). The injured Dr. Stern (Edward Franz) is fed transfusions from two of the other men, in lieu of the plasma stolen by Carrington. As much as the alien's vampirism, this item of the story is an instance of the curious 'blood' motif (broached with Matt and Tess in *Red River,* as well as, obliquely, with Marlowe and the greenhouse-dwelling General Sternwood in *The Big Sleep,* and reiterated in *Land of the Pharaohs, Rio Bravo, Hatari!, Man's Favorite Sport?, El Dorado,* and *Rio Lobo*). As the polar group prepares to meet the alien in final siege, "Mac" MacPherson pugnaciously declares, "Come on, Mr. Martian, and get some nice Scotch blood—one hundred proof! Nothing like it for babies!" (referring to the alien's own procreative ambitions with seedlings at a spot in the greenhouse). Lieutenant MacPherson, the group navigator, is a boyish, "soft," emotional, bookish character who seems to be a fantasy-fiction reader, plays solitaire, and might be delicious prey for the weird alien. (Thus, the hermaphrodite might not be so unerotic after all, taking pleasure in feeding, if missing it in plant-style procreation!)

Ned Scott, for all his preoccupation with taking snapshots, is very much part of the "front-line" group effort, like Nikki, Dr. Chapman, and the young scientist who wears the varsity sweater. The station cook and his assistant are isolated characters, utterly in the background and "out of it." In one scene the friendly cook, in the immediate background, is half obliterated when a door opened by Pat partly covers him, with Mac and Eddie 'converged' there as well, talking with Pat. Since Mac and Eddie are joshing Pat about Nikki, and jokingly offering to go with him to see her, it is in 'quadrangular/triangular convergence' upon her, as she is "replaced" by the shadow/anima figure of the cook there (who, a moment earlier, spoke with Hendrey, but is now half behind the door as well as behind the three men). Next, Hendrey visits Nikki, where he is flustered, and she has the upper hand in a mild quarrel. Just prior to the 'convergence' upon (across) the figure of the cook, Pat brings Mrs. Chapman her box of hairpins from Anchorage. Hence, the shadow/anima-suppressive "cook obliteration" among the three men is compensatory to Hendrey's anima difficulties in the sequence!

Perhaps more than any other film of the series, *The Thing (From Another World)* could be studied for an essential or composite yet detailed revelation of Hawks's method with players—whose character creation consists of interrelated typing, story role, and attendant actions and other directorial treatment according to character: each character in dynamic relation to the others, namely as a peer group.

THE BIG SKY
(1952)

This powerful film is one of the most enjoyable, satisfying, and exemplary films of the Hawks series, recommended as an introduction to his work (ideally billed with a good, comparative feature in one of the comedies, such as *Monkey Business* of the same year). On the negative side, it is unusually violent.

There are many fine things in *The Big Sky*. Everyone is well cast and does a good job. Arthur Hunnicutt portrays Zeb Calloway superbly, rendering one of the finest old (or early middle-aged) "backwoodsman" characters in movies, and his narration on the sound track is an invaluable touch. In a minor way, he is anticipated in McGinnis (Roscoe Karns) in *Today We Live*. Zeb also gives Teal Eye her name, rather as the cowboys "create" Tess in *Red River*.

One or two writers have criticized the lack of character depth or realization on the part of Elizabeth Threatt/Teal Eye, the Indian princess. This is well taken in part. Yet, in addition to one auteur consideration, which favors her portrayal (as a little-spoken, but important figure, sometimes in the background), her broodingly stoical silence with some interjections in Blackfoot and not least, her sign language near the end, work well and at times powerfully. One must strongly disagree with devaluations of Kirk Douglas's portrayal as Jim Deakins (suggesting that Hawks failed to achieve the right creative relationship with him). To my mind, at least, his part could scarcely have been better filled.

The film has an unusually fitting and beautiful musical score by Dimitri Tiomkin, with a "French folk song" and a "French folk dance." Each of these in its way reflects "The Year of Jubilo," a traditional tune which is used when Jim and Boone ride into old Saint Louis. Upriver, the score assumes cool, dark, Prokofiev-like semi-atonalities. The music effectively works *with* the film perhaps more than any other background score of the series.

Elsewhere, in general, prior to his sixties period at least, Hawks seems not to have willingly asserted his background music. (An exception is the eminent music in *Sergeant York*, which is a boon to the film, in conjunction with the latter's pictorial aspect.) This musical moderation goes with Hawks's particular concentration on character dramatics. *Red River's* turgid score, with chorally-rendered theme songs, is discreetly and moderately employed, and is hence tolerable, unlike the obtrusive theme music in the Hawks/MGM project *Come and Get It*.

The Big Sky's music works as well as it does partly because of its easy partnership with the outdoor setting, sequences being filmed in Grand Teton National Park. Like the music, this setting is never featured at serious cost to the peer-group-dramatic centeredness, as the group, by one means or another, 'dramatize/converge' the space (in the pattern). At times, the film leans a little upon the setting (and the music), but not detrimentally. Also, the "folk song" and "folk dance" portions of the score are taken up in the group's own music making (in the motif). In musical and in other ways, *The Big Sky* (which is not strictly a film epic) blends the epical and the dramatic in a more graceful way than *Red River*. Yet the 1952 film is beholden to the grander 'odyssey' exercise of *Red River*. Both pioneer groups travel nearly as far and as long in their odyssey portions.

As tale-teller Zeb begins telling the story on the sound track, we have the initial "woods" scene, with its impressive 'self-encounter/splitting off' instance, one nearly as definitive as the "haystack" instance in *I Was a Male War Bride*. It begins when Jim is alone amidst some woods (where curious things have so often befallen a hero or heroine in folktales). Traveling in his wagon, Jim thinks he sees something in the trees off the road, and "being the curious sort," as Zeb tells us, he parks the wagon and heads briskly in with rifle in hand. He hears a sound like that of a bird, then doubts that he originally saw anything, since a bird would be frightened off by the bear, deer, man, or whatever it might have been. (As it will turn out, the "bird" is Boone whistling, who is thus 'pre-encountered' and "pre-introduced" a little ethereally.)

Turning to head back, the log he steps on gives way and he falls and is stunned (this paralleling Henri's running into the haystack after his stretch of talking to himself in *I Was a Male War Bride*). A rattlesnake there prepares to strike when—as if out of nowhere—Boone Caudell (Dewey Martin) emerges and kills the snake with his knife. Jim, in the act of drawing his too slowly, is thus beholden to the abrupt, young dark stranger, who is in apt contrast with the fairer late-youth and ready ego-symbolism of Jim.

Although it is noted that Boone was aware of the snake and was hence alert to move as he did, the effect is one of a very sudden emergence, the cutting and editing being deft enough so that it is not beyond realism. Boone's sudden emergence parallels Catherine suddenly outside the haystack in *I Was a Male War Bride*. He asks Jim for his knife back and, receiving it, strikes Jim, very hard. Jim is as amused as he is surprised. Boone says that it was for Jim's following him. He clouts him again, as Jim now prepares to get him in turn. Here Boone backs down, noting that Jim is limping from his earlier fall. He says that he will not fight a man with a limp. Jim acquiesces in turn as Boone asks to tag along with him, Jim replying, "I sure don't want to lose you," recalling Tom's quick evaluation of Mickey Kuhn/Matt's precocious pugnacity in their 'fraternal encounter' in *Red River*.

Thus they become immediate 'pals' in the Hawks manner of relationship via violent confrontation. On one level, Boone 'splits off' from Jim, who then beholds his violent or irruptive shadow in Boone—and something of his anima, pointedly through the suggestion being made later that Boone takes after his mother's side. (Too, it is suggested, in the same conversation, that he also takes after his father—"androgynously" hence, on one level.) Also Jim and Boone together 'converge' upon the 'animal/anima'-connected snake in the early scene, in faint ego/shadow/anima 'triangle.'

In view of Marlowe/Jones in *The Big Sleep,* and the infirm Cole Thornton/his horse/Mississippi/and Joey, in *El Dorado,* Boone seems, in part, to be a shadow projection of Jim's minor leg injury (in the 'objectivization' pattern).

In the story, Jim suggestedly replaces Boone's deceased older brother. Boone retains a Blackfoot Indian scalp, clings to it compulsively, as though in vicarious, ongoing revenge for a brave's supposedly having killed his brother.

190

(As it will turn out, his brother did not die in this way.) The scalp is hence a 'friend/foe' instance in its composite, somewhat, of Indian warrior and Boone's brother. Too, he and the Indian princess contend violently over it, she wanting to bury it so that the Blackfoot brave who owned it may be whole (or wholly buried) and thus enter the Hereafter. Again, Jim spontaneously picks up the odd idea (as originally interpreted by Zeb) in 'group contagion,' when drunk and on the point of discovering his sore finger amputated. As a few of the group begin helping him look for the finger—already thrown in the fire—they thus play along with him a little, reflecting the group's playing along with Captain Quincannon's hallucination in the 'dismemberment'-relevant hospital scene in *Air Force.* (Ref. section IV, concerning the 'dismemberment' motif and the Homeric allusion connected with its instance in *The Big Sky.*) Near the end of the film, Boone disposes of the scalp himself, tossing it into the campfire, indicating his greater maturity, as Zeb remarks, "Well, glory hallelujah!" The scalp is thus an intensively dramatized object, in the motif.

Boone's bird calling, and that of others, including the keelboat group's adversaries, is used for signaling under conditions of stealth in the film—good frontier professionalism in the pattern. Why Boone was whistling there with Jim at hand is not explained, though logically it would be to throw him off, as happened. It reiterates Groot's luring the remaining Indian warrior in for Tom's killing in the "raid" scene in *Red River,* as ego/shadow, 'animal/anima,' and 'friend/foe' implications in each and both scenes are reciprocally stressed. 'Bird calling as nonverbal communication in stealth' is also used in *Rio Bravo, El Dorado,* and *Rio Lobo.*

As Zeb relates on the sound track, the reason Jim took Boone along with him was because "he couldn't figure him out," mysteriousness classically characteristic of the shadow when it confronts the ego.

Boone is looking for his Uncle Zeb. Zeb goes on to narrate that Jim and Boone, passing through little towns, "got into trouble pretty near everywhere they went," namely brawling, and not least from Boone's part—in reference, of course, to the sailor 'pals' in *A Girl in Every Port.* This contains a touch of 'sans rites-de-sortie': the woodsman elite pair in rampage upon ordinary, town society. They and Zeb are pointedly drawn as very good men but as social outcasts (as seems to have been true of woodsman types in those times). This unpopular-but-competent/heroic trait is a feature of the "Hawks hero" more generally. Witness Oscar Jaffe, Walter Burns, Doc Holliday, Alvin York (early), Harry Morgan, Phillip Marlowe, Tom Dunson, and others of the series. As much as a maverick shadow touch, this may reflect the director's real life experience with men of heroic bent. Relatedly, Hawks indicates admiration for spirited, capably "bad" youngsters (ref. Billy, Matt as a boy, J.B. in particular, and Colorado, of the series), and for strong, spirited women (such as Lotta, Hildy, Rio, Slim, Catherine, Nikki, Teal Eye, and others).

In Saint Louis (such as it is, in the early 19th century) Jim and Boone go about quarrelsomely, poking fun at the paunchy physiques of town men, Boone briefly attacking an Indian for no reason, save for the belief that one killed his brother. In this sequence, the pair readily clash with members of the monopolistic fur-trading company, rather in "unfraternal/adversarial encounter," since the group will later be their and their group's foes on the river.

Early, inquiring after Zeb, the pair stop at the trading company office and have occasion to be impolite even there. Later, the pair 'fraternally encounter' Zeb and three more of their comrades-to-be, the encounter motif being richly pivotal in the excellent early portion of the film (launched, again, by the spectacular encounter of Boone's 'splitting off' from Jim).

They approach a saloon which Zeb is said to frequent, where outside, a group of black men dance to the music coming from the inside (which is the "French folk dance," being played by a group led by their musical comrade-to-be, Labadie). One of the group of black men says, "White folks comin'," and they all pause and mark time as Jim and Boone leisurely pass them, Jim eyeing them in friendly inquisitiveness. He is somewhat indifferent as to whether or not he and Boone are shown this deference by the dancers (the pair being, after all, anarchic frontier spirits, as well as socially unaccepted themselves). As the group resumes dancing, in the background now, Jim picks up their jigging himself and prances through the swinging doors and around the floor a couple of turns with a handy French girl, before Boone pulls him away (in brief reiteration of Bill's clinging to Spike this way, in *A Girl in Every Port*). We might guess ahead that, in extension of this 'encounter,' the girl will figure 'fraternally' with them in the evening's revelry there (where she emulates their speech and yells).

All this, with the pals, the dancing black group, and the girl, is in the familiar series 'group dynamics/contagion' pattern, which is ultimately an ego/unconscious dynamic. In the same pattern and dynamic, Jim spontaneously, temporarily adopts Teal Eye's idea (learned through Zeb) of physical wholeness as being requisite for entering the hereafter. The encountered dancers, girl, and Indian idea are in the part of irrupting unconscious entities, showing themselves a little before actually affecting the ego (Jim).

This "pre-introductory" dynamic is more emphatic in the case of the shadow/anima figure of Labadie (Henri Letondal) in the saloon, who is a spectacular 'pre-encounter' instance there.

Inside, the pals soon have some pleasant exchange with the French girl—a waitress, a tall, brunette "Hawks type"—who sociably emulates their frontier-style whoops, as "one of the boys," yet neither whorishly nor as a stereotypical waitress. She is able to participate in their drinking song with them ("Whiskey Leave Me Alone," used later in *Hatari!*). Communication across language barriers, of English, French, and Blackfoot, is a pattern in the film, in the tactile-tending, preverbal way (with its oblique relationship to 'second-guessing/merged dramatics'). The French girl shares not Jim's but, significantly, Boone's drink, in reference to his anima aspect, as well as to his being one who (relatedly) will "get the girl" in the end, namely Teal Eye.

As Jim and Boone initially enter the saloon and immediately "bump into" the French girl, she is closely juxtaposed with the musicians, and particularly their leader, the pair's future comrade Labadie, playing a concertina, and placed as her "shadow/animus" here. Although the sequence will center on Jim and Boone's singing at the bar, with a few guests joining in, in a fringe way, Labadie remains prominent, and a prime-moving Center of the room and its activity. Herethrough, he is 'fraternally pre-encountered,' actually meeting Jim and Boone only later, when they remember him as the musician who backed their drinking song (in a shadowy way). As a member of the upriver crew, he is a handy entertainer, and hence on the "effeminate" side, but also "the best cook on the river" in that note of professionalism as well.

The saloon, in its ways of ego/shadow/anima 'encounter' bears some special place-significance. As the Frenchmen are of anima aspect in the film, the place —with the French girl—is lent this aspect, and anticipates the pronounced "anima hotel" in *Rio Bravo*. As the hotel is significantly a place of mishap for the heroes, it may be significant that in the "French saloon," the pals get into trouble and thence into jail again. Both places have a precedent in the saloon in *To Have and Have Not*, which has something of this archetypal focus in its shadow/anima-relevant figures in the musical Cricket and Slim.

The earlier 'encountered' trading company men come to the "French Saloon" to pick a fight with Jim and Boone, whom they know are looking for Zeb, their aim being to break up any free-trading expedition before it can begin. As the pals finish their drinking song, one of the opposing group remarks, "He [Zeb] ain't much, but hog-callin' won't fetch him." Jim and Boone land in jail for the ensuing brawl. The pair are apparently foiled in their quest to find Zeb. But as Boone hops to the upper bunk he lands on a man asleep there, who, roused, is none other than Zeb Calloway. Zeb is both surprised and peeved to be running into his own kin in jail (in Boone Caudell). He and Boone immediately quarrel and have a little skirmish, Zeb beating him to the punch, saying, "You ain't forgot what I learned you, but you're slower 'n scat," indicating the small bullet pouch fallen from Boone's hand. Jim picks it up, saying, "So that's how you can hit so hard"—the bullet pouch being suddenly revealed as a story-involved 'dramatized object' (reiterating the thug Canino's similar use of a roll of coins in *The Big Sleep*). Thus do the pair 'fraternally encounter' Zeb, not ahead of time, but very abruptly. As Jourdonnais (Stephen Geray) and Romaine (Buddy Baer) arrive to rescue Zeb from jail for the trading expedition, one of the pals notes Romaine's great size, as Zeb and Jourdonnais talk through the bars. Romaine waves the pair a smiling greeting, though he and they are not as yet acquainted—save through their being acquainted, and obviously having things in common, with Zeb. Here is a 'fraternal encounter' slightly ahead of time. The combination of the 'encounter' factor and the quiet abruptness of the shot of him as he silently smiles and waves (edited in amidst the scene's conversational busyness) functions a little mandala-Centrically, like a sunrise (considerably recalling the shot of Dutchy as he summarily interjects with "drinks on the house!", in *Only Angels Have Wings*). The anomaly of Romaine's great size also contributes to his mandala-Centrism here.

Jim and Boone get released with Zeb and tag along with him and the Frenchmen, wishing to join them in their plans, whatever they might be. They go to the "French saloon" to get Labadie, who is fairly drunk by now—Jim and Boone expressing some amused surprise in their "retroactive encounter" with the man whom they did not formally meet but now remember (like an unconscious entity previously felt, and now emerging).

Fog is setting in as, from here, there ensues an outstanding sequence. The sequence is a study in stealth, as they row out to the keelboat in secret and slip quietly upriver, past the trading company inspection point, to begin their private venture as yet undetected. As little is spoken, save quietly, the sequence is all the more sensation-functional, with the skillful negotiation in the low visibility.

They get into a rowboat and row quietly out to the *Mandan* (the keelboat's name). As their rowboat goes under a very low pier, moving toward and past the camera, the shadow/anima figure Labadie (in a 'blurred sexual distinctions'/anima note) lies in the bow in such a way as to cryptically suggest a ship's female figurehead! As they signal, back and forth through the fog in low voices, with the word "Mandan," it is with a musical touch, almost ritual-like. As they come aboard and prepare to shove off, Jourdonnais makes the sign of the cross in prayer that they will successfully elude the inspection point in the fog. This is perhaps the only (jointly) congruous, positive, and relatively unmitigated religious point of the series. Like the visual joke of Labadie-as-figurehead, it functions mandala-Centrically, and goes in character with the Frenchmen, who express feeling-function (out of the Jungian quaternity) and "female principle." The fancier Frenchmen are joshed by Zeb, on the trip, though they are not shown to be at a crucial professional disadvantage. Moreover, the French emotionalism rubs off some on the harder Anglo-buckskin types through the story.

The relaxed, studied imagery of the Frenchmen miscellaneously dressed, though with touches of native costume, rowing together in the fog with muffled oars, is inspired, like the entire sequence. (It is one for film connoiseurs.) Later imagery of keelboat teamwork is nearly as good.

Others on deck are told by Jourdonnais to get some sleep there. One Frenchman, the one with the eye patch, restlessly goes below deck for wine or liquor. Here—anomalously popping up amidst the silent stealth at hand—a woman's exclamation of surprise is heard. Hearing this, the men are surprised and concerned that a woman—"Une femme!"—is on board below deck. Zeb, obviously knowledgable of why she (whoever she is) is there, but mum, says to Jim, "Like he says hoss, better get some sleep." The one-eyed Frenchman's running into Her (the anima) in this abrupt, somewhat disadvantageous way, portends ill for him, as the pattern runs. He will be the doomed maverick of the group, as we shall see, an undisciplined one undergoing the initiation/passage of getting killed finally.

The crew have not yet been told of the Indian princess and her part in the business venture at hand; she will be used as a "hostage," in Zeb's quaint way of putting it. Quaintly too, and in character, Jourdonnais puts it, "Hostage.... she will protect us," namely in trade with the Blackfeet upriver, who will be very glad to get her back. (It is, probably in oblique allusion to the Virgin Mary, in the French way. Teal Eye might be considered an unusual, Hawks-style variant of the same!)

Like the classical yin and yang, this point of character contrast in dialogue between Zeb and Jourdonnais exemplifies the contrast between the Anglo types (in Zeb, Jim, Boone, and a minor character called Pete) and the French who, more colorfully clad, are 'always prettyin' themselves up' and, though very spirited, are not so competent nor capably ruthless as Zeb, Jim, and Boone.

Even so, Jourdonnais, at a crisis in the trip, shoots one of the group to keep the rest from turning back, which Zeb reports, adding, "He's got plenty of sand, that Frenchman." (This of course reiterates Tom and wilderness law in *Red River*.) The French/Anglo group dichotomy echoes the contrast between Hildy, with her more compassionate or complex "woman's touch" in her work, and the crudity of the other reporters, in *His Girl Friday*. In general though, Zeb, Jim, and Boone, in that order of competency, are drawn in a better professional light—their adventure-dramatic character contrasting with the somewhat Hawks-comedic pattern of the Frenchmen, at least as exemplified in Jourdonnais and Labadie. The Anglos' gradually partaking, more, of French feeling-function, recalls Geoff's character improvement at the influence of Bonnie in *Only Angels Have Wings*.

The morning after the "fog" scene, they pull ashore, and the probing, archetypally relevant "jug" scene ensues.

As the group, unloading some items, bounce down the gangplank ashore (to the "folk dance" music on the sound track), Jourdonnais brings one of the whiskey jugs up to Jim, Boone, and Zeb (who is drawn as a moderate alcoholic in the story). Just as they start to imbibe, they stop short, as Teal Eye leaves the boat, revealing herself for the first time in the film. Here Jim's hands freeze upon the jug in a statuesque pose, as he refrains from taking it from one of the others. Her face covered with a blanket, she walks past them and the quieted group and into the woods. Everyone is then roused. Jourdonnais, in a fit of agitation, calls the group together, stands on some high ground, and makes an informal speech explaining her presence and revealing the plan, which is to return the Blackfoot nation's lost princess to them for trading privileges, adding that once they start, there is no turning back for anyone, and that no one is to touch the Indian girl, or "Mr. (Zeb) Calloway will shoot." He urges them to talk, to discuss it, for now is the time to turn back if at all. A 'group-delineative/"circular" montage' sequence moves around the group of men, beginning and ending on Jourdonnais. Soon they are all affirmative—although the one-eyed Frenchman expresses befuddlement, mixed feelings. Then—simultaneous with the Indian girl's returning past them to the boat, her face still covered—the jug resumingly is passed around, as cups are out for drinking and nearly all are merrily resolute. Next are two shots respectively of Boone and Jim grinning at one another across a short distance at the cleverness or audacity of the plan, or in some sense of "look at what we've gotten ourselves into now."

The jug, a 'dramatized object' par excellence, is (in a deeper way than the figure of Jourdonnais) a group-focusing Center (and the slightly removed Center of the "circular" montage sequence). It is juxtaposed with the anima in the emerging Indian princess as her (irruptive) passing to and fro brings, respectively, (1) crisis/emergence and (2) a group resolution of the same—as these in turn focus around the jug in a tactile manner and in relation to Her.

Once again, as in many instances in the series, the pattern of the 'transacted/dramatized object' involves the sensation-function, the anima, and mandala-Centrism (or a composite expression of the Self), by way of a 'convergence' upon the object by more than one character (in this case the group).

The same jug (or one exactly like it) figures in the 'dismemberment' scene around Jim as, centrally, he and Zeb get drunk from the jug for Jim's frontier surgery.

Another jug-focusing is part of a sequence for apt comparison with the inceptual "jug" scene: the "song/campfire" sequence, fairly early in the film, with its stark, wry sense of sexual conflict. It includes the encounter of the shadow figure, Poor Devil, with the group. As the group rests around the campfire, Labadie plays his concertina, one man strums a guitar, and another sings the "French folk song" of the film score. It is a lonesome love song, as one Frenchman describes it to Jim and Boone, of a man separated from his woman—to a slow montage around the attentive group. One Frenchman emits a tear, in character. "That music really gets inside a man, don't it?" Boone remarks to Jim. Again Teal Eye passes to and fro in a Centric way.

She comes to the fire carrying a gourd, where the pot is on, stoops down, takes a burning stick from the fire, and as she raises it to blow out the flame, her face firelit thus, she throws a threatening look at Boone (they being in deadly rivalry now over the Blackfoot scalp which he clings to as if it were his lost brother). She dips the stick into the pot (seemingly to check how much food is left), then takes some of its contents in the gourd and leaves the way she came. Jim says to Boone that he thought she was going to shove the burning stick into Boone's face. (Earlier, after Boone's first skirmish with her over the scalp, Jim indicates that he had better sleep with one eye open. "Any good at one-eyed sleepin'?" he chuckles, derisive of Boone's immaturity in the scalp matter.) Thus the anima emerges again, and in the pattern of the love-impulse expressing itself in conflict, as Boone and she later get together, by way of fighting and bloodletting over the scalp, and eventually "marry."

The scene is interrupted by the arrival of Poor Devil (Hank Worden), who is at first shot at by Romaine who is standing watch. We next hear Poor Devil's chronic laughter, ahead of his entering their camp from out of the woods. Poor Devil is a very interesting, focal character: familiarly "Hawksian" somehow, yet not clearly precedented—or not seemingly—though reminding one of the similarly severe alcoholic Eddie in *To Have and Have Not*. (Late in the film we see who, in the series, he reiterates.) Vaguely he anticipates the excellent (nonalcoholic) Red Buttons/Pockets in *Hatari!* each being the odd one of his group, and partaking of more absolute shadow character, verging on archetypal clown/trickster. Norman Alden/John Screaming Eagle accrues somewhat to this standing or category in *Man's Favorite Sport?*

Like Teal Eye, Poor Devil speaks almost no English—though he readily utters, "Whiskey?" As they encounter him, Zeb, well-traveled in Blackfoot country, remarks, "I run onto him every once in a while," in a note of the extended-group pattern. Poor Devil proffers a pair of slain wild turkeys for a few draughts or more from the same (oval) jug. As he prepares to drink, he is sharply interrupted by Teal Eye (as she emerges again). She confronts and reprimands him briefly in their own language for being alcoholically disgraceful there, at which he is submissive, in a touch of the series-comedic 'sex role-reversal' pattern. In her reemergence thus, and focusing on the jug as it does, and with Poor Devil's interruption from drinking, the earlier "jug" scene is reiterated.

Realizing who she is, the derelict Blackfoot will remain with the group throughout the trip, Zeb explains. "We couldn't get shy of him now," he says.

At the successful end of the trip, he is shown in the role of a congenial play-mate/leader of the Indian children in the Blackfoot village. In the trading there, among the Indians and the keelboat group, he has acquired a rifle (in lieu, now, of his bow and arrow) and sports a flashy new blanket. It is one of the three or four he has acquired, and, it is noted, he wears a different one whenever he shows himself. As the tribe gather on the shore, in send-off to the *Mandan* group, he is shown from the rear (significantly at the unexclusive rear end of the Indian assemblage), waving the keelboat group goodbye, raising his new rifle awkwardly up and down.

We see the design on his blanket, a large lateral cross, an x in the motif. Indeed, the half-mad Poor Devil, with his proud new gun and wardrobe of fancy (anima-relevant) blankets, is none other than the gaudy Tony of *Scarface* (who bore an x in the scarred tissue of his cheek), with the Indian children, just earlier, in the part of the gangsters! Thus we finally see who Poor Devil reiterates.

An excellent tracker however, he serves the keelboat group's purpose once or twice—becomes one of them, and not just a tagger-along. Hence the rifle is like a token of "graduation" (initiation/passage), much as the Tommy gun was for Tony, or a boost to the latter's "career," at least. Boone's double-barreled rifle, at which Jim earlier pokes fun (yet which proves very useful at one point), is traded to the Black Foot chief in connection with Boone's marriage to Teal Eye. A shadow/anima-related object, it too reiterates Tony's machine gun.

In character, Jourdonnais sports a flashy blanket from the trading—the flashiest one of all, like the Biblical coat of many colors. Further, it is noted that Poor Devil got his (Indian) blankets from Jourdonnais, in the round-about 'object-transactions' of the trading there.

Midway in the film, the one-eyed Frenchman, in character, makes a pass at Teal Eye and is given some disciplinary lashes at the stake. His bad eye corresponds to Dan's stuttering, early in *Red River*. He later dies, as Streak (Jim Davis) and the trading company group knife him while he inattentively stands his watch—namely as he stoops down to get a drink from the river, his bad eye hence not at fault. Hence, unlike Dan, he is irresponsible. "That were easy," Streak says, in certain derogation, as they abduct Teal Eye and proceed to sabotage the boat.

Earlier, Jim lends Teal Eye his knife for protection against any more violations of the rule that she is not to be molested. Teal Eye and Boone tangle again over the scalp, and she wounds him badly with the loaned knife, then helps nurse him. She pours whiskey in his wound, taking affectionate pleasure at his discomfort at it (as Groot tends a wound of Tom's with the same disinfectant and humor, in *Red River*), and as a jug is focused upon once again. Boone is to be whipped later, after he heals, but this disciplining never transpires.

Jim's loaning his knife to Teal Eye is stage two in the film's series of knife exchanges, in object/tactile communication and relationship, rich with 'friend/foe' overtones. Initially, Boone has his knife handed back to him from Jim after killing the rattlesnake, the exchange closely involved with their getting acquainted in fraternal 'self-encounter.' Next, Jim lends his to Teal Eye who wounds Boone with it. Then Boone, at one point in his initial act of trust toward her, lends his to Teal Eye as they pass through hostile Crow country. There Jim is lost and wounded, and Boone goes in search of him, Teal Eye following, insistent upon helping, hence forming a threesome. In the story there is a minor 'triangular' relationship among them.

Lastly, when Boone goes to her tepee, he hands her his knife in demonstrative peaceful intention and trust, as she then, in a little act of love, cuts the thong holding up the curtain to the entrance, then throws the knife down as the camera lingers on it—this being the consummation of their "wedding."

Immediately the scene cuts to a brave unleashing an ear-piercing cry as the marriage celebration commences—with the curtain having closed on her tepee. The braves begin whooping and dancing around the bonfire, Poor Devil among the most exuberant. Shortly, Boone emerges from the tipi to quizzically regard the celebration, and is informed by Zeb that he is married, simply by having gone into her tipi with the curtain closing. He hovers or wavers between Teal Eye's tipi and the braves dancing around the fire, then goes back inside. Vaguely, this echoes Bonnie starting back to home and hearth but returning to the masculine air-mail group in *Only Angels Have Wings*—only it is reversed here, in reference to Boone's anima aspect.

After Jim is rescued, Boone and he, with Poor Devil and Teal Eye, hide from the Crows in a cave. There Boone operates on Jim by firelight—with a knife again—to remove a Crow bullet, around which the pair's friendship is very focal, there in the medium low-lighting, as Jim thanks Boone for coming after him. The extracted bullet becomes hard proof of Streak's selling guns and ammunition to the Crows and setting them onto the keelboat group. The pals compare it with one of Streak's bullets in the latter's camp (Zeb and others keeping the adversaries at gunpoint). As the evidence is presented that both came from the same bullet-mold, the two groups shoot it out, and the trading company forces are defeated.

Hence, the bullet is an 'object-transactional' focus for Streak's shady doings with the Crows, Boone's fraternal doctoring of his friend, and primitive frontier justice against the trading-company adversaries. In the film, as in the series in general, bloodletting or painful imposition function in adversarial conflict, in friendship, love, and more complex or profound combinations of the same. (Also ref. the 'blood' motif.) This we will note particularly in the 'friend/ foe' patterning in *Rio Bravo*, which is anticipated in *The Big Sky* in Streak and his group, the *Mandan* crew's adversaries. Professional thugs hired by the trading company, they play dirty and are somewhat cowardly, but not particularly villainous. Streak shows concern for his men, more like a good sergeant than the "polecat" that Zeb calls him. His stark patch of white hair, likened to an Indian's white feather, may be said to accrue to some anima allusion, as a Centric thing. He and a resistant, hateful Jourdonnais engage in business talks, just prior to the pals' arriving there with the incriminating bullet extracted from Jim. All in all, the trading company thugs are not so much villains/enemies as they are competitors.

After Streak is killed and his group defeated, his remaining forces are, in the 'friend/foe' way, enlisted to hunt for Teal Eye, who fled the siege on a horse.

Earlier, the *Mandan* group, rifles ready, descend upon an outpost of the trading company to extort beans and flour destroyed in connection with Streak's attempt to burn their boat. In a subtle 'friend/foe' note, Zeb knows where the food is stored, and directs one of their party to those shelves. (Seemingly, he once worked for the trading company.) They have hard words with McMasters (Paul Frees), the company mogul, and with Streak there, which nearly results in Jim's assaulting Streak (which would be a poor tactic under the circumstances). This is interrupted by a fit of laughter on Poor Devil's part—as is his penchant at odd, though appropriate moments, as he vaguely follows the English communication in the film. Jim says to Streak, whom he nearly attacked, "It's a good thing [for you] he laughed." 'Group dynamically/contagiously' here, one member's spontaneous mirth is like an instinct on Jim's own part (in the ego/unconscious dynamic), as he aptly restrains himself. As they are leaving, Poor Devil is grabbed for a hostage. He emits a worried look, as though fearing the group will not consider him sufficiently worth rescuing. They quickly though riskily gain his return to the fold; he then renders another laughing fit.

In this scene, Poor Devil recalls the shadow figure of Uncle Lige in the "porch" scene in *Sergeant York*, as Uncle Lige emits independent utterances of Bible verse which participate aptly in the main dialogue/action. Again, this is in the 'merged dramatics/dialogue' pattern (in which a character or characters participate within one or more others' private dramatic space, often rather demonstrably so). Uncle Lige "adeptly" interjects within the dialogue-space of Alvin, Zeb Andrews, and Gracie, as Poor Devil moves closely with Jim, like a creative shadow entity.

McMasters, Streak's boss, is drawn unfavorably as a frontier czar type who, in Zeb's words, "ain't got sand enough to do his own dirty work, and so he hires polecats like [Streak and his men] to do it for him." A flawed, anima-encumbered character, he is well-spoken, in a French accent, poised and businesslike, though rather defeatist under the circumstances. He is very fancily clad (and dubbed "fancy pants" there, in the derogatory 'fancy apparel' note), and significantly is lame. These features respectively reiterate Dan's thoughts of red shoes and his stuttering, in *Red River*.

The Big Sky features an instance of 'fraternal return.' Near the end of the trip, with Teal Eye, Jim, Boone, and Poor Devil still missing , the boat crew are nearly stalled in their physical progress in shallow water. At this point of seeming defeat, who should show up but a large contingent of Blackfeet on horseback, led by their chief. Thinking at first that it is the Crows again, the crew man the guns, but stop in time as Zeb recognizes the tribe and realizes that Teal Eye must have made it home and sent them. This of course echoes the Abilene trainmen summoning the townsmen out to meet the cowboys and herd in *Red River* (in the extended-group-dynamical pattern). The mass scene is very tastefully handled, de-emphasizing, though not eliminating, panoramic effect, with camera placement closer to and amidst the braves and their chief. The chief earnestly signals friendship then gives curtly gestured commands in the towing of the boat home. Approximately here—and as we have seen the boat's name *Mandan* on the bow—who should come over the hill on the left bank but Jim, Boone, and Poor Devil, showing up in time to behold the boat being thus towed to the Blackfoot shore and village! The crew catches sight of them and waves greeting, in lieu of exclaiming, "You're just in time!", which would be more explicitly in the motif. Just in time they are, though, and displaying the rich accouterment of their adversaries' horses (the anomalous/ "surprise" element). (We know that they are the late Streak's horses, since Zeb, narrating on the sound track just earlier, tells of Jim, Boone, and Poor Devil enlisting Streak's remaining forces to search for Teal Eye. This 'friend/ foe' juxtaposition echoes that of the 'return' motif's prototypical inclusion of the enemy airman in the *Dawn Patrol* instance.)

Altogether, it is a sizeable 'convergence' upon the boat (and its Centrically depicted *Mandan* lettering), involving Teal Eye (ashore) and her Blackfoot emissaries, the crewmen, and particularly the victorious 'returnees' bearing the adversaries' horses.

Although not his best film, *The Big Sky* may well be Hawks's most representative work. Certain of the woods scenes are not as cinematographically naturalistic as the rest of the outdoor sequences, and mar the overall visual style. The dramatics, though seldom outstanding, are at least evenly good.

The series "best" would select portions from numerous works. A fair number of Hawks films are, one way or another, "indispensable," but none are a sufficient composite of quality *and* kind to cover or represent the entire series. The work coming closest to the honor is probably *His Girl Friday,* in its rich and vital mergence of series dramatic and comedic factors. *The Twentieth Century* also achieves this in good measure, as, in its way, *The Big Sky* does in the Anglo/French duality of the group and its interacting, interchanging realms. In turn, the well-rendered Indian factor provides a less talkative but eminent background foil to both Anglo and French.

(The most *dramatically* outstanding Hawks films are, probably, *Only Angels Have Wings* and *To Have and Have Not.* All things considered, *The Twentieth Century* is, I think, a better film than *Scarface;* and *The Thing [From Another World]* is probably Hawks's most comprehensive showpiece of his ensemble-dramatics and the attendant methods with players.)

THE RANSOM OF RED CHIEF
(EPISODE FROM
O. HENRY'S FULL HOUSE)
(1952)

More than the alien in *The Thing (From Another World)*, J.B. (Lee Aaker) is the most central or essential archetypal figure of the Hawks series, in his combination of fantasy and realism and in his being a composite of so many diverse archetypal figures of the series.

In the night scene by the campfire, with a lantern juxtaposed behind him, he aptly constitutes a numinous image. A backwoods boy of seven or eight years, he is precociously formidable, yet ultimately friendly to his two kidnappers (a 'pals' pair of Hawks-comedic types in Oscar Levant/Bill and Fred Allen/Sam). In this shadowy threesome, he echoes the 'triangular,' archetypally-relevant steward in *Corvette K-225*. On the dramatic level and in other ways, J.B. and his switchblade knife reflect Teal Eye in her taciturnity and her knife-wielding violence "contra" Boone (becoming love) in *The Big Sky*.

In the story, J.B. proves too tough for his abductors who finally pay his parents to take him back. As a terror to his backwoods community, he partakes of the ego figure, Alvin York of *Sergeant York*, and the more shadowy Tony of *Scarface*. As a kid fierce beyond what should be considered his state of childhood, he reflects young Matt (Mickey Kuhn), who impresses Tom and Groot with his reckless pugnacity in *Red River*. J.B. is likewise on a certain par with the rather mature boys in *Gentlemen Prefer Blondes*, and of course with the kids who, with Barnaby, play Indian and scalp Hank in *Monkey Business*.

In his fantastic liaison with a dangerous animal (a bear), J.B. links with Susan in *Bringing Up Baby*, and hence solidly with the recalcitrant anima. Yet he could not be more masculine (unless of course he were grown-up). It seems that his prepuberty is the special factor in his series-pattern inspiration. For this reason, he links with the omni-stoical yet anima-linked hermaphroditic alien in *The Thing (From Another World)*. Again, the series patterns reach no higher focus of archetypal relevance than in this child who is an adult, and more than that in turn. He thus partakes of ego, shadow, and anima, and expresses their roots in the Self.

201

MONKEY BUSINESS
(1952)

In the early "kitchen" sequence of this reflective comedy, scientist Barnaby Fulton (Cary Grant) and his wife Edwina (Ginger Rogers) stay home from a trivial social event during which time Barnaby, at his ease, solves part of a lab problem. He does so through his wife's companionability and her more direct assistance as well, in the series theme of professionalism and via the 'pals' motif. Thus, the couple introduce the series' only principal, positive, and relatively unmitigated instance of marriage. (Usually, in the series, marriage is denigrated as an emasculating condition.)

Archetypally, as latent symbol-formation, Edwina's black evening dress, now put aside, hangs on the kitchen wall. Over the stove hangs a rather prominent cluster of kitchen ornaments. The sequence includes the moderately tense, early course of a 'triangle' instance, which ensues after Edwina's ex-suitor, Hank Entwhistle (Hugh Marlowe), phones and drops by. Later, Barnaby and he will come to moderate violence (linking to the film's second 'fraternal return' instance, with Hank as the 'returnee'). Thus, the "kitchen" sequence involves a rich series-pattern cluster, as Edwina's dress, and (not least) the little mandala-Centric grouping of kitchen ornaments, are Centrically irruptive, in the way of pivotal 'triangle' scenes.

Edwina, working over the stove, gives Barnaby the idea that "Heat—plain, ordinary heat," is what is needed for the next step in his vitamin work at the lab. This reiterates Nikki's idea to solve the group's problem by "cooking" (using fire against) the vegetable alien in *The Thing (From Another World)*.

Later, and similarly, Esther, the laboratory ape, participates with Barnaby in his work on one level. A montage of shots moves back and forth between Esther, peering in earnest from her cage as though to direct him, and a three-quarter rear view of Barnaby as he works late at the lab table. This back-and-forth montage links the two of them, Esther being, on one level, a creative part of Barnaby the scientist, as Edwina was a creative partner in a comparable shadow/anima way.

Here however, the pattern and theme—up to now of 'pals' and professionalism—begins to reverse. As Barnaby leaves, Esther escapes from her cage, hops up on the table and randomly mixes the contents of beakers and test tubes. This unleashed 'animal'/anima play results in the super vitamin B-4, which the company and senior executive Oliver Oxly (Charles Coburn) have been fancifully seeking. Anima-irruptively as well, there is, just earlier, an instance of 'sex confusion' with one of the lab apes. This is a result of the caretaker's putting the wrong coveralls on Esther, who is then temporarily confused with a particular male ape. The pointedly dull-witted caretaker—a foil to the learned scientists—is thus a proper shadow/anima figure in the general irruption as well.

Previous to Esther's release from her orthodox-scientific confines as lab animal, a non-comedic contrast/conflict is drawn between the realistic group of scientists and the less scientific (unprofessional and perhaps "effeminate") fancifulness of Oxly and his prepared ad campaign. In short, when Esther takes over the lab, the film leaves a (basic) adventure-dramatic orientation and turns crazy-comedy for the remaining hour and a half. This reflects the adventure-dramatic/comedic dichotomy of *I Was a Male War Bride*, which blends inadequately in that film. *Monkey Business* is saved from this schism by the basically heroic stature of Barnaby and his fellow scientists more or less throughout, providing thus for a more solid story-dramatic form.

Also previous to Esther's science-fictional mischief, Woman is posited in a masculine-supportive role instead of as recalcitrant anima. Although Edwina is essentially a 'pal' to Barnaby throughout, the anima, or Her series-comedic pattern, ensues in "Esther's" remaining portion of the film. In one interlude, Edwina forces him into a feminine garment (in anima-takeover), though in the same sequence he manages to stand up to her formidable mother—to Edwina's rejoicing for him and for themselves as a couple. In other than his spectactular regressions under the miracle vitamin, Barnaby remains a considerable Hawks hero, couched in his professionalism as he is. His comedic points are his name (Barnaby Fulton) and his extremely thick glasses, without which he would contrast somewhat with the indubitable comedy that the film is.

Extraneously and incongruously, Barnaby does an exaggerated "absent-minded intellectual" bit, early in the first scene (reminiscent of Dr. David Huxley in *Bringing Up Baby*, as well as Henri Rochard in his 'sex role-reversal' haziness in *I Was a Male War Bride*. On the precredits sound track, director Hawks himself chides Cary Grant/Barnaby regarding this, as the latter persists in opening his front door before the proper cue. "Not yet, Cary." Hawks repeats, in a soft voice carrying a director's big stick.). Barnaby's quasi-delirium ceases when Edwina does him the comradely favor of suggesting that they stay home from the frivolous (anima-linked) party. He expresses the warmest appreciation of her for this, as the stage is set for the "kitchen" sequence in its 'pals' aspect.

One is inclined to interpret the Esther/Barnaby montage as the ape 'splitting off' from the man, in the motif, like mischievous Eve from Adam, and thence carrying the film into the havoc which follows for all characters, including the scientists. If Barnaby's anima takes over thus, it is ostensively apart from him—comedic victim though he becomes, along with the rest of his colleagues and most of the other characters (who unwittingly ingest the new vitamin which Esther sneaks into the water cooler like a tricksterish child spiking the punch).

Early, we have the short lab interlude with the scientists, important in the film's auteur aspect and that of the series.

Previous to this little scene, Oxly unveils the ad art for the up-and-coming vitamin, which he hopes will go far, even unto restoring youth—not least his youth, that he might better chase his secretary, Lois Laurel (Marilyn Monroe). The ad art pictures a phoenix rising from low flames. In the seclusion of Oxly's office, this ad art forms a 'triangle' factor between him and Barnaby and is lent to negative anima aspect. Barnaby tells Oxly that the ad idea is "lurid and inaccurate" in terms of what their experimentation can realistically hope to produce. (I cannot help feeling, moreover, that the ad art may refer, not only to

Esther, but to the alien surviving the kerosene flames which the group pours on it in *The Thing [From Another World].)*

In the subsequent little lab scene, the scientists together as a group, express pessimism if not scorn for the promotional ideas for Vitamin B-4. Situated near the foreground on either side of the frame, are two mechanical mixers in rhythmic motion. Readily referring to the work at hand and helping to render the scene's group-professional note, they also function like the rocking ship of the storm sequence in *Corvette K-225*, like George Raft's coin flipping in *Scarface*, and other object/tactile activity among players throughout the series, effectively bringing the sensation-function into the dramatic context.

The scientists converse there in the easy, end-to-end dialogue familiar and so effective in Hawks drama. The subject at hand is an unsuccessful past experiment for a hair restorer or salubriant. Aptly, to the foreground is a scientist with a bald head (Henri Letondal). As it is suggested that the Letondal character is living proof of the project's stark failure—Dr. Bruner (Douglas Spencer), to the background and to one side, smilingly adds, "Ah, cut it out fellas!", stroking his own bald head, thus revealing that he participated as a "guinea pig" as well. So ends the short scene.

This partly visual joke recalls the 'verbal/action-simultaneity' instance in the "bottle/George" scene in *Come and Get It*. There, Barney orders the head-waiter to remove the little lamp, which seems to irrupt again in the champagne bottle brought to their table at an apt moment in dialogue and in oblique 'return.' Comparably, the initial bald scientist in the foreground parallels the lamp, as Dr. Bruner's bald head—in its subsequent visual punch line—corresponds to the lamp's similarly abrupt 'return' in the form of the wine bottle. Further, the Centric bald heads seem to reiterate the earlier-scorned (suppressed) phoenix ad art, which is hence irrupted in another form here. This likewise corresponds with the suppressed lamp and irrupting bottle in the "bottle/George" scene in the 1936 film. (Also ref. the ironic, religious-like insignia on the irreligious Vashtar's robe in *Land of the Pharaohs*.)

Douglas Spencer's slim bald head is in fact rather handsome. Fun is poked at it in *The Thing (From Another World)*, and it figures impressively as Spencer/Scotty is introduced in vague 'fraternal return' early in that film. So much the more are (1) the champagne bottle in the "bottle/George" scene in *Come and Get It*, and (2) Spencer/Dr. Bruner's corresponding bald head in the above lab interlude, oblique 'returns' (objects notwithstanding). Since the bald heads of characters figure, just as archetypally, in *Rio Bravo* and *Man's Favorite Sport?*, as we shall see, they constitute a motif.

There are two throughgoing 'fraternal return' instances in *Monkey Business*.

The first, in the board-meeting scene, consists of a 'returning' Barnaby and Edwina, regressed to a childhood level from taking the vitamin, with their 'pal,' Esther the ape, hand-in-hand between them, arriving late to the meeting, with Esther bearing the number *3* on her bib. (Coincidentally, Esther is somewhat a 'triangular' third between the pair.) Traditionally a magic number, it now pops up in relative surprise and in apt wit. Earlier, the caretaker had mixed up the clothes of the lab chimpanzees so that now—and with clear story-dramatic calculation—we have it revealed that Esther's is, aptly, the elixir number (she being the one responsible for the new vitamin). This is the anomalous/"surprise" factor characteristic of important instances of the 'return' motif (as with the pursuit pilot's incongruous rifle in the *Air Force* instance and, originally, Scott's pajama shirt in *The Dawn Patrol*). Too, 'returnees' Barnaby and Edwina are rejuvenated ("resurrected").

No one knows yet that Esther mixed Vitamin B-4. Mistakenly believing that Barnaby has the formula for the miracle concoction, Oxly tries to ply it from him by offering him nice presents, which might successfully woo the child Barnaby has become. Shortly, several principals gather around a baby who has entered the action, who clutches Oxly's proffered watch, and whom they believe is Barnaby regressed physically as well as psychologically now. Forming a chorus and addressing the baby, they sing "The Whiffenpoof Song," theme song of the film, and of sentimental import to Barnaby (and Edwina). This is in an effort to revive him, his adult memory, and hence the formula they believe he has.

A good, warm little scene it is, in its dramaturgy of group 'song session,' and 'transactional object,' the latter mandala-Centric now in the baby's hands, like the bracelet in *Red River*. Later, Edwina, now recovered, comes upon the recovered Barnaby and the same child together, and remarks, "And now there are two of you," for a little instance of the double/*doppelgänger*' motif.

The second 'fraternal return' instance occurs as a result of the regressed Barnaby's playing Indian with some neighborhood children (who, as a girl and several boys, form a characteristic Hawksian group). As the kids contrive successfully to tie Hank Entwhistle to a tree, Barnaby, war-painted, emerges from hiding and descends violently and 'triangularly' upon him, since Hank (backed by Edwina's battle-axe mother) is now an active rival again for Edwina. With a pair of garden clippers, Barnaby prepares to scalp him as the scene cuts. Hank's hands are bound in a prayer-like attitude, in metaphoric allusion to his being a Christian martyr at the stake.

Just how he gets scalped there, we shortly see. Still later, Hank storms into the lab—indeed 'fraternally returns'—with police, and with an anomalous/"surprise" feature appropriate to the motif. It is a fresh, 'initiatory' Mohawk haircut (in lieu of Scott's pajama shirt)! He would seem to be the martyr "returned from the dead" as well. As he and the police enter, the lab is a monkey-cage free-for-all of the principal characters, most of whom have ingested the vitamin from the water-cooler through Esther's earlier enterprise, this being discovered only now. As nearly all the principal characters are there (most of them howling), it takes after the final jail sequence in *Bringing Up Baby*.

At one point, where Barnaby is regressed to an adolescent level, he dons a teenage outfit, buys a hot car, and takes Lois Laurel for a joy ride about town, in a minor 'odyssey' reminiscent of *Bringing Up Baby*—upon which film *Monkey Business* is somewhat patterned. In their psychoanalytic aspect, both projects were apt Hawks-comedy material on the story level. In the case of the 1952 film, the theme is *regression*, from adults to youths, and from industrial civilization to tribalism (in the wild-Indian game with Hank). As psychoanalysis concerns itself with seething unconscious forces, so do certain of the series comedies bring up the same, as the shadow/anima "underside" of the adventure-dramatic hero. As Robin Wood early observed, the adventure-dramatic Tony of *Scarface* bears this comedic aspect. Indeed, the adventure-dramatic and comedic modes merge in a number of films in the series.

Writer Ben Hecht worked on *Monkey Business,* and may be responsible for Barnaby's philosophical line, "What is youth but maladjustment, near-idiocy, and a series of low-comedy disasters?"

GENTLEMEN PREFER BLONDES
(1953)

Gentlemen Prefer Blondes is among Hawks's most "professional" works. This is in terms of its successful collaboration of the more recondite series patterns with a studio-enhanced genre, situation, and story (although the group 'song session' motif and the general Hawks-comedy pattern lend themselves well enough to the musical-comedy genre, in this case). Technicolored, light, gay, and good-naturedly satirical, the film is nonetheless couched in the darker, anima-suppressive parameters of *The Twentieth Century*, on one level; more so than following the shadow/anima-rampant pattern of *Bringing Up Baby* and its descendents.

This is as the "yang" forces of Dorothy, the Olympic team members, the senior Mr. Esmond and his hired detective Ernie Malone, and the French police and judiciaries darkly 'converge' upon the "yin" forces of Lorelei, Gus Esmond (the son), and Lorelei's realm of opulence inclusive of wealthy pursuers like Sir Francis Beekman. These "Yin" forces are centered around the 'dramatized object' of Lady Beekman's diamond tiara.

At the same time, Dorothy, a fellow professional showgirl, is a loyal 'pal' to Lorelei throughout. Moreover, the story culminates in marriage for both of them: to each other, on one level, yet to suitors Ernie Malone and Gus Esmond, who are respective representatives of the yang and yin realms. As we shall see, this general marriage is archetypally launched by considerable 'converging' ritual with the mandala-Centric diamond tiara in the "night court" scene. On a certain level, the wedding is tribal-like, and the object Grail-like, as though adeptly resolving the yin/yang entanglements like an elixir.

The tiara is not without its negative connotation, as a thing of opulence, a source of trouble, and as Ernie Malone gauchely refers to the beautiful, fifteen-thousand-dollar item as "that thing." (Looking over the collection of principal 'dramatized objects' of the series, we may note that each is a source or focus of difficulty, of one sort or another. This is befitting to archetypal emergence, be it shadow, anima, or Self; and properly involves the initiation/passage pattern.)

The film opens with Dorothy Shaw (Jane Russell) and Lorelei Lee (Marilyn Monroe) introducing themselves, as 'pals,' with the song number, "Two Little Girls From Little Rock." It is in two parts, sandwiching the credit sequence which, to the same music, runs in front of a pattern of dark lace (obliquely in the 'fog/rain/shadow' motif, and part of the lace-curtained set where they do the song-number). Initially, they emerge suddenly (irruptively) through dark gauze curtains, dressed in shimmering red gowns, diamonds, and white feathers, the latter in the series 'animal/anima' connection. Between them, they hold white fur pieces, which they toss like a common object toward the camera (in the tactile-functional 'foreground object' pattern) as they begin their close-knit song and dance, as 'pals.'

Juxtaposed with them onstage are two black potted-plant affairs behind them, like their respective shadows. In this note, Dorothy, at two points, moves behind one of the plants, as it shows in front of her, as she (more than Lorelei) is paired with the plant(s), in reference to her being Lorelei's shadow/animus in the film. (During the song, this potted plant is on camera with them more than its mate across the set.) Near the end of the song number, each girl clasps a strip of dark curtain behind her, briefly making a pair of lace columns thus, echoing their 'objectivized' shadows in the potted-plant affairs nearby. Indeed, the lacy pattern behind the credit sequence features two dark lace curtain edges, like a womb opening, yet as though signifying their complementary twosome in the story.

In further ego/shadow/animus juxtaposition, as the girls go backstage, they pass a less glamorous stagehand (their animus) who is to the foreground. He moves briskly past them and onstage to change the sets. On the way to their dressing room, Lorelei accosts Louie, the head waiter, dark-clad in the foreground, and instructs him to show Gus Esmond to their dressing room. In the pair's dressing room, a black dress or slip lies on a chair behind and between them through part of the scene, animus-like, and matching Dorothy's hair in the way that the girls' costumes match.

During the song number, an inserted shot of Gus Esmond (Tommy Noonan) in the night club audience juxtaposes him with a bouquet of flowers on his table, as he cutely waves and throws a kiss to Lorelei onstage. He is admitted backstage by Louie, but is delayed in his forward motion by two women passing him (recalling Professor Potts overwhelmed by the showgirls rushing onstage and leaving him with a feather, in *Ball of Fire*). As the recalcitrant anima stigma is thus upon him, from the flowers and the two women, Gus is in turn 'converged' upon by the girls (and shortly others) in the pair's dressing room. He is, moreover, positioned with the black dress on the chair, the dress matching both his dark suit and Dorothy's hair.

In the dressing room scene, Gus gives Lorelei an engagement ring, which she puts on and reaches across his chest to show Dorothy, who makes a wisecrack about it as she moves to their rear in a resulting encirclement of him. Next, Louie—hastily admitted by Dorothy—interrupts Gus and Lorelei with news of a phone call for Gus from his father. Gus reluctantly, submissively leaves. Dorothy shuts the door behind him and picks up the black garment, which she throws down in another place, nearer the camera—just as she finishes saying that Gus's father would sooner shove him down an elevator shaft than sanction his marriage to Lorelei.

Hence, Gus is 'objectivized' in the garment, in the 'triangular' way, between them, and is generally encircled by the two girls, the senior Esmond on the phone, the latter's emissary in Louis, and in Dorothy's hastily admitting Louie and closing the door behind Gus as she then picks the latter up in the form of the garment he was cryptically paired with!

In the scene, Dorothy busies herself combing her hair, handling costume articles, and moving about the room, in tactile-function contrasting somewhat with her blonde friend who, more stationarily, talks and muses upon/with Gus and diamonds. Dorothy is a little rejected there, and is perhaps a touch envious of Lorelei—along with trying to protect her from her own materialistic silliness and from her outwardly unrealistic aim to marry the wealthy Gus Esmond. In this, the wisecracking Dorothy is Bill seeking to deter the amorous Spike in *A Girl in Every Port*. In kind, the girls wear wrap-around bracelets similar to the epical, 'triangular' bracelet in *Red River*. The other objects are, again, the ('triangular') diamond ring and black dress, both of which Dorothy handles. The scene ends with Dorothy tossing a brown fur piece over her shoulder toward the camera. In general, Dorothy's movements are more masculine-suggestive than Lorelei's.

Next, the girls are off to Paris. Lorelei entertains the idea that Gus will follow her there where his father will not be able to phone him twice a day to deter him from her. In the port scene, Gus and Frizbee, a valet, trail behind the girls toting their fancily-wrapped "bon voyage" gifts (anima-encumberedly).

There, private detective Ernie Malone (Elliot Reid), whose firm has been hired by Gus's father to obtain damning evidence of Lorelei's frivolity, is briefed by a partner who wears an identical suit to Malone's. The partner, austerely professional and short, recalls Bogart/Marlowe of *The Big Sleep*. In a rather gruesome manner, he says to Malone, "The one you're after is the blonde. The brunette's her friend, Dorothy Shaw. Never mind about her; we don't care what she does."

Malone, looking Dorothy over, says "*I* care," as his less handsome colleague replies, in a nasty tone, "Have *fun*, son." and leaves. Herewith, the detective part of the film's general 'convergence' upon the anima (mainly in Lorelei) is in motion.

Dorothy notes the gaping, wolf-whistling Olympic team members preparing to sail with them and says, within their earshot, "The Olympic team? For me?" (as she clasps her purse to her chest). "Now wasn't that thoughtful of somebody. Dibs on the shot-putter." At the "bon voyage" party on board, Gus, worried about Lorelei's behavior on the trip, says, "Dorothy Shaw, I'm counting on you to keep those athletes to yourself." She replies, "What a coincidence. That's my plan too."

Just earlier, Malone, in his initial eavesdropping, interrupts a little love scene between Gus and Lorelei in the latter's compartment (adjacent to Dorothy's). Malone says, "Oh, sorry. Wrong room," as Dorothy, passing him on the way in, remarks on his good looks and expresses the hope that he is sailing with them and not just seeing someone off. Here she pairs off with Malone a little ahead of time. She then brings the Olympic athletes and others in with her for the brief party in their adjoining compartments, thus crowding Gus and Lorelei a little further.

As Gus resumes talking with Lorelei, the latter puts her leopardskin fur piece on her trunk, positioning it between them. Shortly, during the song-number "Bye-bye Baby," Dorothy will momentarily sit on the garment as she sings, as Lorelei takes flight with Gus into the adjoining compartment and closes the door, seeking some minutes alone with him. This is all in variation on the earlier 'triangle' business with the black garment, as Dorothy, once again, symbolically comes between her friend and Gus (via Lorelei's coat, this time).

In a Hawksian manner, "Bye-bye Baby" is rendered at an informal bon voyage party around a phonograph brought into the girls' dual compartment (to feign the musical backing to Dorothy's song number). Dancing in an up-tempo ballroom fashion of the time, Dorothy changes partners while singing to them, and is generally clustered with the Olympic team members, who clap with her and soon pick up the song. She ruffles the curly hair of one athlete and dance partner (which one can do with curly hair without effecting its grooming). He then sits near the camera, the back of his curly head a tactile-functional, 'foreground' Center. Other women join with the fellows in one chorus, as Dorothy moves off-camera with a few of the Olympic men.

In Hawks's stimulating way of interruption (used variously in the series), the musical number commences just prior to, rather than immediately after a steward enters the cabin beating a little gong and giving the first call for all visitors to go ashore. The commencing partiers indicate their annoyance, yet the musical tempo is not interrupted, as Dorothy still begins the song at the right moment. (The steward later returns with the last call, and is vaguely in the 'return' motif—earlier as well as here.)

Thus, the parameters of the song number are less choreographic than action-dramatic, in the way of a 'group-dynamical' chain of occurrence within a small private party and 'song session.' Early, someone is heard to say, "Who has the champagne?" and Dorothy passes Lorelei's and her four glasses around the 'close quarters' for the whole bunch to use, as able.

Midway in the song, the curly-haired athlete places Dorothy atop Lorelei's fur piece and trunk, where she finishes her chorus. Elsewhere in the room, Lorelei and Gus make a retreat to the momentary privacy of the adjoining cabin, where Lorelei sings a slow, romantic interlude of the song to Gus, who is alternately shy, sad at parting, and faint with excitement. (Mutely here, Tommy Noonan performs very well.)

Dorothy looks in at them, anxiously or jealously. Behind her, the partiers are socializing now. She calls their attention to the musically-courting couple, and she and a few of them eavesdrop in a friendly way. Then—interrupting the romantic pair—Dorothy strikes the wall, in the fashion of a drumbeat signaling a tempo change. As the couple look at her, Gus is overwhelmed, but Lorelei is not surprised as, instantly taking the cue from her showgirl colleague, she finishes her chorus in the resumed fast tempo. The partiers barge in, and clustering around the couple, take up the song again in the up-tempo. Gus, still overwhelmed, begins attempting to clap with them—just as the gong and steward are heard (off-camera) with the last call for visitors to go ashore.

Still singing, the entire party of some twenty people races down the corridor and through the dining area, to the visible consternation of older guests there. The gang arrives at the ship's railing, where space is cleared for them, to wave goodbye to those on the dock. Minorly, this rush from the 'close quarters' of the party to the railing is a 'sans rites-de-sortie' instance. (Ref. the main examples of the cattle and elephants invading the towns in *Red River* and *Hatari!* respectively.) As Gus and Lorelei prolong their parting there, Dorothy says to him, "Hey, you'd better go," and shoves him toward the dock a little, just as three ship's officers (one of them rushing up the gangplank) gauchely crowd the girls back from the gangplank, with Gus effectively crowded down it and ashore.

The song sequence ends with the partiers and others at the railing—including Malone—singing the last strains of the song, as the shot cuts to the dock where a few of those seeing the boat off are singing it as well. Gus waves to Lorelei in his cute way, the uniformed Frizbee, his valet, positioned behind him a little like his shadow (as earlier in the sequence).

Summarily then, Gus and Lorelei are 'converged' upon through the sequence by (1) Dorothy and the Olympic team partiers, as well as (2) a few members of the ship's company—much as the detectives earlier draw aim on Lorelei. (Further, in the earlier scene ashore, the passport officials are processing Lorelei [and Dorothy] at the same moment the two detectives are observing them—and with the Olympic fellows looming around the girls at the passport desk.)

Inspirationally couched in the darker parameters of 'convergence,' 'close quarters,' 'triangle,' 'return,' 'sans rites-de-sortie,' and more, the musically and dramatically excellent "Bye-bye Baby" is nonetheless as brisk and colorful a song number as one could wish to behold on the screen.

The next song/dance number is the noted "Anyone Here For Love?", with Dorothy amidst the Olympic team members in the ship's gym where, in characteristic Hawks-comedic 'reversal,' the athletes render effective male chorus lines, dressed in fancily-trimmed flesh-colored trunks. Aside from the song number's noted jibe at "male narcissism and homosexuality" (ref. Andrew Sarris's article, "The World of Howard Hawks"), Dorothy is served, in the scene, with a strong, figurative initiation/passage recalling that of Judith in *Only Angels Have Wings*. Both "initiations" involve flirtation, water, and wet hair. (Also ref. Mme. de Bursak in *To Have and Have Not*, the "toupee" scene in *Man's Favorite Sport*, and Amelita's harsh treatment in *Rio Lobo*.)

The scene begins, very thematically, with a receding shot of the Greek/Spartan soldier, Centrically depicted on the gym wall, as exercising gymnasts successively enter the foreground. As Dorothy sings and dances through the number, the athletes are, on the whole, stoically indifferent to her and her advances as they, very professionally, in the pattern, go about their working out, often in unison "chorus lines." Between two such exercising lines, she struts with a pair of badminton rackets in athletic allusion of her own (in some reminiscence of super-Woman Susan in *Bringing Up Baby*). Finally, Dorothy stoops down at the pool edge as the athletes hurdle over her and into the water, and lastly, she is knocked in herself—rather hard. After this, in a reversed attitude, now that she is thus "hazed," they lift her out of the pool and raise her fondly on their shoulders, as she sings the last strain of the song (although she is a little shaken up in the moment). They carry her a few steps left to an approaching white-coated waiter with a tray of champagne cocktails. The waiter thus emerges/irrupts very Centrically into their midst, in minor 'fraternal return,' as Dorothy takes a glass and raises it trimphantly—"initiated" and one of the fold now.

An interesting production shot of the same gymnasium set has Jane Russell close-knit with three other girls and a dog-in-arms in a commiserative vocal ensemble, the athletes standing (very unchoreographically) in the background. This was evidently rehearsed or tried, but not used in the film. Here of course is an instance of the pattern of sexual peerdom which Dorothy and Lorelei, as 'pals,' and the Olympic team exemplify.

In the ship's lounge, during the cocktail hour, we are introduced to Watson (a positive ego figure, played by the appealing Howard Wendell), Sir Francis Beekman (Charles Coburn), Lady Beekman (Norma Varden), and her fabulous diamond tiara. Malone is there, becoming more interested in Dorothy as he carries on with his job of spying on Lorelei. Watson, the ship's host of social functions, was supportively present at the somewhat wild "bon voyage" party, and stampeded, singingly, to the ship's railing with the others (in the viewer's 'pre-encounter' with him, thus). In the lounge, Watson introduces Dorothy to Sir Francis Beekman/"Piggy," joshing him as a "pigeon" whose special way with the ladies is due to his South African diamond mine (in mild 'convergence' thus, upon the Beekman/Lorelei/diamond cluster of the film). Dorothy, in general, seeks to steer Lorelei away from Piggy and from trouble.

The suavely matriarchal Lady Beekman descends coldly upon the cocktail party. 'Object-transactionally,' she shows Lorelei her tiara, which she places briefly on Lorelei's head. As Lady Beekman drags Piggy away from the cocktail party, Lorelei indicates determination to somehow obtain the treasure.

In a professionalistic note, piggy says of the tiara, "All blue stones. Cozy little job, what?" His wife is a little incensed at his colloquial manner. In a likewise masculine way, Piggy displays not embarrassment but good-natured identification with his nickname, which hence becomes less funny and more dignified. In the scene, however, he is personified/'objectivized' with diamonds, as a special-effects shot superimposes his head with a huge diamond atop his bright red and gold scarf. Along with his porcine nickname, he, a man of some seventy years, is associated again with a pigeon (as well as a python, later), and subsequently assumes the alias of "Amos Finch," in broad shadow/'anima/animal' connection. On deck, at one point, he is expressedly able to "fly on the wings of Mercury" to fetch a drink for Lorelei. Henpecked by his stately wife, he reportedly flees to the African interior (in masculine-escapist 'odyssey') when things come to a crisis over the tiara—although he in fact sneaks back to Paris, under the name of Finch, to steal back the treasure which Lorelei so easily induced him to get for her.

At dinnertime on the boat, Dorothy and Lorelei move undulating through the dining area to the attention of nearly all present (echoing Lotta's, Susan's, and Hildy's anima-consequential traversing of space in earlier films). Aroused but continuing their playing, the violinist and cellist of the small orchestra there follow the girls with their rapt gaze. Leaning across his colleague, the violinist accidentally transgresses upon the cello strings with his bow, the cellist nearly knocking him off his chair for this intrusion. It is an encapsulated 'triangular' clash of ego and shadow via the irruptive anima in the girls. Later in the film, Pierre, the girls' animus cabby, throws a kiss to a nightclub poster of the showgirl pair of Dorothy and Lorelei. Gus, next to him and looking at the poster, thinks this gesture is for him and reciprocally throws a kiss to the startled Pierre, and smiles cutely back as he goes into the club. Here via another 'homosexual joke,' two 'triangles' intermerge: those of Lorelei/Pierre/ Dorothy (see below), and Pierre/the poster pair/Gus here.

'Triangularly' as well, Dorothy and Malone, courtingly arm in arm, go on deck one night and look in the window at Lorelei and Piggy dancing in the lounge. Dorothy remarks that she might go in and break it up and indicates that she is capable of shoving Piggy overboard. After a strong emphasis of loyalty to her friend (at which moment she moves away from Malone) she and the detective have a love scene. (She of course does not know that he is a detective, and that he is spying on her 'pal.') In the relatively shadowed scene, she wears 'initiatory' black lace (in abundance), and on one level she begins teaming with Malone in the film's general anima-suppressive 'convergence' upon the Lorelei/Lord-and-Lady-Beekman/tiara cluster, as Dorothy is, in the moment, Malone's shadow with anima aspect.

In common with Malone's realism and professional audacity is Dorothy's (realism and) wisecracking gaucherie, which she tends to get away with, even in high-class company. In contrast to Lorelei's fuss over wealth and wealthy men, Dorothy, in the dinner scene, says to Malone, "I'm a hobo collector from way back. I may even find room for you." In the same scene, the girls meet Henry Spofford III (George Winslow), a mere boy, whom Lorelei ironically sought as a match for Dorothy, unaware that he was preadolescent. A bright, mature, common-sensical lad, he resembles Dorothy in his deep-voiced directness. After the girls discover that Malone is a detective hired by the senior Esmond, and has clandestine photos of Piggy and Lorelei playing "python and goat," they prepare to retaliate.

Dorothy detains Malone, while Lorelei ransacks his compartment for the "incriminating" roll of film, without success. When she gets stuck while exiting out the porthole, Henry Spofford III happens along and—reasoning that he is too young to be jailed for aiding a burglar, and because Lorelei has "a lot of animal magnetism"—he decides to manually assist her. Piggy comes strolling by; the lad quickly gives her a deck blanket, which he gets behind—in place of her body, as she drapes the blanket from her neck, thus hiding the fact that she is half-in and half-out of a porthole. Piggy begins socializing with her, of course. Taking her hand (Spofford's hand, from under the blanket), he compliments it and kisses it. The boy says, "Stop that!" in his deep voice. Quickly feigning laryngitis, Lorelei sends Piggy for a glass of medicinal sherry, as the boy adds, "Just hurry up," Beekman thence flying "on the wings of Mercury" for her/them. As the boy helps her down from the porthole, he sensibly advises her, "How can you stand that doddering old wolf? Can't you see his intentions are not honorable?"

In view of the evident cross between Dorothy and Spofford, the scene is an effective Lorelei/Spofford/Dorothy/Piggy 'triangle'/*doppelgänger*' entanglement. (This is notwithstanding that two characters posing as one, with one hidden in this way, is a stock movie joke. Again, Hawks is a creative borrower.)

Next, the feminine pair 'converge' upon Malone to pick his pockets for the roll of film. (In the crisis now, Dorothy is behind her friend's wish to marry Gus, though her motivation is sexual antagonism with Malone.) They have Malone in for an ostensive dinner party, feed him a potent drink, spill water on his pants and forcibly remove them, allegedly to put them under the hair drier. Just then, a steward suddenly enters (in service of the "dinner party"), as Dorothy says, "Francois, you're just in time." They put Malone into a fancy housecoat of Lorelei's and send him away with the steward, as Malone explains to him that he's "not a fairy." Francois talks soothingly to him. Next, in close-up on the act, Lorelei removes the box of film from Malone's pants, saying, "Dorothy, I've got it! I've got it!"

Along with the castration allusion, and the 'homosexual joke' in Malone's remark, the "dinner party" scene hosts an outstanding archetypal cluster. In the three principals we have, of course, (1) a 'triangle,' with the two girls as ego and shadow and Malone as their animus. In 'triangle' fashion, Malone is ultimately 'objectivized' in (2) the Centric roll of film, shown in a close-up at the end of the scene, as an animus-linked object between the feminine 'pals.' (3) Forced into the feminine garment, Malone is overwhelmed by the recalcitrant anima, in the pattern, after he is (4) met by a 'fraternal returnee' in the steward. The latter allusion is in view of Francois' abrupt entrance, and Dorothy's line, "you're just in time," characteristic of the subsequent instance with Pierre at the sidewalk cafe (see below), and of the prototypical *Dawn Patrol* instance. Further in the 'return' motif, the incongruous nightgown on Malone seems to replace the pajama shirt of the 1930 instance. Malone's drink —"equal parts Scotch, vodka, brandy, and gin," chased by a glass of vodka which the girls hand him in lieu of water—may be considered metaphorically lethal. In surviving it, Malone thus "returns from the dead," in keeping with the motif.

In terms of its quantity of features, the "dinner party" scene is the most archetypally laden of the entire series.

Malone's drink is mixed by Lorelei, who also obtains the box of film from his pants. In the next scene, she obtains the developed film from the photo shop run by a steward wearing a (ship's) blue coat with an emblem. Here, as though in some retaliation for the "dinner party," she is figuratively 'converged' upon by (the steward, in part, plus) three of the Olympic athletes there, who wear similar coats with emblems—hence as a group. One of the athletes tries to pick her up before she flees after making a joke.

Clandestine photography failing, Malone (assisted by the steward who tends his cabin) succeeds in obtaining a useful tape recording of Lorelei and Piggy together as she talks Piggy into giving her his wife's tiara. Despite Malone's declared intention to continue working against Lorelei if required, Dorothy continues to fall in love with him when the detective lets Dorothy know that he is sincerely interested in her.

The girls disembark in Paris. Pierre the cabby (George Davis) again chauffeurs them about town for sightseeing and shopping. Afterwards the cab is laden with fancily-wrapped packages, as Lorelei remarks, "It's the first time I've been shopping without a man along!", as Pierre, in front, is posed as an ethereal animus figure between them. (Ref. discussion of his 'fraternal return' in section V, and below.)

At their hotel, the manager takes the girls to the 'close quarters' of his office where Malone, Lady Beekman and her insurance man Pritchard (Alex Frazer) confront Lorelei, seeking the tiara, which she refuses to return to them, on the grounds that she did not in fact steal it. Somewhat anomalous shadows, and an ugly, dark sculpture loom behind the action. Anima-suppressively, Dorothy, in retort to Lady Beekman's statement that she "means business" in the tiara matter, says, "Really? Then why are you wearing that hat?"—a bowl-shaped feathery one with a little net.

After this minor 'odd hat' instance, the girls leave, nearly penniless from their shopping spree, their letter of credit having been canceled by the senior Esmond via Malone. Malone offers to help Dorothy, but she tells him to hold his breath in the meantime (i.e., that he may asphyxiate).

Next, the "When Love Goes Wrong" scene ensues, appropriately in the shadowy Latin Quarter, with the girls figuratively down and out. The song number and scene are touched upon in section V, though full details are in order now.

On the set is a tree and its shadow, and a faded cigarette poster behind the accordian player. Early and late in the sequence, the sidewalk cafe setting is medium-low lighted, with the cinematography unobtrusively brightening after the shot of Dorothy, beginning the song, shifts to Lorelei (and thence into the greater song session). Early and late, the lower lighting carries a yellowish tinge. In general, the song/dance number is in the mode/motif of 'close quarters' there. The people in the scene, who (in a positive way) 'converge' upon the girls and extemporaneously join with them in their song, are an essential Hawks group, in the pattern, and are with series-typical variety. They include: a lady flower-vendor, the two dark-clad, white-aproned waiters, a French army officer and a gray-suited man (at the table directly behind the girls), two French sailors, two American soldiers, two American couples on vacation, a gendarme, a French family of four or so, various lower middle-class and working-class Frenchmen—and the two French-African boys who interact closely with the girls; and (not least) the ever-solemn but friendly accordian player who initially comes near them, animus-like, as they begin singing to his background playing in the cafe. As the group picks up a chorus from the girls, they also repeat a "Crazy! Crazy!" portion from the boys (played by Jimmie and Freddie Moultrie), and introduce French interjections of their own (including *"Touche! Touche!"*). It is all very 'group-dynamical/contagious.'

Centric in the scene are Dorothy's pink hat on the little table—matching her ruffled scarf—and her small blue suitcase under the table which similarly figures in a compositional way when the frame expands to take in the entire group 'song session.' Lorelei wears a beret. Both girls are dressed as in the preceding cab and hotel sequences, in dark blue suits. (In a note of Hawksian stoicism, the girls have obviously had to return the things they bought on the shopping spree and loaded into Pierre's cab. Too, these objects, in their ephemeral character, may allude to Pierre's "ghost" status on one level, as he 'returns' in the cafe scene. Ref. section V.)

Tactile-functionally, Dorothy initially orders a single coffee for them both, signaling to the waiter with one finger. They push the lone glass of coffee back and forth behind Dorothy's hat on the table—the two objects juxtaposing with the accordian player who moves closely in behind and between them. When Lorelei sings the line, "When love goes wrong, a man takes flight," she looks mooningly at the hat, then up at Dorothy and her matching scarf, as Dorothy sings a line in turn. This is all very 'triangular' (with the pair's animus in the brunet accordianist, and the man in the song, as well as "objectivized' in the hat and matching scarf). Later, Lorelei sits on the table in front of the hat, as though obliterating the 'objectivized' man who took flight. This is 'triangular' as well, and in some reiteration of Dorothy's early dramatic businesses with the black dress and leopard-skin coat. Indeed, at this point in the story, both girls are estranged from their suitors.

The cafe crowd/group serve to cheer them up, and the song rendition becomes properly jazzy and improvisational in terms of both song and dance, in addition to the "folk" touch of its group participation. Hoagy Carmichael (who played Cricket in *To Have and Have Not*) may have influenced the scene in more ways than as the song lyricist. When Dorothy chantingly interjects with, "No bows, honey, just eight bars and odd!", Pierre's car horn toots—like a few quick notes played on a trumpet, forming a 'words/sounds-simultaneity' instance in the 'merged-dramatical' pattern. He rolls up "just in time," as Dorothy's lines have it, and is greeted in fond 'fraternal return.' The little boys then help load the bags into the cab, and the girls finish the song standing up in the open top, finally turning around to where more people have gathered from the other side of the narrow street. As Pierre and the girls slowly roll away, the cafe/street group wave and sing the last strains, most of them following the cab off camera. This echoes the "bon voyage" party racing through the ship earlier. In the same "spatial-dramatic" way, the rapt boys remain behind, waving after them, doing the most to emphasize the space created by the Parisians following the moving cab. Behind the boys, the flower lady goes back to work with her resplendent cart, and (in a more austere note) the black-clad waiter 'convergingly' removes the girls' Centrically-involved coffee glass from the table (as though to encapsulate the entire scene), as the scene fades out. As certain "suitors" to the girls, and as the girls relate to them a little in kind, the Latin Quarter boys link with the likewise mature/precocious Henry Spofford III on the boat.

All in all, it is a wonderful sequence, one of Hawks's best. It contains a very large part of the series patterns in a nutshell as it were.

The showgirl pair get a job at the "Chez Louis." Backstage, the girls have another 'triangular' bout with Gus who, in the wake of Malone's and the senior Esmond's move against Lorelei, has flown the Atlantic to see her again. The girls are haughty and harsh towards him. As they meet him, immediately backstage, they wear costumes with Napoleonic hats (readily underscoring their 'pal-hood'). In the initial shot inside the dressing room, Dorothy, combing her hair, throws Gus and Lorelei a jealous, sultry look, as Gus is beseeching Lorelei (who is changing behind a screen, shortly to emerge in a white bathrobe). Interruptingly, in the Hawks way, the costume matron—earlier introduced ('pre-encountered') in the background behind the three of them—knocks, looks in, and politely summons Lorelei to the costumers. After Lorelei quickly exits, having thrown more frustrating words at the befuddled Gus, we note (in the next shot) that Dorothy has changed into a similar white robe, off camera somewhere, while Gus was beseeching Lorelei (effectively underscoring, by means of clothing again, the girls' dominant 'pal-hood' there).

Dorothy says to Gus, "Poor Gus. You really have a tough time. You know, if you really want to get upset, go out and see the number she's gonna do next." Here, Gus says, "You mean ...." as he then points to something off-camera in the right foreground. Dorothy feigns a great sigh. He says, "Oh dear!" and rushes out. Dorothy then makes a very sardonic laugh, to herself.

What was Gus pointing to, off-camera? We gather, in the next backstage scene, that it was Lorelei's jewelry box. The song number referred to is "Diamonds Are a Girl's Best Friend," which preaches that men come and go, but the diamonds they may bestow remain (negotiable, in this world of recessions). (Philosophically in turn, at the end of the film, diamond-best-friends are posited as—wedding rings, given by husbands-to-be, with the pillar of marriage implied as a girl's best investment.)

The excellent, highly-staged "Diamonds Are a Girl's Best Friend" includes distant or receded elevated shots, an elevated approach shot, elevated receding shots (!), an upshot of the dancers careening over a rise in the stage, and other spatial dramatics very untypical of Hawks, indicating the influence of other direction (probably that of choreographer Jack Cole). Otherwise, Lorelei is surrounded by suitor-dancers, and commiserates with fellow girls around her, during the number, in the series dramatic/compositional patterns. At one point in the song, a statuesque, relatively silent moment features all dancers raising their hands with Lorelei toward the heavens, in allusion to "worship" of diamonds as Providence itself. This may be viewed as a series-characteristic 'irreligious' note, in its satire. On the scenario level, it may refer, in some part, to the staple commodity that diamonds—like gold—are in conventional economics. (In a secondary-archetypal way, the diamonds/gold standard is the recipient of projections of the supreme Self. Ref. alchemy and the spiritual path from lead to gold.) At the end of the film, this "religious" note in the song/dance becomes linked, conceivably, to holy matrimony, as the Loos-Fields musical deftly turns its playful cynicism to an ideal story-ending. Even so, Hawks renders his own auteur touches to the final wedding scene, as we shall see.

Backstage, after Lorelei's song number, the girls discover that someone has burgled the "jinx tiara" from Lorelei's jewelry box (an agent of Sir Francis Beekman, as we will later be able to surmise). When the gendarmes, sent by Lady Beekman and Prichard, descend upon the club for it and for Lorelei, Dorothy heads out to charm and delay the police. Lorelei receives Gus to try to get the price of the object out of him.

Shortly, there ensues the story-pivotal "night court" scene. Like the night scene on deck with Malone and the lace-clad Dorothy, and the tiara-confrontational scene in the hotel manager's office, the courtroom scene is wrought with a certain amount of shadow (which in all of these scenes does not work very well cinematographically). This is significant on the auteur level, in terms of the motivation or role of the scenes in the film's deeper, archetypal parameters: its darker 'convergence' upon the anima-linked Lorelei/Beekman/tiara cluster. The shadows allude to general *irruption*.

Black-uniformed gendarmes stand 'convergingly' around the austere, wood-paneled room. In the scene and setting, the film's anima-suppresive pattern (in common with *The Twentieth Century*) comes to the fore. Behind the magistrate's bench looms a gothic-like shadow of one of the scene's tree-like coatracks, serving like the black potted-plant affair behind the girls in their initial song number. In a 'pal'-like way, the black-robed, goateed magistrate (Marcel Dalio) is matched with the identically-clad lawyer at hand (Henri Letondal). Upon the magistrate's bench rests an inkwell with a goat statuette (discernible in a good print of the film). As the court business gets under way, a Centric shot of the wall clock shows the time to be 12:45 A.M., the "witching hour"!

217

In view of the scene's summarial, Centric anima-suppression, in common with *The Twentieth Century*, the "gothic" magistrate reiterates Oscar Jaffe of the 1934 film. This is indicated, in part, when at one point in the courtroom havoc, the magistrate comically fires his court clerk (who lapses from duty in falling into participation in the 'song session' which irrupts). This directly recalls Jaffe's recurrent "firing" of Webb, through *The Twentieth Century*.

In the archetypally-laden scene, Dorothy comes to trial shadowily impersonating Lorelei in a blonde wig. In a major series 'double/*doppelgänger*' instance. Pritchard, there in quest of Lady Beekman's missing tiara, begins to recognize the masquerade, but is distracted as Dorothy/Lorelei flies into a chorus of "Diamonds Are a Girl's Best Friend" for him, as the gendarmes appreciatively cluster around her, clapping with the song, all in a shadow/"after hours" version of Lorelei's (and choreographer Jack Cole's) stage rendition in the earlier scene. Dorothy's ruse to save Lorelei is going well.

Malone, still on the job, and the senior Esmond (Taylor Holmes) arrive at the night court expecting to see Lorelei convicted of grand larceny. Dorothy manages to communicate to Malone that she "thinks she's in love with him" but will have nothing to do with him if he foils her plan there to save Lorelei. Instead of exposing Dorothy/Lorelei, Malone immediately resigns the case (less professional now, but very much knowing what he is doing). The senior Esmond is of course surprised and confused.

Knowing that Piggy is at the airport with the recovered tiara, Malone goes there with two gendarmes who drag him to the night court. Piggy wears a prominent pale blue hat. In some fuss over it there, he is ordered, in accordance with court rules, to remove it (in Centric anima-suppression, on one level). Malone—whose professionalism now saves the day for nearly everyone —takes Beekman's briefcase from him and presents the missing tiara. In the concluding bit of court business, Malone gives the tiara to Dorothy/Lorelei, who hands it to the magistrate, who hands it to the attorney, who hands it to Pritchard, who returns it to its rightful place with Piggy, after which—not breaking the rhythm of the roundabout transaction—the magistrate smilingly raps his gavel with the pronouncement, "Case dismissed!", the shot of him here a mandala-Center to the preceding circulation of the "Grail"-like object. (The tiara is of course mandala-Centric as well, but the shot of the magistrate is entirely like the concluding summarial shot of a 'group-delineative/"circular" montage' sequence. In this sense, the tiara transaction, although rendered mainly by camera movement on rhythmic action, is partly a 'group-delineative/"circular" montage.')

The summarily ritualistic, 'convergent' (and anima-suppressive) transaction of course derives from the 'object-transactions' of the dog in *Air Force*, the bracelet in *Red River*, and the wedding ring in *I Was a Male War Bride*.

Next, in a comparable "after hours" setting at the Chez Louis club, with the chairs up on the tables and a custodian in the background, Gus, Lorelei, and the senior Esmond resolve their differences in turn, and at last come to accord on the marriage.

The last scene in the film is the double wedding on the boat home. The opening shot has uniformed stewards 'converged' around the wedding-cake table. In kind, there ensues a 'group-mitigated wedding' instance, headed by the ship's captain with the large group of uniformed ship's officers in close, 'convergent' attendance. Malone and Dorothy make an ego/"shadow" couple while the adjacent Gus and Lorelei make a shadow/anima pair. The captain's lectern-with-Bible slips promptly out of the frame, as the camera moves in on Dorothy and Lorelei side by side in their bridal costumes—as the film ends thus like *A Girl in Every Port,* with the girls as 'pals' Spike and Bill, on one level (with future spouses out of the frame). Their feminine pal-hood is, after all, the most stable or constant feature of the film.

LAND OF THE PHARAOHS
(1955)

It is difficult to understand why Hawks disowned *Land of the Pharaohs*. A generally good film, with some excellent or brilliant moments, it is patterned after *Scarface*, *The Twentieth Century*, and *Red River;* it succeeds as feature-film Egyptology, and manages well with the latter's cumbersome accouterment of the wide screen. It is a principal film in being as frequently accomplished as it is, important in the auteur consideration, and at the same time the odd genre film of the series (more so than *Gentlemen Prefer Blondes*). In these respects, it is a major triumph for the director. Like *Gentlemen Prefer Blondes* (although not so much *The Big Sleep*, with its flaws in the story-telling aspect), the Egyptian project demonstrates Hawks's versatility or professionalism as a film maker.

Like Tony Camonte and Pancho Villa of the series, Pharaoh (Jack Hawkins) perishes out of character or personality failure symbolized in his opulent attachments, in the way of the 'fancy apparel/accouterment' motif. Religious-connected as well, these are the anima trap to which he succumbs, the trap taking the outward form of Nelipher (Joan Collins), the conniving Cyprian princess.

Equally, and like *The Twentieth Century* and *Gentlemen Prefer Blondes*, the film has the underlying pattern of the suppression of the recalcitrant anima. Although Nelipher is very much the death of Pharaoh, his 'pal,' Hamar the high priest (Alexis Minotis), and the mute priests completely subdue Her in turn, with the help of the architect, Vashtar (James Robertson Justice) and his son Senta (Dewey Martin). This anima-suppression is part and parcel of the priests' own religious suicide, which is heroic because of its and their connection with the completed pyramid, in the latter's representation as Man's Work. They link somewhat with those characters who undertake 'fraternal suicide missions' in *The Dawn Patrol*, *Today We Live*, *Ceiling Zero*, and *The Road to Glory*. As the dying airmen/soldiers are survived in the unit or group, which replaces them with new men, so are Hamar and the priests survived by the completed pyramid, which is the more a 'dramatized object,' huge as it is. The pyramid recalls the B-17, *Mary Ann* invested on one level with the soul of the "sacrificed" Captain Quincannon (as borne along by the group) in *Air Force*, and the B-17's descent in Johnson's wallet, in its sacrifice/restoration implication in turn, in *To Have and Have Not*.

Like *Red River*, the story concerns a giant professional task pursued and fulfilled through the main characters' application to it and their developing relationships to one another in the course of the job. The slave-labor factor might seem to be an odd point. Yet, early in the task, the commandeered laborers are shown as having a zealous, comradely morale. For all their multitude, they are given a touch of the peer group, or its extension from the elite circle of Pharaoh, Hamar, Vashtar, Senta, and the mute priests. Later, the laborers reiterate the driven cattle in *Red River*—real enslavement, significantly concurrent with Pharaoh's decline as a man via his materialistic passion and the related Nelipher. The theocracy-deteriorative slave factor—like the science-deteriorative super-vitamin turmoil in *Monkey Business*—is hence, in its odd way, Hawks-comedic, like Pharaoh himself, and like his certain prototype in Tony of *Scarface*.

Initially, there is the splendid, tactile-functional shot of hieroglyphs being inscribed by Hamar the high priest, who on the sound track (in the manner of Groot and Zeb, respectively in *Red River* and *The Big Sky*) begins telling the story of Pharaoh Cheops. Next, Pharaoh, "the living god of Egypt," returns in splendorous procession from war, conquest, and confiscation. The tastefully-rendered portion of military pageantry introduces Pharaoh and, in one shot, "pre-introduces" Vashtar, a captive, walking proudly with his head up.

Inside the palace, Pharaoh greets his compatriot Hamar, who at one point passes in front of the camera in a broad sweep, talking with his lifelong friend in evident close eye contact, though facing more or less toward the camera. It is an excellent moment, both sensation-functionally and dramatically, utilizing the wide screen very well.

As their conversation broaches the subject of the war's spoils, Hamar recalls how, as boys, he and Pharaoh fought over a gold piece, Pharaoh winning, but Hamar finagling it back from him—Pharaoh being obsessed with accummulating gold and treasure ever since. Verbally a 'transacted object' among 'pals,' it reiterates Geoff and the Kid wrestling over the two-headed coin in *Only Angels Have Wings*. In the film, Hamar once or twice 'second-guesses' or anticipates something on Pharaoh's part, in the merged-dramatical fashion.

Next, after Pharaoh has his luxurious bath, he greets his queen. As he is talking with her, Hamar is present. When Pharaoh speaks to him at one point, though not in his direction, he turns toward Hamar to find that he is gone, having discreetly exited, and that in the moment he has been talking to no one. Having been left alone thus (if with his queen) he is a little taken back. It is a magnificent little point, mixedly of 'triangle' and 'self-encounter/splitting off' relevance.

In having been talking, in the moment, to no one, it is a retroactive allusion of Hamar's being "nonexistent," save as part of Pharaoh—namely an allusion that he is Pharaoh's personified shadow. It recalls Henri's riding alone in the sidecar of the runaway motorcycle, talking to Catherine as if she were in the driver's seat, in the 'self-encounter' instance in *I Was a Male War Bride*. Expressed too, is the 'triangle'-related requisite of two (or more) men to keep a curtailment on Woman/anima by their combined ('convergent') presence with Her—such as in Tex's pal coming beside him to assist his standing up to his wife on the phone, in *Ceiling Zero*. As such, the instance with Pharaoh and Hamar is a 'reversal' of the type of instance in which a pal interrupts a love scene between a pal and anima/Her. In this way, Hamar's vanishing on him forebodes Pharaoh's decline and fall at the hands of Nelipher, who enters the film about midway.

This early "vanishing" scene is one of the last really creative moments of Hawks's career, which goes into partial decline after *Land of the Pharaohs*. It is also one of the more creative moments of the series.

Around the palace interiors are leopardskins. Others adorn the mute priests later. This is in allusion to the stoical conquest of rampant instinct/anima, which will climax the film in the sealing up of Princess Nelipher in the pyramid tomb, the leopardskin-adorned priests around her. (Also ref. the bounty-hunting sheriff and his hides in *Rio Lobo*.)

Pharaoh, concerned to have a burglar-proof tomb for his treasure and himself upon death, enlists the captive Vashtar, a brilliant stone-worker and architect. In due exchange for mastercrafting the self-sealing labyrinth, Pharaoh agrees to release Vashtar's people from slavery. Thus they become professional colleagues, in the series-pattern way—although Vashtar will have to be entombed with Pharaoh and the priests because of his knowledge of the labyrinth. Near the end, with Pharaoh murdered and ready for entombment, Hamar overturns part of the agreement and releases Vashtar and his apprentice son Senta, noting that since they did such a good job, it will not matter if they know the soon-to-be-sealed labyrinth route, for it will be impossible for thieves to go through the solid stone which will result. Hamar adds that he knows Pharaoh would have wanted it this way, and intimates that Vashtar probably did the perfect job that he did with this prospect in mind, at which Vashtar tacitly agrees, both sharing the mild humor here—in a deft instance of colleague intimacy, 'second-guessing,' and professional realism.

Earlier, the ruling was that if anyone other than the inner circle of Pharaoh, Hamar, the priests (deprived of their tongues), and Vashtar learned anything about the route of the labyrinth in progress, the person would be killed. Workers were led blindfolded to and from the job by the special priests who, with others of the elite circle, are to be sealed in with Pharaoh. Senta, taking over the tasks of his father, whose eyesight is failing, rescues Pharaoh from a cave-in in the labyrinth, where the usual route to and from the tomb becomes blocked. Senta saves the injured Pharaoh's life by taking him out by another route, thus revealing that he knows more than he is supposed to. In resulting gratitude/camaraderie (yet certain befuddlement and indecisiveness) Pharaoh spares Senta—an instance of character relationship forming around and in the course of professional tasks, overriding formalities.

Early, Vashtar makes a point of not believing in the Afterlife in the 'irreligious' manner of the Hawks hero. As though compensatorily—like the phoenix ad art/idea scorned by the scientists in *Monkey Business*, yet popping up in another form amidst them—this "Afterlife" or religiosity seems irrupted in the odd insignia on his robe. He wears the robe with this insignia early in the film and also at the end, which recalls Mike's sweater with the loud stripe, also worn early and late, in *Tiger Shark*—comparable irruptive Centrism, perhaps. (More mundanely in each case, it is an identifying feature, and thus logically worn when the characters are introduced and when they conclude.)

As work on the pyramid begins, laborers summoned from all parts of the land converge on the site in songful esprit, in a montage sequence—panoramic in its sense of the four corners of the kingdom, but 'group-dynamical,' like the montage of the men at the outset of the river journey in *The Big Sky*. And it is with this sense that the Egyptians 'converge' upon the site as a Center, actually—and relatedly, as the completed pyramid will finally loom as an imbued, transacted, 'dramatized object,' outwardly very different from, but related in function to, the bracelet in *Red River*. Presently, and in part of the same sequence, we have the wonderful panoramic shot of the multitude of craftsmen, engineers. laborers—masters, journeymen, and plumbline-holding apprentices alike—at work on the pyramid amidst a sea of stonework noises ringing away *en masse*. It is one of the finest thirty seconds or so of the Hawks series, and the film's epitomal sequence in terms of its wide-screen medium—supposedly inimical to Hawks's kind of cinema, but not here! Again, something of the same is seen in the scenes of the revolutionaries massing, piling on the train, loading the train, et cetera, in *Viva Villa!*

By contrast, later, and with Pharaoh's decadence, comes these workers' slave-driven oppression—opposite, too, to the willing labor of the keelboat crew of *The Big Sky*, who, as Zeb narrates on the sound track, worked well, "like men do when they believed in what they was doin'." Significantly, Princess Nelipher has shown up at this point, with no Cyprian tithe for the project, but with a hot scheme to ensnare Pharaoh, and at the right time—as, significantly too, he is alienated from his supportive alter-ego/shadow in Hamar. Demonstrably wrapped up in a dandyish preening and his possessions, he is opposite—or will be when he dies—to the Hawks hero who dies leaving but a few meager possessions, as in the 'meager last possessions' instances in *Only Angels Have Wings, Air Force,* and *Red Line 7000*.

In the initial shot of Nelipher, just before she goes in to Pharaoh, she is in the shadows, primping in a mirror held by her muscular, super-stoical slave, Mabula, animus-like here. Later, after she is Pharaoh's new queen and plots to murder him for his treasure and kingdom, Mabula makes an assassination attempt on Pharaoh in his sleep. Though in no way on the story level, this seems to partake of the 'triangle' motif. The scene's action is as dynamic as it is partly because of this deeper, inspirational level of the series' ego/shadow/anima dynamic (via Pharaoh/ego, Mabula/shadow, and Nelipher/anima).

She and Pharaoh first get acquainted violently, in sex-antagonistic strife, in the 'affection/violence' pattern. She leaves her red robe with him over which he broods. There are some fire-lamps in and about, one directly to the foreground, in the familiar frame-compositional pattern, augmenting the scene's tactile dramaturgy. In another, more minor 'object-transaction,' they later drink from a shared cup, founding their relationship.

Nelipher, in collusion with the captain of the guard, graspingly obtains Pharaoh's most prized possession, a jeweled necklace retained with the rest of his treasure in a private room entered by no one save him, his young son, and Hamar. In self-violation of a sort, early, Pharaoh gives in to her persuasion to let her see the room and its priceless, sacred contents (to be buried with him). As will be borne out, the necklace's theft ('transaction') is akin to her obtaining his soul or part of his essence—or "castratingly," in psychoanalytic terms.

The scene of the captain's falling into collusion with her to undo Pharaoh is interesting on a few counts.

Preparing to ensnare the captain by seduction, she turns down the lamp, in keeping with Hawks's cinematographic pattern of lower lighting—as a "morass," in this case, lent to the irrupting unconscious. Medusa-like, her business with the captain is evil. (By contrast, in *Rio Bravo*, Chance and Feathers have good, constructive, or "masculine" business in her hotel room for the cause of local law-enforcement, and as they go in she turns *up* the lamp.

Also ref. 'light/dark cinematography' in Appendix I.)

In the pattern of 'sex role-reversal,' 'fancy apparel/accouterment' and their allusion to negative anima-takeover, the soldierly captain's eyes have cat-like makeup. Anima-takeover is of course to be his lot with Nelipher. In the scene, she has him look at her. She says, "Are you afraid to look into my eyes for what you may see there?" It is a rather nonsensical line—save for auteur significance in its reiteration of Matt and Tess in the "rain" scene in *Red River* where on one level it is suggestive that, as Matt looks at her there, he is looking into a mirror. So it is with the captain, as he and Nelipher echo this earlier 'double/*doppelgänger*' instance.

Mabula, unsuccessful in his attempt on Pharaoh's life, is killed. Pharaoh suspects her and, badly wounded, creeps in unseen, where she is with the captain. She sees Pharaoh's trail of blood and knows it is he, returned. This touches 'pre-encounter,' rather as Tom first encounters Matt in the reaction of his bull to Matt's cow, in *Red River*, and as J.P. Harrah confirms Cole's presence in the saloon by noticing his horse, in *El Dorado*. It is also an important note of Pharaoh and Nelipher's 'friend/foe' bonding, in terms of the 'blood' motif.

Thinking quickly, she sets Pharaoh against the captain. The match is close, but Pharaoh slays him, although he is dying fast. In his delirium he recognizes, amidst the blur, the necklace on her—his "essence" plundered. He knows all as he dies there, for she does nothing to obtain help for him. His last words are, "Hamar, I need you." In a 'reverse' way, this echoes Spike, Bill, and the heart/anchor object in *A Girl in Every Port*, as Woman—rather than the 'pals'—triumph here, and the necklace, which she is wearing, is an 'objectivization' of the dying Pharaoh (in place of an 'objectivization' of Woman/anima between the 'pals').

Hamar, in passive retaliation, simply leaves her in ignorance of the procedure regarding Pharaoh's burial in the completed pyramid. It all goes according to law. She goes into the labyrinth and tomb with Hamar and the mute priests—the latter, with their tongues removed and their heads shaven, recalling the alien in *The Thing (From Another World)*. Speechless, save for their unison gruntings, they are certainly a special series group in their own part! They relate to the 'baldness' motif.

Nelipher, who is only there to claim the treasure (and presumably expects them to tote it back for her), does not realize, as she breaks the earthenware cap releasing the fine sand which lets down the stone sealing Pharaoh's casket, that she is also sealing the room and in turn the entire labyrinth, and the priests and her with it. Only then is she told that according to decree, she must go with her husband Pharaoh and his treasure to death and entombment.

As the room is sealed, she looks around in shock. A montage sequence of a few shots takes in the austere priests as they silently look upon her, a little incriminatingly. Echoing them are the tall male Egyptian statues around the walls of the tomb, looming over the scene. As she falls to the floor in a fitful expenditure of last grief, a longer montage sequence (in certain extension of the previous one) shows the engineering marvel of the labyrinth hydraulically amove (via the fine sand as liquid), lowering great stones into place and thus sealing the labyrinth. In one shot, early in the sequence, some of the fine sand accumulates at a statue's feet as if it were urinating or defecating, like a bull readying to charge (the "charge" here being, of course, the self-sealing pyramid in motion)!

The pyramid is something of a character in its own right, an 'objectivization' of Man-the-measurer-of-all-things. (As such, its self-sealing labyrinth-in-motion conjoins with the priests in the hence two-part 'group-delineative/"circular" montage' around the Centric Nelipher.) Even so, the pyramid's main purpose, on one level, is the shoring up of a male weakness: namely the recalcitrant (compensatory) anima in Nelipher who, as a "total villainess," requires one of the world's greatest architectural achievements to incarcerate her! In the sense of sacrifice/restoration (i.e., restoration in the resulting completed pyramid), she undergoes an initiation/passage, in death with the others. (Ref. Johnson and Mme. de Bursak in *To Have and Have Not.*)

As Vashtar and his people begin their walk to freedom hence, the curious insignia on his robe—earlier like a cryptic resurgence/irruption of his rejection of the idea of the Afterlife—now seems to echo the likewise symbolic pyramid in the distance. As a Hawks hero, he takes no fetishistic pride in the masterpiece, which is merely a job completed. Moses-like, he says, "Come on, we have a long way to go yet," as they set out on their desert hike.

Earlier, Pharaoh is replaced by his tiny son (Piero Giagnoni) who, a little absurdly, and in the same "theocratic-deteriorative" note, is lauded with pomp and ceremony. (Nelipher's attempt on his life failed.) As such, he is not equivalent to the vigorous J.B. of *The Ransom of Chief* nor to Matt as a boy in *Red River*, but is more like the comedic baby and amok children of *Monkey Business*, or the anima triumphant after all!

RIO BRAVO
(1959)

In its slow-paced dramatic concentration—in Dude's struggle with alcohol, in the problematic courtship of Chance and Feathers, and other dramatic action—*Rio Bravo* derives mainly from *To Have and Have Not,* and that film's lower-keyed, drawn-out mode of character/dramatic development. *To Have and Have Not* is superior to *Rio Bravo* in dramatics and dialogue, though by no means in story.

The 1959 film is generally overrated for its story factors. Despite its fine players and story, *Rio Bravo* does not fulfill its excellent outlines. Hawks and his actors frequently fail to work out superior dialogue; but the film's main problem, it seems to me, lies in its mediocre combining of dramatic action with camera placement and frame composition (including cinematographic factors). Often, Hawks's camera is too recessed from the dramatic action. A more liberal use of medium close-ups was probably in order (with attendant additional cutting and/or camera movements). In addition to its excellent story, the film is helped by some endearing light touches—particularly the group's persistent banter and humor through the shootout scene at the Burdett warehouse, which works extremely well. It is the best sequence in the film.

Rio Bravo hosts many points of archetypal/series-pattern importance, which in earlier films work closely with cinematic excellence, but to a lesser extent in *Rio Bravo,* as in other later films of the series.

The celebrated opening sequence, with its dearth of spoken words, derives partly from the tavern brawl in *Sergeant York,* where York is similarly (if accidentally) struck by one of his group (in the 'friend/foe' pattern). Both sequences have a choreographic allusion.

Alcoholic Dude (Dean Martin) comes into a saloon through the side door, to beg drinks as able. At the bar, Joe Burdett (Claude Akins) gestures to Dude to the effect of, "Want a drink?" Dude anxiously nods, as he stands beside and a little behind a post with mounted bull horns (a coat rack) with a cuspidor at the base. Behind Joe at the bar, and in the background behind Dude, are poster paintings of bullfighters in action. Cruelly, Joe tosses a gold coin into the cuspidor, to make Dude demean himself for a dollar's worth of whiskey. (Behind Dude, a barber shaves a man in the adjacent room—where the other bullfight painting is—in more convivial transaction than that of the foreground drama, yet the barber and client metaphorically echoing Joe and Dude. This juxtaposition figures in the sequence's general 'friend/foe' patterning.)

As Dude hesitatingly stoops to retrieve the gold piece, a pair of boots step up, and with a graceful, dance-like movement, the spittoon is kicked away (as the legs make a "figure 4"). Next, is an up-shot of John T. Chance (John Wayne), owner of the boots and the kicking foot, as he looks disdainfully down at Dude. In the next shot of Chance, as he looks at Joe we see his sheriff's badge. Like Dude earlier, Chance is juxtaposed with the mounted bull horns, though he is beside and a little in front of the post, rather than half-behind it—

as ego to the shadow figure in Dude now. The metaphor is, of course, that of a bullfight. Joe wears a pinto horsehide vest. (The general 'animal' allusion of the sequence is one of stoical aspect, matching that of the leopardskin-clad priests in *Land of the Pharaohs*.)

As Chance steps toward Joe to confront him, Dude grabs Chance, whirls him around and clubs him with a heavy stick of firewood he has picked up. Chance falls to the floor unconscious, and Joe, of course, has his cruel laugh on them both (though particularly on Dude, the shadow who overwhelmed his "better half" in Chance/ego instead of aiding him). Out of double frustration, partly stemming from his own misconduct, Dude attacks Joe with the club. Two of Joe's cohorts grab him, and Joe begins beating him with his fists. Another man moves to restrain Joe, and the latter promptly, coolly, draws his Colt forty-five and shoots him at point-blank range. (As we shortly learn, the anonymous outsider was unarmed, thus making it a clear case of murder.)

With Chance unconscious and Dude with the wind knocked out of him, Joe leaves in a cocky manner. Outside, in a significant erotic note (namely, relating to the preceding fracas), Joe brusquely accosts a woman, looks at her, shoves her away, and moves down the street in his town-bully demeanor, similarly eyeing another woman strolling with her husband. This erotic note forms a 'triangle'-type relationship with the previous, general ego/shadow "bullfighting," as the anima factor is brought forth.

Joe enters the Burdett Saloon, where the previous fighting will be concluded. The saloon, owned by Joe's brother Nathan, a wealthy rancher, seems to be an exclusively male establishment, in contrast to the previous saloon which had female employees and served both men and women. The latter place, and later the hotel are anima-linked places of mishap for the heroes in the film—in contrast to the ego/shadow-linked sheriff's office and jail, and in fact the Burdett Saloon. In the Burdett Saloon the lawmen gain tactical victories over the Burdett gang in two scenes (and with deeper 'friend/foe' allusions accruing between the lawmen and the Burdetts in the 'blood' scene there, and via the "Alamo music" played there, as we shall see).

Moments after Joe takes refuge in the Burdett Saloon, Chance, quickly revived and rifle in hand, enters and says, calmly and with a trace of regret, "Joe, you're under arrest." A skirmish follows. Dude, sneaking in behind Chance—as a helpful shadow figure this time—crucially aids Chance in apprehending Joe. As Joe is making an assault on Chance, the latter knocks him unconscious with his rifle, reiterating Dude's earlier club-swinging, though he delivers the blow in a whirling movement, matador-like, thus concluding the general "bullfight" through the two saloons. Chance and Dude then drag the unconscious Joe to jail.

Later however, Pat Wheeler (Ward Bond) says to Chance, "If ever I saw a man holdin' a bull by the tail, you're it," referring to Chance's predicament with Joe and the powerful Burdett gang. (The film has been released with the alternate title, *Bull By the Tail*.) Hence, the "bullfight" metaphor holds, to some extent, for the entire film—a talkative drama of essentially military tactics and strategy, with occasional moves between the few lawmen holding Joe Burdett in jail and the much larger group led by Joe's brother Nathan, who is bent on forcing his release.

The deputies must hold out with their prisoner to deliver him to the U.S, marshal, who will be a few days getting there. The Burdett gunmen blockade the town, preventing Chance from taking the prisoner out and from bringing help in, as the jail, the town, and the deputies' every move are watched in turn.

The Burdetts permit the stagecoach to enter the town, but discreetly sabotage it so that the travelers (and any emissaries friendly to Chance) must stay for a while. Gambler Feathers (Angie Dickenson) stays over, thus. She and Chance eventually become lovers, after a fashion. When the coach leaves, she stays, explaining to the shy, flustered Chance, "I heard somebody say they weren't going. It was me talking." This is in the ego/shadow way of Bonnie's illogical return to the airmail group in *Only Angels Have Wings*.

(Unlike Wayne and Charlene Holt in *El Dorado*, Wayne and Dickenson make, at best, a mediocre dramatic combination, and in general, Hawks's directorial relationship to her was an awkward one. Although she delivers her part reasonably well under the circumstances, she is too recessed from the camera—and her lines are often stiltedly derived from past series heroines and relate awkwardly to the dramatic context. Here the auteur worked against himself.)

The Burdett blockade also lets Pat Wheeler's well-armed freight-wagon train into town. But it stays as well, after Chance's friend Pat—who is drawn as a good trail boss but a blustering hot-head—is shot in the back by a Burdett thug after Pat indiscreetly campaigns to rally gunmen to help Chance. Part of his cargo is dynamite (in shadow/anima-rampant reference to the boss), explosives which prove decisive in the deputies' final shootout with the Burdett group. Early, as Wheeler is having a fit over the Burdett inconvenience to his wagon train, Chance calmly says to him, "Better look out, Pat. You'll blow up and bust."

Colorado Ryan (Ricky Nelson), a Wheeler-employed gunman, eventually hires with Chance as a much-needed deputy. Chance's only regular deputies are Stumpy (Walter Brennan), and Dude.

Stumpy, old, moderately senile, and with a club foot, guards the jail when Chance and Dude are elsewhere in town. Except for his stroll in the town at the very end of the film, the only time Stumpy leaves the premises is when, against orders, he shows up at the final shootout (in an instance of 'fraternal return,' described below). Aptly likening himself to "a gopher or a barn owl," in his 'close quarters' there, Stumpy recalls the old, infirm, greenhouse-dwelling Sternwood, who compares himself with "a common spider," in *The Big Sleep*.

Very trigger-happy—in the shadow/anima-rampant 'gun-lunacy/carelessness' tradition of Clark, Bonnie, Williams, Tess, and others of the series—Stumpy nearly blows Dude's head off by mistake, at one point (in 'friend/foe' reference). Stumpy's regular post in the jail/fortress is behind the locked door of the little cell block, near Joe, for whom he cooks and whose cuts and bruises he tends. He is also assigned to shoot Joe as a hostage, should the Burdetts storm the jail, survive his shotgun blasts from the locked cage door, and break into the cell block. As an expressed "nursemaid" to the prisoner, he and Joe are linked, on a shadow level, and function like the significant (shadowy) background figures Phipps, Sparks, and Bensiger of earlier films. Like Phipps's philosophic association with the soul of the air unit in *The Dawn Patrol*, Stumpy is appealingly juxtaposed with the word "Texas" on a wall map of the state, as he plays harmonica and sings with Dude and Colorado in the bright 'song session' in the jail. Like Nikki in *The Thing (From Another World)*, and Edwina and Esther the chimpanzee in *Monkey Business*, Stumpy, in his shadow/anima aspect, is the ironic source of a couple of bright ideas/innovations in the course of the siege. (On the levels of scenario, dialogue, and dramatics alike, Stumpy is more delimited as a character/portrayal than he should be, as Walter Brennan's fine talents are somewhat sacrificed, although he shines at later points in the film.)

Dude (very well portrayed by Dean Martin), Chance's only other regular deputy, is young and an excellent gunman; but he has been on an alcoholic binge for three years, earning the Spanish nickname "Borachon" (drunk). His long drunk is over a woman who ran out on him. In dialogue, Chance relates that he tried to tell Dude that the girl was "no good," but that Dude, heedless, nearly killed him for it—recalling, of course, the 'triangular' Spike, Bill, and Tessie of *A Girl in Every Port*. Much of the story and drama turn on Dude's fitful initiation/passage back to normal, and to competent deputy responsibility again. In a deeper way than his alcohol problem, Dude is suggestedly a weak-willed type who needs Chance's moral support in general, like a little brother needing a big brother—again, as Chance's inferior shadow.

In an eerie way, he is a shadow figure for the Burdett group as well. He is posited, on a deep level, as the "one flesh" between friend and foe, since the film's marked 'friend/foe' pattern very much turns on Dude. Dude receives severe manhandling from the Burdetts on more than one occasion—to his benefit. In the story, their physical and psychological abuse, and their general threat to the deputy group in the Joe Burdett matter, serve his recovery as much as, or more than, Chance's abiding support. This is of ego/shadow import, as Dude and the Burdett group are partners, on one level.

Pointedly, Dude begins the road back to normal with the advent of Joe's arrest at his and Chance's hands, and in the crisis-context of the archetypally laden "bullfight" sequence. This is richly in the initiation/passage pattern. The next day, as the funeral procession for Joe's victim passes near Dude at his deputy post, he is smiling in his boyish way, via the procession's association with his temporary triumph.

Dude is drying out on beer, with which Chance has stocked the jail in order to keep him out of the saloons. As Dude is partaking of this relative medicine, Joe, from his cell, taunts him, waving another gold dollar at him. Dude throws the bottle at him, which shatters against the bars and over Joe, who says, "Hey Chance! Are you gonna let him do that to me?" The sheriff replies, "I'll do better than that. I'll let him have the key to your cell any time he wants it." (In the end, at the prisoner exchange, Dude overpowers Joe, a considerably larger man, and the shootout then ensues.) When Chance next offers Dude another beer, he does not need it. Throwing the beer at Joe was therapy for the time being.

Later, as Dude at his deputy post confronts Nathan Burdett (John Russell) and a squad of gunmen, he tells Burdett that he is getting practice being sober due to Nathan's brother. Pointedly, Nathan fails to understand what he means.

Early, as Dude begins to feel the sore effects of the lack of hard liquor, Chance chooses the moment to make the evening deputy rounds (as "Burdett therapy"). Suggestedly, however, Dude's nervous condition is rubbing off on Chance (in the ego/shadow, 'group-contagion' way). Although worried, of course, they try to walk tall in making the rounds, each taking one side of the street. At an intersection, a tumbleweed brushes by Dude and rolls behind Chance across the way, an 'object-transaction' between the ego/shadow pair, in its loose way. (Chance is alerted by it, as something which might be a Burdett employee sneaking up on him.) Chance is surprised by an (irruptive) donkey in a stable window, at a point when Dude is near him. When Chance remarks on his own jumpiness, Dude chides him with, "I'll walk along with you and hold your hand."—character being 'reversed' in the moment. In the familiar way of series-pattern clustering, this mild 'double/*doppelgänger*' instance is contiguous with the irruptive entities of the object and the animal.

Previous to this is the 'triangular' "red drawers" sequence. One of Wheeler's men delivers a package to the jail, which Carlos Remonte (Carlos Gonazales Gonzales) is expecting at his hotel. Chance comes to the hotel with the package wrapped in a "plain brown wrapper," just as Carlos is coming down the stairs with some important information for him (the transmission of which will be interrupted for a few minutes). Since the 'fraternal return' line "you're just in time" is used as Chance comes in with the package, the scene perhaps refers to the (likewise 'triangular') "dinner party" scene in *Gentlemen Prefer Blondes*, with its 'return' instance utilizing the same line.

As Chance and Carlos meet at the foot of the stairs, Carlos's wife, Consuela, emerges/interrupts from the downstairs kitchen and remarks on her husband's guilty expression (which is over the package, the contents of which are not yet revealed). In the familiar visual joke of moviedom, Consuela (Estelita Rodriguez) is juxtaposed there with a pair of mounted horns behind her, in stark, comic allusion to their being hers. As we shortly learn, the package contains the bright red drawers Carlos has ordered for her—all in reference to the general "bullfight" again, with the soon-to-be-revealed drawers as a matador cape! (Here, the "bullfight" metaphor assumes an irruptive 'animal'/anima aspect.) As Consuela begins henpecking the resistant Carlos over his guilty look, he quickly takes the sheriff upstairs on their "important business" together. After Carlos tells Chance that he knows women and that Chance does not, he opens the package to show the sheriff his wise purchase—the red drawers. (Here, Carlos echoes Barney's knowledgeable purchase of clothes for Lotta in *Come and Get It*.)

Thus, we have a comic 'triangle' variant, with Chance, Carlos, Conseuela-as-a-bull, and the 'feminine apparel' item 'converged' between the two men. In addition, however, Feathers interrupts them, inquiring for a towel (introducing herself to the film). As Carlos was just holding the drawers against Chance to see how Consuela will look in them, Feathers remarks, "Those things have great possibilities, but not for you." Chance gruffly asks her, a stranger in town, why she is not on the stagecoach. He then learns from Carlos that the wheel is broken (likely sabotaged by Burdett men), which is the earlier "important business." Due to Chance's brusque departure then, and his previous tone with her, Feathers, serving him in kind, calls after him, "Hey Sheriff, you forgot your pants." Chance hesitates, flustered before continuing downstairs.

As discussed in section IV, the drawers function as an anima-irruptive challenge. Again, they are linked with the "bullfight" metaphor, Consuela, and the (irrupting) Feathers, all on the somewhat hen-pecked Carlos's hotel premises. There, Chance will become entangled with Feathers in subsequent scenes, in their awkward courtship (recalling that of Harry and Slim in the hotel in *To Have and Have Not)*. On the uncertain premises of the "anima hotel," Chance—in another touch of 'sex role-reversal' (after briefly playing "Consuela" for Carlos)—will stand behind the bar, at one point, as he serves Feathers and himself, after hours. Shortly, Feathers will stand there as a new employee. Other early business at the hotel is with a card-sharp in a checkered vest (noted at least twice), designating his flawed, "tinhorn" character. Chance also suspects Feathers in the crooked game. He interrogates her in her room, but is bested as she challenges him to search her, to his embarrassment. Yet law enforcement gets served. In the fashion of the interrupting shadow figure, Colorado intrudes on them (thus "saving" Chance), summoning him downstairs to the guilty party—the card sharp. In this way, Chance and Feathers begin their courtship, Hawks-style.

In contrast to the anima-aspected "checkered vest" (and professional gambling) opulence is, again, the heroic 'meager last possessions' motif, of which we have an instance in Colorado bringing the murdered Wheeler's gun and few things to the jail later. Twice, slain Burdett men leave behind their gunman's pay, in similar reference. Repeatedly, their pay is in gold pieces, recalling the object of the original Joe/Dude conflict. The gold pieces are posited as a "Grail"-like metaphor (in the sense, again, of a Centric object ultimately alluding to the Self and masculine Self-realization via Hawksian-type quest/conflict here).

At the scene of Wheeler's ambush, an *x* is prominent on a wooden door adjacent to where his body is dragged from the street, in evident reiteration of this signification in death scenes in *Scarface*. Wheeler's assailant is wounded by Dude before the former flees into the Burdett Saloon. 'Convergingly, ' from the front and side doors, Chance and Dude venture in to apprehend him, and the eerie 'blood' scene ensues. The gunman is somewhere there among mum comrades, and all inside are held at gunpoint as the deputies look for a man with muddy boots. They fail to find him at first, and Dude begins having an alcoholic attack (as he later confesses). In reiteration of the "bullfight" sequence, a Burdett man tauntingly throws a silver dollar into a cuspidor near Dude, who is the more shaken. Then Dude notices blood dripping into a beer resting on the bar near him. He knows the quarry is in the loft. Since Dude is currently drying-out on beer, the Burdett blood is as though medicinally offered to him, on the shadowy 'friend/foe' level! Dude steps forward, and pauses between the camera and the beer, as though in cross-identification with the "proffered" blood! In a moment, he continues his forward motion, whirls, and guns the man down from the loft. After Dude and Chance confirm that the slain man was Wheeler's killer, and prepare to confiscate all guns there, Dude, more boldly now, forces the man who tossed the coin to recover it from the spittoon himself.

In its 'friend/foe' 'blood' content, the scene echoes the motif instances with the vampirous, group-linked alien in *The Thing (From Another World)*, the transfusions among the group in that film, and the blood exchange between Chips and Indian in *Hatari!* Closely involved with Dude's ongoing initiation/ passage, it is one of several archetypally-laden Burdett/deputy exchanges, via Dude, in the film.

Nathan Burdett, well-dressed, visits his brother in jail. There we learn that Stumpy once had some land which Burdett obtained through unfair means. The discussion there between Chance and Burdett is, all things considered, business-like and mutually respectful. Almost convivially, throughout the film, Chance and Dude address the Burdett men they know by their first names (as, in the same oblique 'pals' fashion, Marlowe calls his enemy "Eddie," in *The Big Sleep*). Personal loyalty is a theme in the film. Nathan is acting as he is, going to costly and risky extremes, out of loyalty to his brother. And when Dude is captured, instead of sacrificing him in a cold, military way, Chance agrees to the prisoner exchange also in loyal friendship (although there are other, tactical factors involved). In general, the hired Burdett men express more reluctance than camaraderie in the Joe Burdett matter—save for one hateful man (a "coforeman" of the gang at the time) who expresses loyalty to friends of his whom the deputies have killed.

It may be noted that the entire trouble or "mess" largely stems from Dude's early misbehavior and weak condition. And comparably, Joe, a heavy drinker himself, is designated as "no good." Thus on one level, the ego figures in Chance and Nathan Burdett come to conflict by way of the misdoings of their respective shadows. With Joe in jail—in Chance's "lap," as the Sheriff colloquially puts it—and with Joe somewhat paired with his cellblock mate in Stumpy, and as Dude is repeatedly abused by the Burdett group, the two sides of the conflict each embrace the other's principal shadow figure. Joe/Dude is a dual shadow to both groups.

All in all, the battle is considerably among moral/ethical equals. (Ethics, morality, idealism, pillars of the law, and such are somewhat joshed with Chance's swearing-in of Colorado, where the deputy oath is interrupted by Stumpy with: "(Cackle) Found yourself another knothead who don't know when he's well off?!" Such relates to the series pattern of 'irreligion/anti-cere-mony-and-formality.') In an early conversation with Feathers, Chance suggests that he considers himself not a knightly pillar of the law, but a gunman: a "lazy" one who, instead of selling his gun all over, does so "in one place." The earlier-proposed series 'edict' is indicated: that professionalism and morality/ethics are one; that "right action" tends to come, not from moralism, but from the various "amoral" attributes of professionalism (the latter influenced, of course, by the requisites of the job at hand). The immorality of the "bad guys" is a result of their professional inferiority, and not so much the reverse. This certain moral equality between foes is a broader dimension of the 'friend/foe' pattern, in its sense of "meritocratic gaming" in lieu of a hero/ villain dichotomy.

Too, the opposing groups have commonality in the prospective extermina-

232

tion of nearly all. As Burdett is informed that Stumpy will, ultimately, kill Joe before giving him up, Nathan adds that a court of law would call that murder. Chance adds, "Oh, hell. What's the difference? We'd all be dead by then." Since Nathan cannot risk the deputies carrying out their threat, it is a good tactic on Chance's part to assert it. Yet it is suggestive of the game that, on one level, it all is. This gaming also relates to the pattern of 'characters as portions of one psyche.'

One evening, as the mariachi band in the Burdett Saloon is playing a strange Mexican tune for the umpteenth time, within earshot of the jail, Chance strikes a match and lights the lantern beside the front door of the jail. As he and Dude loiter there, wondering about the music, Colorado comes up and informs them that the tune is the "Degüello" (the "cutthroat" song), which the Mexicans played night and day at the Alamo where the few Texans held out for a long time against the superior military force before ultimate defeat and executions. (An analogy is of course drawn between the Alamo siege and that of the Burdett gang and the lawmen.) Nathan Burdett's message, via the tune, is "no quarter for the losers."

Indeed, as will be retroactively stressed in subsequent scenes, the lighted lamp, juxtaposed with Colorado, Chance, and Dude here, is a pointed symbol of esprit, morale. It combines with the psychological-warfare tune, which will shortly have a positive effect upon Dude who will be on the verge of quitting. As in the case of the souvenir Iron Cross wingtip in *The Dawn Patrol*, a union of opposites (i.e., of foes, adversaries) is alluded to. "Grail"-like, the lantern and tune (combined) Centrically echo the original gold piece between Joe and Dude.

After the "lantern" scene outside the jail, the next shot, within the jail, begins in medium close-up on Chance's feet on a chair, as he taps time to the "Degüello" music down the street. In the cellblock, Stumpy takes up the tune on his harmonica. Chance tells him to stop. "Well, what's the matter?" Stumpy replies, "Is it getting, through to you? (Cackle.)" Herethrough, the "Degüello" tune is embraced.

When Feathers does not leave on the stagecoach, Dude, in recollection of his own hard experience with a woman who came through on the stage three years ago, discreetly chides the sheriff about Feathers. Chance defensively throws an envelope of papers at him. Next, and in certain thematic continuity with this, is the 'triangular' "shaving" scene in Chance's hotel room, among Chance (ego), Dude (shadow), and Feathers (anima), and with a mandala-Centric object (the Self) in the silver hatband among them (with Dude's fine, anima-aspected clothes, and two lanterns figuring as well).

Before they go to the hotel, Chance returns Dude's old guns to him, retained for him—a very appreciated gesture of faith in him and his recovery. At the hotel, Dude also has some of his clothes returned to him, which the sheriff has retained, in meaningful 'object-transaction' as well. In Chance's room, Feathers give Dude a shave, as Chance watches—amusedly (as, in his more "ego-masculine" way, the sheriff proclaims there, "I do my own shaving."). Feathers wears a white blouse, matching the towel around Dude.

Two kerosene lanterns burn in the room. Dude receives her shaving nervously, as though afraid of being slashed. Just earlier, he intimated to Chance that he feared cutting his own throat if he tried shaving himself, due to his hands still shaking from his long drunkenness. Indeed, the Burdett "cutthroat" song and the juxtaposed lantern at the jail, earlier, are comically echoed in the "shaving" scene! (Too, the barber shaving his client in the background of the early strife among Dude, Joe, and Chance seems to be reiterated.) Thus, the features of the friendly "shaving" scene, in their metaphorical juxtaposition with the earlier lantern and adversarial tune, strike another 'friend/foe' chord.

Hence, the three of them make an ego and tactile-functionally-relating shadow/anima 'triangle' in Chance's hotel room. After Feathers concludes Dude's "close shave," he pays her. Dude, dressed in his good clothes again. tosses a silver hatband across the room to Chance in the familiar 'dramatized space' pattern, saying, "I could buy a lot of drinks with that." Chance, agreeing with him, tosses it back to Dude, who says, "I'll let you keep it for me," as he puts it in a drawer—his masculine "essence" thus retained with his friend, on one level. (Shades, of course, of Pharaoh's incarcerated treasure in *Land of the Pharaohs* as well as the mandala-Centric tiara in *Gentlemen Prefer Blondes*, and the epical bracelet in *Red River*.)

Carelessly, Dude goes back to the jail alone. Chance and Feathers then have a mild quarrel. At the jail, the trigger-happy Stumpy—not recognizing Dude in his old, fancy duds—shoots at him in the dark, perforating his hat. This accident sends Dude into his former alcoholically-nervous condition again. Hence, the peril of any "hotel" business, in the film.

Shortly, Burdett's men subdue Dude at his guard post, beat him unconscious, and rob him of his hat and vest. In a ruse, one of them takes his place at the guard spot, impersonating him in his vest and hat at the distance. Others then skirmish with Chance, and Colorado joins in on Chance's side. Feathers aids their tactical victory by throwing a flower pot through the hotel window, distracting the Burdett men.

In the scene where Dude is beaten and his hat and vest are taken, he is washing in the water trough when he is overtaken. He sees the gang's (irrupting) reflections from behind him in the moment before his head is shoved into the water. They then beat him unconscious, and the Burdett man leaves his own hat with Dude who is left bound and gagged in the stable. Dude shortly awakens with the Burdett hat near him, which Chance hands to him as a "souvenir." In view of the "assault from the water reflection," and the clothing exchange, the sequence bears a 'self-encounter/splitting off' reference, and, once again, a note of 'friend/foe' relationship with the Burdett men, who on one level mix identities with their quarry in Dude, the "initiation candidate." (Again, Hawks characters tend to be as components of one psyche.)

The 'clothing exchange' recalls Susan putting on David's hat, David her gown, and both changing into other, odd clothing in *Bringing Up Baby,* in a similar note of identity confusion/reversal between the 1938 pair.

With this humiliation, Dude is ready to quit and start on whiskey again in lieu of medicinal beer. This is simultaneous with Colorado's deputization (after the latter spontaneously helped Chance in the skirmish just earlier). Dude exudes jealousy of Colorado here. Herewith ensues the famous "Alamo music" scene, in which Dude is revived.

As Dude is ready to start on the whiskey bottle, the "Deguello" tune starts again from down the street. He tells Stumpy not to close the shutter, but to let it play. Dude then pours the glass of whiskey back into the bottle without spilling a drop (in oblique 'convergence' upon the liquor), his hand being steady now for the first time in the film. In full 'friend/foe' beneficence, the Burdett psychological-warfare music has all but cured him! His shakes are gone. (Previously, Dude wasted quantities of cigarette tobacco, trying to roll cigarettes—in tactile-functional metaphor of his incompetent condition, as Chance, supportingly, rolled them for him when he failed to roll his own.)

As Robin Wood and others have observed, the closed-in situation of the sheriff's office and jail is series-characteristic, like the heroic/initiatory tomb in *Land of the Pharaohs*, the arctic outpost in *The Thing (From Another World)*, and other 'close quarters,' which sometimes shift with an equal and opposite 'odyssey' mode, like the nighttime garrison in *The Dawn Patrol* and its alternating with spatially-opposite daylight missions and combat. The 'close quarters' intensively focus individual and interpersonal problems among the group as though to functionally launch their different (if similarly tactile-involved) expenditure of work in the field. Another example is the animal-compound residence, with its comedy and conflict, giving rise to the 'odyssey' of daily wild animal chases, in *Hatari!* One may add the implosive anima-intensity of Lotta giving rise to the saloon brawl in *Come and Get It*. In *Rio Bravo*, the group will leave the jail/fortress for a great showdown, with guns and explosives alike. The "anima hotel" is likewise a problematic 'close quarters,' compared to the action outside.

In the jail, Dude is smelling badly due to his earlier abduction and sojourn on the stable floor. The giddy Stumpy (in allusion to the irrupting anima in their midst) suggests that, since he (Stumpy) likes roses, some rose-scented soap would be useful for Dude to bathe with—as, by now, the deputies plan to hole up in the jail completely until the U.S. marshal arrives for Joe, and in the meantime, their confines will be stuffy indeed. Significantly perhaps, Colorado's guitar is painted with—roses, as he, Dude, and Stumpy have a 'song session' there. It is as though the earlier red drawers have emerged anew! Calamitously, Chance and Dude go to the "anima hotel" one more time for Dude to bathe with rose-scented soap, if available, and to pick up supplies. Chance is overwhelmed by Burdett men there. In the subsequent skirmishing, the gang members escape with Dude as a hostage.

A prisoner exchange is arranged, with Chance entertaining last hopes to retrieve Dude and retain Joe via another skirmish. This happens, as Dude, passing Joe in the two-way exchange route, shoves him into some adobe ruins, where he subdues Joe as the gunfight commences between the lawmen in the barn (adjacent to the ruins) and the Burdetts in the warehouse across the way.

The lame Stumpy was left behind to guard the jail, to his complaint and hurt pride. As some Burdett men move from the warehouse toward a position behind Chance and Colorado in the barn, two enormous explosions are heard. The Burdett men are stopped in their tracks. Quickly, in the next shot, Stumpy, cackling, is shown with his shotgun, nicely framed in the adobe ruins, popping up thus in 'fraternal return.' Colorado says to Chance, "Is that who I think it is?" The sheriff replies happily, "Old Stumpy! The fellow I left behind." Immediately, Carlos enters the barn! He bears a gift of more ammunition, to Chance's renewed surprise, thus sharing the 'return' instance with Stumpy. After Stumpy gets the bright idea to assault the warehouse with dynamite (stored nearby with Wheeler's parked wagon train), the lawmen gain the surrender of the Burdett men, after partly destroying the Burdett warehouse/fortress.

In *El Dorado*, the 'returning' Stumpy is paralleled in the irruptive Joey MacDonald, who likewise proves very crucial in the shootout, with two shots. She and Stumpy/Carlos are all anima-associated.

Finally, with the cell block crowded with Burdett men (including Nathan), Chance gets together with Feathers. There in her hotel room, to her pleasure and flattery, Chance jealously has her remove her sexy saloon costume behind the screen (upon which the Sheriff's harsh shadow 'convergingly' looms). This is an initiation/passage of (reversed) 'fancy apparel' (like Geoff's spoiling Judith's hairdo in *Only Angels Have Wings*). As Chance throws her black tights out the window, who should come sauntering by, in apt 'simultaneity,' but Dude and Stumpy. After the latter pair make a joke, Stumpy, cackling, places the tights around his neck, scarf-like, as these 'pals' thus tote the fancy item off with them, which ends the film.

Just earlier, at the jail, Dude intimated to Chance, about to go to the hotel to visit Feathers, that should Chance get into the same sort of woman trouble that Dude did, he will return favors done him and assist Chance back to normal. Archetypally, Dude and Stumpy "rescue" Chance ahead of time, at the hotel. From the short distance away—in the 'dramatized/converged space' pattern—Dude and Stumpy conduct their part of a three-man 'convergence' upon Her, which consists of Chance's making Feathers remove her saloon outfit and throwing her tights out the window, and the others usurping her in turn in her Centric article of clothing. Thus, the film's general, recalcitrant anima, first irrupting in the red drawers, is subdued in the familiarly 'convergent' mandala-Centric pattern.

Hence *Rio Bravo* ends like *A Girl in Every Port*. Yet it also ends like *Land of the Pharaohs*, with Nelipher 'converged,' mandala-Centrically, among priests, statues, tomb, and pyramid, in initiation/passage, as Nelipher "joins" the pyramid cult at last, and as Feathers now belongs to the deputy group.

Midway in the film, we have the comic 'baldness' motif instance with Stumpy. The partly-bald Stumpy, hatless in the moment, sits with a broom in hand, complaining that Chance does not appreciate his service around the jail. Accommodatingly, Chance responds with the "commendation" of quickly kissing the (anima-linked) Stumpy's head, then hastening out the door as the surprised Stumpy swings the broom at him. This recalls Walter Brennan/Groot's swinging his black snake whip at the sugar-pilfering Bunk Kenneally at the rear of the chuck wagon, as the latter nonetheless obtains some of the (anima-linked) sweet stuff in *Red River*. Anima-aspected in *Rio Bravo*, the 'baldness' motif is otherwise a stoically mandala-Centric one. (Ref. the stoically hairless alien in *The Thing (From Another World)*, the Centric instances with Douglas Spencer in that film and in *Monkey Business*, and the stoically bald mute priests in *Land of the Pharaohs*. Note particularly the initiation/passage-related instance with Cadwalader in the "toupee'"scene in *Man's Favorite Sport?*, in the scene's reference to Judith's anima-suppressive, hair-wetting initiation in *Only Angels Have Wings*). After all, baldness is, of course, a masculine attribute and subject to Hawksian pride—not to say ego-idealism!

HATARI!
(1962)

Hatari's humor and outright comedy (of a sort which at times goes beyond realism) combine well with the animal-compound group's business with sundry animals in Tanganyika, as they chase, capture, and hostel them for the zoos of the world. The film's light adventure drama consists partly of antics which remind one of the playful content of home movies. The film moves episodically through a loose story which is much less a plot than a set of series-characteristic character relationships, conflicts, clashes, and their dramatic development. *Hatari*'s manifold concept and potentialities were outstanding—the resulting film less so, enduringly likeable though it is.

The animal chases are very well wrought. (Although John Wayne/Sean Mercer's lines in the field, often, are not. They do not convince one that he is on top of the job as the group "foreman.") In the opening sequence, the group are geographically separated in their field vehicles on the African veldt. Before converging upon a rhino, they 'converge' or dramatize this space in their talk over the two-way radios. It anticipates the tightly edited 'friend/foe' contact in the Rebel troops spying on the Yankees by means of tapped telegraph lines, early in *Rio Lobo* (subsequent to which, after the war, a few of the same Rebels and Yankee Cord McNally embark on a common task together).

In this precredit sequence, the group chases a female rhino. Banteringly, on the intercom, Pockets (Red Buttons) remarks, "Must be a female. She can't make up her mind which way to go." In the same sequence, the animal is also referred to as a "he" or "him"—thus positing the film's thematic 'blurred sexual distinctions' pattern.

Indian (Bruce Cabot) is gored while in the truck. They cease the chase, pull up, and bring out the first-aid bag with its red cross and set it on the truck, its *x* to the foreground of one shot, reiterating those signifying deaths in *Scarface* (although Indian is not dead and will survive). Luis, brunette, and a sort of shadow figure to the group, stands juxtaposed with the Centric aid bag and its *x*. As discussed in the section on the 'fraternal return' motif, Indian's subsequent hospital leave and partial return to the field, still lame, seems to be a latent instance of 'return' "from the dead." (See below the related item of Chip's ethereal entry into the film, at a point when Indian is near death.)

The sex confusion over the rhino, and subsequent instances of the 'blurred sexual distinctions' pattern, are associated with the want of *mastery* in a general sense. (The pattern, of course, involves the troublesome irruptive anima.) The "goat" sequence, in which Pockets attempts to milk a billy goat, is, significantly, one of comic havoc for the group. But it is one of triumph for female newcomer Dallas, who easily solves the problem of feeding the orphaned baby elephant (with goat milk) via her maternal sense and 'woman/animal' connection which triumph at ego-masculine expense, in the sequence. Near the end of the film, when the group break the rhino jinx by capturing one, the animal—although referred to as a "she" at one point in the chase—is very much a "he." Might the "he" allude to the "she" of the pre-

238

credits sequence stoically modified now, namely as the anima 'converged' upon and captured (as, indeed, they shortly hog-tie the male rhino for the compound)? In any case, the second, male rhino in the film is in the role of the recalcitrant anima/'animal' subdued. Altogether, the rhinos reiterate the hermaphroditic alien (with its irruptive anima aspect) in *The Thing (From Another World)*, as well as the bull/cow confusions in *Red River* and *I Was a Male War Bride*, and Esther's confusion with the male lab ape in *Monkey Business*.

The shadow/anima figure, Pockets, is the one most given to sex confusion instances in the film, in reference to more general strife with the problematic anima. The anima is mainly represented in Dallas (Elsa Martinelli), who undergoes several stages of initiation/passage in the story, paralleling Dude of *Rio Bravo* and, particularly, Bonnie of *Only Angels Have Wings*.

As regards the rhino jinx, the earlier rhinoceros victims, before Indian, are noted in dialogue as "that nice Belgian kid" and "Brandy's father." They are archetypal in, respectively, being "nice" (shadow/anima-aspected) and older, and thus prone to accident/death in the field, and with the attendant "archetypal honors" accorded to serious mishap and death. (Ref. discussion of archetypally-prone age extremes, at the end of section V.) Indian is older and, significantly a heavy drinker and a woman chaser. Since these traits are not involved in his accident, his mishap is thus a 'significant happenstansical death (i.e., near-fatal accident)' instance. (Ref. Johnson in *To Have and Have Not*.) In partial contrast, Sean, the group exemplar, is recalcitrantly misogynistic, prior to Dallas's partially curing him (which is simultaneous with her final, turbulent initiation into the group).

In the sequence of Indian's return from the hospital to the compound, still to remain bedridden for a while, he and the younger Sean are posited as warm comrades or 'pals.' They discuss newcomer Dallas, with a fancy white water pitcher at Indian's bedside very Centric between them (underscored in their fairly direct reference to it in dialogue, as it is paired with a liquor bottle which Sean proffers to augment the plain water). At the end of the scene, Sean is rather beautifully juxtaposed with a (reiteratively Centric) lamp beside the door. At this point in their conversation, Indian is indicating his new, semiphobic condition as regards rhino. The shots of him here, propped up in bed next to the large white pitcher, a drink in his hand, are rather comedic and uncomplimentary. Sean is very understanding about Indian's acquired "rhino jinx" attitude. After Sean leaves the room, Indian looks down at the drink in his hand with an expression of regret, as though (unbeknown to Sean, perhaps) he is on the edge of a drinking problem. In general, Indian is treated with a certain directorial "preciousness," as an infirm character, even as though he were bestowed with the honors of one who has died in action.

Brandy Delacourt (Michele Giradon), the other female member of the group, is a curious character, to some extent like an overgrown tomboy (but beautiful), having lived in the veldt all her life. Even so, she is not altogether credible. What Robin Wood criticizes as the undercharacterization of Teal Eye in *The Big Sky* applies more aptly to the unlikelihood of Brandy's rather one-dimensional character. In auteur reference, in her early scene with Kurt, Brandy's reflection in her mirror is embossed with a bad crack in the glass, like an "initiatory" touch of 'fog/rain/shadow.' Too, on one level, she is a shadow/

anima reflection of her late father, former boss of the jungle compound (which she has inherited), and who was, as is stressed, an outstanding professional.

Early, Dallas comes to the animal compound from her native Italy, on a photographic assignment for a zoo. Before this is revealed, Sean discovers her in his bed, wearing Pockets's pajama shirt. (Significantly, Pockets is Sean's anima-linked shadow, as Dallas is his anima in the film. Dallas hence wears an appropriate pajama half in Sean's bed. Too, it is noted that Kurt Mueller (Hardy Kruger) often wears the lower half—hence an involved 'clothing exchange,' as it may be dubbed, as a motif.) Initially, Dallas is well lighted amidst relative shade, with Sean more in shadow—respectively like Jones and Marlowe in their encounter in *The Big Sleep*. This is appropriate to her sudden character introduction. Yet, like Marlowe/Jones, Sean/Dallas is a major 'self-encounter/splitting off' instance, as we shall see.

Sean has no idea who she is. As she speaks to him, he is holding (and retains) one of his shoes in hand, as though in cryptic reference to his 'splitting,' the shoe being his anima 'objectivized' in the moment, quite as She is personified in Dallas across the room. Pockets comes in drunk, and begins to address her as if she were Sean. In the last scene in the film, this part of the scene is quaintly repeated, with Dallas being married to Sean now. As Pockets comes in this time, he begins to make the same mistake, but which he promptly enough corrects—in a note of confusions overcome (more or less) and mastery attained, since their occupational season has ended well, both as regards rhinos and to some extent Woman. Again, psychoanalytic-like, the scenes are dually a wellnigh self-conscious instance of 'self-encounter/splitting off' in view of this "rectification" at the end.

The film's early "morning after" or "breakfast/Dallas" scene begins with a foreground close-up on a glass of bicarbonate of soda. (The shadow figure Luis, of the group, inserts the tablet in the glass—once again in juxtaposition with a mandala-Centric object. Too, the bicarbonate glass and he are paired with the 'empty chair' at the end of the table, which comes into the foreground as the camera moves up and back from the fizzing glass. The 'empty chair' motif is discussed below.) A little in the Hawks way of a "verbal" object popping up, the Centric glass and bicarbonate are meaningful via the previous evening's heavy drinking in celebration of Indian's going off the critical list at the hospital. Pockets, who was perhaps drunker than the others, exudes freshness amidst their moderate hangovers—odd one of the group that he is. He is also a "chow hound," and generally awkward (though very expressive, physically). The unexplained new arrival (who parallels the challenging red drawers arriving at the jail in *Rio Bravo*) has, urbanely, not yet arisen. Independent of her, in the 'pre-encounter' way, Brandy brings her photo equipment in, setting it on the table and inquiring where it might have come from ("a real professional outfit"). In the scene, they puzzle over a letter introducing one "A.M. D'Alessandro," whom, in the sex-confusion pattern, they think may be a man. They try to pronounce the name, but (in unison) they only get to "Dallas..." as, right then, she enters—pops up and completes the pronunciation of her name for them. Even so, on their unwitting cue, she shortly has them call her "Dallas." Hence her nickname, at once created by her and the group, yet neither per se;

240

stoically shortened from the (anima-encumbered) Italian. Thus her name is made peer-familiar previous to their being well-acquainted (if subsequent or consequent to her nocturnal introduction, like a preconscious figure amongst Sean, Pockets and Kurt, via the pajamas). Again, Hawks characters tend to be as portions of one psyche, as the "breakfast/Dallas" sequence exemplifies, in its fine instance of 'merged dramatics/dialogue.'

In this and two other dining room scenes in the film, the main shot of the table features an empty chair in the foreground (its back to the camera). All of these group scenes focus around some pivotal/archetypal business with Dallas, who is absent from the table for at least part of the scene. These "empty chair" scenes are: (1) The above-discussed "breakfast/Dallas" scene of her introduction into the group. (2) The dinner scene following her spectacular initiation into the local African tribe and just previous to its certain reiteration, in 'reverse,' with Sean in her room. (3) The breakfast scene after her secret departure from the animal compound and just prior to the group's "hunting her down" in town (thence unto her final 'initiation' in the group). Items (2) and (3) will be discussed later in this section.

Archetypal figure and "initiation candidate" that Dallas is in the film, these empty chairs refer to her, and in specific allusion to her ethereal/archetypal aspect. They reiterate the 'returning' Scotty's 'empty chair' in *The Thing (From Another World)*, and anticipate that of the deceased Johnny Diamond in *El Dorado:* a rather blatant 'chair' instance which retroactively supports the others as significant motif instances. Hence the 'empty chair' motif, designating an archetypal figure via his/her absence from the particular chair.

Red Buttons/Pockets is the most interesting character in the film. His performance is excellent, one of the finest and most expressive of the series. As a lively, likeable shadow figure, he serves as a 'triangular' go-between for Sean/ego and Dallas/anima in the story. In characteristic ego/shadow tension, Sean is perpetually irritated with him, always vowing to assault him in his repeated line, "One of these days, Pockets...." Too, Pockets continually chides Sean as "Bwana" this and "Bwana" that. 'Triangularly,' he urges Dallas not to irritate Sean too much, since Sean will take it out on him. Pockets is an intelligent character, as Dallas learns more about the mysterious, misogynistic Sean through him, and as he later contrives an ingenious trap and method to capture hundreds of monkeys. Though a full member of the group, he is, amusingly, afraid of animals. A New York City cab driver on the off season, he drives one of the field vehicles.

Anima-encumberedly, he carries Dallas's photo equipment for her, and the thigh pockets of his fatigue pants are a catch-all, in a way contra the material sparseness of the Hawks hero. In the 'song session' scene, he fumbles through sundry pocketed items to find his harmonica, in a 'sex role-reversal' application of the old joke of a woman's purse as a catch-all. At an early point, he starts to tote Dallas's photo equipment for her. Sean tells him not to spoil her, though Pockets ends up carting it for her anyway. Next, and relatedly (along with his being distracted by her half-clothed state), Pockets has a mishap with the vehicle he is driving.

Later, in his general shadow/anima mergence or confusion, Pockets tries to milk a billy goat and still later confuses the sex of one of the baby elephants.

241

Early too, Kurt helps Brandy with her zipper, anima-subserviently, as (connectedly) he reprimands himself for Indian's accident, feeling that he is largely to blame, since he was driving their vehicle. In this scene, he comes to her room with the bad news about Indian, at just the right moment to help her with her zipper and dress, in peer-dynamic 'simultaneity.' There, they are framed together in the earlier-noted cracked mirror.

Like Kid Dabb in *Only Angels Have Wings*, Pockets interrupts the hero and heroine in their growing coziness at least twice. Yet like Sparks and Kid in that film, he assists them when Dallas counsels with him regarding Sean, since Pockets (as Sean/ego's immediate "underside") knows him better than anyone else. Brandy, who is much taller than Pockets, in that touch of 'sex role-reversal,' falls in love with him in a comic, departure-from-realism way. He is also musical, and of course a comedian.

The African word "Hatari!" (Danger!) occurs in the film in connection with Pockets and his invention involving rocket propulsion and explosives, which go off accidentally at one point, to the natives' exclamations. Wheeler, Stumpy, and the wagon-load of dynamite, in *Rio Bravo*, are reiterated. (In other than its juxtaposition in the title sequence with Indian's accident—and its exclamation by Pockets, when the goats harmlessly stampede in one scene—this is the only explicit connection made with the African word. It would seem that "Danger!" is metaphoric and lies mainly within.) In characteristic shadow/anima creativity, Pockets brilliantly, though cumbersomely and comically, delivers the Rube Goldberg device that succeeds in trapping the hundreds of monkeys the group have on order. A feat of engineering, it is yet a shadow/anima irruption, echoing the self-sealing pyramid in *Land of the Pharaohs* of related anima 'convergence' and suppression. The method and device consists of driving the beasts into a large tree, then throwing a gigantic net over it by means of a homemade rocket. After this the tree is cut down, and the group, including Brandy—and Dallas now—having donned bizarre, makeshift suits of armor, extricate the dangerous monkeys by hand. Reference is made in their lines to medieval knights, extraterrestrials, and Cape Canaveral spaceprobing. Pockets, his monkey trap ("Hatari! Hatari!"), and the "knights" are of course one of the finest episodes in the film.

The successive points of Dallas's initiation/passage are as follows:

(1) The first day, she accompanies the group into the field with certain presumptions, designatedly as an amateur with regard to guns, vehicles, driving, etc., initially donning chic and wrong clothes, namely a "funny-looking work outfit." Camera-laden and having hurriedly changed, she gets into the back of one vehicle with Luis and the several African assistants to "Bwana" and the group. In minor 'convergence' upon her, Sean tells the natives in their own language to "take care of her" through the ensuing ride. She insists she needs no caring for, and hence endures the rough ride unpampered. She feels induced to apologize humbly afterward for her presumptuousness, such as it was. Brandy befriends her, prescribing a hot bath for her resulting aches and pains. The group let her stay with her photo assignment, as Sean, to this effect, says, "Rhinos, elephants, water buffalo...and a greenhorn (Dallas)," in the Woman/'animal' connection.

242

(2) That evening they have a 'music session.' Dallas plays some hot piano in company with Pockets's harmonica, and thus contributes something, recalling Bonnie's doing the same to instate herself in the 'song session' in *Only Angels Have Wings*. Prominently in the background is a native shield on the wall. At one point, Sean (in a hint of 'fraternal return') comes in and stands in juxtaposition with it, smiling, wearing his coat with the stark, dark-colored rifle pad on one shoulder: in mandala-Centric reiteration of the shield on the wall.

(3) Dallas, in a maternal way, adopts three motherless baby elephants. Subsequently, the local tribe wish to honor her thus, as "Mama Tembo." Under the auspices of Sean's group, the natives accost her and dress her in tribal costume, after dying her skin brown, and take her through a ceremony initiating her into the tribe. Sean is impressed with the way she goes through with it, noting that it meant a lot to the tribe, and that she is not like other women (whom, like certain other Hawks heroes, he views with fear and suspicion, in the anima-alienated pattern).

Dallas is absent from dinner that night—save for the "initiatory" 'empty chair,' which looms as though in her stead—as she is recovering from the lengthy task of removing the dark paint from herself. Sean visits her in her room to commend her, where—in significant contrast or ego/shadow-type 'reversal' now—she has a pack of (white) cold cream on. Sean, kissing her, gets some on him, uttering, "Women and their contraptions!" Just then, Pockets (who will later build the monkey-catching "contraption") barges in—in the pattern of the shadow interruption of ego and anima in a love scene—and, shying from Sonia, the household Cheetah there, spills Dallas's dinner on Sean, in further tactile relationship! The scene is a little reminiscent of the "signpost" scene in *I Was a Male War Bride*, though (in view of Dallas's earlier African makeup) it corresponds with Barnaby and Edwina's (ego/unconscious) light and dark paint fight in *Monkey Business*.

(4) Suggestive more than explicit, yet persistently compelling, is the seeming content of the "waterhole" sequence. If it is as it seems, it is on the sinister (i.e., cryptically homicidal) side of initiation/passage.

Sean, in his series pattern of "sex antagonism" around Dallas, at one point expresses that he would like to shoot Pockets, "or somebody." On one level, this seems to indicate Dallas. In the scene with the orphaned elephant calf needing to be (mercifully) shot, Dallas intervenes with, "Don't shoot him or you'll have to shoot me too!" Sean replies, "Don't tempt me." Earlier, as Sean is covertly balking at the general decision that Dallas may stay with the group, he wears his jacket with the stark, "anomalous," protective pad on one side, for high-powered rifle shooting—which he wears here and there in scenes, in its prominent, gun-oriented recalcitrance (echoing the Centric, irruptive-like designs on Mike's and Vashtar's clothing, respectively in *Tiger Shark* and *Land of the Pharaohs*).

In the sequence in question, Dallas incorrigibly heads for the local waterhole to bathe her adopted baby elephants without the required armed escort. Sean trails after her, to escort her with his rifle, and wearing his coat with the rifle pad. From a distance and unseen, he fondly watches her with her babies. (In this, he anticipates the neurotic Mike Marsh broodingly watching Gabby from hiding, twice, in *Red Line 7000*. In the second of these scenes, Mike will not toss lead her way but, nastily, his lighted cigarette. In general, Mike is fore-shadowed in Sean of *Hatari!)*

Across the waterhole is a small but cinematographically prominent bush, like some target. Centrically effective, it recalls the script-and-lamp in the violently initiatory rehearsal scene in *The Twentieth Century*, in the way that the bush is retained in the frame in successive shots from different angles. The distant bush rather "looms" in the scene (even, it seems to me, like an obliterated x marking a death as in *Scarface)*. After she joins Sean, some wild elephants approach and bellow threateningly. In anxious conversation, Dallas refers to one of them as a "him," as Sean corrects her with "cow." Previously, in kind, Sean referred to them as "grandfathers" who may be related to the babies and hence dangerous. It is of course the recalcitrant anima irrupting again, via 'blurred sexual distinctions.' Sean has Dallas hide with her babies behind a tree, and frightens the adults off with his rifle.

There seems to be a cryptic, anima-suppressive Sean/Dallas rifle assault here. This is in view of the above-mentioned points of dialogue—as well as the cryptic Tom/Fen "homicide" in *Red River*, and the Roger/Abigail "homicide" in the "pill" sequence in *Man's Favorite Sport?* (These are discussed, respectively, in section IV and the section on the 1963 film.) In any case, Dallas receives another comeuppance in the "waterhole" sequence.

It seems that the irruptive "Hatari! Hatari!" of Pockets and his "Cape Canaveral" explosives going off is in some reference to Sean and his ego/shadow/anima strife. In one scene, Pockets informs Dallas that if Sean is nasty to someone it means that he likes them, and that if he loves someone he is capable of killing them—half seriously, but significantly.

Thus fares Dallas's fourth point of initiation/passage, even like that of the 'significant happenstansical death' of the innocent Fen in *Red River*.

(5) Later, we have the pair of "thorn" scenes, suggestive of passage, and of relationship via the sensation-function. The first consists of Sean removing a thorn from a little deer's foot. In this surgery, the 'dismemberment' instance in *The Big Sky* is echoed. Attendantly, in a 'group-delineative/"circular" montage' sequence, other animals look on as though in intelligent concern. As the (Centric) thorn is extracted, all the animals lurch or race away.

In the Woman/animal connection, this is reiterated with Dallas later, as Sean removes a thorn from her back, in her darkened photo lab with window screens suggestive of a cage (recalling the cage allusion with the shadow/anima-rampant Williams in jail, in *His Girl Friday)*.

(6) In Dallas's thorn scene, she wears a red shirt. She leaves it behind with other clothes, in 'object/apparel'-transaction, as she goes to town to catch the plane for Switzerland. At breakfast, the same 'empty chair' looms in the foreground while members of the group goad Sean into pursuing her. They chase and retain her, recalling the theater group forcing Lily back in *The Twentieth Century*, and which Sean is very anxious to do, being in love with her by now, although having been very short on courtship (hence her leaving the group with mixed feelings). Along with her other clothes, the red shirt is used as "bait" for one of her babies to follow her trail like a bloodhound. In characteristic shadow/anima creativity, Luis and Pockets instigate this idea. The group cart the elephant calf to town in a jeep, and accompanied by a second vehicle,

244

it resembles one of their animal chases in the veldt. Uninvited, the other two elephant calves follow. The babies and the group chase her wantonly, destructively through two retail stores and finally into a hotel, where she is 'converged' upon from two directions, in the lobby. (No police sanctions come down on them in the story!)

It is thus a major 'sans rites-de-sortie' instance, in the group's wanton invasion of normal town society from the bush and the elite realm of the animal compound. It mainly recalls the cattle being herded into the town in *Red River*, and echoes the vigilante uprising in *Barbary Coast*. Obliquely it refers to the comparably violent/'convergent' montage of the pyramid sealing itself upon Nelipher in *Land of the Pharaohs*, which in turn anticipates the colossal and explosive monkey trap in action twenty minutes earlier in *Hatari!*

Thus she is retained, in final initiation/passage into the group. Further, as Pockets exits and Sean and Dallas begin their wedding night, her babies invade the room and break the bed (in the function of the amorous-meddling 'pal'/shadow), ending the film in a "shivaree." At this point, Pockets comes into the room again and stands near Sean, as both minorly echo Spike and Bill at the end of *A Girl in Every Port*.

A fair portion of the drama in *Hatari!* revolves around Chips (Gerard Blain), and him and Kurt, as the two make a friendly yet fighting pair like Spike and Bill of *A Girl in Every Port* and the engine room 'pals' in *Corvette K-225*. Both are of small stature and thus are pugilistically matched. At the end of the film, the two men are off to Paris together, as Kurt explains, "We find we both know a girl there. We go halves.... Another excuse for a fight." They become interested in (tall) Brandy, who somehow ends up going for Pockets, even though Kurt goes so far as to buy her a present. ("One of those things, you know, that women wear with laces on it and some stuff around....") 'Triangularly,' Chips jealously watches them from a doorway as Kurt gives her the object—with Sean watching too, from a point where he can see all three of them (all 'converged' upon Brandy and the fancy item). Sean then has some words with Kurt, warning him that Chips was watching.

Later, Chips saves Kurt's life in the field, shooting a crocodile about to prey on him, which puts them on friendlier terms. That night at the compound, Brandy asks them (i.e., one or both of them) to help her with a baby elephant chore. Alone for a moment, Chips says to Kurt: "*Our* girl looks pretty good tonight, eh?"

Kurt: "I'll flip you to see who goes with her." (tosses a coin).

Chips (grabbing the coin in the air, from him): "Let's go together. I don't trust you."

Kurt: "All right. Then give me my shilling back." (Which Chips does.)

Again, though in a more exemplary way here, they make a 'triangle' with Brandy via a well-transacted object representing Her.

Chips enters the story in place of Indian, who is hospitalized. He and Kurt ride in the same field vehicle alone, as Kurt and Indian did. Yet he early replaces Indian in a deeper way than merely filling his job, as Indian and he archetypally cross in the ego/shadow way.

As the group loiters around the hospital reception room awaiting word on Indian's condition, Chips, a stranger in a black knit shirt, appears very suddenly (like Boone's introduction in *The Big Sky*), juxtaposed with an overhead light. He says, "Who's got a cigarette?" A moment earlier, Luis Francisco Garcia Lopez (Valentin de Vargas) of the group, was searching his pockets for a cigarette pack. Reflexively, Sean tosses his pack to Chips (as though Chips was one of the group), then looks, realizing his mistake. Chips catches it, hesitates as he looks at Luis beside him, and says, "That yours?" Luis curtly says, "Thanks," and snatches the pack from the stranger, rectifying the mistake and the group solidarity. Yet Chips is, on one level, a (spontaneous) member of the group, via this prize 'fraternal pre-encounter' instance by means of the generally group-confined 'transactional object' of cigarettes.

Paired here as Luis's shadow, the stranger is, moreover, Indian (or Indian's shadow) 'fraternally returned' "from the dead." Having heard of the accident, Chips is there seeking Indian's job. Kurt, who feels guilty over Indian's accident (and who is the only one of his small size), takes offense and strikes him for this affront to the group. Indian needs a transfusion. Somewhat incredibly, Chips, as it happens, is the only known source of Indian's blood type within untold miles. After extracting an apology from Kurt, he contributes blood and saves Indian's life. On one level, Chips is Indian's shadow/'double' here, via the 'blood' motif. In addition to his sudden (or irruptive) appearance, Chips is all the more ghost-like in happening by with the right blood type at the right time (namely, like a typically purposive specter). As Indian is, on one level, dead and resurrected via Chips, the latter's dramatic 'fraternal encounter' with the group is, vaguely, Indian's 'return' as well (complete with the Centric accouterment of the juxtaposed overhead light)!

"We're blood brothers now," he later says to Indian, who replies, "Not until I give you some back." Even so, Indian loaned fifteen pounds to Chips (borrowed in turn from the doctor, a group friend). Chips makes good in a shooting match with Kurt (after which he strikes him once, hard, to even things up), and is hired.

Again, he wears a black T-shirt, color perhaps of the uninitiated and/or initiation, like Bill and the "morass" associated with him in *A Girl in Every Port*, like Mike in *Red Line 7000*, in common with Boone's dark clothes in *The Big Sky*, and the garb of numerous female characters in scenes throughout the series. Heroines are sometimes associated with 'fog/rain/shadow' in related reference. Chips is French and brunet while Kurt is German and ego-blond. They hence make a complementary 'pals' instance.

As Kurt begins to seethe in rivalry with Chips over (tall) Brandy, Sean remarks, in familiar disdain: "Spring comes to the bush veldt, and the young bucks start buttin' their heads together ... [Well] don't let it gum up the work around here."

Kurt: "Oh, I won't. But I'm not going to give him a free hand either."

Sean: "Oh, this is gonna be great! The Indian's knocked out, we're stuck with a woman photographer, and you and the Frenchman break out in monkeybites, and we're a month behind already!"

Kurt: "So what?"

Sean: "So don't give him a free hand."

This is an average instance of 'merged dramatics/dialogue' (with Sean abruptly assuming Kurt's concern—i.e., his dramatic/dialogue space). It also

246

stresses the unregimented, informal character of the group. In the series 'group' pattern, the clashing/interrelating energies of the group members prevail, as formalities are often pointedly overruled. In *Air Force* this results in maximum job efficiency—though not in *The Thing (From Another World), Rio Bravo,* nor even *The Big Sky.* Yet the result is a common vitality that is ultimately job-effective. In *Ball of Fire,* the excessively formal, professorial demeanor is reversed with the advent of the personality of Sugarpuss amidst the group, which shifts the story itself—calamitously at first, but finally to the benefit of the Totten House project.

The brunette, taciturn, yet prominent Professor Gurkakoff of that film is paralleled in the shadowy Luis, in *Hatari!* At the end of the season, Luis comes forth in a very 'fancy,' as well as fragrant black suit. Chips and Kurt josh him ambiguously, as though he were either (a) female, and a good date for one of them, perhaps having a sister for the other, or (b) male and, for his obvious "female" qualities, likely to have two sisters for Kurt and Chips, or (c) a bordertown pimp who might be offering his sisters for sale (in the stereotype). Even so, Luis stresses that he is going to town on "business" which, we gather, may be shady or "gangsterish" (as, moreover, Tony of *Scarface* is recalled here). In the past, Luis was a bullfighter.

So much for the mediocre to good *Hatari!* and its diverse, international group: in Sean (originally from Ireland), Dallas (Italy), Pockets (New York City), and Indian (America); Brandy (French-African), Kurt (German), Chips (French), Luis (Mexican), and Brandy's deceased father (French or French-African), and the "nice Belgian kid" who was killed. Peripherally, there are the "boys" (African) and Dr. Sanderson/"Sandy" (apparently German or Austrian, played by Eduard Franz). The film is rich in auteur values and outstanding in its action sequences in the field, where the cast did its own stunt work.

Henry Mancini's music is very good, and the organ rock and roll piece was often heard on disc jockey radio. The most important music in Hawks films is, of course, rendered within the dramatic context, in group-dynamical 'song/music session' instances. More than half the sound films feature these. Even *Scarface* and *Land of the Pharaohs* include them (respectively, in Cesca singing "The Wreck of Old 97" to Guino, and the chanting at the "Ceremony of the Honored Dead" and at other points in the Egyptian project). In addition to two or three native African 'song sessions' and the piano/harmonica session with Dallas and Pockets, the *Hatari!* group sing "Whiskey Leave Me Alone" (used in *The Big Sky*) over the intercom between their two vehicles, in a strong 'dramatized/converged space' instance after the evening's drinking in celebration of Indian's survival at the hospital.

MAN'S FAVORITE SPORT?
(1963)

Once again we may lament the relative mediocrity of a film from Hawks's late period, despite its promise as a project and its wealth of series-pattern material. Like *Hatari!*, *Man's Favorite Sport?* concerns the pursuit of members of the animal kingdom, and self- (and anima-) mastery in connection with the same. It satirizes the urbane, sporting-goods store style of fishing. Like *Bringing Up Baby*, it is a comedy with a psychoanalytic bent (as *Hatari!* has something of the same in the figure of Sean and the self-conscious-like Sean/Dallas 'self-encounter/splitting off' instance).

On a level of comic metaphor and allegory, in the film, the hero's quest is for his masculine-erotic nature and his ego integrity. In terms of the series patterns, the quest concerns his initiation/passage from a kind of dishonesty to ego integrity, the ordeal replete with shadow/anima irruption.

Roger Willoughby (Rock Hudson), a fraudulent but leading fishing expert—who is mainly a successful promoter of costly sporting goods—has never fished in his life. In the story, he is railroaded into a fishing competition at a mountain resort by publicists Abigail Page (Paula Prentiss) and her shadow, Isolde Mueller (Maria Perchy), who is nicknamed "Easy," like a character in *Rio Bravo*.

In the story, they, and particularly Abigail, provide for Roger's psychic harassment—even as metaphorical "fish," in one important scene, in the 'animal/Woman' connection (particularly recalling Susan with her dog and leopard in *Bringing Up Baby)*. In one of the film's many instances of unheroic object-encumbrance, Roger becomes buried in a new-fangled tent which he cannot erect properly. The girls swim up to the shore where Roger is—as 'pals,' yet as "fish." In an ego/shadow way, each wears a diffrent colored bathing cap. They tauntingly confront him just as he emerges from the tangled mass of tent (humiliated by one of the items of equipment he and his firm so espouse). Since he is surprised by them in this stressful way, it is a minor 'self-encounter' instance.

John Screaming Eagle (Norman Alden), a conceptually wonderful character, functions similarly as Willoughby's *shadow*. Like Abigail, he follows or trails Roger about, partly to sell him bogus fishing aids and other rustic items. In the film, he and Isolde/"Easy" serve as go-betweens for Roger and Abigail, in the shadow/anima way.

Prior to his union with Abigail, Roger acts heroically in publically admitting that he is a fake. In the manner of casting his bread upon the waters, all rewards come to him. He soon gets his job back, and Abigail "catches" him. Earlier, as he dines with her, he finds a caterpillar in his salad, in allusion to his being "fished for" with this "bait." As he and Abigail are conjoined in the end, John Screaming Eagle remarks, "...too late to help him now." in reference to female entrapment, and (like the entire character of John Screaming Eagle) reiterating Bill in *A Girl in Every Port.*

At one point, Screaming Eagle, a little in surprise, or in the manner of 'self-encounter,' emerges from the brush to sell Roger a container of "moose blood" for energy in the fishing contest at hand (obliquely in the 'blood' motif). Screaming Eagle develops concern for him in his plights—as when he disconcertedly eavesdrops on Roger's hassling with three females within a very short time—namely, Abigail, "Easy," and Roger's formidable fiancee Tex Connors (Charlene Holt). As an eavesdropper, he is appropriately shadow-like, and in company with Sean in *Hatari!* and Mike in *Red Line 7000*. His changing from "American Indian" talk to ordinary speech, at moments when he doffs his masquerade, touches 'double/*doppelgänger*' (c). (Ref. appendix 1.)

Early, in trying to peddle his junk to Willoughby, John Screaming Eagle remarks in a friendly way that his grandfather once scalped a man named Willoughby—this in a deft touch of the extended group and in the 'friend/foe' pattern. There is the little scene where he gives William Cadwalader (John McGiver) a "valuable historical relic"—a scalp—and adds that, according to custom, he must be given a gift in return, namely twenty dollars. Cadwalader phlegmatically complies. It is an 'object-transaction' of extended-group import, since Cadwalader is Roger's boss, Screaming Eagle Roger's shadow, and the scalp (allegedly, earlier) belonged to a Willoughby of pioneer days.

A more profound tactile/object transaction is the conceptually outstanding "toupee" business among Cadwalader, his loose toupee, and the two women (who 'converge' upon him in effective initiation/passage). In the office, the taciturn Isolde is a background foil to Abigail Page (in the manner of shadows Sierra in *Viva Villa!*, Guino in *Scarface*, and the potted plant affairs behind Dorothy and Lorelei early in *Gentlemen Prefer Blondes*). Isolde's dark hat resembles those of Webb, Mississippi, and Bidey, of the series, and is a minor 'odd hat' instance, and Centric. In the scene, Cadwalader's toupee becomes loose. The girls call his attention to it, and he laments that his wife makes him wear it. All this is in conjunction with Miss Page's knocking an ash tray into the fish tank and splashing water on him, at one point. He is finally led to the manly triumph of removing the contraption, as he then goes off to a business meeting with male peers, walking tall in his 'baldness' (in the mandala-Centric motif). Beautifully reiterated are the "water" initiation/passage instances involving Judith's and Dorothy's hair, respectively in *Only Angels Have Wings* and *Gentlemen Prefer Blondes*.

Likewise conceptually outstanding and fresh is the remarkable "pill" sequence. It involves an 'x' instance, echoing the *x*'s marking the deaths in *Scarface*. As a cryptic, archetypal "homicide," it refers to that of the "waterhole" sequence in *Hatari!*

Preceding it by some time is Willoughby muttering to himself that he will kill Abigail for getting him into his fishing predicament and for her generally besieging and pestering him. In the sequence itself, Abigail goes to his cabin for a sleeping pill, in pretext to get together with him. Not expecting to have to take the pill, she eventually does, for credibility. "I guess it won't kill me," she says significantly.

Prominently near her, and very visible at other times, it is an *x* in the woodwork on the door, and a lateral cross on a nearby appliance. Subsequently she is not murdered, as Roger vowed, but is "dead to the world" from the sedative (with the anima suppressed once again).

Man's Favorite Sport? opens with a smart, energetic credit sequence amove to a jazzy song by a Henry Mancini aggregation, stating that fellows go for many sports but that the favorite one is girls. In lieu of a depicted sportsman is a photomontage of slim young women in vigorous, joyful action at several sports, in oblique, yet resounding echo of Susan of *Bringing Up Baby.* The montage/collage may be the best part of the film.

The opening sequence features Roger's and Abigail's new sporty cars on the streets of San Francisco, as he and she (with Isolde/"Easy" in the car with her) meet ahead of time in automobile/traffic confrontation. Then he and Abigail (still not formally introduced) quarrel over a parking space, she winning. In the course of things here, Willoughby drops his driver's license into her car. After she leaves, he must search for it, looking like a car thief. Accosted by a policeman, Roger shows him Abigail's license by mistake—it being on the floor of her car too, where he picks it up. The officer addresses him as "Abigail Page" (as Roger and she are more formally introduced!). In terms of 'sex role-reversal' and identity confusion with a 'self-encounter/splitting off' aspect, Willoughby thus (retroactively) runs into himself in Her in the preceding automobile clashes.

He is next commiserated with by the officer who, when Roger relates that there were two women, says, "Two of 'em? You were in a spot," echoing, in 'reverse,' the multimale convergence upon Lily in *The Twentieth Century.* His uniformed 'pal' here recalls the delivery man bolstering David on the phone with his fiancee in *Bringing Up Baby.*

Next is the sporting goods store scene, likewise well carried off, and portending a better film than turned out. The scene focuses around one of the most essential player transactions in the Hawks series.*

Major Phipps (Roscoe Karns) comes into the store, and Willoughby and fellow salesmen prepare to descend on him to wheedle out of him all that he may be willing to spend on his pseudo-sportsmanship. Their steady, salesmanlike convergence upon him culminates in their helping him to successfully fly cast in a little canvas pool with a floating ring as a target. In the series compositional pattern, this ring is prominently to the foreground of two or more principal shots. As he works at it, the salesmen casually move in and complete a grouping around him—just as he succeeds in landing the fly in the ring, and as, in unison, they softly utter, "Eureka!"

Although the recalcitrant anima is not explicitly involved here, the sequence is in the mode of group 'convergence' upon the anima, as in the major cases of the theater fellows and Lily in *The Twentieth Century,* and the "night court" scene around the Centric tiara in *Gentlemen Prefer Blondes.* Also recalled are the masterfully self-sealing pyramid and its elite group in *Land of the*

---

*In a recently-viewed print of *Man's Favorite Sport*, this scene seems either to have been replaced by an alternate one or seriously abbreviated by deletions *within* the sequence. I have chosen to trust my memory and discuss the scene as I have recorded it from earlier viewings, in terms of the richer details related here. As regards the particular and general auteur points, my conclusions are, in any case, valid in terms of the other films and film portions cited here in cross-comparison with the "sporting goods store" scene.

Pharaohs, and Tex's 'pal' coming beside him in "osmotic" support, enabling Tex to instantly perk up in the quarrel with his wife on the phone, in *Ceiling Zero*. As a 'group-contagious' assistance to Phipps's successful fly cast, the sequence combines with all the above to suggest that, in the overall series patterns, anima convergence/suppression links with ego/tactile mastery and professional and group mastery.

All of these are linked, in turn, with the Self, the fly-casting sequence being, after all, a dramatic and cinematic mandala. Indeed, Phipps's sales-force-assisted fly cast obliquely yet penetratingly symbolizes the series 'edict'—that of professionalism/competence as a manifold law unto itself, due to its particular rootedness in the all-encompassing Self (in the Hawksian vision or scheme).

The amok "penny arcade" scene diametrically contrasts with the comedic, yet ultimately stoical, "fly-casting" sequence. Yet it has formal similarities. Here, besieged by the two PR women seeking his participation in the tournament, Roger Willoughby admits, semiprivately there, that he has never fished in his life. In preparation for this horrible admission, he races about the room putting coins in every music machine, resulting in a cacophonic hubbub, with the machines' little mechanical figures amove. He needs this chaos of noise going while he utters the unmentionable—"I've never fished in my life!" As he is racing around thus, Abigail says to Isolde, "He's crazy." (Shades of the B-17 warriors in *Air Force*, and other Hawksian adventurers!) Just as he utters the unutterable, the house electricity fails, the lights going out—leaving a female statuette prominently silhouetted in the window. Centric, anima/Self-like, it is the still eye of the just-ceased comedic hurricane.

His mischief's resulting inconvenience to the penny arcade here gives the scene a 'sans rites-de-sortie' aspect, and also recalls the riotous board-meeting scene in *Monkey Business,* centering on Oxly's gold watch. Willoughby's pertinent words, emitted over the noises of each and all the machines going at once, parallels (or rather parodies) the 'overlapping dialogue' technique (which features vocal hubbub with the important lines still coming through).

A minor instance of 'self-encounter/splitting off' occurs where Willoughby, out on the trails on a little motorbike, collides with a bear as the trail passes through some brush, after which the cycle emerges from the other side of the brief tunnel with the bear riding it. Although deriving, in its variation here, from an older, stock movie joke, it compares interestingly with Henri's haystack collision and 'self-encounter' in *I Was a Male War Bride*. (Again, Hawks is a creative borrower from many sources.)

Just before colliding with his shadow in the bear, a girl on a similar motorbike curtly instructs him on how to use it, in parodic Hawksian professionalism.

RED LINE 7000
(1965)

Apart from its serious dramatic flaws, *Red Line 7000,* Hawks's second racing film, is an interesting, "mod"-innovative addition to his later period. It somehow remains likeable after many viewings.

See section IV for some important discussion concerning the Mike/Gabby/Dan 'triangle' and the series-essential 'dismemberment' instance with Ned Arp.

Early, Gail Hire/Holly MacGregor's fiance, Jim Loomis, is killed in a stock-car race, "goes off the deep end" as it is put. This is in dual reference to his having fallen in love and (hence) driving incautiously—going over the "red line" of 7000 R.P.M. (translatable as "Hatari!", or "Danger!"), which leads to his crashing. He leaves behind some pocket change and a cigarette lighter—the latter separately recovered by Lindy at her bar and hangout, for a fresh and geographically split-in-half instance of 'meager last possessions' (utilizing a spatial-dramatic dimension, in the pattern).

Holly's persisting notion that she is a hoodoo to the race drivers she goes with is hence reinforced once again. She is brought to a room by the motel manager—who is later shown in fair rapport with others of the group (or the profession), in the extended-group pattern. In her motel room, Holly tries to drown sorrow and guilt feelings with a bottle and the loud rock and roll music recurrent in the film, the music serving the characters as did the cathartic cigarette smoking/transacting in *Only Angels Have Wings,* and the moderate drinking (by other than boozers Dude and Joe) in *Rio Bravo.* Significantly, the maladjusted Mike Marsh (James Caan) dislikes rock and roll. In shadow/anima complement, Gabrielle Queneau/"Gabby" (Marianna Hill), with whom he will ultimately unite, likes it and is a good dancer.

Holly soon passes out from the imbibed spirits, and Mike takes care of her at the motel for a brief time. He totes her luggage and clothes, and fixes her some breakfast, anima-subserviently, uncomplimentary, and portending ill for him. Further, Mike is a close friend of the deceased, in 'triangle' reference. (Earlier in the film is the dramatically excellent locker-room scene with him and Loomis in close contact, as they discuss her [Her].)

Mike is supportive of Holly and tries to discourage her hoodoo notion of herself, stressing that Jim died not because of her but because he went over the red line, metaphorically linked though they both are. Mike is a very good driver, it is indicated, but he has neurotic problems in the story—along with Holly, and Ned Arp (John Robert Crawford) with his swelled head, and Julie Kazarian (Laura Devon) with her doubts of her femininity. Echoing Boone's dark clothing and countenance in *The Big Sky,* and Chips's shirt in *Hatari!,* Mike wears a black T-shirt, for 'initiation,' marking his indiscipline and moody recalcitrance (subjects of male passage).

Relatedly, there is the slight but deft item of the man on the phone at Lindy's bar, who orders more peach brandy as he broods over his fourth wife, in a series-typical shadow/anima negative-marriage entrapment inclusive of a 'fancy item' (in lieu of, say, "masculine" bourbon, as pointedly in *Rio Lobo*). In the Hawksian scheme of things, "peach brandy" is a condition requiring passage.

In the motel room, Mike and Holly are talking when Pat Kazarian (Norman Alden) enters, interrupting them, asking, "What's going on?" Mike replies, "Well.... I was going to ask her what she's going to do now." Holly then tells them *both*. Thus, Pat is instantly plunged into the conversation, via the 'merged dramatics/dialogue' technique.

This compares well with another, earlier-noted portion of 'merged dramatics/dialogue' in the film. On Gabby's doorstep, she and Dan McCall (James Ward) have broken up. She says: "Are we still friends?"

He (smiling): "What are you doing for dinner tomorrow night?"

She (smiling): "I'm having dinner with a friend."

He: "See you tomorrow night."

Here, Dan and Gabby share one another's personal/conscious space—much as Pat entered the Mike/Holly conversation all too quickly, as though he and Mike were one person.

Again, in the 'merged dramatics/dialogue' pattern and method, characters transact on a nonverbal level, or prematurely, such as in the series instances of 'second-guessing' (the simplest example of the pattern). This is as a character or characters assume dramatic space ordinarily of the personal space of another character or characters. Generally this flies in the face of the more salient functions of orthodox, "isometric" drama and dialogue. In terms of the close-knit group, and its extensions one way and another, it functions thematically in the Hawks series. Stemming from the scenario of *A Girl in Every Port*, it bears reference to the pattern of 'characters as portions of one psyche.'

Similarly, characters prematurely transact via 'fraternal encounter/pre-encounter.' Early, two race drivers are trying to pick up Gabby at Lindy's bar. Dan, a stranger to the two men, comes up, and a mild confrontation ensues over her. (The pair do not know that Dan is her boyfriend, meeting her there for a date.) A few moments later, Pat comes up and says, "I didn't know you fellows had met." Dan answers, "We haven't." Pat then introduces Dan to the pair. Indeed, they *have* met, of course, ahead of Pat's introduction, in the 'fraternal encounter' way. Too, Dan is somewhat pre-introduced ('pre-encountered' by the pair) through Gabby, his anima. (There she is generally 'converged' upon in a 'triangular/quadrangular' note as well, in series-typical archetypal clustering.) As it quickly becomes clear who Dan is, namely Gabby's boyfriend (and, not least, the driver pair have also heard of Dan McCall), the limbo and moderate hubbub of strangeness among the characters richly congeals in new acquaintance. In the Hawks way, the acquaintance thus comes about prior to formal/verbal introductions, in terms of deeper confrontation.

At an early point, Dan has car trouble on the road and Holly gives him a lift (in a touch of 'sex role-reversal,' since women are usually the ones with car trouble in movies). Although this is their first meeting, she knows who he is through the grapevine, in the 'fraternal pre-encounter' way. On one level, she is his irrupting anima (via the 'sex role-reversal' factor). Later, it is for Holly that he will break up with Gabby.

Very shortly, Holly and Gabby first meet in Dan's motel room. Holly and she find that they both speak French, Gabby's native language, and they both launch into a cheerily energetic conversation in the same, semi-comically excluding Dan, who protests. Evasively, on one level, he goes to the phone to call the Kazarian garage regarding his stalled car—thus fleeing to the haven of masculine peerdom! A manner of 'triangle' instance is afoot, among Holly, Gabby, and Dan—with characteristic emphasis on an odd, deep transaction between the pair in rivalry for a member of the opposite sex. Later sensing that Dan has fallen for Holly, Gabby alludes in an oblique way that she is a little jealous of her. This is as she says, "I'm not jealous of *Holly*. I'm jealous of *you*." (Italics mine.)

Holly's fear of becoming a hoodoo to Dan comes between them, of course. In one scene in Lindy's, she acts her superstition out in a rock and roll number—"Wildcat Jones"—accompanied by several uniformed waitresses (a peer group). The ingredients of the song are: Wildcat Jones, in his ten gallon hat and overalls, is good with cars but not with the girls, which proves his downfall. Along comes a girl who "takes Jones for a ride," keeping him out all night before a race. Thence he crashes and "sails out of town with her." This is of course a parable of the anima compensatorily irrupting, verily as Death. Possibly, the ten-gallon-hatted Jones and she directly recall Tom and Fen (and Matt and Tess in the "rain" scene) in the cowboy-epical *Red River*.

Like her hoodoo notion in general, the song number echoes Bonnie, guilt-ridden for her indirect involvement in Joe's death in *Only Angels Have Wings*. In that film, her sense of guilt and the general loss of their comrade are expended in the group 'song session' which follows ("The Peanut Vendor"). In kind, Holly, again, earlier turns up the rock and roll music to help drown out Jim Loomis's death. His quiet fifteen-second-long funeral scene is followed by one character's reference to rock and roll, as "better than a hymn for some people"—as the funeral is, retroactively, mitigated by this touch of 'irreligion.'

A prominent supporting character is Lindy Bonaparte (Charlene Holt), proprietress of Lindy's. Though echoing Sparks of *Only Angels Have Wings*, in a minor way, she mainly takes after the heroine Hildy of *His Girl Friday*. The little scene in which she is introduced is a good one, and somewhat wrought in Hawks's old black and white, medium-lighted cinematography, successfully within color. Her name, Bonaparte, that of the old conquerer, is a significant character touch. To reveal this allusion, we need to look ahead to the scene of Mike and Gabby's main encounter. This scene successfully utilizes shadow (a fair amount of it) in a fresh way, for Hawks.

Mike and Gabby have communicated earlier, though from his part in a curt, unfriendly way. The "Pepsi" scene is outdoors at the posh motel, with loud rock and roll music coming from somewhere (or from Gabby's room, as I recall). 'Pre-encounteringly,' both characters happen outside at once. Echoing Sean eavesdropping on Dallas in the "waterhole" scene in *Hatari!*, Mike, broodingly in the shadows, watches Gabby dancing a little by herself to the music as she comes to get a Pepsi from the vending machine. She confronts him, and they become better acquainted there. He has a Pepsi too. Between them, it is a 'shared drinks in common' instance (like Slim and Cricket's scotch and sodas in *To Have and Have Not)*. In an effort to bring him out, she round-

254

aboutly begins taunting him about his name, Mike Marsh. This is by way of her belief that people's names influence who they become: for example that Napoleon Bonaparte had to be a great conqueror; that Oscar Wilde "had to be..." (wild). (I.e., gay? Although not directed at Mike, he is uncomfortable at this 'homosexual joke,' as he coughs nervously here.) She alludes that a "Marsh" might have to be a bogged-down sort (a shadowy sort). Thus he and she begin courting, Hawks-style.

Lindy Bonaparte is hence conqueress-like, as a proprietress might need to be. In her introductory bar scene and at times thereafter, she wears, like a Medal of Honor, a stopwatch belonging to her late husband, a race driver who died in action. After a series-typical transaction of drinks with those at the table, who include Holly, she relates that she is now *safely* married: not to an automobile hero, but to a (professionally "inferior") bank teller, implying her anima or female-egoistic dominance. In this and in other ways, she is in the heroine mode of Hildy of the series (who, again, was going to exit from the vortex of the newspaper business by marrying Bruce the insurance man).

Lindy's Hawksian drink transactions in the film consist of (1) bringing up a tray of them and serving herself one, and at another point, (2) as one man takes the tray of drinks she is holding, he takes one and offers/gives it to her—"mixing it up" thus, in the 'merged dramatical' way.

Behind her and strikingly, in her introductory scene's key shot, is one of the automotive advertising posters or signs which adorn the film's mod/pop setting. As a somewhat hardened race driver's widow, she makes a flippant remark about the deceased Jim Loomis's girlfriend left behind, then senses that it is Holly there. She emphatically apologizes, as they are thus preintroduced in the 'fraternal pre-encounter' way. Soon they are in partnership together in Lindy's, which correspondingly, as a twosome, they expand. Later, Lindy is rough on Holly in her persisting hoodoo idea; but it is helpful to Holly, and helps to intervene for Dan and her.

In the course of the dramatic development of the violent Mike/Gabby/Dan 'triangle,' it may be that a new motif comes to light, although I consider 'anima-ego' to be questionable or tentative.

Mike and Gabby are dating in his car. She sings and he whistles with her, in a 'song session' instance between them—as a two-way montage sequence, back and forth between them from opposite sides of the parked car, alternates each of them in light and shadow. Altogether, Gabby's greatly contrasting liveliness is dominant. Hence, the moments in which Mike is in shadow there are more emphatic, making him all the more "Marsh"-like. Yet she is like a certain "vanguard" or process on *his* part, like a flower growing out of him—in an "ego" position thus, with Mike as her personified unconscious (her shadow/animus, say). Very suggestively, here and subsequently, she forms the "ego-channel" of his eventual jealous assault on Dan, as Mike (as unconsciousness) irrupts through her. Indeed, this relates to the 'triangular' saloon brawl in *Come and Get It*, where the eminent Lotta becomes an anima-*ego* and an "ego-channel" for Barney and Swan's brawling, as they irrupt through her, like one or more unconscious entities.

As these sequences suggest an 'anima-ego' motif, the Marlowe/Jones 'self encounter' in *The Big Sleep* suggests a 'shadow-ego' variant. As Marlowe's shadow, Jones, takes the ego position over him, Marlowe irrupts in turn upon Jones's killer and singlehandedly defeats the gang as well.

Jung has referred to cases, or a category, in which a subject's anima yields, in turn, a legitimate animus (or vice versa). Conceivably, then, Hawks projects his anima in Gabby and his anima's animus in Mike, in the sequence.

Later, on their date, Gabby wants to drive Mike's road car very fast around the deserted night track. As she is thence in the driver's seat of the speeding car, they constitute a more overt 'sex role-reversal.' She alludes to the car as a "beast." As the car spins out, it may be in allusion to sexual climax on her part, with her increasing speed as building up to the same—as, herethrough, Mike coaxes and guides her driving, as if he were the woman, guiding a male partner in Gabby and the "beast."

Thus is she vivacious and active and he "dormant" in the sequence, recalling his earlier watching her from hiding and shadows as she danced by the Pepsi dispenser. In this passive and hidden way, Mike spies on her a second time, just prior to his assault on Dan the next day on the track. (Again, ref. discussion of the Mike/Dan/Gabby crisis and the attendant 'dismemberment' instance with Ned Arp, in section IV.)

As Mike's eventual "quarry," one or more things associated with Dan McCall are target-like, as though to accommodate Mike's irruptive, assaultive shot at him! Mandala-Centrically, these are the round, sun-like white form on the side of Dan's street vehicle, and his blond hair and blazer jacket emblem.

In the scene of Gabby's seeming, to Mike, to have gone back to Dan, Mike renders a deft, ugly 'object-transaction' with her. As he begins upbraiding her, he throws his cigarette at her. As he goes up to her, he crushes it underfoot, the camera in medium close-up on it, thus grounding the short scene. Metaphorically, he "rubs her out" here!

It supports one's darker suspicions of the eavesdropping "waterhole" scene with Sean, his high-powered rifle, and Dallas, in *Hatari!* Moreover, this scene with Mike and Gabby commences with his having spied on her a second time.

There is the unusual instance of 'sex role-reversal/confusion' with Julie Kazarian (Laura Devon) who is concerned about her female identity. She and Ned cross paths in a quarrelsome encounter, in the Hawks way. He is seeking the deceased Jim Loomis's job with her brother's stock-car racing team as she comes up on a motorcycle. Ned remarks to her that he thought, at first, that she was a boy, since she drives like one. Because she is hyperconcerned about being feminine and sexy, a little tiff ensues. Pat is disinclined to try him out. Then, for some enigmatic reason, she *supports* Ned there—urges Pat to let him show what he can do on a clear track. Afterwards he is hired, partly through his and Julie's 'friend/foe' encounter thus. For Julie it is an instance of 'the love impulse initially expressing itself in conflict,' then acquiescing to receptivity. Whence they become an important couple in the story.

In an initiation/passage, "hazing" note, Ned is given a mechanically unbalanced car to drive. During his trial run, a piece of paper passes in front of him, well to the foreground (in the familiar compositional pattern). Later in the film, it is remarked that at high speeds a driver can be fatally disoriented by something as minor as a piece of paper, thus linking the two portions.

At a few points, the announcer's booth at the track is shown—containing several men and one woman at work, in the familiar 'convergence' of two or more men upon Her.

The last scene in the film (previous to more outstanding footage of racing stock-cars interedited with medium closeups of driver characters) is a charming one indeed, and rendered from the girls' point of view. It is just after the scenes of character problem resolutions—subsequent to Ned's losing his hand in a crash, and Mike's lunatic attempt on Dan's life and its 'triangle' and other archetypal features. (Ref. section IV.) This general or group resolution of problems is, again, symbolized in the last sequence's opening shot of Ned Arp's prosthetic hand on the wheel as he drives ably in the race, in the way of sacrifice/passage via 'dismemberment' and its subsequent adaptation and wholeness (i.e., "restoration").

Related to Ned Arp and his renewal are the three girls in the stands. Holly is freed of her hoodoo idea through Dan's surviving his earlier crash, and Julie and Gabby have achieved hard-won reconciliation with their boyfriends. They sit there looking smilingly cool and calm in the face of their men risking their lives anew on the track. This is a "mod" sort of 'reverse' of Lee and Ann's (contrasting) aloofness near the end of *The Crowd Roars*, Hawks's other racing film. Holly, Julie, and Gabby are good supporters now. Directorially, they seem to be cutely showing it off for the camera—in a touch of the casual, playful manner of much of *Hatari's* dramatic style. In this way the story concludes very happily, save that in the subsequent short racing sequence, the film (literally) ends on another crash.

EL DORADO
(1966)

Rio Bravo, El Dorado, and *Rio Lobo* are companion films in being action dramas of essentially military (or tactical/strategic) contention between two groups, set wholly or in major part in Western towns and featuring common points of story and situation (e.g., the sheriff's office and jail as a fortess in the siege, yielding to a prisoner-exchange drama). All were filmed in color between 1958 and 1970, and star John Wayne. The later films, though lacking the story-dramatic depths of *Rio Bravo,* surpass it in certain visual, dramatic, and action-dramatic aspects (save that Wayne's *Rio Lobo* performance is on the mediocre to poor side).

El Dorado is rich in settings, cinematography, costuming, and frame-composition (including ample medium closeups and effective camera movements). Likewise in contrast to *Rio Bravo, El Dorado* is more briskly paced. In view of the lighter story, this is advantageous. *El Dorado's* generally low-keyed dramatic force is sometimes broken by injections of senseless banter/humor—obvious "padding" which mars rather than enriches the film (in contrast to the apt bantering humor of the groups in *The Thing (From Another World),* particularly, and to some extent *Rio Bravo).*

The 1966 film has a few bad scenes, of careless, slipshod story development. (There is the improbable business of Cole Thornton being returned, bound and gagged, to his comrades at the jail and held hostage at the same time via guns trained on him from across the street.) Improbable or anachronistic for a Western town of the time is the set of Joey and Mississippi's combative "roll in the hay" (recalling that of Billy and Rio in *The Outlaw).* It is in a stable, at night, and yet the place is fully lighted! James Caan is imperfectly cast and/or inadequately directed in the carelessly conceived role of Alan Bourdillon Traherne/"Mississippi." Christopher George's portrayal as the gunman Nelse McLeod is dramatically good and visually excellent. Wayne, Robert Mitchum, and Charlene Holt are in good form. Disappointingly, Arthur Hunnicutt/Bull Harris is too restrained from his loquacious expressiveness as a Western type.

The film opens with the rich "W.C." sequence, with its 'friend/foe' and 'triangle' dramatics in contention around a mandala-Centric object.

El Dorado sheriff J.P. Harrah (Robert Mitchum), aware that his old friend Cole Thornton (John Wayne) is in town, notes the latter's appaloosa horse outside a saloon, and thus ('pre-encounteringly') knows that Cole is inside. Uneasily, but in competent stealth, he steals into the W.C. where Cole is washing, and confronts him at gunpoint. 'Pre-encounteringly' as well, Cole recognizes J.P.'s voice before looking up from washing. Drying his face with a towel as he turns, he then stares in surprize at J.P.'s rifle trained upon him. The story is thus launched with great dramatic tension, since the two characters are supposed to be good friends.

J.P. heard that Cole has hired with the outlaw rancher, Bart Jason, in the latter's impending range war with the MacDonald family over the latters' waterhole. Cole cancels his tentative plans to hire with Jason after hearing

J.P's version of the conditions of the Jason/MacDonald quarrel. Both pals fondly express that they are glad not to be on opposite sides. Cole notices that J.P. has customized his rifle after Cole's own—with a circular rather than an oblong cocking lever; a large ring. J.P. tosses the rifle to Cole who then tosses it back to him in 'object-transaction'—saliently a handshake. The gun's stark mandala-Centric feature becomes all the more symbolic as J.P. intimates that he copied Cole's rifle because Cole was *lucky* with it.

Also, it may be significant that Bart Jason's name is that of the mythical hero who sought the golden fleece, in common with the quest for Eldorado in the Edgar Allen Poe poem, used in the film.

Cole's spotted horse and the "Grail"-like object between the two men acquire further 'triangle' aspect when Maudie (Charlene Holt) barges in and embraces Cole in reunion—to J.P.'s comic consternation, since he likes her too, and her obviously more than friendly relationship with Cole is news to him. As she suddenly enters, after announcing herself through the door, J.P. slips behind the opening door: as, on one level, she "becomes" or 'splits off' from J.P.! She does not come between the two men in the story. There she passes the remark that she will leave them both if they quarrel over her. After Cole leaves to sever with Jason, J.P. and Maudie lovingly discuss Cole. Here, close in the foreground of the two-shot, J.P. for a few moments gazes off in the direction of Cole's exit. Alone shortly, Maudie utters "Hell!" to herself, since a consummated relationship with Cole (or with either of them) is 'triangularly' thwarted now.

The scene shifts to the MacDonald waterhole and a few of the MacDonalds and their Mexican cowhands amidst a herd of horses being watered. In the foreground is a vaquero with a lasso, in a professionalistic note (as though cognizant of the historical fact that Mexican stockmen taught the trade to American cowboys). The water curves around a mountainous rock (a boundary marker to the MacDonald ranch land). Word comes to them that the elite gunman, Cole Thornton, has hired with Bart Jason and is on his way to the latter's ranch nearby. (In truth, Cole is going there to refuse the employment.) Expecting trouble, Kevin MacDonald, the father (R.G. Armstrong), sends nervous young Luke MacDonald (Johhny Crawford) to the top of the rock to observe, and to fire a warning shot as needed, while the rest begin driving—stampeding—the horses home. The overall image here, of shots of the horses plowing through the shallow water and around the rock, with the boy on top (as one of the shots moves upward to him) is indeed a mandala-pattern; a stupendous one. Significantly, Luke, a 'gun-careless' "green kid" type, will shortly be killed there. Here, ahead of time, he is lent "archetypal honors," as the pinnacle/Center of the overall composition, just as his subsequent, dramatically excellent death scene is (hence) one of the archetypal passage. (See below.) He, the rock, and the horses below seem to reterate the pyramid of *Land of the Pharaohs.*

A few miles away, Cole rides up to Jason's ranch, and tosses his partly-spent bag of advance wages to Bart Jason (Edward Asner), who shortly tosses it to his foreman behind him, in series-typical 'object-transaction. In the conversation, Jason suggests that Cole is quitting because he does not want to go against Sheriff J.P. Harrah due to the latter's expertise. Cole, laughing at this considerable truth, says, "You know, you're just about right!", leaving out the friendship factor. Cole insults the gang members, who loiter there in a slovenly way, as being evidently not tough enough "to stomp a stringy jack rabbit," let alone go against the professional likes of J.P. Harrah. One recalcitrant man begins to pull a rifle from a saddle scabbard. Cole catches him at it and warns him, derogatorily calling him "Fancy Vest." Jason orders the fancy-vested man to move away from the rifle, which he does, sullenly, leaving it half out of its scabbard.

Anima-aspected in terms of the 'fancy apparel' stigma, the man and his action of partially drawing the rifle, are shortly reiterated by the film's recalcitrant anima figure Josephine MacDonald/"Joey" (Michele Carey). She too, partially draws a rifle, leaving it half out of its scabbard, but subsequently ambushes Cole with it. (See below.) Thus, "Fancy Vest" and she form a shadow/anima pairing, around their action with the rifles, against the ego figure Cole Thornton: the essentially common 'object'/action (the rifles) serving as a mandala-Center. Holistically, the Jason gunman performs an incomplete action with the object which Joey completes when she eventually shoots Cole. The action-in-progress is of course stressed by the half-in, half-out positions of the scabbarded rifles in the respective ranch scenes previous to the shooting. Holistically as well, "Fancy Vest" and Joey are, on one level, the same entity.

Riding back from the Jason ranch, Cole passes the rock by the waterhole. Luke MacDonald is asleep at his post. Awakened by the sound of Cole's horse, he jumps up and begins shooting wildly. Cole hastily shoots him from a distance. On top of the rock, Thornton is mortified to find that his assailant and victim is only a boy. He prepares to bring him home to the MacDonald ranch, but Luke, in agony from his gut wound, pleads for Cole not to move him. (Johnny Crawford's performance and directorial treatment are very strong here.) As Cole goes to prepare some way to transport him, Luke shoots himself with a concealed handgun. At the MacDonald ranch, they hear the sequence of shots and, from the distance, realize that Luke has fared badly (in a minor note of 'dramatized/converged space'). The family and hired hands take cover and prepare for a siege with Jason men: but Cole rides in alone with Luke's body draped over the latter's horse. From points around, the MacDonalds and employees neatly 'converge' on Cole and the body. Thornton upbraids Kevin MacDonald for leaving a boy to do a man's job (and for the father's too-pessimistic advice to the boy on the nature of gut wounds). More covertly, Cole upbraids himself for the tragedy.

As part of the scene's general 'convergence' upon the body of Luke, Joey and her brother Jared ride in from a far corner of the ranch. Her brother dismounts, but Joey stays on her horse. She expresses distrust of Cole and his account of her brother's death, and begins to draw her rifle from its saddle scabbard. Stopped in this act by one of her brothers and ordered inside the house by the father, she instead gallops off with the rifle half out of its scabbard—all in basic reiteration of "Fancy Vest's" earlier action.

On Cole's return, Joey waits in hiding for him in some rocks across from the tall rock by the waterhole. Ambushed, Cole feigns dead, as his appaloosa stud waits faithfully near him in the foreground of the shot. Joey comes beside Cole and says, "I reckon you won't shoot any more little boys, mister!" Cole springs to life and knocks her off her feet. He tosses her rifle out into the pond. After giving her some professional advice on not coming near a gunned-down quarry until she is certain they are dead, he wipes some of his blood on her shirt and leaves (in a very Centric instance of fraternal 'blood' exchange). Near the end of the film she will, significantly, save Cole's life (saying afterwards, "I owed you something.").

In town, Doc Miller (Paul Fix) informs Cole that he is not a good enough doctor to remove the bullet—precariously lodged against Cole's spine—and that he will have to be operated upon by "one of those new-fangled squirts" to have it safely removed. Doc Miller's flippant remark, lending a shadow/anima stigma to refined surgery and surgeons is significant. At points in the film, Cole undergoes temporary paralysis of his gun hand due to the lodged bullet, a predicament which of course carries a sense of ego failure. As a result of this ego failure, compensatory unconscious material irrupts—as indeed, the progressively deteriorating infirmity is lent to shadow/anima association in the film. Even its prescribed surgery is lent to this stigma. Throughout the film, and even at the end, Thornton refuses to "stoop" to any new-fangledness concerning the lodged bullet. (Basic first aid of the military kind, which the ego figure Doc Miller provides, seems to be the Hawksian-heroic limit here!)

Initially of course, the recalcitrant anima figure Joey, in her way of 'gun-lunacy/carelessness' (in extension of the shadowy "Fancy Vest" at Jason's ranch), is responsible for the wound and the condition. As we shall see, the infirm hand is an object of some archetypal focus—as an oblique 'dismemberment' instance, with Joey, Mississippi, and Cole's horse figuring as "personifications" as well as "restorations" of the lame hand.

As Cole relaxes in a bordertown cantina, Nelse McLeod and three gunmen enter and brusquely order dinner. Outside, Alan Bourdillon Traherne/"Mississippi," introducing himself to the film as well, rides up and hitches his horse near Cole's appaloosa. The latter is in the foreground, juxtaposed with Mississippi, in the film's second 'pre-encounter' via Cole's horse. (Shortly, Mississippi will tag along with Cole as his "son/younger brother"/shadow.)

Inside, the recalcitrant Mississippi confronts Charlie of Nelse's group, challenging him for once having teamed with three others in killing Mississippi's guardian/friend Johnny Diamond, whose odd black hat Mississippi wears cherishingly (reiterating Boone's obsessive clinging to the scalp in *The Big Sky*). Nelse orders Charlie to face the young stranger, saying, "Like he says, Charlie, it shouldn't have taken four of you." As Charlie draws, Mississippi (who is gunless) draws a knife from behind his neck and throws it impaling Charlie before he can shoot. The young stranger is then threatened by Milt of the group. Here, Cole suddenly intervenes from across the room, shooting the gun from Milt's hand. (He says to Milt, "I'd let it drop, friend.") Like his advice to Joey earlier, Cole's intervention here is not so much idealistic or knightly, but *professional.* In terms of Cole's character, it is in behalf of a more mature professionalism, whether in tactical or strategic terms. In this case, he moves to keep the "score" even, preventing the escalation of revenge-homicide on the behalf of murdered friends, which beyond a certain point is obviously bad for the gunman trade.) Concerning Charlie and Milt, Nelse says, "It always seems to take more than one, doesn't it?" Cole philosophically replies, "That's because they're no good," in the same professional note.

Herethrough, Cole and Nelse have recognized each other as professional gunmen of renown, which allows a rather friendly exchange to follow. Nelse buys Cole and Mississippi a drink, as the latter (standing) replace Nelse's men around the table. Nelse and his men are on their way to El Dorado to work for Bart Jason in his range war with the MacDonalds. Nelse offers Cole a job with him in the same, which he refuses. Here Cole learns that Sheriff J.P. Harrah has become a drunk, over a "wandering petticoat" who jilted him.

The other McLeod men lie in ambush for Mississippi outside, but are 'second-guessed' in the same by Cole. Nelse is induced to call his men off. Out of "professional courtesy," as he puts it, he also lets Cole confiscate some of their guns for temporary retention with the sheriff (an old friend of Cole's).

Cole and Mississippi then dine in another cantina. Johnny Diamond's black hat hangs on the third, vacant chair, as the deceased gambler is present by way of Mississippi's reminiscence upon him there (as well as in the young man's general compulsive attachment to the hat). Clustered with the Centric 'odd hat,' this 'empty chair' instance recalls that of Scotty's oblique 'return' "from the dead" at the poker table, in *The Thing (From Another World)*. Both link, of course, to the 'chair' instances of initiation/passage reference in *Hatari!*, and the "death/resurrection" aspect of the initiation pattern is, once again, underscored. In a complementary, Centric way, a candle burns there at Cole and Mississippi's table in a sense of vigil.

Mississippi asks to ride along with Cole, who refuses him flatly and leaves for El Dorado to rehabilitate and help J.P. against the Jason/McLeod gang. Earlier, it was hinted that one or each of the pals had saved the other's life in the past. Also, Cole feels beholden to the MacDonalds for Luke's death—all in the same professional note of "keeping the score even," whether in terms of favors or otherwise.

On the trail, Cole has a painful paralysis attack. Falling from his horse beside a waterhole, he coddles his temporarily infirm right arm, talking to his horse, Cochise, who lingers at his right side like a faithful dog—a 'pal' and a shadow thus, juxtaposed with Cole's infirmity there. Almost simultaneously, Mississippi comes riding over the hill, following him, in the Hawksian role of the lost son looking for a father/older brother. A conversation ensues over Cole's lame gun hand, and when Mississippi helps Cole back on his horse, the infirmity becomes personified in Mississippi as well as the horse. Cole's hand is, again, an unconscious entity, and an oblique 'dismemberment' instance. Near the end of the film, Joey, who caused the condition, comes to Cole's rescue at a time when his hand is lame again, thus linking with it a second time. Earlier having "taken" his hand, she does the most to "restore" it in the final shootout scene, where she 'fraternally returns' as well. (See below.)

The younger man succeeds in tagging along with Cole this time, to the latter's certain ego/shadow resistance mixed with flustered compliance. Mississippi generally makes Cole angry, it is noted. On the trail, Mississippi recites part of Poe's "Eldorado," an allegory of the Grail quest, and one of the late Johnny Diamond's favorite poems. Irritatedly, Cole scorns the poem, saying, "… it don't work out that way" (i.e., in that idealistic way, in the wild west), rather echoing the scorned phoenix ad art and its attendant ad campaign in *Monkey Business*, and touching the series 'irreligion' pattern.

Ghost-like, Johnny Diamond, by way of the shadow figure in Mississippi (who wears his hat and vaguely assumes his identity), recites the poem at points in the film. "Eldorado" is a 'fancy item/accouterment' in its own right, along with the Johnny Diamond hat. In the course of events, the hat is derogated by Cole, Bull Harris, and Joey, but Mississippi never parts with it. In addition, Mississippi obtains an appropriately comical hand-shotgun, a wide pattern firearm able to compensate for the young man's poor marksmanship, recalling Boone's double-barreled gun in *The Big Sky*, and Tony's machine gun in *Scarface*: all shadow/anima-rampant and anima-encumbered objects.

In the film, the sobering-up J.P. repeats over and over, "Who is this Mississippi?", or "who *are* you?", or "who the hell are *you?*" (as formal introductions are delayed, due to pressing, unfolding events). This is in keeping with the classical mysteriousness of the irrupting shadow. Part of the difficulty is Mississippi's shadow/anima-encumbered proper name, Alan Bourdillon Traherne, around which considerable fuss is made. (Ref. "A.-M. D'Alessandro," in *Hatari!.)*

Compared to his stately, gracefully strong condition earlier, Mitchum/Harrah is virtually another character in the "drunken sheriff" sequence, as he plays his own shadow. This has resulted, again, from Her who jilted him. In other reference to J.P.'s condition, his hat has been taken by someone and he is left with an older, less dignified one, in the 'clothing exchange' motif, of identity confusion. (Ref. Dude's archetypally-relevant impersonation by the Burdett man, via 'self-encounter/splitting off' and 'clothing exchange,' in *Rio Bravo).*

In a 'friend/foe' way recalling Stumpy's accidentally shooting at Dude in *Rio Bravo*, deputy Bull Harris, at his nighttime guard post outside the jail, threateningly halts the pair, before recognizing Cole. J.P. is in a drunken sleep on a jail bed, as Cole approaches his old pal—throwing a large, ominous shadow over the incapacitated sheriff. Awakened, J.P. says, "What the hell are you doin' here?" Cole replies, "I'm looking at a badge with a drunk pinned on it." The thrown-shadow feature, the indicated object-predominance, and the pair's subsequent fight, recall, of course, Spike and Bill, and the latter's eminent association with the Centric heart/anchor monogram, in *A Girl in Every Port*.

Again the ethereal figure of the late Johnny Diamond enters the story—in the form of a new motif and by way of Mississippi, when the latter recalls an alcoholism cure, learned from the Mississippi River gambler. It is an extraordinary, comical concoction of virtual inedibles including a dose of gun powder. "I hope you don't blow him up," Cole says, as Mississippi and Bull complete the mixture which in fact aids J.P.'s cure. Reiterated are Pockets and his elaborate monkey trap driven by explosives in *Hatari!*, and the self-sealing pyramid in *Land of the Pharaohs*. Among these, we have another series motif, one of shadow/anima-irruptive violence: the 'elaborate contraption/devising' motif. In *Rio Lobo*, it is also expressed in Shasta's huge medicine-show wagon

263

(employed somewhat like a tank), and obliquely in Phillips's shotgun with the triggers wired back for reckless, "customized" action by means of thumbing the hammers only. Other odd and extreme firearms, like Boone's and Tony's, of the series, and Mississippi's colossal handgun, are related to the motif.

McLeod and his men arrive and link up with Jason's men in town. Three of the latter seriously wound Jared MacDonald and take cover in the church. Cole, Bull, Mississippi, and a half-sobered-up J.P. besiege them. Initially, Bull shoots at the three foes in the bell tower, ricocheting bullets off the bells, in noisy, 'object-transaction.' In general, as the bells get rung, one way and another, in the fight, and are visually focused upon, they figure Centrically in the sequence. The Jason men begin fleeing downstairs just as J.P. and Cole storm through the front doors. The destructive (not to say 'irreligious') fight through the venerable place has a 'sans rites-de-sortie' aspect.

When the last Jason man flees the church, Mississippi chases him and fires his hand cannon after him. This mainly dislodges a sign which falls down and strikes the man, who is still able to flee into the Jason Saloon. The sign reads "Dressmaking/Notions," and some of the man's blood is found near it. One may interpret a 'triangle/blood' instance here between Mississippi and his quarry, with the 'feminine apparel' sign as the anima representation. Subsequently, the four heroes convene near the object in 'triangle'-type 'convergence.'

Inside the saloon, the recovering J.P. manages to kill the man in a gunfight and arrest Bart Jason, as Cole, Mississippi, and Bull retain the other gang members, including McLeod, at gunpoint. As the four heroes take Jason to jail, Mississippi notices someone with a rifle in a window in the stable across the way. In the 'blurred sexual distinctions' way of the series, the armed "fellow" turns out to be, not a man, but (apty) the masculinely-clad, tomboyish Joey MacDonald. In a scuffle with her in the barn, Mississippi's hat falls off and lies juxtaposed with Joey's hair as he pins her to the hay-strewn floor. In her recalcitrant, 'gun-careless' way, she was gunning for Bart Jason as he was being taken into jail, but could not get a clear shot at him. She insults Mississippi's odd hat. He retorts by designating her hair as being like that of a "wild mustang that needs a currycomb and a brush," for which she strikes him. Manhandling her in turn, he warns her that he can hit harder than she can. Thus, in the Hawksian way of "sex antagonism" and the 'friend/foe' pattern, augmented by an 'animal/anima' note (coupled in turn with the young man's 'odd hat'), she and Mississippi get acquainted, and will become friendlier subsequently. They are, of course, on the same side of the fight.

While J.P. gets some needed recuperative rest, Cole and Mississippi prepare for the evening deputy rounds. Bull deputizes them for the same, saying, "I forgot the words, but you better say "I do," which they do, in another series dig at marriage and formality/ceremony. Bull wittily adds that the badge will give an enemy a good mark to shoot at.

The scene with J.P. taking a bath in the jail very successfully utilizes humor. Robert Mitchum is very good in the scene. He wants privacy, but is besieged by Joey and then Maudie, and by bars of soap. As he is using the bar which Bull brought him, Joey comes in with soap (one bar from Doc Miller, and one from her), clean clothes for J.P., and news that her brother Jared is recovering well. J.P. refuses the soap, which she leaves with the clothes. As Joey exits, Maudie enters before the door closes. She tosses a bar of soap to him—into the camera, in the 'foreground object/action' pattern—which J.P. catches and retains, since it is in his hands (though, on one level, it is due to Maudie's more initiated status with the group than the wild-and-wooly Joey MacDonald, at this time).

Later, the four lawmen prepare to rescue Saul MacDonald, who is being held hostage by the Jason/McLeod group. Cole's arm is paralyzed, and J.P. is hobbling on a crutch with a wounded leg. Cole plans a ruse. The deputies take two wagons into town—J.P., Mississippi, and Bull in one, and Cole alone in the other. Cole must somehow deter the gang in front of the saloon as the others move from the back alley to rescue Saul. Maudie wants to ride with Cole as far as he will permit her to accompany him. "[You'll] give me something to lean on," he says to Maudie beside him. Mississippi chooses this apt moment to recite part of Johnny Diamond's poem to the couple:

> And when his strength
> failed him at length
> He met a pilgrim shadow,
> "Shadow," said he,
> "Where can it be,
> This land called Eldorado?"

Cole is tolerant, but not moved to any poetic reverence. Maudie is, of course, posited as the "pilgrim shadow" here. Just earlier, in a "Grail"-like note, she was juxtaposed with a wagon wheel in the foreground.

As J.P., Bull, and Mississippi mount their wagon in turn, the young man continues his recitation:

> "Over the mountains of the moon,
> Down in the valley of the shadow.
> "Ride, boldly, ride," the shade replied,
> "The search for Eldorado."

As the second wagon shoves off, Bull blows his old cavalry bugle—a Centric object which he retains from Indian-war service, echoing Papa Laroche's fetishistic bugle in *The Road to Glory*. Earlier, Bull heralds his entry into the film in playing "The Girl I Left Behind Me" as, 'pre-encounteringly,' he is recognized by his musical approach.

Prior to sneaking into the rear of the Jason Saloon, where the MacDonald hostage is tied to a chair amidst Jason/McLeod men, Mississippi removes his huge handgun, puts Johnny Diamond's hat atop Bull's, and dons a quick disguise, pilfered from a clothesline. He feigns being Chinese to fool the guard posted at the back door. Knocking him out, he throws the black garment over the unconscious Jason man and retrieves his hat from Bull (all in sundry 'clothing exchange' augmented by the 'double/*doppelgänger*'/[c] instance). The three creep inside and momentarily hide in the storeroom.

In front of the saloon, Cole drives up, parks, and has some last words with McLeod and Jason, displaying his lame hand. They expect no contest from him. Jason is rightly concerned; but the overconfident McLeod is incautiously "curious." As the three deputies move to overcome the gang inside, to Bull's bugle call (those outside being distracted by it), Cole sends the horses and wagon forward as he grabs a hidden rifle and tumbles from the wagon. Shooting it with his good left hand, he fells McLeod and Jason's foreman. Inside, in the course of the brief fight, Mississippi fires his colossal scattergun. Some of the shot, coming through the window, wounds Cole (in the 'friend/foe' way). Later in the jail, this accident is dwelt on in a humorous tone.

As Cole, in the street, struggles vainly to fire again, Jason, taking his dead foreman's gun, is about to shoot him. Suddenly Joey MacDonald emerges/irrupts from beside the building and shoots Jason, saving Cole's life (covering for the latter's infirm hand in shadow/anima extension of it, paralleling her earlier responsibility for the injury). Here, Joey reiterates Stumpy's crucial 'fraternal return' at the shootout in *Rio Bravo*. Both instances anticipate Pierre Cardona's more graphic 'return' instance and intervention in the saloon fight in *Rio Lobo*.

Bull summons Cole over to Nelse McLeod who has some dying words for his professional compatriot, Cole. Unlike Luke MacDonald, earlier, Nelse displays no pain from his gutwound.

McLeod: "You didn't give me any chance at all, did you?"

Cole: "No, I didn't. You're too good to give a chance to."

McLeod: "Yeah.... Letting a one-arm man take me" (upbraiding himself as he dies).

In the film, Cole and McLeod are posited virtually as "friendly enemies," in the 'friend/foe' pattern, in their mutual professional respect, which is very focal. They are akin to Matt and Cherry in *Red River;* Pat, Billy and Doc in *The Outlaw;* and ultimately the battling 'pals,' Spike and Bill, of *A Girl in Every Port.* Nelse approaches being a hero figure, despite his taking the wrong side in the range war. This "blurred moral/ethical distinction" via Cole and Nelse touches the series edict again, of professionalism constituting ethics and morality in its own right. The film's "villains" are Jason, who cannot use a gun well and must hire whoever will work for him in his unfair schemes, and the Jason/McLeod hirelings who show poor nerve in a pinch, who for their poorer competence, must gang up on adversaries one victim at a time, and for whom McLeod himself indicates disrespect. (Ref. the bordertown cantina scene.)

The eminent feature of Nelse's facial scar recalls Tony of *Scarface,* Hawks's favorite film. McLeod's professional flaw is, pointedly, his (thinking-functional) *curiosity,* given to incaution. (Ref. the subsection on the quaternity of mental functions and attitude types.) Early, curious as to how the gunless Mississippi intended to kill Charlie, he sent the latter to his death, losing a useful employee. At the final shootout, Nelse was curious as to what the infirm Cole Thornton was going to do, which proved fatal. Comparably, Tony's downfall, in *Scarface,* is his thinking-functional beginnings of education and self-awareness (e.g., attending the theater): "curiosity" which arrests his primitive strength in the end.

At the end of *El Dorado,* Mississippi, suggestedly, goes out to court Joey, who is angry with him. Cole suggests that he will quit wandering and settle in town—with Maudie, perhaps, though she is angrily estranged from him by now. In the last shot in the film, J.P. and Cole walk along the street, each with a crutch to assist a wounded right leg, in a strong 'pals' note. Cole's gun hand is normal again, for the time being. He has told the "new-fangled" Dr. Donovan (Anthony Rogers) that he will let him remove the progressively incapacitating bullet against his spine as soon as his leg heals. ("Fat chance!", the viewer is inclined to think.) Again, the oblique 'dismemberment' is "restored" in the film via its personification in protagonist-heroes and not by way of 'fancy' surgery by a "new fangled squirt."

RIO LOBO
(1970)

This third member of the "Rio Bravo Trilogy" falls short of the dramatic values of *Rio Bravo* and *El Dorado* (as well as those of *Hatari!* and *Red Line 7000*), though its technical and action-dramatic competence generally saves the film from utter mediocrity. The result is a dignified, though not outstanding finish to Hawks's directorial career.

The early Rebel train robbery, in its resourceful, "Rube Goldberg" devising and execution (utilizing a hornets' nest for a Molotov cocktail, among other unusual tactics), is rendered in an action-montage sequence with nearly as much character expression as action on the part of the Confederate guerrillas. (Second-unit director Yakima Canutt contributed to the sequence.) One of the series' more finely-crafted action sequences, it strikes the auteur chords of elite professionalism, the tactile-function, 'elaborate contraption/devising,' and the shadow—as the Rebels in general make a tricksterish, ape-like counterpart to the blue-clad formalism of Col. Cord McNally (John Wayne) and the Union cavalry men.

The Union soldiers' careful handling of the gold shipment, and the raiders' skillful descent and whooping 'convergence' upon the (Centric/"Grail"-like) Yankee gold suggest, reiteratingly, a metaphor of the "Eldorado" quest. (Ref. *El Dorado* and its use of the Poe poem.) Later, Cord McNally and the same Rebels clash and gradually interrelate in a 'friend/foe' way. This is richly foreshadowed in the Rebels' intercepting Colonel McNally's directives regarding the gold shipment by tapping the Union telegraph wires (in deeper, ego/shadow communication, on one level).

As the train is being robbed, the event is detected at a Union town ahead. There, a Union soldier, a bugler, quickly passes the news to Colonel McNally that the telegraph lines (sabotaged by the gold raiders) are dead. McNally tells him to "call in [his] outposts." McNally and a lieutenant then pass in front of him as the bugler, having moved to another position, sounds "Assembly," effectively flaunting his gold-braided tunic, juxtaposed with a lantern near him, in a series-typical, mandala-Centric action-dramatical composition. While McNally and a Union detachment are following the train robbers, one corporal finds a Rebel coat button on a bush. As they resume their pursuit, the same corporal's chevrons pass close to the camera (the shot taking in the piece of cloth with the button, in his hand): this as though in dual 'object'/Centric reference to the McNally/Rebel 'friend/foe' crossing of paths shortly.

Separated from others of the search party, and riding alone up a stream, McNally sees Confederate Capt. Pierre Cardona (Jorge Rivero), who is unarmed and with a bandaged leg. Accosting Cardona at gunpoint, McNally is then jumped by Sergeant Toscarora (Chris Mitchum). Next McNally awakens in the cave-hideout of the Rebel train robbers, dressed in a Confederate coat. Here, it is noted that Cardona's leg was not wounded; that he got the loan of a bandage, one "with real blood, made by a Yankee bullet," from the wounded Corporal Bidey (Dean Smith), constituting a Yankee-involved Rebel 'blood' exchange instance. Bidey also wears a black 'odd hat' like that of Mississippi/-Johnny Diamond in *El Dorado*. Though no verbal mention is made of it in the film, it is visually, Centrically prominent in the earlier train robbery sequence.

In view of McNally's expressed humiliation in being taken, and his awkward dress in the Confederate coat, the 'clothing exchange' instance here bears reference to the subcategory of instances involving a male protagonist's being comedically forced into an item of feminine apparel. As Colonel McNally awakens in the cave, the first voice he hears is that of Capt. Pierre Cardona, who is the first man he sees. Juxtaposed with a flaming wall torch, in Centric/archetypal reference, Cardona, as McNally's shadow here and throughout the film, is a 'self-encounter/splitting off' instance. (Too, their meeting alone on the stream recalls, somewhat, the instance with Jim and Boone in *The Big Sky*.) Pierre and Cord met four years ago in Abilene and had a quarrel over a horse staked in a poker game, recalling Doc and Billy in *The Outlaw*.

They have dressed Colonel McNally in the Rebel hat and coat to motivate him to lead them to safety—away from Yankee troops in the vicinity—riding at the head of their party. On the journey, Cardona (for some reason) wears a Union coat and hat, presumably Cord's. The colonel leads them into the camp of the Tenth Ohio Cavalry, and Cardona and Toscarora are captured. Herethrough, McNally shared some of their corn liquor, and their relationship or exchange was more sporting and respectful than hostile, in the 'friend/foe' way.

At the war's end, Colonel McNally meets Cardona and Toscarora at their prison release. He buys them a drink, to confer with them to learn the identity of the fifth columnists who sold them information about Union gold shipments. Because McNally's "younger brother"/'pal,' Lieutenant Forsythe (Peter Jason), was killed in the earlier train robbery, the colonel is particularly motivated to apprehend the Union traitors. (Ref. Marlowe, the murdered Jones, and the Mars gang, in *The Big Sleep*.) There in the saloon, some fuss is made over a 'fancy' bottle of planter's rum the bartender tries to sell them—to McNally's blunt refusal, in favor of the more "ego-masculine" (and less expensive) whiskey, in the familiar Hawksian symbolism.

Cord McNally lends Toscarora money to return home to his guardian's ranch in Rio Lobo, Texas. Toscarora replies, "Colonel, I never thought I'd want to kiss a Yank." Further, the ex-Confederates agree to communicate with Cord, via the sheriff of nearby Blackthorn, if they should run into either of the fifth columnists (whose names they do not know). As a civilian, Cord will hire with the Union Army as a gunman to apprehend them.

Next, Cord rides to Blackthorn, having been summoned there by Cordona on undisclosed business. Cardona, as it will turn out, is seeking Cord's help against some Rio Lobo gangsters who are taking over the community—including Toscarora's guardian's ranch—by means of cheap monetary purchases backed by brute force. The man behind it is ex-Union Sergeant Major Gorman, alias Mr. Ketcham (Victor French), who, as it will turn out, is one of the sought-after fifth columnists. The other quarry is gang member Whitey Carter (Robert Donner), a "deputy" of Rio Lobo "Sheriff" Tom Hendricks (Mike Henry), who works for Ketcham. Ketcham stays more or less in hiding at his ranch.

Arriving in Blackthorn, Cord talks with Sheriff Pat Cronin (Bill Williams), juxtaposed with some wolf pelts which the sheriff has obtained for bounty money (in anima/'animal'-suppression between the two men). Very shortly, Shasta Delaney (Jennifer O'Neil) gets off the stagecoach and storms into the sheriff's office seeking Cronin's help against Hendricks's men, who killed her guardian, a medicine-show operator. The Blackthorn sheriff can legally do nothing for her. In the scene, she has a few pugnacious words with Cord, whom she successfully intimidates, in the ego-masculine anima-alienated pattern (recalling, in particular, David and Susan of *Bringing Up Baby*).

Cord and the sheriff go to the hotel to see Cardona who is in one of the rooms with a girl, having paid the proprietors two dollars not to be disturbed. "Two dollars'll buy you a lot of sleep around here. Well, I guess we can wait awhile," says Cord. They go into the hotel saloon for a drink. In one corner, Shasta—"little Miss Busybody" in Cord's words—sits with a large white cup of coffee. Her rather flat, saucer-like light-purple hat combines with the stark white cup in a striking composition. After earlier storming the sheriff's office, in the fashion of Hepburn/Susan of the series, she now presides here as a powerful anima/Center.

Several of Hendricks's men, wearing deputy badges, ride into town and enter the hotel saloon to arrest Shasta on false charges (she having witnessed the murder of her guardian). The Blackthorn Sheriff insists on a warrant for her arrest. George (George Plimpton), a Rio Lobo gunman, comes in the back way, forcing Pat to disarm. In a moment, Shasta takes a derringer from her purse and, from under the table, shoots gang-member Whitey Carter. (Since it is a reckless move, Shasta joins the anima- and shadow/anima-rampant 'gun-lunacy/carelessness' figures of the series.) In the ensuing gunfight, as Cord is about to be shot from behind, Pierre Cardona suddenly emerges/irrupts from upstairs and shoots the man in time. "I heard the racket and somehow knew it was you." he says to Cord, in 'fraternal pre-encounter' reference. Cardona wears only a leather shirt and light-purple long johns, this odd, 'fancy' getup serving as the anomalous feature of his irruptive 'fraternal return' instance here (particularly reiterating those of Stumpy and Joey, respectively in *Rio Bravo* and *El Dorado*).

Significantly perhaps, his long johns match the color of Shasta's hat. In her Centric eminence in the sequence, combined with her earlier, stormy emergence in the Sheriff's office, Shasta recalls Lotta and her 'anima-ego' eminence in the saloon-brawl sequence in *Come and Get It*, as both women effectively assume an "ego" position through which the predominantly masculine fight irrupts, in the fashion of Her irrupting shadow/animus.

Cardona identifies the slain Whitey Carter as one of the fifth columnists Cord is after. Shasta has fainted, and Cord and Cardona take her up to the latter's hotel room (as the other woman is tossed out). The Blackthorn Sheriff tells the hotel people to go and get the undertaker, who, in 'word/action-simultaneity,' enters at that moment. "Never mind, here he comes," the sheriff says. Like Cardona, the undertaker heard the noise and moved to the job.

As related in subsequent dialogue, Cord and Pierre, in the 'triangular' way, flip a coin to see who is to undress Shasta (who, having fainted, needs to have her clothing loosened, before being put to bed). (Ref. Chips, Kurt, Brandy, and the coin, in *Hatari!*). In complementary 'clothing exchange' reference, Shasta is lying on Cardona's pants, in the bed.

Cord decides that Cardona's and Toscarora's (as well as Shasta's) business with "Sheriff" Hendricks's gang may bear common cause with his quest for the remaining fifth columnist. They set out for Rio Lobo as a wholesomely friendly, egalitarian threesome, as ego/shadow/anima (Cord/Cardona/Shasta). Pierre Cardona, as a Gallic Latino and ladies' man, is anima-aspected shadow material for Cord, an older, Anglo, less sexy "comfortable old man." As they make camp, Pierre makes a mild pass at Shasta, as he wraps her in his sarape. She rejects him, then tells him a Hawks-heroine "hard-luck story" of marital and sexual woes, then makes a pass at him in turn—before shoving his proffered sarape back to him in a curt way ('object-transactionally') and in partial rejection again. Before she goes to sleep, however, the Man/Woman "pendulum" swings back his way when he gives her a scare by telling her that they are camped on an (evident) Indian burial site—thus hitting her with an ego-masculine, Hawksian item concerning "the honored dead." (Ref. the "Ceremony of the Honored Dead" and the pyramid cult in general, in *Land of the Pharaohs*.) She anxiously moves from the spot—where she was "probably sleeping on the skull of some brave" (in possible archetypal reference to her earlier lying on Cardona's pants in the hotel). In general, their campsite reiterates the pyramid of the 1955 film. She passes the night close to (moderately drunk) Cord McNally, some yards away, who is old and "comfortable." Throughout her major introductory scene here, Jennifer O'Neil/Shasta is cinematographically treated in a series-characteristic light/shadow mixture, of the general 'fog/rain/shadow' sort so often associated with Hawks heroines (in vague 'initiatory' reference). (I once talked with an actress who interviewed with Hawks for a part in *Red Line 7000*. Interestingly, Hawks conducted the meeting with her in a room that was extremely dark.)

Jennifer O'Neil/Shasta's bright performance and exuberant personality contributes much to the film. With certain exceptions, the film's performances are competent to good. John Wayne/Cord is generally "wooden" and at times inept. Hawks seems to try to mask this by adding heavy drinking to Colonel McNally's character, yet it does not mask his below-par performance. (Wayne considerably makes up for it in his Rooster Cogburn portrayal, under Henry Hathaway, in *True Grit*, 1969.)

Arriving in Rio Lobo at night, Cardona puts their horses away and, dodging two of the town's terrorist "deputies," barges into the house of Amelita (Sherry Lansing) to hide. Very suddenly, and simultaneous with Cardona's opening the door, the shot shifts abruptly to Amelita in the act of tossing back her hair and looking around—constituting a sharp 'self-encounter/splitting off' instance, with Amelita as his irrupting, personified anima. Moments later, after a dearth of conversation, they part on rather intimate terms, as he leaves to rejoin his comrades (recalling the 'self-encounter/splitting off' instance with Matt and Tess in the latter's introduction scene in *Red River*). Later, Cardona pours water over Amelita's hair for washing; and "Sheriff" Hendricks mars her face with a long scar, for which she kills him in the final-shootout sequence. Herethrough, the dramatic business with Amelita directly recalls Judith's and

Dorothy's "wet hair" initiation/passage instances, in *Only Angels Have Wings* and *Gentlemen Prefer Blondes* respectively, with Amelita's horrible scarring an added anima-suppression on one level.

Of special reference, in terms of mandala-Centrism, is the scene of Toscarora and some ranch hands bringing his and his guardian's horses into town to the livery stable corral. Toscarora rides in front of the cantering herd, which, guided by the other riders as well, races around the corner past the stable and into the corral. Tosararora pulls aside and pauses directly in front of the sign on the stable wall (reading "Livery Stable" in old-fashioned script) as the herd passes him. Here the camera zooms in on him and the juxtaposed sign, the racing horses close in the foreground. This is in stark reiteration of the comparably Centric and doomed Luke MacDonald atop the mountainous rock with the horses passing in a curved path around its base, in *El Dorado*. In a few moments, Toscarora, after a brief reunion with his girlfriend, Maria (Susana Dosamontes), is beaten and jailed by Hendricks deputies on false charges—corresponding with Luke's sacrifice/passage in the *El Dorado* instance.

Cord, Cardona, and Shasta rescue Phillips, Toscarora's guardian, from Hendricks men who are in the act of confiscating his and the younger man's ranch. In a crude but successful tactic, they use Shasta's huge medicine-show wagon in the process. The wagon is an anima-rampant 'elaborate contraption/devising' instance, complete with a female-figure logo on one side! Cumbersome, comical, and harmless as it is, it is yet a vague tank. His ranch momentarily secured, the heavy-drinking, sado-comical Phillips (a lively portrayal by Jack Elam) joins Cord and Cardona in capturing Mr. Ketcham—who is, again, ex-Union Sergeant-Major Gorman, the remaining fifth columnist sought after by Cord. They use him as a hostage to force Hendricks and several gang members from the jail where the heroes then release Toscarora, jail Ketcham, and board up to await Union soldiers (to be summoned from a nearby fort by Cardona).

Cardona is captured by Hendricks men before he can reach the army fort. At the subsequent prisoner exchange, a shootout ensues. Here, Ketcham is shot by Hendricks himself when it is revealed that Ketcham, under coercion from the heroes, signed the Rio Lobo ranch deeds back over to their rightful owners, thus selling out his and the gangsters' plans. Townsmen, including Civil War veterans (ex-Corporal Bidey, of the original gold raid, among them), join the siege effectively. Lastly, Amelita (paralleling Joey in *El Dorado)* emerges to shoot Hendricks for scarring her face. Hendricks dies beside a wagon-wheel, juxtaposed with him as a possible x instance, like those marking the gangster deaths in *Scarface*.

Would-be robber-baron Gorman/"Ketcham" is, of course, a negative character in the film—sneaky, traitorous, cowardly, greedy, and not least, unprofessional (in his getting others to do too much of the work for him while he hides at home). In contrast, the crooked and unnecessarily cruel "Sheriff" Hendricks and his gang are depicted with fair dignity as professional gunmen, and are rendered with cinematic/dramatic effectiveness, as a series-characteristic group. The (interspersed) shot of them after they are forced from the jail—grouped along the front of a building, with Hendricks standing in strong juxtaposition with a post—is very striking and memorable in its shadowy way, as a rather inspired wedding of composition and content. It recalls the shot of the cowboys loitering on the Abilene sidewalk awaiting news of the cattle trading in *Red River*. The earlier scene of the Hendricks group converged around a table, with a low-slung lantern in their midst, as they assess their situation and quickly plan tactics, is likewise memorable as a series-typical union of form/content. It is also a "classical " type of Hawksian composition. When the meeting breaks up, the camera moves toward Hendricks and his second in command, with the mandala-Centric lantern behind and between them, as the gang members exit, passing in the foreground of the shot.

At the prisoner-exchange walk, Ketcham's belt is taken from him by Cord, requiring the prisoner to hold up his pants, rendering his hands useless. As Cardona escapes, and Hendricks (presently) shoots Ketcham, the latter's pants come partly off, in the mode of a Hawks-comedy protagonist in the throes of a humiliating, shadow/anima-irruptive mishap. Thus, dually 'converged' upon by the ego-masculine/group counterparts of the McNally group and Hendricks alike, the anima-villainous Nelipher and the converging priests in *Land of the Pharaohs* are vaguely echoed.

At the very end of *Rio Lobo*, Cord befriends Amelita in her distraught condition over having killed Hendricks. They leave together—as the film and the series end on this note of senior-masculine gallantry/charity. Also, she helps him along in place of a crutch for his wounded leg. The scar on one side of her face is, vaguely, a 'transacted object' between them. As he leans on her to walk, she recalls Maudie in the role of Cole Thornton's "pilgrim shadow" in *El Dorado*.

AFTERWORD

Herethrough, at points, the writer's critical/analytical tools may seem to be ferreting out more than is significantly contained in the material being viewed. This is because the auteur dimension's sweep and import are often less apparent in particular cases than via several cases in series. The reader of course needs to view the films in series. In the auteur approach to film, this is nearly as important as the individually outstanding works taken in themselves.

Jungian psychology for all its high-philosophical categories and seeming mysticism is mainly a practical method. Its ideas are time-tested probes and guides and, not least, a sweeping confessional by a psychiatric guru whose terms and method have been gained in *reflective experience* and are not easily passed on, whether in media or to colleague successors. The ostensively grandiose ideas apply in an often uncannily intimate or particular way, as in the case of the Hawks films. (As related in the Introduction, my application of Jung arose out of the project rather than being brought to it *a priori*—or before the fact.)

Hawks's auteur vision and essential situation, of the small, diverse, essentially masculine group living out their special peer dynamics in strife with the job at hand as well as with the manifold, comedic "underside" of heroism, is a considerable chronicle. Not least essential, perhaps, is the inferred or derived *edict:* again, that solid professionalism tends to entail morality/ethics with it in its own part, and vice versa, and that these are inseparable, or One, like a manner of Kharmic entity—ultimately entailed with the archetypal Self. All this is well-personified in the shadow/Self figure of Schindler (Martin Miller) in *I Was a Male War Bride,* whose craft-professionalism automatically hates the black market as it loves the Allied Occupation, and overrules the ethical offense of his (suggestedly) having informed on his black market associates, in the film. Like an allegorical representation of Self-realization, Schindler is the sudden (irruptive), unexpected, though fitting end/culmination of Henri and Catherine's 'odyssey' through the first half of the film. A lens grinder by trade, Schindler states, "I am a scientist." This slight misnomer may be significant. One wonders if, directorially, he echoes the well-publicized Albert Einstein, of the time (although the film character resembles Steinmetz).

The series edict involves a fair number of films, and the rest, one way or another, are consistent with it. *The Dawn Patrol,* and other war and aviation films, set the stage for it with extreme, life-and-death circumstances which ennoble skill, competence, nerve, and group loyalty, shoving aside the relative luxury of abstract morality/ethics and other high-mindedness. More probing however, are the projects in which Hawks collaborated with writer Jules Furthman, particularly *The Outlaw, To Have and Have Not,* and *Rio Bravo* (and thence the *"Rio Bravo* Trilogy" which, in collaboration with other writers, follows).

In *The Outlaw,* gunman competence is more humane than hot-headed "law and order." Harry Morgan, of the 1944 film, follows the righteous path through business considerations, businesslike loyalties (more or less), and professional responsibility. In the *"Rio Bravo* Trilogy," the "good guys" are less

274

distinguished from the "bad guys" by morality/ethics than by professional caliber. The real series "villains" are within, in the irruptive shadow/anima (in Dude and Joe in *Rio Bravo,* and in Gorman/"Ketcham" in *Rio Lobo).* In kind, the airmen make a comrade of the captured enemy flier in *The Dawn Patrol,* while the panicky fellow in the same scene is the film's negative character. Negatively epitomized by Nelipher in *Land of the Pharaohs* (arguably the series' only thoroughly villainous character), shadow/anima- and anima-aspected characters are given to initiation/passage in the series. Otherwise shadow/anima and anima irruption is given to the Hawks comedy pattern.

This pragmatic Hawksian world view is not ahistorical, but wrought in the broken world of modern times, particularly in our severance from the family and its community extensions. Yet the auteur's male supremacism, of the archetypal patterns and motifs with which we have been concerned, is classical, almost mythic in character.

In another way, his characters and groups are *vestiges,* as Peter Wollen notes, even though constituting a vision of people very much as people and as "human animals" in a perennial way. Despite their being born of the age of World War—"the greatest mass-action of all" (Jung)—Hawks's people (as much as the nostalgic-tending familial/traditional outlook of John Ford) are peculiarly counter to all that smacks of manipulated masses in the modern world. Hence, Hawks and his counterpart in John Ford belong to the fairly recent past, and to the last vestiges of our pioneer heritage.

APPENDIX 1
SUMMARY AND DESCRIPTION OF SERIES MOTIFS AND PATTERNS

MOTIFS (Alphabetical Listing)

ANIMA-EGO, SHADOW-EGO
ANIMAL, WOMAN/ANIMAL
BALD HEAD/BALDNESS
BINDING
BIRD CALLING
BLOOD (EXCHANGE)
CHARACTER IMPERSONATING A FELLOW CHARACTER OR LEAP-
   ING INTO A RADICAL CHARACTER CHANGE
CLOSE QUARTERS/ODYSSEY
CLOTHING EXCHANGE
DISMEMBERMENT/RESTORATION
DOUBLE/*DOPPELGÄNGER*
ELABORATE CONTRAPTION/DEVISING   .
EMPTY CHAIR
FANCY OR FEMININE APPAREL/ITEM/ACCOUTERMENT
FLOOR MARKING(S)
FOG/RAIN/SHADOW
FRATERNAL ENCOUNTER/PRE-ENCOUNTER, "PRE-
   INTRODUCTION"
FRATERNAL RETURN
FRATERNAL SUICIDE MISSION
GROUP-DELINEATIVE/"CIRCULAR" MONTAGE
GROUP-MITIGATED WEDDING CEREMONY
GUN-LUNACY/CARELESSNESS
MEAGER LAST POSSESSIONS
MUTELY OR WORDLESSLY EXPRESSED CONCERN AT A PAL'S
   NUPTIAL PLANS OR AMOROUS INVOLVEMENT
ODD HAT
ODYSSEY
OVERLAPPING DIALOGUE/"SPEED," END-TO-END DIALOGUE
PALS
SANS RITES-DE-SORTIE
SELF-ENCOUNTER/SPLITTING OFF
SHARED DRINKS IN COMMON
SIGNIFICANT HAPPENSTANSICAL DEATH/MISHAP
SONG/MUSIC SESSION
TRAMP (STIGMA)
TRIANGLE, "QUADRANGLE"
TWOSOME SIGN
WET HAIR INITIATION/PASSAGE

PATTERNS (Alphabetical Listing)

ANIMA
BLURRED SEXUAL DISTINCTIONS, SEX CONFUSION, SEX ROLE-
    REVERSAL
CHARACTER INTERACTION/DEVELOPMENT AS A STORY FACTOR
CHARACTERS AS PORTIONS OF ONE PSYCHE
CINEMATOGRAPHIC-DRAMATIC LIGHT/SHADOW
CONVERGENCE
DRAMATIZED/CONVERGED SPACE, SPATIAL DRAMATICS
FOREGROUND OBJECT/ACTION
FRIENDS/FOES, AFFECTION/VIOLENCE, LOVE/VIOLENCE, "THE
    LOVE IMPULSE IN MAN EXPRESSING ITSELF IN CONFLICT"
GROUP, PEER GROUP, GROUP-DYNAMICS/CONTAGION, EX-
    TENDED GROUP
GROUP/PALS TRICKSTERISM
HOMOSEXUAL JOKE, HOMOSEXUAL ALLUSION/UNDERCURRENT
INITIATION/PASSAGE, SACRIFICE/PASSAGE, SACRIFICE/RES-
    TORATION
IRRELIGION/ANTI-CEREMONY-OR-FORMALITY
MANDALA-CENTRISM, CENTER, SELF, "GRAIL"
MERGED DRAMATICS/DIALOGUE (pattern and technique inclusive
    of SECOND-GUESSING, and VERBAL-, VERBAL-ACTIONAL, and
    other SIMULTANEITY)
OBJECT/OBJECTIVIZATION, TRANSACTED/DRAMATIZED OBJECT
PROFESSIONALISM, SERIES EDICT, "BLURRED MORAL/ETHICAL
    DISTINCTIONS"
REVERSAL
SENSATION/TACTILE-FUNCTION
SHADOW, EGO/SHADOW, SHADOW/ANIMA

Summary and Description of Series Motifs
(Criterion: three or more instances in two or more films.)

ANIMA/EGO, SHADOW/EGO
    The 'anima/ego, shadow/ego,' motif is hypothetical. Its ingredients described
here may not be separable from, but variations of the 'pals' and 'triangle'
motifs, and of other categories below.
    An anima figure—or, in the case of Jones in *The Big Sleep,* a shadow
figure—assumes an ego-dynamical position in the cinematic/dramatic situation in place of the protagonist, protagonists, or protagonists and adversaries
combined, who thence irrupt through his/her ego domain in an unconscious-
dynamical fashion. In the series archetypal patterns, anima and (often)
shadow figures are essentially provocative (irruptive). Hence, ego protagonists
may be given to special aggression by way of assuming the part of an un-

conscious figure. Mike Marsh of *Red Line 7000* (notwithstanding that he is an unconscious, shadow figure in the first place) "subsumes" to the temporarily ego-dynamical Gabby to subsequently explode upon Dan—much as the ego-figure Marlowe subsumes to the shadowy Jones to irrupt upon the Mars gang in *The Big Sleep* (in a way different than in the Chandler novel).

Discussed in the section on *Red Line 7000* this seeming motif is revealed in *Come and Get It, The Big Sleep, Red Line 7000,* and *Rio Lobo.*

ANIMAL, WOMAN/ANIMAL

The 'animal, woman/animal' motif is effectively the use of an animal or animals in a tricksterish anima function, or a linking of Woman (i.e., the anima) with the animal kingdom. The job-companionable sled dogs in *The Thing (From Another World),* and in general horses, are exceptional in being more as ego/shadow-heroic peers. The fancy roan horse in *The Outlaw* is both 'pal'-like and drawn in association with Jane Russell/Rio. Also, the cattle in *Red River* are less tricksterish than they are cowboy peers. In certain instances, animal skins represent the anima subjugated. (Ref. the leopardskins adorning the priests in *Land of the Pharaohs,* and Sheriff Pat Cronin's wolfskins obtained in gainful bounty hunting, in *Rio Lobo.*) The bird calling in *Red River, The Big Sky,* and later Westerns is mixedly with shadow/anima and ego-pragmatic reference—like Cole's horse in *El Dorado,* a shadow/anima figure and a 'pal.' However, the feminine furs, leopardskin apparel, and feathers, in *The Twentieth Century, Gentlemen Prefer Blondes,* and elsewhere, are anima-dominant.

Instances of this motif occur in *Fig Leaves, Scarface, Tiger Shark, Viva Villa!, The Twentieth Century, Bringing Up Baby, The Outlaw, Sergeant York, Air Force, The Big Sleep* (ref. the Marlowe/Sternwood and Marlowe/Mars business-meeting scenes), *The Thing (From Another World)* (ref. section IV), *The Big Sky, The Ransom of Red Chief, Monkey Business, Gentlemen Prefer Blondes, Land of the Pharaohs, Rio Bravo, Hatari!, Man's Favorite Sport?, El Dorado,* and elsewhere.

BALD HEAD/BALDNESS

In basic instances, a character's bald head is mocked, yet is posited, on another level, in ego-masculine mandala-Centric reference. (Ref. particularly the Douglas Spencer characters in *The Thing (From Another World)* and *Monkey Business.*) See also, ODD HAT.

See *The Thing (From Another World), Monkey Business, Land of the Pharaohs* (the stoically bald, mute priests), *Rio Bravo, Man's Favorite Sport?*

BINDING

A character may be bound (or, in the case of Captain Hendrey in *The Thing (From Another World),* simulates being securely bound, as part of a jest), in initiation/sacrifice reference, on one level. The important dual instance in *The Big Sleep* and the instance in *The Thing (From Another World)* are closely related. (Ref. section IV.)

The Outlaw (Rio's "disciplinary" binding, drawn-and-quartered style, not noted in the text), *The Big Sleep, The Thing (From Another World),* and *Rio Bravo* (Dude's subjugation) make use of the 'binding' motif.

BIRD CALLING

Bird calling is used, in an ego-pragmatic way, as signaling under conditions of stealth. The major instances in *Red River* and *The Big Sky* are closely involved with 'animal'/anima, 'friends/foes,' 'object-transaction' and, in the latter film, with 'self-encounter/splitting off.' See also, ANIMAL.

This motif occurs in *Red River*, *The Big Sky*, *Rio Bravo*, *El Dorado*, *Rio Lobo*.

BLOOD (EXCHANGE)

Blood figures in transaction and particularly in *relationship*, among friends, lovers, or between a protagonist and an antagonist. See also, FRIENDS/FOES.

'Blood (exchange)' occurs in *The Big Sleep* (obliquely, in the Marlowe/Sternwood interview scene, particularly in terms of the General's cross-reference with the vampirous alien in *The Thing (From Another World)*; *Red River*, *The Thing (From Another World)*, *Land of the Pharaohs*, *Rio Bravo*, *Hatari!*, *Man's Favorite Sport?* (in John Screaming Eagle's offering Willoughby "moose blood" for energy in the fishing contest), *El Dorado*, *Rio Lobo*.

CHARACTER IMPERSONATING A FELLOW CHARACTER OR LEAPING INTO A RADICAL CHARACTER CHANGE; see DOUBLE/*DOPPELGÄNGER*

CLOSE QUARTERS/ODYSSEY

Situational, dramatic close-confinement sometimes alternates closely with a story-level quest (odyssey) over a distance of ground (or air). *The Thing (From Another World)* and *Rio Bravo* notably feature 'close quarters' more in itself; and *Bringing Up Baby*, *Air Force*, *Corvette K-225*, *Red River*, and *The Big Sky* are more exclusive 'odysseys.' Other films cross these.

This motif appears in *The Dawn Patrol*, *The Twentieth Century*, *Ceiling Zero*, *Bringing Up Baby*, *Only Angels Have Wings*, *Ball of Fire*, *Air Force*, *Corvette K-225*, *Red River*, *I Was a Male War Bride*, *The Thing (From Another World)*, *The Big Sky*, *Land of the Pharaohs*, *Rio Bravo*, *Hatari!*, and elsewhere.

CLOTHING EXCHANGE

A character may don another's item or items of clothing in archetypal (ego/unconscious) allusion of shared identity, identity confusion, or, in the several instances of the comedic forcing of an item of feminine apparel onto a male character, in allusion to his own severe anima irruption.

See also FANCY OR FEMININE APPAREL/ITEM/ACCOUTERMENT regarding instances of female-male clothing imposition in *Bringing Up Baby*, *I Was a Male War Bride*, *Monkey Business*, and *Gentlemen Prefer Blondes;* the E. F. Edinger excerpt on Odysseus, Ino's veil and "transvestism" in section IV; and Romaine's female impersonation fit in *The Big Sky* (ref. the section on *I Was a Male War Bride*).

Clothing exchange figures in *Bringing Up Baby*, *I Was a Male War Bride*, *The Big Sky* (ref. the section on *I Was a Male War Bride*), *The Thing (From Another World)*, *Rio Bravo*, *Hatari!*, *El Dorado*, *Rio Lobo*.

DISMEMBERMENT/RESTORATION

A severed limb or appendage, with the associated idea or fact of its compensation or restoration, is a Hawks motif. The basic instances consist of: (1) the folkish idea of the amputated member needing to be retained for the Afterlife; which retainment is (2) subsequently acted out, one way or another, in allusion to an archetypal restoration (and hence the Self). Other important instances lack the folk idea, and feature the limb's replacement or compensation in some physical way, yet in allusion to the same archetypal restoration, on one level. (Ref. discussion in section IV.)

This motif is found in *Tiger Shark, Barbary Coast, Air Force* (obliquely, in the B-17 as an extension and restoration of the perished Captain Quincannon), *The Big Sleep* (obliquely, in Marlowe's car as an extension of himself; ref. the *Air Force* instance), *The Thing (From Another World), The Big Sky, Red Line 7000*, and *El Dorado* (obliquely in the recurring paralysis of Cole Thornton's gun hand and its evident shadow/anima personifications which serve as compensation/restoration). *Hatari!* contains an oblique instance.

DOUBLE/*DOPPELGÄNGER*

The 'double/*doppelgänger*' motif takes several forms in the series:

(a) A more or less direct reference to a character as being the "double" of, or of the same identity as, another character, in *Scarface, To Have and Have Not, Red River, Land of the Pharaohs.*

(b) A less explicit but evident borrowing of the older literary, dramatic, and film motif of the "double," as in *A Girl in Every Port.*

(c) An instance of the sub-motif of a 'character impersonating a fellow character or leaping into a radical character change' (self-explanatory). (See also, SELF-ENCOUNTER/SPLITTING OFF.) In *Come and Get It, Bringing Up Baby, The Big Sleep, I Was a Male War Bride, Gentlemen Prefer Blondes, El Dorado,* and minorly elsewhere.

ELABORATE CONTRAPTION/DEVISING

'Elaborate contraption/devising,' an unusual, often comically complex, and effective practical device, is occasionally used in the series. A violent unconscious irruption, on one level, the motif stems mainly from the self-sealing pyramid in *Land of the Pharaohs*, and is also used in *Hatari!, El Dorado,* and *Rio Lobo.* The unusual firearms of Tony, Boone, Mississippi, and Phillips of the series, relate to this motif. See also, GUN-LUNACY/CARELESSNESS.

EMPTY CHAIR

An empty chair, shown in the foreground for at least part of the scene, at an otherwise occupied table, is used in effective allusion to an archetypal figure either dead, present-but-"ethereal" (as in the case of Scotty in *The Thing (From Another World)*, or absent in the moment.

The empty chair motif is found in *The Thing (From Another World), Hatari!,* and *El Dorado.*

FANCY OR FEMININE APPAREL/ITEM/ACCOUTERMENT

Fancy or feminine apparel or items or accountments frequently appear in the series as an objectivization of the recalcitrant anima. See also CLOTHING EXCHANGE, OBJECT/OBJECTIVIZATION, TRANSACTED/DRAMA-TIZED OBJECT.

This motif occurs in *Fig Leaves, A Girl in Every Port, The Dawn Patrol* (ref. section V), *Barbary Coast, Come and Get It, Bringing Up Baby, Sergeant York, Ball of Fire, Red River* (ref. Dan, discussed in section IV), *I Was a Male War Bride, The Big Sky, Monkey Business, Gentlemen Prefer Blondes, Land of the Pharaohs, Rio Bravo, Red Line 7000,* and minorly elsewhere.

FLOOR MARKING(S)

Chalked or painted line(s) on a floor directing foot movements is a minor motif stemming from Jaffe's highly transactive chalkings on the stage floor in the archetypally laden rehearsal sequence in *The Twentieth Century*. This motif relates to 'transacted/dramatized object.' It is found in *The Twentieth Century, Sergeant York,* and *Ball of Fire*.

FOG/RAIN/SHADOW

An association of fog, rain, or other "murky" substitute may be used with Woman or (as in the important instance with Bill-as-shadowy-morass in *A Girl in Every Port*) an anima-associated male character. Dark clothing, whether on women or men, pertains to the motif. The motif seems to denote anima or shadow/anima initiation or "candidacy" for the same, and relates, of course, to the 'cinematographic-dramatic light/shadow' pattern. Note the Hawks-comedic instance with Tony Schwerke and Evvie in *Come and Get It*, and the odd, "cracked mirror" instance with Brandy and Kurt in *Hatari!*

A Girl in Every Port, Scarface, Today We Live and *The Road to Glory* (Diana and Monique as Red Cross soldiers, uniformed near the wet, dark front lines), *Barbary Coast, Come and Get It, Only Angels Have Wings, The Outlaw* (Rio in the dark barn), *Red River, The Big Sky, Hatari!, Red Line 7000, Rio Lobo,* and elsewhere.

FRATERNAL ENCOUNTER/PRE-ENCOUNTER,
"PRE-INTRODUCTION"

Hawks often launches an association between characters with an abrupt or violent clash. Or there may be a preliminary encounter that is coincidental or indirect. There may also be a combination of these. Often, *premature intimacy* is an ingredient. Archetypally, the encountered one is an unconscious figure ir-rupting, perhaps after having made himself/herself prematurely (preconscious-ly) felt to the protagonist. The basic instance is that of Spike and Bill in *A Girl in Every Port*. See also, SELF-ENCOUNTER/SPLITTING OFF.

Examples of this motif occur in *Fig Leaves, A Girl in Every Port, Scarface* (minorly, with Tony and the waiter in the "spaghetti" scene), *Bringing Up Baby, Only Angels Have Wings, His Girl Friday, The Outlaw* (Doc and Billy, via Doc's stolen horse), *The Big Sleep, Red River, I Was a Male War Bride, The Big Sky, Hatari!, Man's Favorite Sport?, El Dorado, Rio Lobo,* and elsewhere.

FRATERNAL RETURN

In the 'fraternal return' motif, a character (or, in instances, more than one character) suddenly arrives or emerges (irrupts) upon a group scene unexpectedly and/or after some absence, often bearing some special accoutrement providing an additional (irruptive) "surprise" element (as Center) and/or being himself or herself an archetypal figure. The latter allusion is often in terms of a "return from the dead," on one level, as the motif is basically one of "death/resurrection." (Ref. section V, on the motif.)

The Dawn Patrol, The Twentieth Century, Barbary Coast, Ceiling Zero, Come and Get It (obliquely, in the "bottle/George" scene), *Only Angels Have Wings* (obliquely, in Bonnie's return to the group as her "other half" catches the boat for home), *Sergeant York, Ball of Fire, Air Force, Red River* (obliquely, in the appearance of the maimed, miraculously survived victim of the Missouri-border raid), *The Thing (From Another World), The Big Sky, Monkey Business, Gentlemen Prefer Blondes, Rio Bravo, Hatari!* (obliquely, as Chips 'fraternally encounters' the group as the nearly-deceased Indian's shadow), *El Dorado,* and *Rio Lobo.*

FRATERNAL SUICIDE MISSION

The 'fraternal suicide mission' motif has one or more members of a close-knit group embarking on a fatal or suicidal mission in place of a comrade (i.e., to spare him), or making an otherwise noble or heroic gesture resulting in death. More generally, the groups in the adventure dramas are a touch suicidal in being "crazy" in pursuing their course or profession without much logical consideration. (Ref. section on INITIATION/PASSAGE. See also, SACRIFICE/PASSAGE, SACRIFICE/RESTORATION.)

The Dawn Patrol, Ceiling Zero, The Road to Glory, Only Angels Have Wings (Kid Dabb's last job), *Air Force* (obliquely, in Captain Quincannon's self-sacrifice for the B-17 *Mary Ann*), and *Land of the Pharaohs* (the high priests' self-sacrifice for the pyramid).

GROUP-DELINEATIVE/"CIRCULAR" MONTAGE

Hawks sometimes uses a more or less rapid montage sequence of members of a group or scene, to group/"circular" rather than "linear" effect. This "circular" effect is importantly aided by a 'convergence/Center' factor, or by an adjacent contextual factor which lends "circumferential" effect (as in the *Red River* instance), or both.

Barbary Coast, His Girl Friday, Sergeant York, Air Force, Red River, A Song is Born, The Thing (From Another World) (obliquely, in the scene of the discovery of the flying saucer, where the instance is rendered mainly with camera-movement), *The Big Sky, Gentlemen Prefer Blondes* (obliquely, in "night court" scene with the tiara, where the instance is rendered mainly with camera movement), *Land of the Pharaohs,* and *Hatari!*

GROUP-MITIGATED WEDDING CEREMONY

Wedding guests and/or attendants, one way or another, may assume an inordinately insertive part in the normally bride/groom/clergyman-centered event, to unorthodox or tricksterish effect. See also, IRRELIGION/ANTI-CERE-

MONY-OR-FORMALITY.

Tiger Shark, Today We Live (obliquely in Diana and her rings), *Ball of Fire* (obliquely, in the scene of Potts's announcing his engagement with Sugarpuss, in addition to the group interruption of her and Joe Lilac's wedding, later), *I Was a Male War Bride, The Thing (From Another World)* (obliquely, in the group's assertiveness in getting Hendrey to discuss marriage with Nikki), *Gentlemen Prefer Blondes,* and *El Dorado* (obliquely, in Bull Harris's comic allusion to the swearing in of deputies as a wedding ceremony).

GUN-LUNACY/CARELESSNESS

An insane or wildly heedless character, or a woman, sometimes handles a loaded gun wantonly or carelessly, usually resulting in one or more casualties; a motif of violent anima or shadow/anima irruption. See also, the related ELABORATE CONTRAPTION/DEVISING.

Scarface (Tony and his "new toy" in the Tommy gun), *The Twentieth Century, Only Angels Have Wings, His Girl Friday, The Outlaw* (Rio), *Red River, El Dorado* (Mississippi and his reckless hand-shotgun, as well as Joey), *Rio Lobo* (Amelita, as well as Phillips and his reckless modified shotgun), and elsewhere.

MEAGER LAST POSSESSIONS

A deceased character's last possessions, usually few and penurious, are curtly noted or gloomily contemplated in a number of films. See also, OBJECT/OBJECTIVIZATION, DRAMATIZED/TRANSACTED OBJECT.

The Dawn Patrol, Tiger Shark, Only Angels Have Wings, Air Force, To Have and Have Not (Johnson's wallet and, obliquely, Mme. de Bursak's jewelry passed along), *Rio Bravo, Red Line 7000, El Dorado* (obliquely in Johnny Diamond's hat and watch, left behind).

MUTELY OR WORDLESSLY EXPRESSED CONCERN AT A PAL'S NUPTIAL PLANS OR AMOROUS INVOLVEMENT

After witnessing a pal's expressed nuptial or amorous concern, a character ('pal') may mutely shake his or her head, in vague or mysterious misgiving. See also PALS, and particularly TRIANGLE.

This motif is found in *A Girl in Every Port* (Bill, for Spike and Tessie), *The Twentieth Century* (Webb, for Jaffe and Lily), *Bringing Up Baby* (obliquely, in Susan, hearing of David's marriage plans, where she laughs at him in an enigmatic way), *Sergeant York* (separately: George York and Mother York, for Alvin and Gracie), *Red River* (Groot, for Tom and Fen), *Man's Favorite Sport?* (John Screaming Eagle, for Willoughby's woman troubles).

ODD HAT

A character may persist in wearing an unorthodox dark-colored hat—a derby or a small plug hat—despite inconveniences around it or stemming from it. In *Red River* and *El Dorado,* the 'odd hat' is the occasion for fighting and quarreling. In the instances in *The Twentieth Century* and *El Dorado,* the hat is with major Centric/archetypal focus. In its mandala-Centrism the motif has features in common with BALD HEAD/BALDNESS.

The Twentieth Century (the basic and prototypical instance), *Red River, Gentlemen Prefer Blondes* (oblique reference in Dorothy's jibe at Lady Beekman's hat), *Man's Favorite Sport?* (minorly), *El Dorado, Rio Lobo* (minorly).

ODYSSEY; see CLOSE QUARTERS/ODYSSEY

OVERLAPPING DIALOGUE/"SPEED," END-TO-END DIALOGUE

Hawks sometimes has two or more characters agitatedly talking at once or "stepping on each other's lines," with the important words or phrases engineered to come through on the sound track. In instances, the lines do not overlap but occur "end to end." See Hawks's own comments on the technique in Appendix 3.

This motif is used in *Ceiling Zero, Bringing Up Baby, His Girl Friday, The Thing (From Another World)*, and in spots elsewhere.

PALS

Along with the closely related 'triangle' motif, 'pals' is the most important and prevalent motif of the series. Two characters of the same sex (though sometimes not) are close or inseparable friends and essentially or ultimately with ego/shadow or ego/shadow/anima allusion. In *Bringing Up Baby*, the allusion is of David/ego perpetually overwhelmed by Susan/anima as, in this Hawks-comedic subjugation, he is "fallen" to his shadow and is thus a shadow/anima figure. It is also a partial instance of 'anima-ego' with "animus" —namely short of David irrupting through Her ego domain. In *Monkey Business*, Barnaby and Edwina, though husband and wife, are Hawks-stylistic 'pals'—even as Alvin York and his mother, in *Sergeant York*, are a solid 'pals' instance, in the first half of that film. See also, DOUBLE/*DOPPELGÄNGER*, TRIANGLE, SELF-ENCOUNTER/SPLITTING OFF.

Pals is a motif in *Fig Leaves, A Girl in Every Port, The Crowd Roars, Scarface* (Tony and Guino, and Tony and Cesca in the last-shoothout scene), *Tiger Shark, Ceiling Zero, Come and Get It, Bringing Up Baby, His Girl Friday, Sergeant York, To Have and Have Not, Red River, I Was a Male War Bride, The Big Sky, The Ransom of Red Chief, Monkey Business, Gentlemen Prefer Blondes, Land of the Pharaohs, Rio Bravo, El Dorado*, and in some part, nearly all the remaining films.

SANS RITES-DE-SORTIE

In a number of instances in the series, a close-knit, elite group disruptively or destructively moves upon or within a more established or sedately normal community or situation. This motif more or less merges with the general 'group/pals tricksterism' pattern as exemplified in Susan and David amok in *Bringing Up Baby*. The important instances are in *Red River, Gentlemen Prefer Blondes*, and *Hatari!*

Barbary Coast (the vigilante uprising), *Come and Get It* (Barney, Swan, Lotta and the saloon brawl), *Sergeant York* (York and his pals interrupting the church meeting), *Red River, Gentlemen Prefer Blondes, Hatari!*, and *El Dorado*.

SELF-ENCOUNTER/SPLITTING OFF

A character may 'fraternally encounter' or otherwise transact with another in such a way as to allude to his thus encountering a personification of a part of himself—that is, more pronouncedly than in purer 'fraternal encounter' instances, and in a more abrupt and cinematically intricate way than in 'double/*doppelgänger*' motif instances of types (a) and (b). Even so, Spike's sudden discovery of his old sexual rival in Bill via discovery of the latter's heart/anchor signet ring, in *A Girl in Every Port* (part of a type [b] 'double' instance), is very close to 'self-encounter/splitting off,' in the way that it occurs. See also, DOUBLE/*DOPPELGÄNGER* type (c).

Self-encounter/splitting off is a motif in *Ceiling Zero* (vaguely at least, in Dizzy's 'return'/ 'encounter' with the Federal agent), *The Big Sleep, Red River, I Was a Male War Bride, The Big Sky, Monkey Business, Land of the Pharaohs* (obliquely, or in 'reverse,' in the early scene with Pharaoh, his queen, and Hamar), *Rio Bravo, Hatari!, Man's Favorite Sport?* (minorly, in places), *El Dorado*, and *Rio Lobo.*

SHARED DRINKS IN COMMON

Characters rather pointedly may purchase the same drink in "fraternal" emphasis and, in instances, in character reference (e.g., bourbon as more "masculine" than Scotch or fancy planter's rum). See also, OBJECT/OBJECTIVIZATION, TRANSACTED/DRAMATIZED OBJECT.

This motif occurs in *A Girl in Every Port, Only Angels Have Wings, His Girl Friday, The Outlaw* (the most emphatic instance), *To Have and Have Not, Red Line 7000, Rio Lobo*, and minorly elsewhere.

SIGNIFICANT HAPPENSTANSICAL DEATH/MISHAP

In the series, a character may be violent killed, or nearly so, through no specific fault of his or her own but with just-previous or subsequent focus on a professional or character shortcoming, thus providing, on one level, a "reason" for the character's death or figurative death.

Significant happenstansical death/mishap is found as a motif in *Tiger Shark* (Manuel, "a good fisherman," but old and religious), *Air Force* (the "green kid"), *To Have and Have Not, Red River* (Fen and Dan, discussed in the section on *To Have and Have Not* as well), and *Hatari!*

SONG/MUSIC SESSION

An informal or otherwise personally-contactual making and sharing of music among a group or pair was used frequently by Hawks. Dramatically, the motif is part of the 'group dynamics/contagion' pattern.

This motif is found in *The Dawn Patrol* (ref. section IV), *Scarface* (noted in section on *Hatari!*), *Tiger Shark* (singing in the foc's'le; not noted in the text), *Today We Live, Come and Get It, Bringing Up Baby, Only Angels Have Wings, Sergeant York* (singing among York and his drinking pals; not noted in the text), *Ball of Fire, Corvette K-225* (singing in the foc's'le), *To Have and Have Not, A Song is Born, Red River* (singing in the bunkhouse), *The Big Sky, Monkey Business, Gentlemen Prefer Blondes, Land of the Pharaohs* (noted in the section on *Hatari!*), *Hatari!, Red Line 7000*, and elsewhere.

285

TRAMP (STIGMA)

A female character may react or over-react to a real or imagined insinuation that she is "cheap" or "just a tramp." In variation, Lotta insinuates this of herself, in *Come and Get It,* and Shasta volunteers the information, lamentingly, that she used to work in a saloon, in *Rio Lobo.* The motif often serves to launch an initial yet more intimate character interrelationship. See CHARACTER INTERACTION/DEVELOPMENT AS A STORY FACTOR.

The tramp (stigma) motif occurs in *The Crowd Roars, Barbary Coast,* (Mary "Swan" Rutledge, as a saloon employee; not noted in the text), *Come and Get It, Ball of Fire* (Sugarpuss breaking her engagement with Potts, to his scorn for her, when she must leave with the gang; not noted in the text), *To Have and Have Not* (Slim and Harry), *Red River* (Tess and Matt), *Rio Bravo* (Feathers and Chance), and obliquely elsewhere.

TRIANGLE, "QUADRANGLE"

'Triangle, "quadrangle"' refers to a relationship among three or four characters, at least one of them of the opposite sex to the others, with unusual and varying complexity, depending on the instance. The Hawks 'triangle' generally serves, or deeply focuses the 'pals' or sexual-peer factor over an existing or impending love relationship on the part of one with the sexually opposite member—with whom the other pal may be involved as well, or at another point in the story.

In *Hatari!,* Kurt relates that he and his 'pal' Chips are going to Paris at the end of the working season, since they have found that they both know a girl there. "We go halves," he says—"another excuse for a fight." In the same film, Sean's 'pal,' Pockets, twice interrupts a budding love scene between Sean and Dallas, in cryptic jealousy. ("Pal interrupting a love scene" could be listed as a submotif here, with several instances.) In *Land of the Pharaohs,* this is 'reversed,' as Hamar discreetly exits from Pharaoh and his queen to the former's mild consternation when he suddenly discovers Hamar's absence. In *El Dorado,* Maudie 'triangularly' barges in on Cole and J.P.'s reunion in the washroom, in another 'reversal' of the submotif.

The sexually opposite member (usually female) may be an "ethereal" go-between for the pals. Or one pal may simply serve as a go-between for the other and the woman, in a neat or ideal ego/shadow/anima dynamic (as with Sean, Pockets, and Dallas in *Hatari!*). Man-man love is often underscored; yet man-woman love is almost always a factor. To make a long discussion short, compare the "classical" and prototypical instance in *A Girl in Every Port* with the variants in *Tiger Shark, The Road to Glory, Come and Get It, His Girl Friday,* and *I Was a Male War Bride.* Then compare these with the 'quadrangular' relationship in *Today We Live,* and with the jumble amongst Joe, Lee, Eddie, and Ann in *The Crowd Roars,* and the instance with the ethereal steward—seemingly a "proxy" for the Ella Raines character in the naval-officer quarrel between her brother and the Randolph Scott character—in *Corvette K-225.*

Almost every instance is story-dramatically different, so that the motif is virtually a pattern: one always of ego/shadow/anima-or-animus import, and often involving a Centric object in 'objectivization' of one of the 'triangle' par-

286

ticipants (ref. particularly: *A Girl in Every Port, Come and Get It, Only Angels Have Wings,* and *Red River*). In this regard, the "raid" scene in *Red River* is particularly complex and probing. See also OBJECT/OBJECTIVIZATION.

The triangle/"quadrangle" motif is used in *Fig Leaves* (minorly, in the "socio-drama" scene), *A Girl in Every Port, Tiger Shark, Today We Live, The Twentieth Century, Ceiling Zero, The Road to Glory, Come and Get It, His Girl Friday, Ball of Fire, Corvette K-225, Red River, A Song is Born* (directly after the instance in *Ball of Fire*), *I Was a Male War Bride, The Big Sky, Monkey Business, Gentlemen Prefer Blondes* (ref. section V), *Land of the Pharaohs, Red Line 7000* (ref. section V), *El Dorado, Rio Lobo,* and elsewhere.

TWOSOME SIGN

The 'twosome sign' is a minor motif of body language indicating a pair's status as good 'pals.' One of them, or in the instance in *I Was a Male War Bride,* a third, supporting character, holds up two fingers, signifying that the pair is a solid twosome.

At the beginning of *Only Angels Have Wings,* there is the shot of an officer on the bridge of the incoming banana boat as he holds up two fingers to the helmsman in a nautical signal. Significantly perhaps, the immediately-following sequence involves two airman pals and Bonnie in 'pals'/'triangle' business reminiscent of *A Girl in Every Port,* in which the motif was an ongoing signifying trademark of Spike and Bill's pal-hood.

A Girl in Every Port, Come and Get It, Only Angels Have Wings, Red River (obliquely but implosively in the early "raid" scene), and *I Was a Male War Bride* use this motif.

WET HAIR INITIATION/PASSAGE

There are certain 'initiation/passage' instances which involve a character's hair being doused with water. Usually the "candidate" is a woman. In the oblique but highly significant instance in *Man's Favorite Sport?,* the ingredients are: (1) William Cadwalader 'converged' upon by two women, (2) his being splashed with water from the fish tank, (3) his loose toupee (which his wife makes him wear), and (4) his final decision not to wear the silly thing as he leaves for a business meeting. In this important connection, see BALD HEAD/BALDNESS.

Only Angels Have Wings, Gentlemen Prefer Blondes, Man's Favorite Sport?, and *Rio Lobo* use the wet hair initiation/passage motif.

WRITTEN AGREEMENT

A business agreement or contract sometimes figures in a story-dramatically pivotal way. The motif stems from the Centric piece of paper containing Lily's new contract in the 'return' sequence in *The Twentieth Century.* Oblique instances (in *The Big Sky* and *Land of the Pharaohs*) are verbal agreements functioning in a story-dramatically pivotal way.

This motif is found in *The Twentieth Century, Sergeant York, Red River, The Big Sky,* and *Land of the Pharaohs* (Pharaoh's agreement with Vashtar for the latter's commitment to the pyramid project).

X

Hawks sometimes uses an *x* or a cross, formed by some means or other, spatially-temporally proximal to a death or deaths, to a near-death or, in the mock instances in *The Twentieth Century* and *Man's Favorite Sport?*, a feigned or parodic death.

The *x* motif is found in *The Dawn Patrol* (ref. section V), *The Criminal Code*, *Scarface*, *Tiger Shark* (Manuel's crucifix returned, some days later, to Quita), *The Twentieth Century* (ref. section V), *Only Angels Have Wings* (the *X* scene, possibly an '*x*' instance), *To Have and Have Not* (the eminent overhead fans turning, throwing shadows at the scene of Johnson's death; not noted in the text), *The Big Sky*, *Rio Bravo*, *Hatari!*, *Man's Favorite Sport?*, with instances elsewhere.

Summary and description of Series Patterns (general, or otherwise innumerable in their instances throughout the series).

ANIMA

Various, essentially provocative expressions of male-psychic female principle, in the series, range from the character of Susan in *Bringing Up Baby*, and the animal pets associated with her, to the (male) dog in *Air Force*, to certain dramatized objects, like the red drawers in *Rio Bravo*. The heart/anchor insignia in *A Girl in Every Port*, and the bracelet in *Red River* are of anima aspect—like the male characters Swan in *Come and Get It*, the steward in *Corvette K-225*, Cricket in *To Have and Have Not*, and Boone in *The Big Sky*. In the series patterns, anima/Woman tends to be either recalcitrantly dominant or ego-masculinely suppressed. In the deeper analytical psychology of the series patterns, anima irruption overwhelms the ego, causing the latter to fall to its shadow form—hence the frequent crossing of shadow and anima, or male and female, in many characters of the series (such as Boone of *The Big Sky*, and Hildy of *His Girl Friday*). Pierre the cab driver in *Gentlemen Prefer Blondes*, by a 'reversal' of the 'triangle' motif, is an animus between the two feminine 'pals' (ref. section V). See also BLURRED SEXUAL DISTINCTIONS, SHADOW.

BLURRED SEXUAL DISTINCTIONS, SEX CONFUSION, SEX ROLE-REVERSAL

Hawks uses a special pattern constituted of the irruptive anima within the ego-masculine ken. In *His Girl Friday*, Hildy is referred to as a "newspaperman," the newsmen variously as "bridesmaid" material and "gossiping old ladies," and Bruce as eligible marriage material for Walter Burns. In *Red River*, *I Was a Male War Bride*, *Monkey Business*, and at several points in *Hatari!*, the sex of an animal (or a person) is confused. In *The Big Sky*, Boone admonishes that he takes after his mother's side, in shadow/anima reference. (Significantly, in terms of series archetypal clustering, this occurs in the archetypally-probing 'dismemberment' scene with Jim.) Similarly elsewhere, a male character assumes some part of a feminine pattern, or is tagged with a feminine association, or dons or is forced into an article of feminine clothing (ref. CLOTHING EXCHANGE motif).

288

One of the gentlest examples is John Chance's taking a position behind the bar where Feathers will shortly be employed in the hotel, in *Rio Bravo*. In *Red Line 7000*, Julie is initially taken for a boy by Ned Arp because of the masculine way she drives her motorcycle. Also refer to the hermaphroditic alien in *The Thing (From Another World)*, and perhaps the prepubescent J.B. in *The Ransom of Red Chief*. See discussion at the end of section IV; see also, REVERSAL pattern.

CHARACTER INTERACTION/DEVELOPMENT AS A STORY FACTOR

Wherever possible, Hawks relegates plot, as such, aside (or into secondary priority) and moves a story through character interaction, unfoldment and development between a pair or among a group of characters. In its best examples, this occurs around relatively trivial things or emotional matters, as the characters thus reveal themselves, deepen their relationships, and thence act more meaningfully in the story's situational crisis or crises. The most illustrative examples (variously involved with the trivial and the monumental) are: Jaffe and Lily in *The Twentieth Century;* Goeff, Kid, and Bonnie in *Only Angels Have Wings;* Walter, Hildy, and Bruce in *His Girl Friday;* the business among Lieutenant Rader, the B-17 crewman, and the latter's sister in *Air Force;* Potts, Oddly, and Sugarpuss in the 'triangle' sequence in *Ball of Fire;* Harry and Slim in *To Have and Have Not;* Tom and Matt in *Red River;* Dude's personal struggle—and the frustrated Stumpy's ultimate heroism—in *Rio Bravo;* and *Hatari!* and *Red Line 7000* in general.

CHARACTERS AS PORTIONS OF ONE PSYCHE

Ego/shadow/anima/Self dynamics played out by their personifications in characters may be referred to as 'characters as portions of one psyche.' Personification is not always specific, nor clear-cut in terms of archetypal entities, but a function of a general ego/unconscious dynamic, as in 'group dynamics/contagion' and 'merged dramatics/dialogue.' Importantly, in basic 'triangle' instances, an object becomes 'mandala-Centrically' personified (ref. OBJECT/OBJECTIVIZATION). The ego/shadow/anima/Self scenario with Spike, Bill, Tessie, and the heart/anchor insignia, in *A Girl in Every Port,* is prototypical. Another comprehensive example is the cross-sexual complication amongst Joe, Eddie, Lee, and Ann, as focused in Lee's remarkable line, fairly late in *The Crowd Roars*. There Joe's girlfriend Lee (who was put aside due to Joe's interest in coaching his younger brother Eddie) encouraged her 'pal' Ann to steal Eddie from Joe, so that Joe would know what it was like to lose someone he loved—that is, to know what it was like for Lee to lose him (Joe). Herewith, ego, shadow, and anima intermingle with a characteristic 'blurred sexual distinctions'-pattern touch.

See also TRIANGLE, SELF-ENCOUNTER/SPLITTING OFF, and ANIMA-EGO/SHADOW-EGO.

CINEMATOGRAPHIC-DRAMATIC LIGHT/SHADOW

'Cinematographic-dramatic light/shadow' refers to various, characteristically Hawksian uses of lighting, particularly the use of medium lighting, medium shadow, and shadow, as cinematographic context in many scenes and films—of archetypal import, though not always neat or simple in its archetypal reference (as in the case of the archetypal series patterns and motifs more generally).

Initially, there is the penchant of medium-low lighting and shadow to lend dramatic action to unconscious dynamics. Then there are the instances of light/shadow contrast readily alluding to an emergence from unconsciousness to the lighter ego/conscious realm. Witness the well-lighted Dallas, compared to the mixedly light-and-shadowed Sean as she 'splits off' from him in the early bedroom scene in *Hatari!* (More mundanely, her well-lighted cinematic treatment serves to properly introduce her to the film as a new character.) The alternating light/dark cinematography upon Mike and Gabby plays a part in delineating their 'anima-ego' motif instance in *Red Line 7000,* as with Matt and Tess, initially, in delineating their 'self-encounter/splitting off'/'double' example in *Red River*.

Relatedly, there is the scene of the anima-emergent Dutchy and Bonnie, well-lighted and contrasted with the dark yet ego-masculine realm of the fog-bound flier in trouble outside, in *Only Angels Have Wings.* Again, this is compositely indicated in the lighted and shadowed sides of Geoff's face there: one side "indoors," and the other "outside" with the shadow-aspected and doomed Joe. In variation, there is the "morass" effect in the pivotal 'triangle' scenes in *A Girl in Every Port, The Road to Glory, Come and Get It, Only Angels Have Wings,* and elsewhere, consisting of expressionistic light/dark contrast (in instances, combining with an object)—in differing ways, but in common allusion to acute ego/unconscious irruption and the transcendent function amove upon the ego realm.

In further regard, shadow is often employed in connection with the ("morass"-aspected) 'rain/fog/shadow' motif, in reference to 'initiatory' anima-suppression. (Ref. Shasta's excellent light/shadow cinematography as she tells her "hard-luck story" in *Rio Lobo*.)

CONVERGENCE

'Convergence' is a very frequent dramatic-actional tendency for two or more characters to descend upon a common Center, often an object or some tactile business, or suppressively upon an anima representation or a shadow/anima figure. Note, particularly the priests, the self-sealing pyramid, and Nelipher in *Land of the Pharaohs,* and the "fly-casting" sequence in *Man's Favorite Sport?* This pattern merges with those of 'object/objectivization'-'trans-acted/dramatized object,' and 'mandala-Centrism' and with important variants of the 'triangle' motif.

DRAMATIZED/CONVERGED SPACE, SPATIAL DRAMATICS

'Dramatized/converged space, spatial dramatics' is an extension or emphasis of the pals/group ken over a considerable distance of ground in which contact/transaction is markedly or pointedly retained or extended. For example, Webb, Jaffe, and Lily in the rehearsal scene in *The Twentieth Century,* Lotta and the saloon-brawl sequence in *Come and Get It,* Tom, Groot, the wagon master and gunmen, and Fen, in 'convergence' upon/with Her and the bracelet, over the distance of ground, early in *Red River,* and Gabby on the dance floor in *Red Line 7000* (ref. page 102).

FOREGROUND OBJECT/ACTION

Foreground object/action is a compositional pattern (sometimes dramatic as well) in which an object and/or an action is employed starkly in the foreground, in tactile-functional reference and effect, and sometimes semiologically, as in the "morning after" or "breakfast/Dallas" scene's initially focusing on Luis's making a glass of bicarbonate, shown in fair close up, in *Hatari!* (Herewith, the camera recedes to take in the entire set, and Dallas's 'empty chair' motif instance pervades in the foreground in Centric references as well.) Other key examples of the 'foreground' pattern are the mechanical mixers in the brief lab scene with the scientists in *Monkey Business* and, in variation, the foliage rising in the foreground as Joe crashes and the "green kid" parachutes to the ground, respectively in *Only Angels Have Wings* and *Air Force*. The instances of the pattern are varied and innumerable.

FRIENDS/FOES, AFFECTION/VIOLENCE, LOVE/VIOLENCE "THE LOVE IMPULSE IN MAN EXPRESSING ITSELF IN CONFLICT"

The latter aspect of this pattern is rendered verbally as a theme in *Bringing Up Baby*, and less explicitly in *I Was a Male War Bride, Hatari!*, and elsewhere. A pattern of violence and opposition as *relationship*, with instances of moderate or major violence among friends, foes, and (in the way of 'fraternal encounter') among friends-to-be, and soon-to-be lovers. Chief examples are Spike and Bill in *A Girl in Every Port*, Tom and Matt and Matt and Tess in *Red River*, the group and the vampirous alien in *The Thing (From Another World)* (discussed in section IV, and in the section on the film) and their reiteration in the 'blood' scene with Dude and the Burdett gunman in *Rio Bravo*. See also, FRATERNAL ENCOUNTER motif and CHARACTERS AS PORTIONS OF ONE PSYCHE pattern, in terms of their ego/unconscious dynamic in common with the 'friend/foe' pattern. See PROFESSIONALISM-SERIES EDICT regarding the pattern's sense of cryptic union between series protagonists and antagonists.

GROUP, PEER GROUP, GROUP-DYNAMICS/CONTAGION, EXTENDED GROUP

Hawks's general thematic, dramatic, and cinematic basis in and of the close-knit peer group, is referred to here as 'group, peer group, group-dynamics/contagion.' It includes other, group-external characters sometimes partaking of the same dynamic in communication with the protagonists—like the traffic cop in *Ball of Fire* (noted in section V). In this regard, note the telling cases of Williams and Clark (who are shadow figures to the respective groups) respectively in *His Girl Friday* and *The Twentieth Century;* and the language barriers readily crossed in *The Big Sky*. 'Group contagion' is exemplified in the basic "sacrifice/restoration" instances of 'dismemberment' (in *Tiger Shark, Air Force*, and *The Big Sky*), and in the "When Love Goes Wrong" 'return' scene in *Gentlemen Prefer Blondes*. See also MERGED DRAMATICS/DIALOGUE, FRATERNAL ENCOUNTER/PRE-ENCOUNTER, FRIENDS/FOES, and CHARACTERS AS PORTIONS OF ONE PSYCHE.

291

GROUP/PALS TRICKSTERISM

'Group/pals tricksterism' is the disruptive or destructive behavior of pals or a group against outsiders or social norms, as in York and his drinking pals ("assisted" by Zeke) disrupting the church meeting, and the former trio's brawling in the tavern (specifically in their driving the dancers off the floor), in *Sergeant York;* and Stumpy's interrupting the deputy swearing-in in *Rio Bravo.* See also, SANS RITES-DE-SORTIE and, obiquely, IRRELI-GION/ANTI-CEREMONY-OR-FORMALITY, and GROUP-MITIGATED WEDDING CEREMONY. See also the subsection on the shadow.

HOMOSEXUAL JOKE, HOMOSEXUAL ALLUSION/UNDERCURRENT

Homosexuality comedically or derisively hit upon, at points in *Bringing Up Baby, His Girl Friday, Gentlemen Prefer Blondes, Red Line 7000,* and elsewhere not noted in the text, fall in the pattern referred to here as 'homosexual joke, homosexual allusion/undercurrent.' Also the rather frequent sense of a homosexual undercurrent in films throughout the series, notably Spike and Bill in *A Girl in Every Port,* Swan in *Come and Get It,* the tavern brawl in *Sergeant York,* Potts and Oddly in *Ball of Fire,* and the 'triangle' motif and the 'blurred sexual distinctions' pattern more generally. Though arguably a pattern of repressed homosexuality, the pattern is, in part at least, a more superficial impression had from ego/shadow/anima dynamics and their personifications. In terms of analytical psychology, "gayness" is not indicated, in the Hawks series, so much as "homosexuality" as a more ordinary part of unconscious life. (Ref. discussion in the section on *A Girl in Every Port*—in reference too, to the pattern's archetypal linking in male adolescent initiation/rites-of-passage. See the text subsection on the latter.)

INITIATION/PASSAGE, SACRIFICE/PASSAGE, SACRIFICE/RESTORATION

Generally, 'initiation/passage, sacrifice/passage, sacrifice/restoration' refers to the hazing and testing of characters, as focused in the rough "shaping up" of an odd character to group standing and/or ego-masculine responsibility. (Ref. Lieutenant Cartwright in *Corvette K-225,* and Dude in *Rio Bravo.*) Archetypally, this aspect of the pattern links, ultimately, with the "death/resurrection" ('sacrifice/passage') allusion in important 'fraternal return' instances, and with 'dismemberment' instances (the latter of 'sacrifice/restoration' aspect). Perhaps the most comprehensive instance of the overall pattern is Mme. de Bursak's anima-suppressive "shaping up" with a parodic death and a 'meager last possessions' motif instance, and not least, her association in turn with Johnson and his blatant 'significant happenstansical death' (the latter of 'sacrifice/passage' aspect), in *To Have and Have Not.* (See the text subsection on initiation/rites-of-passage.)

IRRELIGION/ANTI-CEREMONY-OR-FORMALITY

'Irreligion/anti-ceremony-or-formality' is the emphatic or more tacit deriding or mitigation of religion, ceremony, and formality in the series. The prayerful Monique in *The Road to Glory* is the only unmitigated exception. In *Rio Lobo,* Cord McNally casually remarks to Susana that she might pray for him and Cardona in their impending siege with Hendrick's men. Later, she says to him, as he is leaving her house, "I will pray for you." Not seeming to have heard her, he says, simply, "G'night," curtly, as he exits—canceling the earlier religiosity. Refer also to: 'group-mitigated wedding ceremony,' and discussion of religion's mainly group-dynamical function in *Sergeant York,* as well as Mike Mascarenas's "folk" sea-burial service in *Tiger Shark* (ref. section IV). See also, discussion of the theocratic aspects (their derision and, in ways, their heroic mitigation) in *Land of the Pharaohs,* in the section on the film, in section I, and in the subsection on the quaternity of mental functions and attitude types. See the section on *The Big Sky* for notes on Jourdonnais' functional religiosity (noted also in the subsection on the quaternity), and the section on *Red River* for general discussion of series religion/irreligion.

MANDALA-CENTRISM, CENTER, SELF, "GRAIL"

'Mandala-Centrism' refers to the dramatic- or cinematic-compositional formation of a mandala pattern—whether in certain acute 'convergence' pattern instances, like the "flying casting" sequence in *Man's Favorite Sport?* and the business with the tiara in the "night court" sequence in *Gentlemen Prefer Blondes,* or more drawn out 'dramatized object' instances like the bracelet and dog respectively in *Red River* and *Air Force,* or such as the 'group-delineative/"circular" montage' upon the Centric airman doll in the latter film. Because of the ego-masculine orientation of the Hawks series, and in view of mandala-Centrism's representation of the Self, I have referred to Centric objects of the series as the "poor man's Holy Grail," after the classical, knightly, and "yogic" symbol of projected Self realization.

Of special interest are the dramatic-actional/compositional instances with Luke MacDonald in *El Dorado* and Toscarora in *Rio Lobo* (which are also of 'sacrifice/passage' aspect). Similarly, 'fraternal returnees' (in their "death/resurrection" allusion), like Scott in *The Dawn Patrol,* Rader/Quincannon in *Air Force,* and Pierre in *Gentlemen Prefer Blondes,* are Centric—like the ethereal subjects of the 'empty chair' and 'bald head' motifs. J.B. of *The Ransom of Red Chief* is Centric in his transcendent-functional *composite* of numerous, diverse archetypal figures of the series. The anima-aspected objects of important 'triangle' instances are Centric. All of these, in their shadowy (ultimately shadow-aspected) way, allude to the archetypal Self.

MERGED DRAMATICS/DIALOGUE (pattern inclusive of SECOND-GUESSING, and VERBAL-, VERBAL/ACTION- and other SIMULTANEITY)

'Merged dramatics/dialogue' is an implosive dramatic method in which characters essentially share action and/or dialogue more normally separated between characters' respective kens. Often it is an effective sharing of awareness of things by more than one character, and occurs to the effect of an abrupt revelation of this shared consciousness, as in the simple instances of 'second-guessing' (e.g., the "servant/fishing" instance in *Come and Get It*). There is the 'fraternal encounter' example with Gabby, the two race drivers, and Dan, in *Red Line 7000* (ref. discussion of the pattern and technique in that section), and Dallas's and the group's rather inadvertent creation of her

293

nickname in the "breakfast/Dallas" scene in *Hatari!* The 'merged dramatics' method is 'verbal/action-simultaneous' and 'verbal-simultaneous' respectively in the "Brooklyn" example early in *Only Angels Have Wings,* and the dramatic business with Uncle Lige in the "porch" scene in *Sergeant York.* 'Simultaneity' instances feature two more or less independent events which occur in physical/temporal proximity so as to dramatically link in common cognitive process, on one level (in a manner of characters/events as portions of one psyche). The easily resolved language barriers in *The Big Sky* relate to the 'merged dramatics' pattern, particularly in the case of Poor Devil's appropriately occurring laughing fits.

Merged dramatics/dialogue are probably Hawks's most outstanding contribution to cinema and drama. See also, CHARACTERS AS PORTIONS OF ONE PSYCHE.

OBJECT/OBJECTIVIZATION, TRANSACTED/DRAMATIZED OBJECT

In the 'object/objectivization, transacted/dramatized object' pattern, an object (or, in the case of *Air Force,* an animal) is employed as a means of character transaction, in the sensation/tactile-functional pattern, often anima-linked, and often an alluded objectivization of a character. The bracelet in *Red River* alludes to Fen (as well as to Tom's deceased mother), as the modified brand insignia at the end of the film "replaces" Tess. In *El Dorado,* the recurring paralysis of Cole's gun hand is personified in his horse, as well as in Mississippi and Joey. In *Air Force,* the restored B-17, *Mary Ann* is, on one level, a "resurrection" of the deceased Captain Quincannon and/or a restoration of a physical part of him (in the 'dismemberment' allusion). In terms of 'meager last possessions,' a deceased character's remaining possessions are an 'objectivization' of him, on one level. Transacted/dramatized objects tend to be Centric. Other various examples include the heart/anchor insignia in *A Girl in Every Port,* the hatpin in *The Twentieth Century,* the serving-tray keepsake in *Come and Get It,* the two-headed coin in *Only Angels Have Wings,* Henri's wig ("Florence") in *I Was a Male War Bride,* the scalp and the knives in *The Big Sky,* and the tiara in *Gentlemen Prefer Blondes.*

PROFESSIONALISM, SERIES EDICT, "BLURRED MORAL/ETHICAL DISTINCTIONS"

Hawks's chief story-dramatic and situational factor is the job and its professional requisites and demands, which are the main concern and reason-for-being of his characters and groups in the chief instances of this pattern, in both drama and comedy. The pattern ranges from the gangsters in *Scarface* to the soldiers, sailors, and airmen of war and action films, to the comedic professors and their encyclopedia project in *Ball of Fire,* to the showgirls and their camaraderie in *Gentlemen Prefer Blondes,* to the "idiotic" but dedicated lawmen in *Rio Bravo.*

All in all, professionalism is, in effect, posited as an ego-masculine ideal—countered by psychically-opposite, irruptive shadow and particularly anima factors (which tend to dominate in the Hawks comedy pattern, from *Bringing Up Baby* on). The "ideal" partly overrides enmities between protagonists and antagonists, rendering them less than enemies and even "sporting comrades," on one level (in the 'friend/foe' pattern). 'Professionalism' tends to entail ethics and morality in its own, pragmatic part. As such, ethics and morality are covertly eliminated as independent abstract entities—much as religiosity, ceremony, and formality are derided, suppressed, or mitigated in some way, in the series (in the hence related 'irreligion/anti-ceremony-or-formality' pattern). This certain 'professionalism as entailing ethics/morality in its own right' is the proposed Hawksian edict. "Blurred moral/ethical distinctions" is a more superficial impression had from the same.

One basis for Tom's being spared rather than killed off in *Red River,* despite his villainous deterioration, is in his basic part in the ultimate success of the herd and the cattle drive. See particularly, *His Girl Friday, The Outlaw, Rio Bravo,* and *El Dorado*—where "villainy" (such as it is, in the series) is constituted more in lesser professional caliber, one way or another, than in breaches of a separate ethics/morality. (Ref. particularly to Doc and Billy contra Pat, the hotheaded, less competent sheriff who, rather than the two outlaws, becomes responsible for the harm and bloodshed in *The Outlaw;* and Cole and Nelse and their professionalistic 'friend/foe' example in *El Dorado.*) The real villain in the series is the irruptive unconscious on the "underside" of both heroes and foes, the extreme example being the negative anima figure Nelipher in *Land of the Pharaohs.*

REVERSAL

'Reversal' is a general Hawksian method of reversing or altering usual role types and typical situations. For example, *A Girl in Every Port* was rendered, genrewise, as "a love story between two men" (Hawks's designation); Barrymore and Lombard, the attractive leads in *The Twentieth Century,* rendered their own low comedy in lieu of supporting comic players doing it; Hildy, a man in *The Front Page,* was cast by Hawks as a woman in the derivative *His Girl Friday.* (Ref. in particular to BLURRED SEXUAL DISTINCTIONS/SEX ROLE-REVERSAL pattern.)

SENSATION/TACTILE-FUNCTION

The sense of *touch,* and the corporeal in general, are prevalent in Hawksian dramatics and cinema. (Ref. OBJECT/OBJECTIVIZATION, TRANSACTED/DRAMATIZED OBJECT patterns; discussion of the quaternity of mental functions and attitude types in the subsection on the same.)

SHADOW, EGO/SHADOW, SHADOW/ANIMA

The various expressions of the archetypal shadow in the series patterns: in the ego/shadow-involved 'pals,' 'fraternal encounter/pre-encounter,' 'double/*doppelgänger*' and 'self-encounter/splitting off' motifs (which are sometimes anima-involved as well); in certain characters like Kid Dabb and Sparks in *Only Angels Have Wings,* Bensiger in *His Girl Friday,* Jones in *The Big Sleep,* Boone in *The Big Sky,* Pockets in *Hatari!,* and John Screaming Eagle in *Man's Favorite Sport?* In a more general way, it is expressed in the situationally various male-adolescent initiation/passage pattern, of the series. (Ref. to the text subsection on the same.)

In many instances, shadow and anima merge in a character, as in the figure of Tony in *Scarface*, Mike in *Tiger Shark*, Mother York in *Sergeant York*, and even Dorothy in *Gentlemen Prefer Blondes*. Again, this is ultimately a function of the dynamic of the anima irrupting upon and overwhelming the ego which, in its disadvantage, falls to its shadow half or underside (which is hence expressed in a figure with androgynous touches or reference).

In keeping with the male-supremacism of the series, all archetypal expression in Hawks films—including mandala-Centrism/Self—is shadow-aspected, or "seen through a glass darkly (i.e., shadowily)."

See also, of course, the section on the shadow.

APPENDIX 2

Red River as Mythos.

From *Howard Hawks, Storyteller,* by Gerald Mast, pp. 334-337.

Like Homer and the Old Testament, *Red River* is a juxtaposition of legend and history, myth and fact, oral tradition and written record. Like Homer and the Old Testament, *Red River* is an attempt to tell (or retell) to the culture a story of how that culture developed, what and where it had been, so its members could know what it was and, therefore, what it is. Just as these earlier historical myths came to and spread through the culture by the primary means of popular dissemination—the Greek singer and the Hebrew cantor (note the importance of singing in both)—Hawks used the most common form in his day for "singing" his culture's historical myths—the moving picture. Once one begins to think of *Red River* as the kind of historical myth which we call today "epic," it is amazing how many parallels one can find in the film to those epics.

The journey, of course, provides the structure for both *The Odyssey* and the Old Testament's Exodus. As in Homer, *Red River* develops the tension between the commander and his men, and the fact that, although the enemy appears to be natural, geographical, or external, the real enemy is psychological—in the hearts and minds of the travelers themselves.... As in Exodus, the travelers cross a body of water called the "Red," and the magnificent crossing of Hawks's men and beasts through the real waters of the Red River seems far more miraculous than the crossing of Cecil B. DeMille's Hebrews through the process-shot waters of the Red Sea in *The Ten Commandments*. Once the travelers in both *Red River* and Exodus reach the wilderness on the other side of the Red, their troubles increase. Like Moses' reaction to the prostrate Israelites at the feet of the Golden Calf, Dunson's inflexible commitment to duty, honor, and the written law keeps him from understanding the weaknesses that have driven his weaker but equally mortal followers to the false idol. Like Moses, Dunson condemns his erring followers justly but harshly and, like Moses, he is repaid for his hubris, his harsh and inhuman sense of justice, by being deprived of his command. Joshua, not Moses, takes the children of Israel to the Promised Land, and Matthew, not Dunson, takes the men and the herd to Abilene.

And there are still other parallels. The union of calf and bull in the film's prologue, a marriage which also implies a kind of marriage between Matthew and Dunson (an implication supported by the gift of the bracelet as well as the male-female oppositions in the characters), evokes the mythic couplings of gods, humans, and animals in the Homeric world.[1] Dunson's commitment to "read over" the men he kills reveals the same kind of doing honor to the remains of one's fallen adversary as the warriors perform for the corpses of Hector and Patroclus in *The Iliad*. Dunson's "signing on" the men to make the drive parallels the commitment of honor that the Achaian princes pledged to Menelaus before the journey to Troy. Nadine Groot is the film's choric Nestor or Mentor, its old, wise man whose age and wisdom give him the privilege to console, criticize, and advise. As the men leave Texas for Missouri, their exuberant "yahoos" are an American western's translation of a warrior's vaunting on the Homeric field of battle. Finally, if *The Iliad* sings of the unbending, single-minded anger of Achilles, *Red River* sings of the unbending, angry single-mindedness of Dunson—quite literally sings of it, since song is very much a part of the film's soundtrack, its folkloric evocations, and its heroic spirit.

How conscious was Hawks of these parallels? Christian Nyby, the film's editor, never heard any references to such epic works, although he believed the parallel to *Mutiny on the Bounty* was conscious. And that sea story, with a screenplay by Jules Furthman, who also worked on *Red River*, is a much more obvious direct descendant of *The Odyssey*. Hawks's background and classical education, as well as his fondness for reading and for stories, probably led him to read these epic stories at some point in his life, perhaps at Phillips Exeter. That he knows something of the classic world becomes clear in one of Hawks's interviews where he refers to the original property of *El Dorado* as "a story that was sort of a Greek tragedy." Perhaps the one concrete indication that Hawks might have been conscious of his story's epic parallels was his title, *Red River*, which no one else seemed to like or even find relevant to the narrative. The film's associate producer urged Hawks to change the title, either to something more specifically geographical (such as *In Old Texas*) or more specifically related to the film's heroic task (such as *The Great Cattle Drive*). Hawks's title is a deliberate (and unexplicated) metaphor—like *Only Angels Have Wings* or *The Big Sleep*. Its most specific connection is not to a geographical body of water but to that Biblical body of water in Exodus. It is difficult to explain Hawks's insistence on keeping the title *Red River* except as a deliberate play upon the parallel between a Red River and a Red Sea.[2] Once this single Biblical parallel falls into place, the others fall in line behind it.

What is significant, however, is not Hawks's consciousness of these epic parallels but the way that the particular narrative task he set himself called them forth. He might not have known he was going to make a classical epic, but he knew he was going to make a very big film. Its narrative would be a synthesis of historical fact and fictional story, of a culture's geographical history and its guiding moral myth, of social purpose and personal psychology, of external dangers and internal tensions. Hawks may well have realized, as did his friend John Ford, that the western was America's guiding historical myth, our cultural equivalent of the Trojan War or the exodus from Egypt.

Significantly, these allegorical westerns which affirm the virtue and value of the American enterprise were made in the years that bracket the Second World War, when the strength and future of that enterprise was severely tested. Hawks certainly realized that the making of his film was as immense, as epic a task as the action which the narrative depicted, so that the making of the film in the present was not just a retelling of the past but a reenactment of it, bringing the cultural myth of the past into the cultural reality of the present.

It may just be that in telling immense stories of this type, stories which develop the unity of humans, animals, and nature, of past and present, of external and internal dangers, these mythic, epic parallels might necessarily arise.³ Whatever their source, the *Red River* that results from them is one of the major translations of classical epic and myth into American terms. Like Twain's *Huckleberry Finn*, Melville's *Moby Dick*, Keaton's *The General*, and *As I Lay Dying*, *Red River* finds its closest epic affinity with *The Odyssey*, the comic rather than the tragic epic model: the long and arduous journey that tests the strength of the leader and the travelers from outside and inside. At the end of many of these American odysseys, the leader and the travelers pass those severe tests, learn a great deal about the dangers both outside and inside, and, like Odysseus, finally arrive "home."

COMMENT

This writer agrees with Professor Mast's proposed likelihood of Hawks's borrowing from Biblical, classical, and/or movie-epical material for *Red River*'s story-framework.

In section IV, I discuss certain other mythic parallels in *Red River*, *The Big Sky*, and in the cluster obtaining between portions of *The Big Sleep* and *The Thing (From Another World)*. Significantly perhaps, these parallels are nearly all contemporaneous with or subsequent to the filming of *Red River*. It is very possible that the literary/mythical-influenced framework discussed above by Professor Mast served to evoke the other parallels discussed in section IV by stimulating the recall of old story material on Hawks's part. (Also note the "Prometheus" allusion with Bunk Kenneally and the maimed lone survivor of the border raid, in terms of the latter's oblique 'return' "from the dead" in *Red River*, discussed in the section on the film.) In *The Thing (From Another World)*, Scotty refers to the flying saucer as "the greatest (news) story since the parting of the Red Sea," underscoring Professor Mast's suggested DeMille-and/or-Biblical consciousness on Hawks's part regarding *Red River*'s title.

Even so, the Homeric and Northern European mythic parallels discussed in section IV are, again, constituted of well-precedented series motifs and patterns as much as they resemble integral secondary-archetypal mythic material. Hence, my own Jungian approach to Hawks, in terms of archetypal series patterns and motifs over one of integral borrowing, on Hawks's part, from outside mythic material. Although such borrowing is very legitimately proposed of the Biblical/epical framework of *Red River* (1948), the film is a special case in being Hawks's first "DeMille"-type movie epic, and the only one outside of *Land of the Pharaohs* (1955). In both films, the broader epical/mythical framework is not very typical of the series—whereas the sundry archetypal motifs and patterns summarized in Appendix 1 reside abundantly at the heart of Hawksian cinema from 1928, cumulatively to 1970.

See also, reference to Professor Mast's posited Matt/cowboy-and-herd/Tom visual-dramatic metaphor via the bracelet, in the section on *Red River*.

---

[1]Ref. My own discussion of Tom, Matt, Groot, the cowboys and herd (plus the bracelet) as a kind of male-archetypal "family," in section IV.

[2]It should be noted that *Red River* is, in truth, a very good title, and that the Red River is a real river in Texas—these being, certainly, very likely factors in Hawks's choice of a title.

[3]Focused here is the issue of independent cultural parallelism, attributable to "mechanical" factors common to all cultural enterprise, and—according to analytical psychology—attributable to common psychogenic, archetypal factors as well.

APPENDIX 3
CAREER AND FILMOGRAPHY

(Source: Joseph McBride, *Hawks on Hawks*.)

Born Howard Winchester Hawks, May 30, 1896, in Goshen, Indiana; to Frank and Helen Hawks. Two sisters, Grace and another, died young, of illnesses. Brothers Kenneth and William, both in the film business, died respectively in 1930 and 1969. Hawks grew up in Neenah, Wisconsin, and Pasadena, California; attended high school in Glendora, California; Phillips Exeter Academy in New Hampshire; then Throop College (now California Institute of Technology) in Pasadena, and Cornell University, where he studied engineering. Served in the U.S. Army Air Service in Texas during World War I. Marriages to: Athole Shearer Ward (Norma Shearer's sister), 1928 to 1940; Nancy Gross, 1941 to 1948; Dee Hartford, 1953 to 1959. Four children—David, Barbara, Kitty, and Gregg; adopted Peter Ward, the son of his first wife. Died December 26, 1977, at home in Palm Springs, California.

During vacations from Cornell, 1916 and 1917, Hawks worked in the property department of Famous Players-Lasky Studio (then the production arm of Paramount) and directed several scenes of Marshall Neilan's *The Little Princess*. After the war, he worked as a race car driver, aviator, and airplane builder, and directed several short comedies and independently produced films for Marshall Neilan and Alan Dwan. He joined the story department at Paramount in 1922 and worked on the scripts of about sixty films, usually uncredited. In 1924 he moved to the MGM story department for a year before signing a directing contract with William Fox Studios. He received writing credit on four features before becoming a director: *Quicksands* (1923), American Releasing Corporation, directed by Jack Conway; *Tiger Love* (1924), Paramount, directed by George Melford; *The Dressmaker From Paris* (1925), Paramount, directed by Paul Bern; and *Honesty—The Best Policy* (1926), Fox, directed by Charles Bennett.

Throughout his career he produced many of the films he directed, and worked (usually uncredited) on the scripts of most of his produced and directed films. He produced *Corvette K-225* (1943), directed by Richard Rossen, and *The Thing (From Another World)* (1951), directed by Christian Nyby—with uncredited directorial participation on the latter film (and, as observant opinion may have it, on *Corvette* as well). He apparently also participated in the writing on both films. Directed, without credit, part of *The Prizefighter and the Lady* (1933), directed by W. S. van Dyke, *Viva Villa!* (1934), directed by Jack Conway, and *The Outlaw* (1940-43), directed by Howard Hughes. Hawks related that he contributed to the scripts of *Underworld* (1927), directed by Josef von Sternberg, and four Victor Fleming films: *Red Dust* (1932), *Captains Courageous* (1937), *Test Pilot* (1938), and *Gone With the Wind* (1939). Hawks reportedly has script/scenario participation on a number of other films, without credit.

Hawks's *The Dawn Patrol* won the Academy Award for the best screen story of 1930. In 1941 he was nominated for Best Director, for *Sergeant York*.

Gary Cooper, starring in the film, won the Oscar for Best Actor. In 1974, the Academy of Motion Picture Arts and Sciences awarded Hawks a special Oscar for his work as "a master American film-maker whose creative efforts hold a distinguished place in the world of cinema."

Excerpts from *Hawks on Hawks* By Joseph McBride (Text portions in parentheses are the interviewer's; ellipsis-point indications and words paraphrased in brackets are the present writer's.)

(A) From the Introduction by Joseph McBride

[Hawks's] sense of humor is more than just a junction of his desire to be entertaining: it is an essential part of his view of human existence. Comedy and tragedy are interrelated in his work, the drama often coming from a character overcoming tendencies to ridiculousness, and the comedy typically arising from the descent of a dignified person into absurdity....

Hawks's work can be faulted for its narrowness of thematic range, in contrast to the breadth of vision one finds in Renoir or Ford or Rossellini, and the lack of thematic development in his work over such a long career is evidence of a self-centered, relatively unquestioning personality. But if these limitations prevent Hawks from reaching the highest level of cinematic greatness, they must also be recognized as essential elements in his artistic strength. Like his utilitarian style, which avoids superfluous flourishes to concentrate on presenting a scene in the clearest and most economical way, Hawks's thematic simplicity enabled him to concentrate on nuances of human behavior with a rare degree of richness and complexity....

[His] greatness was in his ability to make people come alive on the screen. We understand his theme through the complexity of his people, rather than seeing his people as reductive illustrations of his themes. And though he is often misleadingly categorized as an "action" director, probably because of the genres in which he chose to work, Hawks showed remarkably little interest in action for its own sake; he should more accurately be placed alongside behavioristic directors such as Ozu, McCarey, and Rohmer in his intimate concentration on the subtleties of character as revealed through the texture of dialogue and physical expressiveness....

[Confronted] with questions about his intentions in creating such-and-such a scene, he would almost invariably reply with an anecdote illuminating *how* he created the scene rather than what it was supposed to mean. He often expressed surprise and amusement at the things people were finding in his work, at the deep levels of meaning and symbolism critics were unearthing in what seemed to him to be 'just good stories'....

Hawks's attitude was partly a pose. Like many directors of his generation, he preferred to present himself as a craftsman rather than an artist....

302

[And yet] 'Something I feel that's very interesting with Hawks,' Truffant said on [one] occasion, 'is that in all those interviews, he always criticizes, he raps the intellectuals, and in my opinion he is one of the most intellectual filmmakers in America. He often speaks in terms of film concepts. He has many general theories. He doesn't belong to the school of instinctive filmmakers. He thinks of everything he does, everything is thought out. So somebody ought to tell him one day that despite himself he is an intellectual and that he has to accept that.' (*Grand Illusions*, Winter 1977, pp. 31-32.) [Pp. 2-5.]

(B) Portions from McBride/Hawks Interviews.

Q: What kind of experiences did you have during the war?

H: There wasn't very much. We went through what they called ground school. I was commander of a squadron. While I was waiting to be called I went out and got about an hour's experience flying. And then when we got down to flying school I think I got about an hour and three-quarters flying, and they made me an instructor.... And it was awfully slow because there were two thousand cadets down there (in Texas) and only seven airplanes. ... The chance of getting into combat was very futile, and I went into a course in big gun spotting, flying and spotting artillery shelters. I had a hell of a time getting sent to the spotting place because they wanted me as an instructor. Then the war was over. [Pp. 13-14.]

H: I learned right in the beginning from [John] Ford, and I learned what not to do by watching Cecil B. De Mille....
I remember one time in the 1920s when [Ford] and I were talking with some executive, and the executive said, "Christ, Howard, how come you know so much about stories?" And [Ford] said, "He reads books".... I wrote titles till I was blue in the face. If you didn't like a story, you could change it just by writing different titles. There was one picture (*Lucretia Lombard, 1923)* that had Irene Rich and Norma Shearer, and I didn't think much of Irene Rich, so I made Norma the heroine and reversed the whole thing. The director (Jack Conway) was very pleased with it. [Pp. 15, 16, 17, 18.]

H: I told John Wayne when we started to work together, "Duke, if you can make three good scenes in this picture and don't annoy the audience the rest of the time, you'll be good." He said, "Do you believe that?" I said, "Yeah. If I make five good scenes in this picture, and don't annoy the audience, I think I'll be good." So he started to work on that. And he always comes up and says, "Hey, is this one of those scenes?" I'd say, "This is the one where you get it over with as quickly as you can and don't annoy the audience." "OK." We work that way, and now he preaches that as though it's gospel, and he does a great job of not annoying the audience. As we got to be better friends working together, I could hear him telling some actor who was trying to ham it up, "Like the boss says this. You see that you do it. Get it over in a hurry. This is one of those scenes." I never realized that he was playing policeman for me on the last two or three pictures. [P. 29.]

Q: You said once that Ernst Lubitsch was one of your three favorite directors (the other two were John Ford and Leo McCarey). Which of Lubitsch's films did you study most when you were starting out?

H: I studied them all. He was at Paramount when I was there.... [P. 20.]

H: [Writers] Hecht and MacArthur were just marvelous. The first picture we worked on they said, "Oh we're all through now." I said, "No, tomorrow we start on something new." The fellows said, "What?" I said, "Different ways of saying things." And they had more fun, we had more fun for about three days saying things in different ways. I'd say, "How do you say this—you've got a line, 'Oh, you're just in love.'" One of them came up with, "Oh, you're just broke out in monkey bites." The audience knows vaguely what you're saying, they like the method of saying it. We go through the entire script in sequence: one of us suggests something, and what you suggest somebody else twists around. I learned it from Hemingway. Noel Coward came to see me once when I was over at Columbia, introduced himself, and said, "What do you call the kind of dialogue you use?" And I said, "Well, Hemingway calls it oblique dialogue. I call it three-cushion. Because you hit it over here and over here and go over here to get the meaning. We discussed it for quite a while. Another time Capra and I spent a couple of hours talking about it, and he went off and made I think the finest example of that kind of dialogue. Jean Arthur was in love with Jimmy Stewart in *Mr. Smith Goes to Washington*, and she was trying to persuade Thomas Mitchell to marry her because she was in love with Stewart. That was oblique if ever there was one. We talked it over until he got the line, then he went and did it better than I did. I believe that this particular method makes the audience do the work rather than coming out and making a kind of stupid scene out of it.

Q: Plots tend to be more important in films than characters. Quite often the characters behave according to the dictates of the plot. But you usually did it the other way around.

H: There's a very simple theory behind that. There are about thirty plots in all of drama. They've all been done by very good people. If you can think of a new way to tell that plot, you're pretty good. But if you can do characters, you can forget all about the plot. You just have the characters moving around. Let them tell the story for you, and don't worry about the plot. I don't. [Plot] movements come from characterization....

Q: Hemingway said that the best storytelling is like an iceberg—only one-eighth of it is above water, the rest is down below.

H: Yeah....You make a picture, you draw a picture of it. See, if you're gonna do something, do it with characters. Do 'em a little differently. Everything's been done. Now your job is to do 'em a little differently.... [Pp. 32-34]

Q: You're fond of giving your characters nicknames. Does Bogart call Bacall "Slim" in *To Have and Have Not*, even though the character's name is Marie, because you called your wife (Nancy Gross, Hawks's second wife) "Slim?"

H: Yes.

Q: And why does Bacall call Bogart "Steve," even though his character's name is Harry?

H: Because my wife called me that.

Q: Didn't you once say that Victor Fleming and you used to call each other "Dan?" Why was that?

H: Well, I think we just started. He'd say, "Dan, what are you gonna do?" And I'd say, "Dan, I don't know." And we'd go out and get into some kind of trouble.... [P. 34.]

Q: How do you rehearse actors?

H: Part of it is if I'd think of something, I'd go to the actor and say, "Don't tell this other guy about it, but read such-and-such a line." He throws the line to the other actor, and the other actor at first doesn't know what to say and then he responds in his own way, and it always works out well. You don't have to do a lot of rehearsing with any good actor. You merely tell them what you're trying to get out of a scene, then you just turn them loose and let them go.... [P. 39.]

H: The greatest drama in the world is really funny. A man who loses his pants out in front of a thousand people—he's suffering the tortures of the damned, but he's awfully funny doing it. I had a damn good teacher, Chaplin. Probably our greatest comic. And everything he did was tragedy. He made things funny out of tragedy. I work a lot on that. I wanted to do *Don Quixote* with Cary Grant and Cantinflas, and people said, "But that isn't a comedy—that's a tragedy." I'd have to go into a long explanation. I think we could have a lot of fun with it. I think that Don Quixote's the basis really for the Chaplin character... [Pp. 65-66.]

Q: [Concerning 'overlapping dialogue'/"speed":] In *His Girl Friday* the dialogue was much faster than normal. And the actors were stepping on each other's lines throughout the film. How did you make that work?

H: If you'll ever listen to some people who are talking, especially in a scene of any excitement, they all talk at the same time. All it needs is a little extra work on the dialogue. You put a few words in front of somebody's speech and put a few words at the end and they can overlap it. It gives you a sense of speed that actually doesn't exist. And then you make people talk a little faster.... [Pp. 80-81.]

Q: [On the "Potts/Oddly/Sugarpuss" motel scene in *Ball of Fire:*] One especially good scene was in *Ball of Fire,* when Gregg Toland did a close-up of Barbara Stanwyck with everything in darkness except her eyes.

H: He was a hell of a cameraman. We had a marvelous scene where Cooper had to come in and say something to the girl. She was in bed, and you couldn't see her face, you could just see her eyes. I said to Toland, "How the hell can I do that? How can I light her eyes without lighting her face?" And he said, "We'll have her do it in blackface".... Oh, God, it was a good scene. [Pp. 82-83.]

Q: I was talking to Truffaut about *Hatari!* the other day, and he made an interesting remark about it. His film *Day for Night* is about the making of a film. And he said he thought *Hatari!* was really a film about filmmaking and you used hunting as a metaphor for that. He said you were perhaps conscious of doing it, because John Wayne is like the director of a film. They sit around at night and write on a blackboard what they're going to do the next day, and he tells the crew how to do it, and then they all go out the next morning in a convoy of trucks, and it shows them staging these scenes. Then they come back at night they go to the bar and relax just like a film crew on location.

H: Probably that had a lot to do with the thing, because there wasn't much story. I accept anything anybody says about it. The Frenchmen are so funny. They attribute things. I can't even understand the words that they use in talking about why you arrive at such a thing.... [P. 142.]

Filmography; Principal Films Produced and/or Directed (in whole or in part) by Hawks (additional sources: Belton, Poague, Wood).

The Road to Glory (Fox, 1926)

Producers: Fox Film Corporation, William Fox
Assistant Director: James Tinling
Screenplay: L. G. Rigby, story by Hawks
Cinematographer: Joseph August
Cast: May McAvoy (Judith Allen), Leslie Fenton (David Hale), Ford Sterling (James Allen), Rockliffe Fellows (Del Cole)
Running Time: 70 minutes
Released: February, 1926

Fig Leaves (Fox, 1926)

Producer: Howard Hawks
Supervision: Winfield Sheehan

Assistant Director: James Tinling
Screenplay: Hope Loring, Louis D. Lighton, story by Hawks
Titles: Malcolm Stuart Boylan
Cinematographer: Joseph August (two sequences in Technicolor)
Art Directors: William S. Darling, William Cameron Menzies
Costumes: Adrian
Editor: Rose Smith
Cast: George O'Brien (Adam Smith), Olive Borden (Eve Smith), Phyllis Haver
    (Alice Atkins), Andre de Beranger (Joseph Andre), William Austin (An-
    dre's Assistant), Heinie Conklin (Eddie McSwiggen)
Running Time: 72 minutes
Released: August, 1926

The Cradle Snatchers (Fox, 1927)

Producer: Howard Hawks
Assistant Director: James Tinling
Screenplay: Sarah Y. Mason, from the play by Russell Medcraft and Norma
    Mitchell
Titles: Malcolm Stuart Boylan
Setting: William Darling
Costumes: Kathleen Kay
Cinematographer: L. William O'Connell
Editor: Ralph Dixon
Cast: Louise Fazenda (Susan Martin), J. Farrell MacDonald (George Martin),
    Ethel Wales (Ethel Drake), Franklin Pangborn (Howard Drake), Dorothy
    Phillips (Kitty Ladd), William Davidson (Roy Ladd), Joseph Striker (Joe
    Valley), Nick Stuart (Henry Winton), Arthur Lake (Oscar), Sally Eilers,
    Diane Ellis
Running Time: 70 minutes
Released: May, 1927

Paid to Love (Fox, 1927)

Producer: Howard Hawks
Assistant Director: James Tinling
Screenplay: William M. Conselman, Seton I. Miller, story by Harry Carr
Adaptation: Benjamin Glazer
Titles: Malcolm Stuart Boylan
Cinematographer: L. William O'Connell
Art Director: William S. Darling
Editor: Ralph Dixon
Cast: George O'Brien (Crown Prince Michael), Virginia Valli (Dolores/Gaby), J.
    Farrell MacDonald (Peter Roberts), Thomas Jefferson (King), William
    Powell (Prince Eric)
Running Time: 80 minutes
Released: August, 1927

A Girl in Every Port (Fox, 1928)

Producer: Howard Hawks
Assistant Director: William Tummel
Screenplay: Seton I. Miller, Reginald Morris, Sidney Lanford, from a story by
Hawks and a screenstory by James K. McGuiness
Titles: Malcolm Stuart Boylan
Cinematographers: L. William O'Connell, R. J. Bergquist
Art Directors: William S. Darling, Leo E. Kuter
Costumes: Kathleen Kay
Editor: Ralph Dixon
Cast: Victor McLaglen (Spike Madden), Robert Armstrong (Bill), Louise
Brooks (Tessie), Leila Hymans, Sally Rand, Myrna Loy, William
Demarest
Running Time: 64 minutes
Released: February, 1928

Fazil (Fox, 1928)

Producer: William Fox
Assistant Director: James Tinling
Screenplay: Seton I. Miller, Philip Klein, from the play *L'Insoumise,* by Pierre
Frondaie, and the English adaptation, *Prince Fazil*
Cinematographer: L. William O'Connell
Editor: Ralph Dixon
Cast: Charles Farrell (Prince Fazil), Gretta Nissen (Fabienne), Mae Busch
(Helene Debreuze), John Boles (John Clavering), Tyler Brooke (Jacques
Debreuze), Vadim Uraneff (Ahmed)
Running Time: 95 minutes
Released: June, 1928, released in both sound effects plus musical score, and
silent versions

The Air Circus (Fox, 1928) (part talking)

Producer: William Fox
Assistant Director: William Tummel
Codirector: Lewis Seiler (talking sequences)
Dialogue Director: Charles Judels
Screenplay: Seton I. Miller, Norman Z. McLeod, from a story by Graham Baker
and Andrew Bennison
Dialogue: Hugh Herbert
Titles: William Kernell
Cinematographer: Dan Clark
Editor: Ralph Dixon
Cast: Louise Dresser (Mrs. Blake), David Rollins (Buddy Blake), Arthur Lake
(Speed Doolittle), Sue Carol (Sue Manning), Charles Delany (Charles
Manning), Heinie Conklin (Jerry McSwiggen), Earl Robinson (Lieu-
tenant Blake)
Running Time: 100 minutes
Released: September, 1928

Trent's Last Case (Fox, 1929)

Producer: Howard Hawks
Supervision: Bertram Millhauser
Assistant Director: E. D. Leshin
Screenplay: Scott Darling, Beulah Marie Dix, from E. C. Bentley's novel
Titles: Malcolm Stuart Boylan
Cinematographer: Hal Rosson
Costumes: Sophie Wachner
Cast: Donald Crisp (Sigsbee Manderson), Raymond Griffith (Philip Trent),
      Raymond Hatton (Joshua Cupples), Marceline Day (Evelyn Manderson),
      Lawrence Gray (Jack Marlowe), Anita Garvin, Edgar Kennedy (Police
      Inspector)
Running Time: 67 minutes
Released: March, 1929, in both sound effects plus musical score, and silent ver-
sions

The Dawn Patrol (First National-Warner Brothers, 1930)

Producer: Robert North
Screenplay: Howard Hawks, Dan Totheroh, Seton I. Miller, story by Hawks but
      credited to John Monk Saunders
Cinematographer: Ernest Haller
Aerial Sequences: Leo Nomis
Assistant Director: Elmer Dyer
Art Director: Jack Okey
Music: Leo F. Forbstein
Editor: Ray Curtiss
Special Effects: Fred Jackman
Cast: Richard Barthelmess (Dick Courtney), Douglas Fairbanks, Jr. (Douglas
      Scott), Neil Hamilton (Major Brand), William Janney (Gordon Scott),
      James Finlayson (Field Sergeant), Frank McHugh (Flaherty), Gardner
      James (Ralph Hollister)
Running Time: 95 minutes
Released: August, 1930

The Criminal Code (Columbia, 1931)

Producers: Howard Hawks, Harry Cohn
Screenplay: Seton I. Miller, Fred Niblo, Jr., from the play by Martin Flavin
Cinematographers: James Wong Howe, L. William O'Connell
Art Direction: Edward Jewell
Sound: Glen Rominger
Editor: Edward Curtiss
Cast: Walter Huston (Warden Brady), Phillips Holmes (Robert Graham), Con-
      stance Cummings (Mary Brady), DeWitt Jennings (Gleason), John
      Sheehan (MacManus), Boris Karloff (Galloway), Clark Marshall (Runch),
      Andy Devine
Running Time: 97 minutes
Released: January, 1931

Scarface (Atlantic Pictures/United Artists, 1932)

Producers: Howard Hawks, Howard Hughes
Assistant Director: Richard Rosson
Screenplay: Ben Hecht, Seton I. Miller, John Lee Mahin, W. R. Burnett, from
        the novel by Armitage Trail
Cinematographers: Lee Garmes, L. William O'Connell
Art Director: Harry Oliver
Production Manager: Charles Stallings
Music: Adolph Tandler, Gus Arnheim
Sound: William Snyder
Editors: Edward Curtiss, Douglas Biggs
Cast: Paul Muni (Tony Camonte), Ann Dvorak (Cesca Camonte), Karen Morley
      (Poppy), George Raft (Guino Rinaldo), Osgood Perkins (Johnny Lovo),
      Boris Karloff (Gaffney), Vince Barnett (Angelo), C. Henry Gordon
      (Guarino), Inez Palange (Mrs. Camonte), Edwin Maxwell (Chief of Detec-
      tives)
Running Time: 90 minutes
Released: April, 1932

The Crowd Roars (Warner Brothers, 1932)

Producer: Bryan Foy
Screenplay: Kubec Glasmon, John Bright, Seton I. Miller, Niven Busch, story
        by Hawks
Cinematographer: Sid Hickox
Art Director: Jack Okey
Music: Leo F. Forbstein
Editors: John Stumar, Thomas Pratt
Technical Effects: Fred Jackman
Cast: James Cagney (Joe Greer), Joan Blondell (Ann), Ann Dvorak (Lee Mer-
      rick), Eric Linden (Eddie Greer), Guy Kibbee (Dad Greer), Frank
      McHugh (Spud Connors), Charlotte Merriam (Spud's wife), Harry Hartz,
      Fred Frame (drivers)
Running Time: 85 minutes
Released: April, 1932

Tiger Shark (First National/Warner Brothers, 1932)

Producer: Bryan Foy
Assistant Director: Richard Rosson
Marine Supervision: Guy Silva
Screenplay: Wells Root, from the story "Tuna" by Houston Branch
Cinematographer: Tony Gaudio
Art Director: Jack Okey
Music: Leo F. Forbstein
Costumes: Orry-Kelly
Editor: Thomas Pratt
Cast: Edward G. Robinson (Mike Mascarenas), Richard Arlen (Pipes Boley),

Zita Johann (Quita Silva), Vince Barnett (Fishbone), J. Carroll Naish (Tony), William Ricciardi (Manuel Silva)
Running Time: 80 minutes
Released: September, 1932

Today We Live (MGM, 1933)

Producer: Howard Hawks
Screenplay: Edith Fitzgerald, Dwight Taylor, William Faulkner, from the story "Turnabout" by Faulkner
Cinematographer: Oliver T. Marsh
Editor: Edward Curtiss
Cast: Joan Crawford (Diana), Gary Cooper (Bogard), Robert Young (Claude), Franchot Tone (Ronnie), Roscoe Karns (McGinnis)
Running Time: 113 minutes
Released: March, 1933

Viva Villa! (MGM, 1934)

Producer: David O. Selznick
Directors: Jack Conway and, uncredited, Howard Hawks
Assistant Director: James D. Waters
Screenplay: Ben Hecht, from the story by Edgcumb Pinchon and O. B. Stade
Art Director: Harry Oliver
Sets: Edwin B. Willis
Music: Herbert Stothart, Juan Aguilar
Editor: Robert J. Kern
Cast: Wallace Beery (Pancho Villa), Leo Carrillo (Sierra), Fay Wray (Teresa), Stuart Erwin (Johnny Sykes), Donald Cook (Don Felipe), Henry B. Walthall (Madero), Joseph Schildkraut (General Pascal)
Running Time: 115 minutes
Released: April, 1934

The Twentieth Century (Columbia, 1934)

Producer: Howard Hawks
Screenplay: Ben Hecht, Charles MacArthur, from their play, based on the Charles Bruce Milholland play *Napoleon on Broadway*
Cinematographers: Joseph August, Joseph Walker
Editor: Gene Havlick
Cast: John Barrymore (Oscar Jaffe), Carole Lombard (Lily Garland), Walter Connolly (Oliver Webb), Roscoe Karns (Owen O'Malley), Charles Levison (Max Jacobs), Edgar Kennedy (McGonigle), Etienne Giradot (Matthew J. Clark)
Running Time: 91 minutes
Released: May, 1934

Barbary Coast (Goldwyn Productions/United Artists, 1935)

Producer: Samuel Goldwyn
Assistant Director: Walter Mayo

Screenplay: Ben Hecht, Charles MacArthur, Edward Chodorov
Cinematographer: Ray June
Art Director: Richard Day
Music: Alfred Newman
Costumes: Omar Kiam
Cast: Miriam Hopkins (Mary "Swan" Rutledge), Edward G. Robinson (Louis
    Chamalis), Joel McCrea (James Carmichael), Walter Brennan (Old
    Atrocity), Frank Craven (Colonel Cobb), Brian Donlevy (Knuckles),
    Harry Carey (Slocum), Donald Meek (McTavish)
Running Time: 91 minutes
Released: September, 1935

Ceiling Zero (Cosmopolitan/First National-Warners, 1935)

Producer: Harry Joe Brown
Screenplay: Frank Wead, from his play
Cinematographer: Arthur Edeson
Art Director: John Hughes
Music: Leo F. Forbstein
Editor: William Holmes
Special Effects: Fred Jackson
Technical Advisor: Paul Mantz
Cast: James Cagney (Dizzy Davis), Pat O'Brien (Jake Lee), June Travis (Tom-
    my), Stuart Erwin (Tex Clarke), Isabel Jewell (Lou Clarke), Henry
    Wadsworth (Tay)
Running Time: 95 minutes
Released: January, 1936

The Road to Glory (Twentieth Century-Fox, 1936)

Producer: Darryl F. Zanuck
Associate Producer: Nunnally Johnson
Assistant Director: Ed O'Fearna
Screenplay: Joe Sayre, William Faulkner, from the film *Les Croix de Bois*, by
    Roland Dorgeles
Cinematographer: Gregg Toland
Art Director: Hans Peters
Sets: Thomas Little
Music: Louis Silvers
Costumes: Gwen Wakeling
Editor: Edward Curtiss
Cast: Fredric March (Lt. Michel Denet), Warner Baxter (Capt. Paul Laroche),
    Lionel Barrymore (Papa Laroche), June Lange (Monique), Gregory
    Ratoff (Bouffiou), Victor Kilian (Regnier)
Running Time: 95 minutes
Released: June, 1936

Come and Get It (Goldwyn Productions/United Artists, 1936)

Producer: Samuel Goldwyn
Directors: Howard Hawks, William Wyler
Assistant Directors: Richard Rosson, Ross Lederman
Screenplay: Jane Murfin, Jules Furthman, from the novel by Edna Ferber
Cinematographers: Gregg Toland, Rudolph Mate
Art Director: Richard Day
Sets: Julia Heron
Music: Alfred Newman
Costumes: Omar Kiam
Editor: Edward Curtiss
Special Effects: Ray Binger
Cast: Edward Arnold (Barney Glasgow), Frances Farmer (Lotta Morgan, Lotta Bostrum), Joel McCrea (Richard Glasgow), Walter Brennan (Swan Bostrom), Frank Shields (Tony Schwerke), Andrea Leeds (Evvie Glasgow), Mary Nash (Emma Louise Glasgow), Mady Christians (Karie)
Running Time: 105 minutes
Released: October, 1936

Bringing Up Baby (RKO, 1938)

Producer: Howard Hawks
Associate Producer: Cliff Reid
Assistant Director; Edward Donahue
Screenplay: Dudley Nichols, Hagar Wilde, from a story by Wilde
Cinematographer: Russell Metty
Art Directors: Van Nest Polglase, Perry Furguson
Sets: Darrell Silvera
Music: Roy Webb
Editor: George Hively
Special Effects: Vernon L. Walker
Cast: Cary Grant (David Huxley), Katharine Hepburn (Susan Vance), Charles Ruggles (Maj. Horace Applegate), Walter Catlett (Constable Slocum), Barry Fitzgerald (Gogarty), May Robson (Aunt Elizabeth), Fritz Feld (Dr. Lehmann), Virginia Walker (Alice Swallow). George Irvin (Peabody)
Running Time: 102 minutes
Released: February, 1938

Only Angels Have Wings (Columbia, 1939)

Producer: Howard Hawks
Assistant Director: Arthur Black
Screenplay: Jules Furthman, from a story by Hawks
Cinematographers: Joseph Walker, Elmer Dyer
Art Director: Lionel Banks
Music: Dimitri Tiomkin
Gowns: Kalloch
Editor: Viola Lawrence

Special Effects: E. Roy Davidson, Edwin C. Hahn
Technical Advisor and Chief Pilot: Paul Mantz
Cast: Cary Grant (Geoff Carter), Jean Arthur (Bonnie Lee), Thomas Mitchell (Kid Dabb), Richard Barthelmess (Bat Kilgalen/"McPherson"), Sig Ruman (Dutchy), Rita Hayworth (Judith), Victor Kilian (Sparks), John Carrol (Gent Shelton), Allyn Joslyn (Les Peters), Noah Beery, Jr. (Joe Souther)
Running Time: 121 minutes
Released: May 1939

His Girl Friday (Columbia, 1939)

Producer: Howard Hawks
Assistant Director: Clifton Broughton
Screenplay: Charles Lederer, from the play *The Front Page,* by Ben Hecht and Charles MacArthur
Cinematographer: Joseph Walker
Art Director: Lionel Banks
Music: Morris Stoloff
Gowns: Kalloch
Editor: Gene Havlick
Cast: Gary Grant (Walter Burns), Rosalind Russell (Hildy Johnson), Ralph Bellamy (Bruce Baldwin), Gene Lockhart (Sheriff Hartwell), Abner Biberman (Diamond Louie), Porter Hall (Murphy), Ernest Truex (Bensiger), Clarence Kolb (mayor), Roscoe Karns (McCue), Frank Orth (Duffy), John Qualen (Earl Williams), Helen Mack (Molly Malloy), Alma Kruger (Mrs. Baldwin), Frank Jenks (Wilson), Regis Toomey (Sanders), Billy Gilbert (Joe Pettibone), Edwin Maxwell (Dr. Egelhoffer)
Running Time: 92 minutes
Released: January, 1940

Sergeant York (Warner Brothers, 1941)

Producers: Jesse L. Lasky, Hal B. Wallis
Screenplay: Abem Finkel, Harry Chandler, Howard Koch, John Huston, from *War Diary of Sergeant York,* edited by Tom Skeyhill, and *Sergeant York—Last of the Long Hunters,* by Skeyhill
Cinematographers: Sol Polito, Arthur Edeson (war sequence)
Art Director: John Hughes
Sets: Fred MacLean
Music: Max Steiner
Musical Director: Leo F. Forbstein
Sound: Nathan Levinson
Makeup: Perc Westmore
Editor: William Holmes
Cast: Gary Cooper (Alvin C. York), Walter Brennan (Pastor Rosier Pile), Joan Leslie (Gracie Williams), Margaret Wycherley (Mother York), George Tobias (Pusher Ross), Stanley Ridges (Major Buxton), Ward Bond (Ike Botkin), Noah Beery, Jr. (Buck Lipscomb), June Lockhart (Rosie York),

Dickie Moore (George York), Clem Bevans (Zeke), Howard da Silva (Lem), Charles Trowbridge (Cordell Hill), Robert Porterfield (Zeb Andrews), Erville Alderson (Nate Thomkins), Tully Marshall (Uncle Lige)

Running Time: 134 minutes
Released: September, 1941

Ball of Fire (RKO, 1941)

Producer: Samuel Goldwyn
Assistant Director: William Tummel
Screenplay: Billy Wilder, Charles Brackett, from the story "From A to Z," by Wilder and Thomas Moore
Cinematographer: Gregg Toland
Art Director: Perry Ferguson
Assistant: McClure Claps
Sets: Howard Bristol
Music: Alfred Newman
Costumes: Edith Head
Editor: Daniel Mandell
Cast: Gary Cooper (Bertram Potts), Barbara Stanwyck (Sugarpuss O'Shea), Richard Haydn (Profedssor Oddly), Oscar Homolka (Professor Gurkakoff), Dana Andrews (Joe Lilac), Dan Duryea (Duke Pastrami), Henry Travers (Professor Jerome), S. Z. Sakall (Professor Magenbruch), Tully Marshall (Professor Robinson), Leonid Kinskey (Professor Quintana), Aubrey Mather (Professor Peagram), Mary Field (Miss Totten), Kathleen Howard (Miss Bragg)

Running Time: 111 minutes
Released: January, 1942

The Outlaw (RKO, 1943)

Producer: Hughes Productions, Howard Hughes
Directors: Howard Hughes and, uncredited, Howard Hawks
Screenplay: Jules Furthman
Cinematographer: Gregg Toland
Editor: Wallace Grissell
Music: Victor Young
Cast: Jane Russell (Rio McDonald), Walter Huston (Doc Holliday), Jack Buetel (Billy the Kid), Thomas Mitchell (Pat Garrett)

Running Time: 123 minutes
Released: February, 1943

Air Force (Warner Brothers, 1943)

Producer: Hal B. Wallis
Assistant Director: Jack Sullivan
Screenplay: Dudley Nichols, William Faulkner
Cinematographer: James Wong Howe
Aerial Photography: Elmer Dyer, Charles Marshall
Art Director: John Hughes

315

Sets: Walter F. Tilford
Music: Franz Waxman
Musical Director: Leo F. Forbstein
Editor: George Amy
Special Effects: E. Roy Davidson, Rex Wimpy, H. F. Koenekamp
Technical Advisor and Chief Pilot: Paul Mantz
Cast: John Garfield (Sgt. John B. Winocki), John Ridgely (Capt. Michael A.
    Quincannon), George Tobias (Corporal Weinberg), Harry Carey (Sgt. R.
    L. White), Gig Young (Lt. Xavier W. Williams), Arthur Kennedy (Lt. T.
    C. McMartin), Charles Drake (Lt. M. W. Hauser), James Brown (Lt. T. A.
    Rader), Richard Lane, Edward S. Brophy, Faye Emerson, Ann Doran,
    Dorothy Peterson
Running Time: 124 minutes
Released: March, 1943

Corvette K-225 (Universal, 1943)

Producer: Howard Hawks for Universal
Direction: Richard Rosson and, uncredited, Hawks (opinion)
Screenplay: Lt. John Rhodes Sturdy, RCNVR
Cinematographers: Tony Gaudio, Harry Perry
Editor: Edward Curtiss
Art Director: John B. Goodman, Robert Boyle
Music: David Buttolph
Cast: Randolph Scott, Ella Raines, James Brown, Barry Fitzgerald, Andy
    Devine, Fuzzy Knight, Noah Berry, Jr., Richard Lane, Thomas Gomez,
    Walter Sande, Robert Mitchum
Running Time: 99 minutes
Released: October, 1943
(Additional source for credits: John Belton)

To Have and Have Not (Warner Brothers, 1944)

Producer: Howard Hawks
Assistant Director: Jack Sullivan
Screenplay: Jules Furthman, William Faulkner, suggested by the novel by
    Ernest Hemingway
Cinematographer: Sidney Hickox
Art Director: Charles Novi
Sets: Casey Roberts
Music: Leo F. Forbstein, Songs by Hoagy Carmichael and Johnny Mercer
Editor: Christian Nyby
Special Effects: E. Roy Davidson, Rex Wimpy
Technical Advisor: Louis Comien
Gowns: Milo Anderson
Cast: Humphrey Bogart (Harry Morgan), Walter Brennan (Eddie), Lauren
    Bacall (Marie Brown/"Slim"), Hoagy Carmichael (Cricket), Marcel Dalio
    (Frenchy Gerard), Walter Sande (Johnson), Dan Seymour (Captain

Renard), Walter Molnar (Paul de Bursak), Dolores Moran (Mme. Helene de Bursak)
Running Time: 97 minutes
Released: January, 1944

The Big Sleep (Warner Brothers, 1946)

Producer: Howard Hawks
Assistant Director: Chuck Hansen
Screenplay: Jules Furthman, William Faulkner, Leigh Brackett, from the novel by Raymond Chandler
Cinematographer: Sidney Hickox
Art Director: Carl Jules Weyl
Sets: Fred MacLean
Music: Max Steiner
Musical Director: Leo F. Forbstein
Wardrobe: Leah Rhodes
Editor: Christian Nyby
Special Effects: E. Roy Davidson, Warren E. Lynch
Cast: Humphrey Bogart (Philip Marlowe), Lauren Bacall (Vivian Sternwood/Rutledge), John Ridgely (Eddie Mars), Louis Jean Heydt (Joe Brody), Elisha Cook, Jr. (Harry Jones), Regis Toomey (Bernie Ohls), Sonia Darrin (Agnes Lowzier), Bob Steele (Canino), Martha Vickers (Carmen Sternwood), Charles Waldron (General Sternwood), Tom Rafferty (Carol Lundgren), Dorothy Malone (bookstore girl), Peggy Knudsen (Mona Mars), Theodore von Eltz (Arthur Gwyn Geiger)
Running Time: 114 minutes
Released: August, 1946

Red River United Artists/Monterey, 1948)

Producer: Howard Hawks
Executive Producer: Charles K. Feldman
Assistant Director: William McGarry
Second Unit Director: Arthur Rosson
Screenplay: Borden Chase, Charles Schnee, from the book *Blazing Guns on the Chisholm Trail,* by Chase
Cinematographer: Russell Harlan
Art Director: John Datu Arensma
Music: Dimitri Tiomkin
Editor: Christian Nyby
Special Effects: Don Steward
Special Photographic Effects: Allan Thompson
Cast: John Wayne (Tom Dunson), Montgomery Clift (Matthew Garth), Walter Brennan (Groot Nadine), John Ireland (Cherry Valance), Joanne Dru (Tess Millay), Noah Beery, Jr. (Buster), Chief Yowlatchie (Quo), Paul Fix (Teeler), Hank Worden (Simms), Harry Carey, Sr. (Melville), Harry Carey, Jr. (Dan Latimer), Ivan Parry (Bunk Kenneally), Coleen Gray (Fen), Mickey Kuhn (Matt as a boy), Hal Taliaferro (Old Leather), Paul

Fiero (Fernandez), William Self (wounded wrangler), Dan White (Laredo),
Ray Hyke
Running Time: 125 minutes
Released: August, 1948

A Song is Born (RKO, 1948)

Producer: Samuel Goldwyn
Assistant Director: Joseph Boyle
Screenplay: Harry Tugend, based on Hawks's film *Ball of Fire*
Cinematographer: Gregg Toland (in Technicolor)
Art Directors: George Jenkins, Perry Ferguson
Music: Emil Newman, Hugo Friedhofer
Songs: Don Raye, Gene DePaul
Editor: Daniel Mandell
Special Photographic Effects: John P. Fulton
Cast: Danny Kaye (Prof. Robert Frisbee), Virginia Mayo (Honey Swanson),
    Steve Cochran (Tony Crow), O. Z. Whitehead (Professor Oddly), Mary
    Field (Miss Totten), Esther Dale, Benny Goodman, Hugh Herbert, Buck
    and Bubbles, Louis Armstrong, Mel Powell, Lionel Hampton, Tommy
    Dorsey, Charlie Barnett, The Page Cavanaugh Trio, The Golden Gate
    Quartet, Russo and the Samba Kings
Running Time: 113 minutes
Released: November, 1948

I Was a Male War Bride (Twentieth Century-Fox, 1949)

Producer: Sol C. Siegel
Assistant Director: Arthur Jacobson
Screenplay: Charles Lederer, Leonard Spiegelglass, Hager Wilde, from the story
            by Henri Rochard
Cinematography: Norbert Brodine, O. H. Borrodale
Art Directors: Lyle Wheeler, Albert Hogsett
Sets: Thomas Little, Walter M. Scott
Music: Cyril Mockridge
Musical Director: Lionel Newman
Editor: James B. Clark
Special Photographic Effects: Fred Sersen
Cast: Cary Grant (Capt. Henri Rochard), Ann Sheridan (Lt. Catherine Gates),
    William Neff (Capt. Jack Rumsey), Marion Marshall (Kitty), Martin
    Miller (Schindler)
Running Time: 105 minutes
Released: September, 1949

The Thing (From Another World) (RKO/Winchester, 1951)

Producer: Howard Hawks
Associate Producer: Edward Lasker
Directors: Christian Nyby and, uncredited, Hawks (opinion)

Assistant Directors: Arthur Siteman, Max Henry
Screenplay: Charles Lederer, from the story "Who Goes There?" by John W.
Campbell, Jr.
Cinematographer: Russell Harlan
Art Director: Albert S. D'Agostino, John Hughes
Sets: Darrell Silvera, William Stevens
Music: Dimitri Tiomkin
Editor: Roland Cross
Sound: Phil Brigandi, Clem Portman
Special Effects: Donald Steward
Special Photographic Effects: Linwood Dunn
Special Photography: Lee Nelows
Cast: Kenneth Toby (Capt. Patrick Hendrey), Margaret Sheridan (Nikki
Nicholson), Douglas Spencer (Ned Scott/"Scotty"), Dewey Martin (Bob,
Tech Sgt.), Robert Cornthwaite (Dr. Carrington), James Young (Lt. Eddie Dykes), Robert Nichols (Lieutenant MacPherson), John Dierkes (Dr.
Chapman), William Self (Corporal Barnes), Eduard Franz (Dr. Stern),
Sally Creighton (Mrs. Chapman), James Arness (the alien), David
McMahon (General Fogarty)
Running Time: 85 minutes
Released: April, 1951

The Big Sky (RKO/Winchester, 1952)

Producer: Howard Hawks
Associate Producer: Edward Lasker
Assistant Director: William McGarry
Second Unit Director: Arthur Rosson
Screenplay: Dudley Nichols, from the novel by A. P. Guthrie, Jr.
Cinematographer: Russell Harlan
Art Director: Albert S. D'Agostino, Perry Ferguson
Sets: Darrell Silvera, William Stevens
Music: Dimitri Tiomkin
Costumes: Dorothy Jeakins
Editor: Christian Nyby
Special Effects: Donald Steward
Cast: Kirk Douglas (Jim Deakins), Dewey Martin (Boone Caudell), Arthur
Hunnicutt (Zeb Calloway), Elizabeth Threatt (Teal Eye), Hank Worden
(Poor Devil), Jim Davis (Streak), Buddy Baer (Romaine), Steven Geray
(Jourdonnais), Henri Letondal (Labadie), Paul Frees (McMasters), Barbara Hawks
Running Time: 120 minutes
Released: August 1952

The Ransom of Red Chief (episode in *O. Henry's Full House*) (Twentieth
Century-Fox, 1952)

Producer: Andre Hakim
Screenplay: Nunnally Johnson, from the O. Henry short story

Cinematographer: Milton Krasner
Art Director: Chester Goce
Music: Alfred Newman
Editor: William B. Murphy
Narrator: John Steinbeck
Cast: Fred Allen (Sam), Oscar Levant (Bill), Lee Aaker (J.B.), Kathleen
    Freeman (J.B.'s mother), Alfred Minar (J.B.'s father), Robert Easton
Running Time: 25 minutes
Released: September, 1952

Monkey Business (Twentieth Century-Fox, 1952)

Producer: Sol C. Siegel
Screenplay: Ben Hecht, I.A.L. Diamond, Charles Lederer, from a story by Harry
    Segall
Cinematographer: Milton Krasner
Art Directors: Lyle Wheeler, George Patrick
Sets: Thomas Little, Walter M. Scott
Music: Leigh Harline
Musical Director: Lionel Newman
Editor: William B. Murphy
Special Photographic Effects: Ray Kellogg
Cast: Cary Grant (Dr. Barnaby Fulton), Ginger Rogers (Edwina Fulton),
    Charles Coburn (Oliver Oxly), Marilyn Monroe (Lois Laurel), Hugh
    Marlowe (Hank Entwhistle), Robert Cornthwaite (Dr. Zoldek), Esther
    Dale, Harry Carey, Jr., George Winslow, Heinie Conklin, Howard
    Hawks (voice), Henri Letondal
Running Time: 97 minutes
Released: September, 1952

Gentlemen Prefer Blondes (Twentieth Century-Fox, 1953)

Producer: Sol C. Siegel
Assistant Director: Paul Helmick
Screenplay: Charles Lederer, from the musical by Anita Loos and Joseph Fields,
    based on the Loos novel
Cinematographer: Harry J. Wild (in Technicolor)
Art Directors: Lyle Wheeler, Joseph C. Wright
Sets: Claude Carpenter
Choreography: Jack Cole
Songs: Jule Styne, Leo Robin, Hoagy Carmichael, Harold Adamson
Musical Director: Lionel Newman
Costumes: Travilla
Editor: Hugh S. Fowler
Special Photographic Effects: Ray Kellogg
Cast: Marilyn Monroe (Lorelei Lee), Jane Russell (Dorothy Shaw), Charles
    Coburn (Sir Francis Beekman/"Piggy"), Elliot Reid (Ernie Malone),
    Tommy Noonan (Gus Esmond), George Winslow (Henry Spofford III),
    Marcel Dalio (magistrate), Taylor Holmes (Mr. Esmond), Norma Varden

(Lady Beekman), Howard Wendell (Watson), Steven Geray (hotel manager), Alex Frazer (Pritchard), George Davis (Pierre, the cab driver), Henri Letondal, Jimmie and Freddie Moultrie, Harry Carey, Jr., Robert Nichols, Kenneth Tobey, James Young
Running Time: 91 minutes
Released: August, 1953

Land of the Pharaohs (Warners/Continental Company, 1955)

Producer: Howard Hawks
Associate Producer: Arthur Siteman
Assistant Director: Paul Helmick
Second Unit Director: Noel Howard
Screenplay: William Faulkner, Harry Kurnitz, Harold Jack Bloom
Cinematographer: Lee Garmes (interiors), Russell Harlan (exteriors) (Cinemascope and Warnercolor)
Art Director: Alexandre Trauner
Music: Dimitri Tiomkin
Costumes: Mayo
Editors: Rudi Fehr, V. Sagovsky
Special Effects: Don Steward
Cast: Jack Hawkins (Pharaoh Cheops), Joan Collins (Princess Nelipher), Dewey Martin (Senta), Alexis Minotis (Hamar), James Robertson Justice (Vashtar), Piero Giagnoni (Pharaoh's young son), Luisa Boni, Sydney Chaplin, Kerima
Running Time: 101 minutes
Released: July, 1955

Rio Bravo (Warner Brothers/Armanda, 1959)

Producer: Howard Hawks
Assistant Director: Paul Helmick
Screenplay: Jules Furthman, Leigh Brackett, from a short story by Barbara Hawks McCampbell
Cinematographer: Russell Harlan (in Technicolor)
Art Director: Leo K. Kuter
Sets: Ralph S. Hurt
Music: Dimitri Tiomkin
Songs: Tiomkin, Paul Francis Webster
Costumes: Marjorie Best
Editor: Folmar Blangsted
Cast: John Wayne (Sheriff John T. Chance), Dean Martin (Dude), Walter Brennan (Stumpy), Angie Dickinson (Feathers), Ricky Nelson (Colorado Ryan), Ward Bond (Pat Wheeler), John Russell (Nathan Burdett), Pedro Gonzales-Gonzales (Carlos), Estrelita Rodriguez (Consuela), Claude Akins (Joe Burdett), Harry Carey, Jr.
Running Time: 140 minutes
Released: April, 1959

Hatari! (Paramount/Malabar, 1962)

Producer: Howard Hawks
Associate Producer and Second Unit Director: Paul Helmick
Assistant Directors: Tom Connors, Russ Saunders
Screenplay: Leigh Bracket, from a story by Harry Kurnitz
Cinematographers: Russell Harlan, Joseph Brun (Technicolor)
Art Directors: Hal Pereira, Carl Anderson
Sets: Sam Comer, Claude Carpenter
Music: Henry Mancini
Editor: Stuart Gilmore
Special Effects: John P. Fulton
Special Mechanical Effects: Richard Parker
Technical Advisor: Willy deBeer
Cast: John Wayne (Sean Mercer), Elsa Martinelli (Dallas), Hardy Kruger (Kurt
    Mueller), Gerard Blain (Chips), Red Buttons (Pockets), Michele Girardon
    (Brandy Delacourt), Bruce Cabot (Indian), Valentin de Vargas (Luis),
    Eduard Franz (Dr. Sanderson/"Sandy")
Running Time: 155 minutes
Released: June, 1962

Man's Favorite Sport? (Universal/Gibralter/Laurel, 1963)

Producer: Howard Hawks
Associate Producer: Paul Helmick
Assistant Director: Tom Connors, Jr.
Screenplay: John Fenton Murray, Steve McNeil, based on the story "The Girl
    Who Almost Got Away" by Pat Frank
Cinematographer: Russell Harlan
Art Directors: Alexander Golitzen, Tambi Larsen
Music: Henry Mancini
Editor: Stuart Gilmore
Special Effects: Ben McMahon
Cast: Rock Hudson (Roger Willoughby), Paula Prentiss (Abigail Page), Maria
    Perschy (Isolde "Easy" Mueller), John McGiver (William Cadwalader),
    Charlene Holt (Tex Connors), Roscoe Karns (Major Phipps), Norman
    Alden (John Screaming Eagle), Forrest Lewis, Regis Toomey
Running Time: 120 minutes
Released: January, 1964

Red Line 7000 (Paramount/Laurel, 1965)

Producer: Howard Hawks
Second Unit Director: Bruce Kessler
Assistant Director: Dick Moder
Screenplay: Hawks, George Kirgo
Cinematographer: Milton Krasner
Art Director: Hal Pereira, Arthur Lonergan
Music: Nelson Riddle

Editors: Stuart Gilmore, Bill Brame
Special Effects: Paul K. Lerpae
Cast: James Caan (Mike Marsh), Laura Devon (Julie Kazarian), Gail Hire (Holly MacGregor), Charlene Holt (Lindy Bonaparte), John Robert Crawford (Ned Arp), Marianna Hill (Gabrielle/"Gabby"), James Ward (Dan McCall), Norman Alden (Pat Kazarian), George Takei (Kato)
Running Time: 110 minutes
Released: November, 1965

El Dorado (Paramount/Laurel, 1966)

Producer: Howard Hawks
Assistant Director: Andrew J. Durkus
Screenplay: Leigh Brackett, from the novel *The Stars in Their Courses* by Harry Brown
Cinematographer: Harold Rosson
Art Directors: Hal Pereira, Carl Anderson
Music: Nelson Riddle
Editor: John Woodcock
Special Photographic Effects: Paul K. Lerpae
Cast: John Wayne (Cole Thornton), Robert Mitchum (Sheriff J.P. Harrah), James Caan (Alan Bourdillon Traherne/"Mississippi"), Charlene Holt (Maudie), Michele Carey (Joey MacDonald), Arthur Hunnicutt (Bull Harris), Christopher George (Nelse McLeod), R.G. Armstrong (Kevin MacDonald), Edward Asner (Bart Jason), Paul Fix (Doc Miller), Jim Davis (Jason's foreman), Johnny Crawford (Luke MacDonald), Anthony Rogers (Dr. Donovan)
Running Time: 122 minutes
Released: December, 1966

Rio Lobo (Cinema Center/Malabar, 1970)

Producer: Howard Hawks
Associate Producer: Paul Helmick
Assistant Director: Yakima Canutt
Screenplay: Leigh Brackett and Burton Wohl, story by Wohl
Cinematographer: William Clothier
Art Director: William R. Kiernan
Production Design: Robert Smith
Sets: William Kiernan
Music: Jerry Goldsmith
Editor: John Woodcock
Special Effects: A.D. Flowers, Clifford P. Wenger
Cast: John Wayne (Cord McNally), Jorge Rivero (Pierre Cardona), Chris Mitchum (Toscarora), Jack Elam (Phillips), Jennifer O'Neil (Shasta Delaney), Susana Dosamantes (Maria), Sherry Lansing (Amelita), Victor French (Ketchum), Mike Henry (Hendricks), Bill Williams (Sheriff Cronin), David Huddleston, Jim Davis, Robert Conner, George Plimp-

ton, Hank Worden, Edward Faulkner
Running Time: 114 minutes
Released: November, 1970

NOTES

1. *From page 14.* C.G. Jung writes, in his noted passage in *Psychology and Alchemy* (par. 30, p. 5), "In nature the opposites seek one another...and so it is in the unconscious [by virtue of the latter's *undifferentiated* character], and particularly in the archetype of unity, the self [by virtue in turn of the latter's operant potential for effecting ego/unconscious mergence and harmony, thus bringing the said undifferentiation to a higher order and unity]. Here, as in deity, the opposites cancel out. But as soon as the unconscious begins to manifest itself they split asunder, as at the Creation; for every act of dawning consciousness is a creative act, and it is from this psychological experience all our cosmogonic symbols are derived." [And, less dramatically, other symbols and patterns as well.]

2. *From page 14.* Edward Edinger, *Ego and Archetype,* pp. 132-33.

3. *From page 15.* "So we can take your introvert-extrovert category and describe the introverted sensation type, the extroverted sensation type, the introverted thinking type, and so on," interviewer Richard I. Evans addressed Jung. Jung replied, "It is just a sort of skeleton to which you have to add the flesh. Or you could say it is like a country mapped out at triangular points.... It is a means to an end. It only makes sense when you deal with practical cases." (William McGuire and R.F.C. Hull, eds., *C.G. Jung Speaking,* "The Houston Films," pp. 311-12.)

4. *From page 17.* Laurens van der Post, *Jung and the Story of Our Time,* pp. 69-70.

5. *From page 21.* C.G. Jung, Psychological Reflections; A New Anthology of His Writings, Jolande Jacobi, ed., p. 119.

6. *From page 21.* Ibid., p. 115.

7. *From page 27.* Among the more articulate of the "Front Generation" was ex-airman and maverick British politican Sir Oswald Mosley, who is portrayed in his autobiography (*My Life*), and in a biography by Robert Skidelsky, who therein relates of Mosley's "nostalgic yearning for, and idealization of, the 'spirit of the trenches.' Mosley's real problem," Skidelsky writes, "was that his sense of political mission awakened by the war coexisted with an inability to settle down again to normal civilian life, with its conventional standards of success and achievements, its conventional pace and morality...." And its betrayals and failings; whence: "Under the traumatic impact of [the Labour Party's 1930-31 collapse], the emotional syndrome reasserted itself: the emptiness of civilian life, the fraudulence of politics. Mosley fled back to the trenches." [that is, via the new and "ultramodern" movement of fascism.] See, Robert Skidelsky, *Oswald Mosley* (New York: Holt, Rinehart and Winston, 1975.), p. 21.

8. *From page 27.* Peter Wollen, *Signs and Meaning in the Cinema,* p. 81.

9. *From page 30.* C.G. Jung, *The Collected works of C.G. Jung,* R.F.C. Hull, trans., vol. 12: *Psychology and Alchemy,* pars. 49-50, pp. 44-46.

10. *From page 31.* Joseph Campbell, *The Hero With a Thousand Faces,* pp. 193-96.

11. *From page 33.* C.G. Jung, *The Collected Works of C.G. Jung,* R.F.C. Hull, trans., vol. 7: *Two Essays on Analytical Psychology,* "The Relation Between the Ego and the Unconscious," par. 261, pp. 169-70.

12. *From page 41.* See *Man, Myth & Magic; An Illustrated Encyclopedia of the Supernatural,* s.v. "Germanic Mythology," by H.R. Ellis Davidson, "Ring," by Venetia Newall, "Scandinavia," by H.R. Ellis Davidson, "Thor," H.R. Ellis Davidson.

13. *From Page 42. Ibid.*

14. *From page 42. Ibid.*

15. *From page 46.* Joseph Campbell, *The Hero With a Thousand Faces,* p. 73.

16. *From page 50.* Gerald Mast, *Howard Hawks, Storyteller,* p. 7.

SELECTED BIBLIOGRAPHY
(OF WORKS CONSULTED)

On Hawks and Film

Belton, John. *Howard Hawks, Frank Borzage, Edgar G. Ulmer. The Hollywood Professionals, vol. 3.* New York: A.S. Barnes, 1974.

Corliss, Richard, ed. *The Hollywood Screenwriters.* New York: Discus Books (Avon), 1972. Contains sections on Jules Furthman, Ben Hecht, Borden Chase, Dudley Nichols, and others who wrote for Hawks.

Haver, Ron. Program notes for the Howard Hawks film retrospective at the Los Angeles County Art Museum, 1974.

Mast, Gerald. *Howard Hawks, Storyteller.* New York, Oxford: Oxford University Press, 1982.

McBride, Joseph, ed. *Focus on Howard Hawks.* Englewood, New Jersey: Prentice-Hall, Inc., 1972. Contains articles on Hawks by many writers.

———. *Hawks on Hawks.* Berkeley, Los Angeles, London: University of California Press, 1982. Contains extensive interviews with Hawks by the author, with detailed filmography.

Poague, Leland A. *Howard Hawks.* Boston: Twayne Publishers, 1982. Provides an informed, valuable though rather strained polemic contra the "Wollen/Wood" overview on Hawks cinema. Features discussion on hitherto "lost" or little-available Hawks films from the silent period.

Sarris, Andrew. *The American Cinema; Directors and Directions, 1929-1968.* New York: E.P. Dutton & Co., 1968. Contains sections on Hawks and many other directors, with discussion of the auteur approach to film. One of the most important books in the field of film studies.

———, ed. *Interviews with Film Directors.* New York: Discus Books (Avon), 1967. Contains a Hawks interview.

———. "The World of Howard Hawks," in Joseph McBride, ed., *Focus on Howard Hawks,* pp. 35-64. A well-oriented discussion covering most of Hawks's films.

Thompson, Rich. Program notes for the Howard Hawks film retrospective at the Los Angeles County Art Museum, 1974

Tudor, Andrew. *Theories of Film.* New York: Viking Press, 1973. Contains a good discussion of the auteur approach to film

Willis, Donald C. *The Films of Howard Hawks.* Metuchen, New Jersey: The Scarecrow Press, Inc., 1976. Reviews most of Hawks's films, with discussion of the auteur approach to film and a Hawks interview.

Wollen, Peter. *Signs and Meaning in the Cinema.* Bloomington, Indiana; London: Indiana University Press, 1972.

Wood, Robin. *Howard Hawks.* Garden City, New York: Doubleday & Co.; London: Secker & Warburg; 1968.

On Analytical Psychology

Books Consulted on Jung and Analytical Psychology. (Particularly recommended is Jacobi's *The Psychology of C.G. Jung.*)

Bennet, E.A. *What Jung Really Said.* New York: Schocken Books, 1967.

Bertine, Eleanor. *Jung's Contribution to Our Time (Collected Papers).* New York: G.P. Putnam's Sons for the C.G. Jung Foundation for Analytical Psychology, 1967.

Cox, David. *Modern Psychology; The Teachings of Carl Gustav Jung.* New York, Evanston, San Francisco, London: Barnes & Noble Books (Harper & Row), 1967.

Edinger, Edward. *Ego and Archetype.* Baltimore: Penguin Books, 1974.

Fordham, Frieda. *An Introduction to Jung's Psychology.* Baltimore: Penguin Books, 1975.

Franz, Marie-Louise von. *C.G. Jung; His Myth in Our Time.* Boston, Toronto: Little, Brown & Co., 1975.

Harding, M. Esther. *The I and the Not-I; A Study in the Development of Conciousness.* Princeton, New Jersey: Princeton University Press, Bollingen Series LXXIX, 1973.

Harding, M. Esther. *Journey into Self.* New York: David McKay Co., 1973.

———. *Psychic Energy, Its Source and Transmission.* Princeton, New Jersey: Princeton University Press, Bollingen Series X, 1973.

Hochheimer, Wolfgang. *The Psychotherapy of C.G. Jung.* London: Barrie & Rockliffe for the C.G. Jung Foundation for Analytical Psychology, 1969.

Jaffe, Aniela. *From the Life and Work of C.G. Jung.* New York, Evanston, San Francisco: Harper Colophon Books (Harper & Row), 1971.

———. *The Myth of Meaning.* New York, Baltimore: Penguin Books, 1975.

Jacobi, Jolande. *Complex/Archetype/Symbol in the Psychology of C.G. Jung.* Princeton, New Jersey: Princeton University Press, Bollingen Series LVII, 1972.

———. *The Psychology of C.G. Jung.* New Haven, London: Yale University Press, 1975.

Kirsch, James. *Shakespeare's Royal Self.* New York: G. P. Putnam's Sons for the C.G. Jung Foundation for Analytical Psychology, 1966. A Jungian Analysis of three of Shakespeare's principal tragedies.

Meir, Carl Alfred, M.D. *Jung's Analytical Psychology and Religion.* Carbondale and Edwardsville: Southern Illinois University Press; London, Amsterdam: Feffer & Simons, Inc.; 1977.

Odajnyk, Volodymyr Walter. *Jung and Politics; The Political and Social Ideas of C.G. Jung.* New York, Hagerstown, San Francisco, London: Harper Colophon Books (Harper & Row), 1976.

Post, Laurens van der. *Jung and the Story of Our Time.* New York: Vintage Books (Random House), 1977.

Progoff, Ira. *Jung's Psychology and Its Social Meaning.* Garden City, New York: Anchor Books (Doubleday), 1973.

Singer, June. *Boundaries of the Soul; The Practice of Jung's Psychology.* Garden City, New York: Anchor Books (Doubleday), 1972.

Stern, Paul J. *C.G. Jung; The Haunted Prophet.* New York: Delta (Dell), 1977.

Storr, Anthony. *C.G. Jung*. New York: Viking Press, 1973.

Basic Writings by C.G. Jung Consulted:

Jung, C.G. *The Collected Works of C.G. Jung*, R.F.C. Hull, trans., vols. 5, 7, 8, 9(I), 9(II), 10, 12, 13, 14, 18. Princeton, New Jersey: Princeton University Press, Bollingen Series XX, 1954-76.

——. *The Collected Works of C.G. Jung*, R.F.C. Hull, trans., vol. 15. New York: Bollingen Foundation in conjunction with Pantheon Books (Random House), 1966.

——. *The Portable Jung*, Joseph Campbell, ed., R.F.C. Hull, trans. New York: The Viking Press, Inc., 1971.

Numerical listing of works consulted from *The Collected Works of C.G. Jung:*

Bollingen Series XX (Ref: above.):

Vol. 5, *Symbols of Transformation.*
Vol. 7, *Two Essays on Analytical Psychology.*
Vol. 8, *The Structure and Dynamics of the Psyche.*
Vol. 9(I), *The Archetypes of the Collective Unconscious.*
Vol. 9(II), *Aion: Researches into the Phenomenology of the Self.*
Vol. 10, *Civilization in Transition.*
Vol. 12, *Psychology and Alchemy.*
Vol. 13, *Alchemical Studies.*
Vol. 14, *Mysterium Coniunctionis.*
Vol. 15, *The Spirit in Man, Art, and Literature.*
Vol. 18, *The Symbolic Life: Miscellaneous Writings.*

Other Writings by C.G. Jung Consulted:

Jung, C.G. *Analytical Psychology: Its Theory and Practice.* New York: Vintage Books (Random House), 1968.

——, with C. Kerenyi. *Essays on a Science of Mythology.* Princeton, New Jersey: Princeton University Press, Bollingen Series XXII, 1973.

——. *Memories, Dreams, Reflections.* New York: Vintage Books (Random House), 1963.

——. *Modern Man in Search of a Soul.* New York: Harvest Books (Harcourt, Brace & World), no publication date given (first published in 1933).

——. *Psychological Reflections; A New Anthology of His Writings, 1905-1961.* Jolande Jacobi, ed., in conjunction with R.F.C. Hull. Princeton, New Jersey: Princeton University Press, Bollingen Series XXXI, 1974.

McGuire, William; and R.F.C. Hull, eds. *C.G. Jung Speaking; Interviews and Encounters.* Princeton, New Jersey: Princeton University Press, Bollingen Series XCVII, 1977.

Additional References

Campbell, Joseph. *The Hero With a Thousand Faces.* Princeton, New Jersey: Princeton University Press, Bollingen Series XVII, 1973.

Cavendish, Richard; ed. *Man, Myth & Magic; An Illustrated Encyclopedia of the Supernatural*, vols 1-34. New York: Marshall Cavendish Corporation, 1970.

Jung, C.G.; with M.-L. von Franz, Joseph L. Henderson, Jolande Jacobi, Aniela Jaffe. *Man and His Symbols*. Garden City, New York: Windfall/ Doubleday, 1976.

GLOSSARY OF CINEMATIC AND DRAMATIC TERMS (WITH APPLICATIONS)

(Source: Thurston C. Jordan, Jr., *Glossary of Motion Picture Terminology*, Menlo Park, California: Pacific Coast Publishers, 1968.)

BUSINESS (n). Actions by which an actor or actors-in-ensemble interpret a character or characters, and/or the dramatic action of a sequence. Includes movements, acts, gestures and facial expressions.

CINEMATIC (adj.) Pertaining to cinema, especially in addition to the dramatic (which pertains more specifically to actorial business). The cinematic entails the factors of photography, camera placement and movement, lighting, sound, cutting and editing, special photographic effects, and narrative factors peculiar to the medium of the feature film as distinguished from stage drama.

CINEMATOGRAPHY (n). Factors of photography and lighting; technical/mediumistic factors pertaining to the same.

CLOSE-UP (n). A shot, taken within a very short distance from the subject (e.g., one to two feet). Hawks seldom shoots so close as to eliminate all context of the greater setting/action. (Ref. the opening of the "accordian" scene in *Come and Get It.*)

CUT (n). The sharp transition from one shot to another resulting from the joining of the two shots (i.e., physically, in the editing lab). In *The American Cinema*, Andrew Sarris notes, "Hawks will work within a frame as much as possible, cutting only when a long take or an elaborate track might distract his audience from the issues in the foreground of the action." (p. 55.)

DRAMATIC (adj.) Pertaining to all factors of script performance exclusive of strictly cinematic factors: namely, all actorial business and its direction. In Hawks cinema, dramatic factors run proportionately high.

EDITING (n). The part of the production stage in which the recorded sights and sounds are variously selected, mixed, and linked together unto the final product: the film and its sound track. (Editing work can take place previous to the end of all shooting, of course.)

ELEVATED SHOT, DOWN-SHOT (n). A. shot aimed down from a high angle (i.e., significantly higher than eye level). Hawks shoots mostly at eye level. (Ref. however the elevated shot at the opening of *The Outlaw.*)

EXPRESSIONISM, GERMAN (n). In film, an older "genre" and style of cinema given to contrived distortions (of set, lighting, and story/drama), to sharp cinematographic contrasts and shadow, and in one sense or another, imaginative content (e.g., caricature, or projected phantasy), as well as nega-

330

tivity. Part of the result is a tending "triumph of form over content." The best Expressionistic film is, perhaps, F.W. Murnau's American-made *Sunrise (A Song of Two Humans)* (1927). John Ford's *The Informer* and *The Hurricane* are considerably in this style, like parts of Hawks's *A Girl in Every Port.*

EXPRESSIONISTIC (adj.) Given to remnants or moderate traces or influence of older, filmic German Expressionism. (Ref. early portions of Hawks's *Viva Villa!*)

FADE IN/OUT (n). The gradual picture transition from or to picture blackness, and/or the corresponding effect in sound recording.

FOREGROUND (n). For our purposes, the portion of a scene near the camera and occupied. (Ref. 'foreground object/action' pattern in Appendix 1.)

FRAME (n). An individual picture on a filmstrip. The formal content of the motion-picture screen at any given time. The frame changes when the camera moves, when a shot cuts, or the action-dramatic composition alters significantly. (2) (v). To directorially/cinematographically compose a shot, with reference to set and dramatic-actional composition.

LOW LIGHTING, MEDIUM-LOW LIGHTING, SHADOW (n). General low-level ("low-keyed") illumination of the subject. With shadow(s) the light/dark contrasts are, of course, sharper. Hawks is fond of using lower lighting and sometimes shadow/contrast. They may be said to be important to his cinema.

STORY/DRAMA (n). The narrative dimention of a script in performance.

TAKE (n). A term denoting the photographing, recording, etc., of a shot. Takes are numbered sequentially and identified on a slate, and on the sound recording, by voice.

TRUCKING SHOT (n). A shot resulting from the camera moving in a vehicular way over a distance of ground (e.g., in following a character's motion). Hawks seldom used trucking shots before *Hatari!*, where they were necessary in the animal chases. (Ref. however Hildy's introduction sequence in *His Girl Friday,* and Dorothy and Lorelei's promenade through the ship's dining room in *Gentlemen Prefer Blondes.)*

TWO-SHOT (n). A fairly close shot covering two actors. (Ref. particularly the professor and hipster in the montage sequence in *A Song is Born.*)

UP-SHOT (n). A shot aimed upward from a lower angle to the action. (Ref. the "authoritarian" up-shot of Mother York from Alvin York's viewpoint, more or less, as he arrives home from drinking and brawling, feeling guilty and embarrassed. Also, the two or more up-shots of John Chance from the viewpoint, more or less, of Dude, particularly in terms of the latter's shame and disgrace, at points. See *Sergeant York* and *Rio Bravo* respectively.)

ZOOM, ZOOM-SHOT (n). Rapid movement, real or apparent, of the camera toward a subject. Late in his career, in *El Dorado* and particularly *Rio Lobo,* Hawks used a zoom lens, in a striking way, to artificially produce the rapid forward movement of a shot—to inferior results, mainly. Note however, the effective zooming-in on Toscarora against the "Livery Stable" sign, past the galloping horses in the foreground, in *Rio Lobo*. This zoom-movement corresponds to the moving up-shot past the galloping horses to Luke Mac-Donald on top of the rock, in the parallel portion of *El Dorado*. (Ref. 'mandala-Centrism' pattern in Appendix 1.)

CLARK BRANSON is a graduate of the University of California at Los Angeles where he studied behavioral science and folklore. He has written book reviews for the Los Angeles Times, and has produced and edited two musical/folkloric/literary documentaries for Folkways Records: *Leave Her Johnnie, Leave Her,* and *Al Tocar Diana/"At Break of Dawn."* With Mary Anneeta Mann he co-produced the 1984 edition of *The Los Angeles Theatre Book.* He resides in his home town of Pasadena, California.